To Iain

Margaret & Iain —

— on his happy release
OCT. 2004

PARRY TO FINZI

TWENTY ENGLISH SONG-COMPOSERS

PARRY TO FINZI

TWENTY ENGLISH SONG-COMPOSERS

Trevor Hold

THE BOYDELL PRESS

First published 2002
The Boydell Press, Woodbridge

ISBN 0 85115 887 0

The Boydell Press is an imprint of Boydell & Brewer Ltd
PO Box 9, Woodbridge, Suffolk IP12 3DF, UK
and of Boydell & Brewer Inc.
PO Box 41026, Rochester, NY 14604–4126, USA
website: www.boydell.co.uk

A catalogue record for this book is available
from the British Library

Library of Congress Cataloging-in-Publication Data
Hold, Trevor.
  Parry to Finzi : twenty English song-composers / Trevor Hold.
    p. cm.
Includes bibliographical references (p.) and index.
  ISBN 0–85115–887–0 (alk. paper)
    1. Songs, English – England – History and criticism.   2. English
poetry – Musical settings – History and criticism.   3. Vocal
music – England – History and criticism.   4. Composers – England.
I. Parry, C. Hubert H. (Charles Hubert Hastings), 1848–1918.   II. Finzi,
Gerald, 1901–1956.   III. Title.
ML2831 .H65 2002
782.4′3′092242–dc21   2002008051

Typeset by Joshua Associates Ltd, Oxford
Printed in Great Britain by
St Edmundsbury Press Ltd, Bury St Edmunds, Suffolk

Contents

To the memory of John Bishop (1931–2000)
sine qua non

Preface

> I would rather spend my life trying to achieve one book of little songs that shall have a lasting fragrance, than pile up tome upon tome on the dusty shelves of the British Museum.
>
> Peter Warlock: letter to Bernard van Dieren, 14 January 1920

Hilaire Belloc ended his essay 'On Song' with the words: 'It is the best of all trades to make songs', going on to say 'and the second best to sing them' (*On Everything*, 1909). Though not wishing to belittle the role of the singer, I think Belloc got the matter the right way round. And he should know: he was, after all, an enthusiastic singer himself, as well as being a 'maker'. (Someone has to 'make' the song before another can sing it.) In the time of Campion it was possible, in theory, for a song to be written, words and music, and performed, singer and lute, by one person. The days of the singer-songwriter, in the art-song at least, are long gone; the genre has become far too refined and sophisticated. None of the twenty song-composers covered in this study was a professional singer in as much as he performed his songs in public, though one or two – Bax, Quilter, Bridge, Browne – were capable enough as pianists to accompany singers in recitals. Likewise, 400 years ago, it was not uncommon for the composer to be the poet too. With the exception of Ivor Gurney – an outstanding exception – none of the composers included in this book were practising poets. Even Gurney himself kept the two arts separate; 'Severn meadows' is the only published song for which he wrote both words and music. Thus, today, we need two independent artists to 'make' a song – poet and composer – and two more – singer and accompanist – to perform it.

At the time of the first great flowering of English Song in the late 16th century, even if the composer didn't write his own texts then at least he knew the requirements of words-for-music. Conversely, Shakespeare, who was no musician as far as we know, could fashion lyrics 'apt' for musical setting, having learned the skill (as all lyric-writers should) by the art of contrafactum: writing new words to existing tunes. Sadly this accomplishment has been all but forgotten by 'serious' poets in the last 200 years, and few poets today understand the craft of the composer, or vice versa. The resulting rift between poet and composer has created many problems. Because poets do not write words for musical setting, composers tend to choose their lyrics 'off-the-peg'

– not always sensibly. In this study I have attempted to highlight this aspect of the songwriting art, emphasising the relationship between poem and musical setting.

Few topics in the field of aesthetics have engendered as much controversy as 'words-for-music'. There are two schools of thought on the matter: those who believe that 'words-for-music' is a specialised craft and that composers should only set poetry that has specifically been framed for musical setting; and those who believe that the idea of 'words-for-music' is a myth and that composers are morally justified in setting to music anything that takes their fancy. The most authoritative spokesmen for the two sides in recent times have been Victor Clinton-Baddeley – in his book *Words for Music* (1941) – and Gerald Finzi – in his hitherto unpublished Crees lectures, *The Composer's Use of Words*, which he gave at the Royal College of Music in the summer of 1955. Both have argued their cases with cogency and passion; anyone coming fresh to the subject is likely to be persuaded by either. It is only when the arguments are read side by side that it will be realised how conflicting their views are. By and large, it would seem to be the poets who advocate a special craft of 'words-for-music', the composers who do not. Clinton-Baddeley's views are shared by Thomas Campion (1601 and 1613), John Dryden (1691) and, in our own day, W. H. Auden (1957) and Cecil Day Lewis (1961). Finzi's views have been echoed by Benjamin Britten (1945) and Michael Tippett (1960). Though the argument is unlikely to be resolved, one thing is clear. The composer who sets poetry that was never intended for the purpose is in danger of being branded by the poet as an arrogant philistine. Song is the wedding of the two arts of Poetry and Music. How can such a union be healthy when poet and composer are at loggerheads? For this reason, I am myself a convinced adherent of the 'words-for-music' school. I have placed my cards on the table: the bias of this book is towards the first position.

A book such as this has to have clearly-defined limits, and the reader deserves to know what these limits are: what the book is about and what it is not about. The twenty song-composers in this study range chronologically from Hubert Parry (b. 1848) to Gerald Finzi (b. 1901) and represent what we now acknowledge as a Second Golden Age of English Song: the Age of English Romantic Song. All composers are British-born – there is no Grainger and no Kelly – and the songs considered are to *English* texts – no Welsh or French or Latin – concentrating on published *solo* songs – no duets – with piano accompaniment. The latter form the mainstream of the repertoire, though clearly solo songs with chamber or orchestral accompaniment – e.g. *Sea-Pictures* and *The Curlew* – are included too. Folksong arrangements are not considered, nor are translations unless they are especially relevant or if the translations themselves are of literary merit. My criterion for the twenty songwriters chosen has simply been *major* songwriters. *Major* has nothing to do with quantity, everything to do with quality. I have been completely unswayed by 'sheer weight of numbers': hence, no Granville Bantock, no Josef Holbrooke, no Cyril Scott; hence, too, the chapters, albeit short, on George Butterworth and Denis Browne.

Some may question the inclusion of Elgar and Delius. Admittedly neither can be described as a major songwriter, but as the major composers of their generation, it is inevitable that they had something important and individual to say when they did turn to the solo song.

We have had two Golden Ages of Song in this country. The first came at the turn of the 17th century, in the last years of Elizabeth's reign and the first years of the reign of James I (c.1590–1620), with composers such as Dowland, Campion, Daniel and Rosseter. The second came at the end of Victoria's reign and lasted until the latter part of the reign of George V (c.1880–1930), spanning the careers of Parry, Stanford, Somervell and Warlock. The two ages were quite different in character. The first was the age of lute-song, songs written for solo (invariably male) voice accompanied by lute. The emphasis was on vocal line; the majority of songs were strophic in form, the words specially written for setting by contemporary poets, but sometimes, as in the case of Thomas Campion, by the composer himself. The second was what we now identify as the era of English Romantic Song, songs written for a wide range of voices (male and female) with piano accompaniment. Though strophically based, they are rarely in simple strophic form, the words neither written 'to order', nor even by contemporary poets (with a few rare exceptions): indeed they were frequently composed to texts chosen from the trove of lyrical poetry written during the First Golden Age. From the 1880s to the 1930s, hundreds of such songs were written for a growing outlet of professional and amateur singers. Publishers found it a lucrative market, promoting the songs through famous singers of the day – 'As sung by . . .' – and almost every British composer of the period, whether adept at word-setting or not, contributed to the genre at one time or another. Appendix 1 lists 117 song-composers born in the 50 years between the births of Parry (1848) and Finzi (1901).

What are the characteristics and qualities of English Romantic Song? At the risk of being simplistic, a typical song could be described as follows:

It lasts about 2½–3 minutes.

It has a text either by a 19th-century or early 20th-century poet. (Shelley/Tennyson/Housman) or from the great treasure trove of 16th/17th-century English verse, notably that great twosome, Shakespeare and Anon. (With the exception of Burns and Blake, it is unlikely to be by a poet born between Dryden and Wordsworth, Dryden and Wordsworth not excluded.)

Great care and emphasis will have been placed on 'just note and accent' in the word-setting. The poem will be set syllabically, with melisma reserved for special words or for cadences. Word painting will be used discreetly: in pastel/watercolour fashion rather than oils.

The vocal line will be lyrical and eminently singable, but never with *bel canto* virtuosity.

The piano part will be a discreet companion to the voice – a gentleman's gentleman – buoying it up but never intruding when the voice is in motion and coming to the fore only at preludes, interludes and codas. Like the accompaniments of Schubert and Schumann, it favours the middle range of the keyboard, taking on the major 'landscape painting' for the setting, with short arabesques for bird-song, running semiquavers for water-mills and streams. The pedal is used to great effect to blur arpeggiated figurations.

In form, it follows the invariably terraced stanzas of the poets. So, varied strophic is the favourite form – exact strophic is most unusual – except in poems of three stanzas or more where ternary (A(A)BA) or an 'Abgesang' shape (AAB) is often used. Through-composed ('durchcomponiert') patterns are less usual, though more common later in the age. There will be a short (2–4-bar) introduction, the strophes divided by (2–4-bar) interludes, with a short (2–4-bar) coda to conclude.

The harmonic language is rich and expressive, but not until Delius, Bax and Bridge does it progress much beyond the occasional 9th or more exotic Ravelian discord. The idiom is predominantly harmonic – contrapuntal techniques are kept well out of the way; the realisation and exploitation of such resources were the rediscovery of later songwriters.

The English Romantic Song is fundamentally lyrical, its subject-matter serious. It prefers the mask of tragedy to that of comedy. There are few 'comedies' (as opposed to comic songs) in the repertoire; a song such as Warlock's 'Away to Twiver' is exceptional. Wit and humour are not what one associates with English Romantic Song – indeed with Romantic Art in general. Matthew Arnold's 'High Seriousness' reigns. The levity or wry, ironic questioning found in the songs of Hugo Wolf or Francis Poulenc has no place.

What links these 20 composers, other than the desire to set English poetry to music? In all cases they lived through, and were affected by, the First World War. Butterworth and Browne died in it, and Gurney and Moeran suffered for the rest of their lives from fighting in it. Many lost friends and relatives: in Ernest Farrar (himself a talented songwriter), Finzi lost his teacher and Bridge one of his greatest friends. Elgar never recovered from the trauma; Delius had to leave his home in France to live 'in exile' in his native England. Vaughan Williams gave up four years of his career to enlist in the Royal Army Medical Corps. World War One cast a shadow over all, and in doing so shaped the music and the choice of poetry for setting.

Secondly, these songwriters are linked by the influence of the two pioneers, Parry and Stanford: Parry by example, Stanford as a teacher. Stanford's extraordinary tally of students who later distinguished themselves as composers is referred to in Chapter 2. Parry's inspiration, if not immediate – as in the case of Somervell, Vaughan Williams, Holst and Finzi – was indirectly one of the most potent. His *English Lyrics,* published between demurely reticent, dove-grey covers, symbolically garlanded with oak-leaves and acorns, acted as a marker and touchstone for English Romantic Song.

Thirdly, these composers were complemented and inspired by a generation of talented British singers: not only the great names of Gervase Elwes, John Coates, Muriel Foster, Ada Crossley, Clara Butt, Plunket Greene and Steuart Wilson, but lesser lights, some now all-but-forgotten, such as Denham Price, Agnes Nichols, Mark Raphael and Philip Wilson.

There are no distracting footnotes to this book. The references cited in the text (e.g. Hold, 1901: 5) can be found in the Bibliography. Dates of composition and publication of songs are differentiated by Roman and Italic types (e.g. Delius's 'I-Brasil' (1913, *1915*)).

Finally, a brief note about the Epigraphs appended to each of the main chapters. All are taken from poems set by the composer in question and are chosen because they have special significance or symbolism. They encapsulate the composer's life/character/personality (as with Parry, Stanford and Holst); or his songwriting career (Somervell, Vaughan Williams and Bridge); or they come from a key song in his output (Gibbs, Browne, Howells and Warlock).

It is impossible in a book of this kind to mention everyone to whom one is indebted: all the song-composers who have delighted the ears over the past sixty years, all the singers and accompanists who have brought those songs to life, the writers who have opened my ears and pointed the way. But, specifically, I would like to thank the following, without whom the book would not have been written:

The late John Bishop, who asked me to write the book in the first place and who was ever ready to furnish me with copies of songs and to answer queries – if he did not know the answer himself, he invariably knew who did; Lewis Foreman, who has always been generous in giving his time and sharing his vast knowledge of English music; Michael Pilkington, for sharing with me his encyclopaedic knowledge of English song; Michael Hurd, who meticulously read through my original draft and whose professional eye tidied up loose ends and unravelled some of my awkwardly-written sentences; Stephen Banfield, whose pioneering study of English Romantic Song, *Sensibility and English Song*, has been a constant reference and guide; all the singers who have put up with my accompaniments over the years and with whom I was able to explore the English song-repertoire, notably John Potter, Kate and Malcolm Bown, Susan Jenkins, Kenneth Park and David Wilson-Johnson; Edward Storey and Bill Forster, with whom I tutored many enjoyable weekend courses devoted to the ever fascinating topic of Words-and-Music; Bruce Phillips, Caroline Palmer, Pru Harrison and the staff at Boydell & Brewer, for taking on the publication and seeing it through the press; those musical trusts and societies who so generously gave financial subsidy towards the production of the book – the Frank Bridge Bequest, the Delius Trust, the Ivor Gurney Society, G. & I. Holst Ltd, the John Ireland Trust, the R.V.W. Trust, and the Peter Warlock Society; and last, but never least, my wife Sue – far more gifted than I at writing prose, she has corrected my grammar and syntax and curbed my flights of poetic fancy as well as going Box-and-Cox with the typing.

Trevor Hold
June 2002

Introduction: Setting Poetry to Music

Words move, music moves
Only in Time.
           T. S. Eliot: *Burnt Norton*

Song lives a mermaid-like existence, half in words, half in music, the offspring of the marriage of two quite different parent arts, poetry and music, which can and do exist perfectly happily on their own. But for some reason the two arts have always been attracted to each other; no songless people, as far as it is known, has ever been discovered (Scholes, 1955: 971). They have their own distinctive techniques and logic: indeed, as in so many marriages, it is the differences that attract. But even so, to effect a 'harmonious meeting', they need something in common, and here the most important link is that both are temporal arts, wherein attention is thrown forward in time in a 'fixed and determinate succession' (Hadow, 1928: 224). They both rely on the passing of time in order to be understood, as distinct from the spatial arts of painting and sculpture. Without this fact, no marriage would be possible. One could hardly set a painting to music . . . 'The organisation of sound into rhythm is fundamental to both' (Pattison, 1948: 76). But there the affinities cease, for music relies far more on the passing of time than poetry. As W. H. Auden succinctly put it, 'In music . . . the movement is the expression; in poetry it is but a very small part of it' (1957: ix). Whereas when reading a poem, you are able to go back and re-read, with a song this is not possible, for the ongoing movement *is* the experience, and once the singing is over, the lyric has flown. There are other crucial differences. Poetry relies for its comprehensibility on the gradual unfolding of ideas through a logical network of words and phrases. Though, within these words and phrases, 'sound' is important, through alliteration, rhyme and assonance, it is a subsidiary function. It is the *meaning* of the words that is paramount. Poetry's subject-matter is the world of ideas, not the world of sound – the sounds of the words are the means to an end, not the end itself. By comparison, music is, to borrow Dryden's description, 'inarticulate'. It can suggest but never discuss or narrate ideas. Its appeal is to structure rather than content, relying for *its* comprehensibility on the repetition (reprise/recapitulation), variation or adaptation (development) of musical ideas. Repetition of ideas is essential in music; in poetry it is usually to be avoided.

Even in areas where a meeting-point is possible, it is often more of an illusion than reality. The art of songwriting is essentially one of artistic deception. It is like a person walking towards his own reflection in a looking-glass, to the point where he almost touches that reflection. The two images meet – *almost*, but never *quite*. So it is with the song: the words and the music can, in a masterpiece such as Dowland's 'In darkness let me dwell' or Britten's *Serenade*, blend until we cannot distinguish one art from the other; but they only blend, never unite. It is the masterly illusion of a master conjuror. But the same can be said of all art. Take rhythm, for example. Rhythm in poetry is not the same as rhythm in music. For the variety and subtlety of its rhythm, poetry relies on different pressures of accent over what are basically simple metrical schemes. If an iambic pentameter is being used, there must always be ten syllables, five stressed, five unstressed, and though there is some 'counterpointing' of the rhythm of the words with the metre, this is insignificant. For metre to be treated with such naivety in music is unthinkable. Music is able to admit a wide variety of durations within a basic metrical pattern; moreover, it is able to avoid direct contact with the underlying stress. This flexibility of rhythm is one of music's greatest assets. Nevertheless, it is technically through rhythm and form that the two arts effect a liaison, though both have to compromise to achieve this. In order to write words for musical setting successfully, the poet has to craft his words with care and keep in mind some basic rules-of-thumb. These can prove restrictive and irksome, as even a master-craftsman such as John Dryden discovered to his annoyance: 'I have been obliged to cramp my verses, and make them rugged to the Reader, that they may be harmonious to the Hearer', adding, as an insurance, 'I flatter myself with an imagination, that a judicious audience will easily distinguish betwixt the songs wherein I have complied with [the composer], and those in which I have followed the rules of Poetry' (Preface to *King Arthur*, 1691). It might appear that it is poetry that has to make most of the compromises in this marriage. Indeed, some might argue that Song is the offspring of a morganatic marriage, Poetry the poor partner, Music the high-born partner with all the rights of decision. But Music, too, has to make adjustments. There is a fundamental difference between writing vocal music and instrumental music. Composers have always understood this, even if they have not always acted upon it. Thomas Morley, in his *A Plaine and Easie Introduction to Practicalle Musicke* (1597), makes a simple division between music made 'on a ditty' and music made 'without a ditty'. When writing music 'without a ditty', i.e. abstract instrumental music, a composer can allow his imagination to fly freely, following its own abstract aural logic, and to experiment with form, harmony, texture. When writing music 'on a ditty', however, his primary concern must be the conveyance of the poetic text: not only fidelity to 'just note and accent' but also to the poem's structure. The core of the matter is this: in music where words are set, there is, before a note of music is written, already a logical structure in place, formed by the pattern of words. This pattern of words will articulate ideas, situation and mood. If the words chosen for setting are poetry, there will also be a clear-cut formal structure, articulated by line-length, stanza-shape and poetic form, aided and abetted by rhyme, assonance and alliteration. The composer may well decide to ignore this framework. Some, like Michael Tippett, may even advocate that the poetic framework should be destroyed (1960: 466). Often the formal structure of a poem will be submerged or transfigured, as, for example, when a composer sets a poetic form such as the sonnet. But when a poet has deliberately written words-for-music and gone out of his way to supply melo-poetic features, such as repeated words, phrases, refrain-lines, etc., the composer would be obtuse not to match the poem's shape in musical terms. A composer chooses to set a poem not just for what it says, but for the way in which it is said, and the shape of a poem is intrinsically bound up with the way it is said.

There are four possible ways in which a song can come into being: the songwriter can write both words and music; the poet and the composer can collaborate directly with each other; the composer can set a poem to music that he has come upon in his reading; the poet can write words to a melody that he has come upon in his listening. One of the most popular questions about songwriting, pulled perennially like a chestnut out of the fire, is 'What comes first – the words, or the music?' In the case of popular song, there is no clear answer: sometimes it is the words, sometimes the music. We have it from no less an authority than Ira Gershwin that in his collaboration with his brother, George, it was often George who would come up with the tune first, and Ira who would then fit lyrics to it. (See his commentary on 'It ain't necessarily so' in *Lyrics on Several Occasions* (1977: 147–150).) The art of contrafactum, writing words to existing melodies, is an ancient one. Folksongs have regularly been dressed up with new verses; the writers of topical ballads, hawked in the streets of London in the 16th, 17th, 18th and 19th centuries, all did this: new words to existing tunes, so well known that they were printed without music, with simply the instruction 'To be sung to the tune of Jenny Adair, Lillibulero, The Grey Goose, etc., etc.' Many of the finest lyric-writers amongst our poets learned their trade by this means: Shakespeare, Gay, Clare, Hardy all indulged in contra-factum at one time or another, and became the better lyric-writers for it. But as far as art-song is concerned, the answer is the opposite: the words come first, the music second. The examples of contrafactum in art-song – for example, Bax's 'The enchanted fiddle' – are so exceptional as to be curiosities. Of the other three options mentioned, the idea of the poet-composer, though ideal, is idealistic. The artist with the dual talents of Thomas Campion or Ivor Gurney is exceedingly rare. More realistic is the direct collaboration between poet and composer, and the advantages of this are many and obvious. As with clothes, the tailor-made affords a better fit than the 'off-the-peg'; if the suit doesn't fit, you can always send it back for alterations. Such direct collaboration was common practice up to the end of the 17th century. Since then, however, with the growing rift between poets and composers, as both went their own ways developing their arts independently, art-song has relied upon the last option – of composers turning to pre-existing poetry for their inspiration. By the end of the 19th century and the period of English Romantic Song under discussion, the choice of poetic clothes was becoming more and more antique in cut; composers were favouring lyrics from earlier centuries, particularly the great 16th- and 17th-century depositories of song-lyrics, as much as and, sometimes, more than their own poetic contemporaries.

What are a composer's touchstones in choosing a poem for setting to music? This is not the appropriate place to discuss in detail the vexed and thorny question of 'words-for-music' – this I have already done in my article ' "Words for Music": an old problem revisited' (1986/7: 283–96). Therefore I shall summarise the matter briefly. There are basically two schools of thought: on the one hand those who believe that composers are justified in setting to music anything they wish; on the other, those who believe that 'words-for-music' is a specialised craft. By and large, it is the poets who advocate a special craft of 'words-for-music', the composers who do not. To take one extreme, it is clear that anything written *could* be set to music, prose as well as poetry: dinner menus, shopping lists, book indexes. Indeed, they have. (I wouldn't be surprised if someone hasn't set portions of a telephone directory.) But is it worth it? As we have seen, words and music approach each other most closely in lyric poetry, and it is there that art-song for the most part dwells. What a composer is looking for is poetry that suggests and hints, but has no need to explain. Philip Larkin once observed (1981) that poems which are 'self-sufficient as eggs' are hardly likely to be suitable for musical setting, for there is nothing left for the composer to add. The Elizabethans knew this and differentiated between words to be read and words to be set. Compare, for example, the two versions that Sidney made of his famous poem 'My true love hath my heart':

(i)   My true love hath my heart and I have his,
          By just exchange one for another given;
      I hold his dear, and mine he cannot miss,
          There never was a better bargain driven.
            My true love hath my heart and I have his.

      His heart in me keeps him and me in one,
          My heart in him his thoughts and senses guides;
      He loves my heart, for once it was his own,
          I cherish his, because in me it bides.
            My true love hath my heart and I have his.
                        Art of English Poesie, 1589

(ii)   My true Love hath my heart, and I have his,
      By just exchange one for the other given:
      I held his dear, and mine he cannot miss;
      There never was a better bargain driven.
      His heart in me keeps me and him in one,
      My heart in him his thoughts and senses guides:
      He loves my heart, for once it was his own;
      I cherish his because in me it bides.
      His heart his wound receivëd from my sight,
      My heart was wounded with his wounded heart;

For as from me, on him his hurt did smart.
So still methought in me his hurt did smart.
    Both, equal hurt, in this change sought our bliss:
    My true Love hath my heart, and I have his.
Arcadia, 3rd ed., 1598

Basically they are the same poem: the language is the same, as are the ideas and many of the phrases. The first, however, is a lyric, a poem to be sung; the second is a sonnet, a poem to be read.

Cecil Day Lewis has written that the business of the song-lyric is 'to make words sing and dance, not to make them argue, moralise or speechify' (1961: 11). It follows that didactic, ruminative and satirical modes of thought are alien to it. Nor can music deal with complex or involved ideas: it needs to go straight to the heart of the matter. Therefore the poetic device of irony is extremely difficult to handle in song. Despite their attractiveness in so many other respects, the lyrics of Heine and Housman have caused problems for song-composers in this respect. Take, for example, 'Is my team ploughing?' from Housman's *A Shropshire Lad*:

'Is my friend hearty,
    Now I am thin and pine,
And has he found to sleep in
    A better bed than mine?'

Yes, lad, I lie easy,
    I lie as lads would choose;
I cheer a dead man's sweetheart,
    Never ask me whose.

Has any song-composer managed to capture the correct tone-of-voice for that final stanza? What began as an elegiac poem ends ironically, spoken with the tongue in the cheek, a sting in the tail. But how can music deal with this abrupt and subtle change of mood? Neither Butterworth's setting (elegiac) nor Vaughan Williams's (hysterical) is satisfactory. Take another example, Hardy's 'The self-unseeing':

Here is the ancient floor,
Footworn and hollowed and thin,
Here was the former door
Where the dead feet walked in.

She sat here in her chair,
Smiling into the fire;
He who played stood there,
Bowing it higher and higher.

Childlike, I danced in a dream;
Blessing emblazoned that day;
Everything glowed with a gleam;
Yet we were looking away!

At first glance, this is a simple, straightforward lyric – deceptively so, for further reading shows it to be threaded through with subtleties of thought and allusion. Take, for example, those personal pronouns: who is doing what, when and where? This is a poem which needs to be read and re-read for all its layers of meaning to be understood, and any attempt to set it to music – where such re-perusal is impossible – is unlikely to succeed. Gerald Finzi's setting, in *Before and After Summer*, merely skims the surface of Hardy's thinking and trivialises the poem.

Songs can, of course, be ironical, but it is a quite different sort of irony to poetic irony, consisting usually of deliberate mismatching of text and music. John Ireland's setting of Sylvia Townsend Warner's poems, 'The soldier's return' and 'The scapegoat', in *Songs Sacred and Profane*, demonstrates this, as do many songs by Benjamin Britten (*A Charm of Lullabies* (1947) is full of such ironical cross-graining, uneasy music contradicting the mood of the cradle-poetry). Such ironical modes are a feature of much music post World War I, but relatively rare in English Romantic Song, where composers sought to match mood with mood.

A fundamental problem common to all vocal music, whether opera, oratorio or solo song, is the audibility and comprehension of sung words. This requires special technical considerations. The poem should be written in simple and precise language, with plenty of open vowels, not over-clogged with sibilants or consonants, short words in preference to long, and short sentences with strong verbs and nouns; repetitions, alliteration, assonance and onomatopoeia are all helpful, as are refrains which, Pattison reminds us, are 'one of the oldest and most universal concessions of the poet to the composer' (1948: 155), and (always a welcome bonus) aural imagery – references to musical instruments and natural sounds (the wind – falling rain – the sea – bird song). Campion, Shakespeare and those anonymous Elizabethan lyricists knew exactly what was required. In the intervening centuries the art seems to have been lost, and today, with the outstanding exception of musical theatre, it is very difficult for a composer to find a poet who has even the basic knowledge of the craft. (Why is it, I wonder, that some of the most effective 20th-century 'words-for-music' are not original English poetry, but the translations from the Chinese by Arthur Waley or the Latin by Helen Waddell?)

Why does a composer set a poem to music? What is his justification and objective, and what are his criteria? Gerald Finzi, in a letter to Howard Ferguson (December 1936, Ferguson and Hurd, 2001: 139), wrote: 'But the first & last thing is that a composer is (presumably) moved by a poem & wishes to identify himself with it & to share it.' Too often composers choose to set a poem simply because they like it: they are touched by its sentiments, its subject-matter, its imagery. But this is not enough. The composer should ask himself whether the poem needs music adding to it. If the poem is a 'complete', satisfactory work of art, 'self-sufficient' as Larkin's egg (as, for example, a Shakespeare sonnet or Keats ode), is it not an impertinence, a 'gilding of the lily', to impose music on it? Much better to choose poetry which is deliberately conceived for musical setting, or poetry which is adaptable to musical treatment and which has within it 'sufficient room to tolerate the presence of music' (Barbier, in Bernac, 1977: 40). Arthur Hutchings has pointed out the distinction between 'The man who wants to set a poem, and the man who wants a poem to set' (1963: 34). I think that we must deplore the latter – though, heaven knows, in practice it is all too common – and encourage the former.

Having justified his choice of poem, what are the composer's aims and objective in setting it to music? The answer will vary considerably, ranging from high ideals – to give a musical interpretation of the poet's thoughts; to add, through music, an illumination to the poet's ideas; to add emotional depth to the poet's sentiments – to more mundane aims, such as fitting the words with an attractive melody, or setting them with great care for prosody and 'just note and accent'. All these objectives are, of course, desirable, but none sufficient in itself. Something else is needed. No matter what the literary quality of the text – whether doggerel verse or Shakespeare sonnet – the composer must be able to transform his creation into a convincing new art-form: Song. This, in the end, can be the only justification for setting words to music.

Ever since the Renaissance, one of the main criteria for judging a solo song was on its faithfulness to its text: its attention to declamation and its expressiveness. Until the early 19th century, the onus here was on the vocal line; the role of the accompaniment, whether lute or harpsichord, was secondary. With the development of the piano in the early 19th century and the simultaneous emergence of the Romantic movement in poetry, perceptions changed. The expressive qualities of the piano were harnessed as a vital means of bringing to life the pictorial and emotional elements of the poetry. Though the singer obviously maintained the key role in the declamation of the text, the piano acted as a running commentary. In this partnership between voice and accompaniment lie the origins of the Romantic art-song as we know it, pioneered, if not invented, in the German *Lied* by Schubert, developed and consolidated by Schumann, Brahms, Wolf and Strauss, and emulated and translated into their own national traditions by Fauré, Duparc, Debussy and Ravel in France, Grieg in Norway, Mussorgsky and Tchaikovsky in Russia. In Britain, the art-song was slow to take root for a variety of reasons (see Temperley and Bush (1988) and Banfield (1985)), but when it eventually did, in the last decade of the 19th century, the result was one of the most remarkable flowerings of English song since, and in every way comparable with, the Golden Age of the late 16th, early 17th century. This period, stretching roughly in time from 1890 to 1940, represents English Romantic Song, which forms the subject of this book.

How do we judge a successful art-song? Though there can be no definitive answer, the following touchstones are useful. First and foremost is the composer's ability to respond to the text. Secondly, his ability, by the process of imaginative alchemy, to combine words with music to create the new art-form of song. The fulfilment of these basic demands may require the following:

(1) the realisation of an apposite musical form which will illuminate and encompass the shape of the original text;
(2) fidelity to the interpretation of the text and to its declamation;
(3) an imaginative (and therefore memorable) and well-shaped vocal line;
(4) an accompaniment which is both idiosyncratic and illuminating to the text.

Not every successful song will contain all of these ingredients at one and the same time. It is possible to produce a good song where the 'note and accent' of the word-setting is not 'just' – *vide* Stravinsky's *In Memoriam Dylan Thomas* – or where the composer's interpretation may not quite be the same as the poet's – *vide* Britten's setting of Wilfred Owen's 'Strange meeting' (*War Requiem*) or John Ireland's setting of Masefield's 'Sea fever' – and there are many examples in the repertoire that are hampered by awkward vocal lines and poor accompaniments. But one could hardly imagine a masterpiece of song that did not contain most of these ingredients.

In the art-song, the relationship between vocal line and accompaniment is crucial. The singer's role, because it is the conveyor of the words, must always be *prima inter pares* and the accompaniment should partner but never dominate the vocal line. Over-written, over-elaborate accompaniments are a fault which plagues many songs in the English repertoire, as we shall see in the case of the early songs of Arnold Bax. Although the setting of the words must be the song-composer's prime concern, it is not necessarily his first task. For many composers, the priority is to establish the mood of the poem, and this may involve conceiving ideas for the accompaniment before they set a single word to music. Composing the vocal line is a balancing act, juggling the competing requirements of poetry and music. How do you achieve a memorable musical line without harming the poetic line? And how do you achieve 'just note and accent' without abandoning the musical line? The setting of the words always has to be uppermost: after all, why set a text to music unless you absolutely need to, when you could write a piece of instrumental music instead? If you choose to set a text, then, *noblesse oblige*, you should honour it by matching in your music its mood and meaning, and declamation. On the other hand, unless you are writing recitative, in which the text itself acts as the main structural prop, the music will require its own structures to give the song sense and integrity. As Peter Warlock wrote, 'If words are set to music, the music must be as independent an entity as the poem' (Heseltine, 1917: 46). There is a distinction, however, between a self-contained vocal line and a catchy tune, though, as Vaughan Williams confessed:

> We composers are an unconscientious crowd and are much too apt to use the great poets as mere pegs on which to hang our silly little tunes (Letter to Philip Henderson, 31/1/1937, quoted in Kennedy, 2/1980: 254).

Elgar is a songwriter whom one often feels is guilty of pegging his tunes to his texts rather than setting his texts to music.

The art of declamation – the mirroring of the rhythms of poetry into the rhythms of music – is an essential tool of the trade. Thomas Morley succinctly explained this over 400 years ago:

> We must also have a care to applie the notes to the wordes . . . that we cause no sillable which is by nature short to be expressed by manie notes or one long note, nor no long sillable to be expressed with a short note (*A Plaine and Easie Introduction* . . . (1597)).

With some composers, one senses a strain and struggle to mirror the prosody of the text in the music. But with all the great song-composers it is a natural talent: one feels that they hardly have to give it a thought. It is not necessary to follow the example of Gerald Finzi, who took fastidious care to capture natural nuances and subtle inflections of speech in his songs. On the other hand, the views advocated by the young Benjamin Britten that:

> the composer should not deliberately avoid unnatural stresses if the prosody of the poem and the emotional situation demand them, nor be afraid of a high-handed treatment of the words (1945: 8)

are rather high-handed themselves and certainly not to be recommended to a would-be songwriter. (I am sure that Britten would be the last person to advocate the treatment of English prosody which he so amusingly satirised in the 'Play of Pyramus and Thisbe' in his opera *A Midsummer Night's Dream*.) Occasionally, however, unexpected or 'unnatural' word-setting can produce magical results. Who but the sourest puritan would begrudge Britten the evocative way in which he separates the words 'And she is not afraid of their foot-fall' in his setting of Wilfred Owen's 'The kind ghosts' in *Nocturne* (Ex. 1)?

Ex. 1

That there is enormous leeway and scope in setting words to music can be seen by comparing the settings of the same text by different composers. Take, for example, the treatment of Shakespeare's 'It was a lover and his lass' by Quilter, Warlock and Finzi (Ex. 2).

Ex. 2(a)

Ex. 2(b)

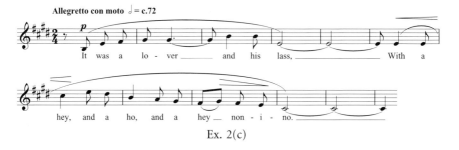

Ex. 2(c)

The best advice on the matter is the *res media* advocated, not by a composer, but by that musically-aware poet, Ezra Pound, in the 'briefest set of rules on which we may assume that intelligent musicians and poets are alike agreed':

> First, that the words of a song sung should be intelligible.
> Second, that words should not be unreasonably distorted.
> Third, that the rhythm of poetry should not be unreasonably ruined by the musician setting it to music (1912: 343–4).

Another quality found in all the best songwriters is the ability to allow the words to breathe. So many composers, once they have embarked on setting a poem, seem to have only one end in view: to get the words set and done with as quickly as possible. They hurtle through the text like steeplechasers, as though to reach the finishing line was their only purpose. 'Words take longer to sing than to speak', wrote W. H. Auden (1957: x) and words sung take longer to make their point than words read. The more breathing space given to the words, the more likely is the listener to comprehend them. Ivor Gurney was a songwriter with an impeccable sense of timing, who knew exactly how to pace the setting of words in a song. He never rushes his word-setting, with the result that his songs are spacious and airy. He is not afraid of silence: 'those silences that amount to genius', as Herbert Howells perceptibly wrote (1938: 15). He breaks up the vocal line between phrases and sentences to allow the music to fill in what he reads as the poet's unsaid, inexpressible thoughts. Take, for example, such songs as 'The Lent lily' (*Ludlow and Teme*) and 'The folly of being comforted'. But, of course, Gurney was a poet himself.

There are two technical features in songwriting that have been hallowed by composers through the centuries but equally abhorred by poets: the use of melisma and the use of text-repetition. W. B. Yeats's injunction, 'A musician who would give me pleasure should not repeat a line, or put more than one note to one syllable' (1922) sums up the poet's attitude. Melisma – the singing of more than one note to a syllable – has for centuries been accepted as a vocal technique not only in art-song but also in folk and popular song. It can, if overused or handled indiscreetly, distort and obscure the sense of the words, making them difficult to be heard clearly. This is certainly the case in vocal writing of the Baroque period, and it led to a reaction by 19th-century songwriters such as Parry and Stanford, who stuck to the almost Cranmerian one-syllable/one-note style of declamation. But this puritanical restriction is unnecessarily limiting and precludes the expressive aspects of melisma. For melisma is a means not only of underlining important words but also of expressing emotional feelings of joy, ecstasy and the like. When handled sensitively and imaginatively, as by English composers such as Purcell, Britten and Tippett, it does not obscure but rather illuminates the text. Generally speaking, however, melisma is by no means a common feature of English Romantic Song, conspicuous perhaps by its absence; when encountered it is often used for quasi-archaic purposes, as 'historical' imagery, as in Finzi's 'Come away, death' (see Ex. 20.12).

The question of repetition of text is a different matter. The poet's complaint is that composers often repeat parts of his poem – not just words and phrases, but whole stanzas, '[making] me say twice what I have only said once', as Tennyson once remarked. The problem arises because music, unlike poetry, is an art which thrives on repetition and reprise. Many poets, appreciating the importance of this, have tried to help composers by deliberately including repetitions in their song-lyrics; they realise that, in the transitory flight of a poem when sung, repetition of key words and phrases may be essential to their comprehension. Shakespeare's song-lyrics are full of verbal repetition: 'Merrily, merrily', 'Come away, come away', 'jog on, jog on', 'Arise! Arise! Arise!', 'Blow, blow . . . Freeze, freeze', 'Reply! Reply!', 'Come hither! Come hither!', 'Cuckoo! Cuckoo! Cuckoo!' He did not repeat the words for fun, but for emphasis. Tennyson tried to circumvent the unauthorised repetition that he deplored by supplying his own: 'Break, break, break' is the opening of one of his most powerful lyrics, and the repetition of the word 'dying' in 'The splendour falls' has been a god-send to every composer who has set it. Repetition of entire stanzas, though less common, is also to be found, as in Matthew Arnold's 'Come to me in my dreams' and R. L. Stevenson's 'The vagabond'; in both cases the poets repeat their opening stanzas at the end. It is unsanctioned, mere-tricious repetition that annoys the poet. There are even cases of composers repeating repetitions. Britten adds four extra 'dying's to his setting of 'The splendour falls', and, not content with Housman's repetition of ''Tis true, 'tis true' at the end of 'When I was one-and-twenty', Butterworth adds another. In both cases the repetitions are justified by the musical results. Even so, it suggests that the poet can never get it right: 'give the composer and inch . . .'! Far less excusable are the instances where composers repeat whole stanzas of a poet's text for purely musical reasons. This often takes the form of the repetition of the opening stanza with its original music at the end of a song, to give the song a musical framework. Quilter, usually a fastidious respecter of the poet's intention, does this in his setting of Herrick's 'Cherry ripe', and Butterworth in his setting of Housman's 'Think no more, lad'.

Equally unacceptable is the reverse procedure, where a composer omits portions of a poem. One of the most notorious instances is in Vaughan Williams's *On Wenlock Edge*, where the composer omits two stanzas from Housman's dialogue poem, 'Is my team ploughing?' This infuriated Housman, who asked how Vaughan Williams would like it if two bars were cut out of his music. Vaughan Williams replied:

> The composer has a perfect right artistically to set any portion of a poem he chooses provided he does not alter the sense.

adding cheekily:

> I feel that a poet should be grateful to anyone who fails to perpetuate such lines as:
>> The goal stands up, the keeper
>> Stands up to keep the goal
>>> (in Grant Richards, 1941: 221).

As Ernest Newman commented, the omission of these stanzas destroys the poet's effect of 'a gradual, almost casual, transition from the ghost's questions about the common things of life to the question about his sweetheart' (1918: 397). One can see, however, why Vaughan Williams jibbed: those two footballing stanzas are prosaic and low-key and consequently difficult to set to music, though both Butterworth and Orr managed to accommodate them perfectly satisfactorily. One extreme example of both omission and commission is found in Frank Bridge's setting of Yeats's 'When you are old and grey'. Not only does Bridge omit the final stanza of the poem, but he compounds the offence by repeating the first stanza in its place, thus adding insult to injury. In doing so, he commits the crime of altering the sense of the poem. And yet the song, in the 'sense' that Bridge gives it, is beautifully attractive and convincing, even if it is not the song that Yeats had in mind.

The function of the accompaniment in song-setting takes many forms. At a very basic, practical level, it is to give support to the singer, by supplying the initial intonation and thereafter to help keep the singer in tune. But, of course, in the development of the art-song it has taken on many other roles: rhythmic, harmonic, dramatic and illustrative. By taking over some of the aspects of the text-setting – by establishing mood and atmosphere, underpinning the song's harmonic structure, underlining the text through word-painting, etc. – the accompaniment frees the singer to concentrate on the prime task of the song: the conveyance of the text. Just as the vocal line can capture the 'jizz' of the lyric, so the piano can reflect the poem's subject-matter and mood through musical analogy. This it can do particularly when there are aural references in the text: the swaying of a boat – the sound of bells – a dance in progress – soldiers marching, etc. The piano accompaniment is thus able to enlarge on pictorial detail in the poem, using some figure or motive to create a picture in sound: the sound of a mill-wheel (as in Vaughan Williams's 'The water mill'); the various entertainments at a country wedding (Warlock's 'Away to Twiver'); the motion of a steam train (Britten's 'Midnight on the Great Western'); a woman dancing (Browne's 'To Gratiana, dancing and singing'). Thus, as Colles expresses it, 'The verbal picture passes through the voice to the instrument' (1928: 140), and in doing so, the piano is linked not only to the text but to the singer, emphasising the partnership between the two. In addition, through its ability to supply instrumental preludes, interludes and codas, the accompaniment provides other crucial functions: giving continuity to the musical flow of the setting; re-enforcing the formal shapes of the song; and, at a very practical level, allowing the singer breathing space within and between strophes without sacrificing continuity, while at the same time giving the poem 'breathing space'.

The reference to the piano's capability to convey pictorial detail raises another danger-fraught issue in song-composition, word-painting: that is, matching poetic imagery with musical analogy. Though it applies to both the vocal line and the accompaniment, in art-song it is mainly the concern of the accompaniment, and for that reason does not upset the poets as much as the other contentious issues discussed earlier. Word-painting is an essential – and natural – ingredient in the art-song, as Thomas Morley long ago realised:

> You must have a care that when your matter signifieth ascending, high heaven, and such like you make your musicke ascend; and by the contrarie when your dittie speaketh of descending lowenes, depth, hell, and others such, you must make your musicke descend, for as it will be thought a great absurditie to talke of heaven and point downwarde to the earth; so will it be counted great incongruitie if a musician upon the wordes *he ascended into heaven* should cause his musicke descend, or by the contrarie upon the descension should cause his musicke to ascend (1597).

Word-painting can range from an individual word – for example, the word 'frosted' in Howells's 'The Lady Caroline' (bar 9) – to an entire song – the military march which underpins Somervell's 'The street sounds to the soldiers' tread'. But the use of word-painting can easily lead to naivety and an over-concern with detail. All of the great song-composers wielded the word-paintbrush with extreme care:

> The musical composer who catches at every particular epithet or metaphor that the part affords him to show his imitative power, will never fail to hurt the true aim of his composition (Charles Avison, 1752).

'To underline a poem word by word,' wrote Warlock, 'is the work of a misguided schoolmaster'. Though attention has to be given to each detail, it is the overall mood and shape of the song that matters; otherwise, sight of the wood will be lost for the trees. For example, just because a cuckoo is referred to in the text does not necessarily mean that we must hear it sing. If it must call, then let it do so in an imaginative and tasteful way. In his setting of Shakespeare's notoriously cuckoo-dominated lyric 'When daisies pied', Warlock himself gets round the problem by saturating his texture with cuckoo calls. There is hardly a bar without one. In this way he conceals any possibility of meretriciousness, for the cuckoo-call becomes the basic musical motive of the song. (At the same time he manages to combine the cuckoo with the cuckolded – the underlying theme of the song – by wittily concealing a reference to Mendelssohn's 'Wedding March': see Ex. 18.20(c)).

The experienced song-composer knows that, as with any technical device, word-painting is effective in inverse ratio to its use. There are so many fine examples in English Romantic Song that it is invidious to make a selection, but outstanding moments, subtle yet tellingly effective, include Denis Browne's 'To Gratiana dancing and singing' (a 17th-century *almand* measure acting as a background music to the dance); Somervell's 'The street sounds to the soldiers' tread' (soldiers passing by to the strains of a military march); Vaughan Williams's 'Bredon Hill' (bells ringing) and 'The water mill' (the sounds of mill-wheel and clocks). All of these might be described as 'continuous musical metaphors' in that they act as the piano's musical material throughout the song. A more sophisticated example, which defies Warlock's reprimand about the misguided schoolmaster, is Holst's 'The floral bandit', which picks up image after image from Humbert Wolfe's poem, yet still manages to work through sheer musical wit.

Related to word-painting is the composer's response to the poet's use of simile and extended metaphor. Apart from the fact that long similes are very difficult to accommodate and make sense of in musical setting, they can often take attention away from the real point and meaning of a poem. This is illustrated in two poems which have both received several musical settings: Shelley's 'Music, when soft voices die' and Edward Shanks's 'The fields are full'. Shelley's poem is *not* about music, but about memory. The three images in the poem – music, violets, rose-leaves – represent the three senses of sound, smell and sight which are used as metaphors for the eventual subject of the poem, which is (unsurprisingly) love:

> And so thy thoughts, when thou art gone,
> Love itself shall slumber on.

Edward Shanks's poem is in two stanzas, and parallels imagery of a late summer landscape and a devoted old couple:

> The fields are full of summer still
> And breathe again upon the air
> From brown dry side of hedge and hill
> More sweetness than the sense can bear.

So some old couple who in youth
With love were filled and overfull,
And loved with strength and loved with truth,
In heavy age are beautiful.

The second stanza acts as a metaphor for the first – or is it the other way round? The problem for the songwriter is to decide which is the central image – the summer fields or the old couple. (For a detailed discussion of the setting by Gibbs, Gurney and Warlock, see Banfield, 1985: 217–18.)

Reference has already been made to composers' misinterpretation of a poet's text. One of the most famous examples of this in English song is probably John Ireland's 'Sea fever'. Masefield's poem – indeed, the very title – suggests a feverish longing for the sea. You would expect, therefore, the music to be fast and feverish, with a sense of urgency to match. In Ireland's setting (marked *Lento*) there is certainly no sense of urgency; rather, it is sturdy and stoical, so that 'Sea melancholy' would be a more appropriate title. Yet the song-setting is so well known – it is and always has been the composer's most popular song – that it is almost impossible to read the poem without having Ireland's music in your ears. What can we conclude from this? Logically, from an interpretational viewpoint, Ireland's setting is wrong; emotionally, from audience reaction, it works perfectly well. That poet and song-setter can genuinely differ in interpretation is evident from Howells's setting of James Stephens's 'The goat paths'. Most people reading the poem would, I think, judge that Howells's evocation of the haze and daze of a summer noon has perfectly encapsulated the mood of Stephens's poem. Yet when Howells heard Stephens himself read the poem aloud, he was surprised: 'he made of it something unbelievably like a dynamo, utterly unlike the leisurely pastoral idyll I'd conceived it as' (Palmer, 1978: 16). Quite clearly, then, different interpretations of the same poem are possible – not just possible, but essential, for what would be the point of a poem being set more than once? A classic instance occurs in the two settings of John Fletcher's lyric 'Come, sleep' by Gurney and Warlock. Whereas Warlock's (1922) is classical and restrained, Gurney's (1913) is passionate and romantic. Yet both are valid interpretations and masterpieces in their own right (see Hold, 1980: 26–35). A similar difference of interpretation can be heard in the settings of Humbert Wolfe's 'Journey's end' by Bridge and Holst, and of Housman's 'Look not in my eyes' by Butterworth and Ireland. Perhaps one of the most striking examples of such 'cross-interpretation' are the settings of Hardy's 'Proud songsters' by Finzi and Britten. On cursory acquaintance, Britten's setting (the sixth song from *Winter Words* (1953)) sounds rushed – it is over and done with in less than a minute – and seems trivial and lacking in sensitivity, the texture no more than a continuous sequence of trills. Finzi's setting (from *Earth and Air and Rain*), on the other hand, is broad and spacious – it lasts nearly three and a half minutes – and the words are set with great care and deliberation, with a long prelude (15 bars of 4/4, at crotchet = 69) and an ample interlude (six bars) between the two verses, and quite different musical ideas for the two stanzas. 'How could Britten be so lacking in imagination?' one might ask. The answer, of course, is that he is not; as always, the clue to his setting lies in the words. The poem describes the brevity of the birds' existence as seen through the eyes of the poet-onlooker: these 'brand-new birds of twelve-months' growing' singing their hearts out 'As if all Time were theirs' – who less than two years before were only 'particles of grain,/And earth, and air, and rain', and by implication, of course, in less than two more years are not likely to be singing. That unspoken message is poignant, and it is that aspect that Finzi, as the outside human observer, endeavours to capture – the transience of beauty and of life, and inevitable thoughts of human mortality – and does so in one of his finest, most moving songs. Britten, on the other hand, is not concerned with the human observer, but with the birds themselves. His song *is* the song of the birds, in all their joyous trilling and whistling and piping, as the words fleet by. But, paradoxically, in doing so, his music captures the irony beneath Hardy's deceptively simple words: things are not what they seem – 'something lies beyond the scene'. Who is right? Neither, or each. Yet one marvels that the same poem can be set in two such completely different ways. How can one composer take three times as long as another to set the same lyric? Both are perfectly valid, perfectly effective settings. Such is the mystery of song.

In the final analysis, however, with all the 'ifs' and 'perhaps' and 'buts', the 'neverthelesses' and 'howevers' set aside, the masterpieces of English song are those in which all the parameters work together: where the composer has successfully captured the mood, interpreted the meaning, set the words with due care for their prosody and created a vocal line that is shapely and a delight to sing, a piano accompaniment that fits it like a glove yet remains idiomatic and pianistic, and a musical shape which reflects the poem's shape; where, in fact, he has found the magic alchemy to match poem and music so that the two arts are so inextricably entwined that they are metamorphosed into a new art-form altogether, song. For me such moments are not uncommon in English Romantic Song. I think of two George Butterworth songs: 'Loveliest of trees', in which the shape as well as the sentiments and mood of Housman's poem are reflected in music, so effortlessly that one almost takes it for granted; and 'On the way to Kew', where Henley's subtle use of refraining lines are brilliantly caught and 'explained' by the musical refrains; of Denis Browne's 'To Gratiana dancing and singing', where the music adds a new dimension to the poem which could never be achieved in words: a motion, a dance, a feeling of living presence; of Warlock's 'The fox', which transforms a simple rural image into a masterpiece of darkness and foreboding; of Gurney's 'On the folly of being comforted', in which Yeats's sweet-sad love-song is turned into a poignant drama; of Quilter's 'Go, lovely rose', with its subtle counterpointing of music and text; of Ireland's 'The trellis', where youthful love and the languor of a summer's day are caught forever in a point of time . . . In such cases, image and reflection do seem to meet, to such an extent that it is impossible to say which is which.

1

Hubert Parry (1848–1918)

> I hear the feet below
> In the dark street;
> They hurry and shuffle by,
> And go, on errands bitter or sweet
> Whither I cannot know.
>
> Langdon Elwyn Mitchell:
'From a city window'

Both in his life and in his music, Hubert Parry comes across as a knight-errant, a St. George battling to slay the Dragons of vulgarity, philistinism and frivolity. In an article, 'The present condition of English song-writing', published in *The Century Guild Hobby Horse* in 1888, he described the state of songwriting in England as a 'Slough of Musical Despond such as can rarely have been provided for any other nation under heaven', berating the perpetrators in no uncertain terms:

> The very facilities which song-writing has offered for making money with the very least trouble has been its curse . . . The makers of the patent trade-song, from which one may exclude successful composers in other branches of art, have been for the most part helpless dullards whose sentiment is sodden with vulgarity and commonness, whose artistic insight is a long way below zero, whose ideas of declamation are an insult to the language, and whose musical incapacity is tragi-comic; and these have been thy gods, O Israel! (Parry, 1888: 69)

One can understand and sympathise with him. Perhaps in his desire to establish an art-song tradition one detects academic earnestness and a sense of historical destiny, but there was no tradition of serious art-song in this country to match the thriving, healthy tradition of the German *Lied* or the quickly-flowering French *mélodie*: good, vulgar (in the best sense) songs for the music-hall, sentimental popular ballads for the drawing-room, but little else. Sterndale Bennett, Sullivan and Pierson had attempted to establish a tradition in different ways, with varying success, but the seeds sown had not germinated: fallen, it would seem, on stony ground. By the time he was writing his article, Parry had published his first two sets of *English Lyrics* and his Four Shakespeare Sonnets. Over the next 25 years, he was to establish almost single-handedly an English art-song tradition, laying down, for better or for worse, its ground rules and patterns: the poets to set; the method for setting English words; its scope and its special English 'sensibility'. This he did through his twelve sets of *English Lyrics*. These songs established a basis for a tradition of lyrical song on a wide front, serious and frivolous, love-songs and narrative ballads, pictorial and personal, setting a wide diversity of English poetry from song-lyrics to sonnets. The one genre that he failed to establish was an English equivalent of the *Liederkreis*. This was left to his pupil, Arthur Somervell, with his song-cycles *Maud* and *A Shropshire Lad*. Parry as a composer embodies the characteristic English sense of reticence and caution. He was unable to wear his heart on his sleeve. One often feels that he was more concerned to do justice to the poet's text than to reflect his own personal involvement in it. If, as Colles suggested (Graves, 1926 II: 168), Parry's songs were 'a sort of private diary in which he expressed his most intimate thought', then he had the diarist's ability to be selective. In his best songs, however – 'Nightfall in winter', 'From a city window', 'Through the ivory gate' – he throws caution aside and manages to open up his feelings.

Parry wrote songs throughout his career, the earliest, 'Fair is my love' (1864) and 'Why does azure deck the sky' (1865), when he was still at Eton, his last, 'The sound of hidden music', in February 1918, eight months before he died. There are some 150 songs in all. Because he had no serious English precedents to follow – the examples of earlier English song-composers such as Dowland and Purcell would have been outside his orbit of experience – Parry's models in songwriting were the masters of the German *Lied*, Schubert, Mendelssohn and particularly Schumann and Brahms. It is significant that his early settings of Shakespeare's sonnets were written not to Shakespeare's original poetry, but to German translations by Friedrich Bodenstedt; it was only afterwards that he adapted them to the original words. There were two reasons for this: to be taken seriously as a songwriter one had to set German texts or, if the poems chosen were in English, to have German translations made (as in the case of Sterndale Bennett). The second reason was that Parry found it easier to set the poems in German, as he confided to his diary on 19 November 1874 (Dibble, 1992: 116). Parry had steeped himself in the German repertoire, so not unexpectedly he adhered to German models in his songwriting. This is apparent in an early song, 'Angel hosts, sweet love, befriend thee' (1866), where the two stanzas are set to different music, i.e. '*durchkomponiert*', following the German model. His earliest acknowledged song, 'Fair is my love' (1864) has a strong Mendelssohnian flavour to it, but the influences in his first mature songs are Schumann and Brahms. In a song such as 'Take, O take those lips away' he follows the Schumannesque trait of leaving the harmonic sense of the singer's final line incomplete so that a piano postlude is necessary to round the song off. Schumann's legacy can be detected in other early songs such as 'Good night' and 'Willow, willow, willow'. Plunket Greene (Graves, 1926 II: 169) refutes the influence of Brahms, and Geoffrey Bush has pointed out (1982: xv) that, in his careful word-setting and careful choice of poetry, Parry is closer to Hugo Wolf than to Brahms. But in his musical reactions he is far closer in spirit to Brahms, and there is little doubt of Brahms's example in late songs such as 'Dirge in woods', 'The witches' wood' and 'Sleep', and even in an early song such as 'No longer mourn'. (Taken by itself, the piano part of this song could be a Brahms Intermezzo.)

Parry's first published song was a setting of Thomas Moore's 'Why does azure deck the sky' (1865, *1866*), his first songs of importance the *Three Songs*, op.12. These were turned down by Novellos but published in 1873 by Lambourn Cock. They show the influence of Schumann's songs, but are somewhat insipid by comparison. The best known is Tennyson's 'The poet's song', cast in a lightly-varied strophic form, with rather four-square writing for voice and piano. Both this and 'More fond than cushat dove' (words by 'Thomas Ingoldsby', the alias of Richard Barham (1788–1845), author of *The Ingoldsby Legends*) reside close to the Victorian parlour. More interesting is 'Music', a setting of Shelley's 'Music, when soft voices die', which attempts to raise the artistic status of the accompaniment by quasi-imitation with the vocal line (reflecting the music which 'vibrates in the memory') and some neat overlapping of voice and piano at the cadences. But by comparison with his later part-song-setting of the same text (*Six Modern Lyrics, 1897*) it is dull and penny-plain. (Dibble, 1992, reproduces the solo setting on pp. 90–1.) His discovery of Wagner and his growing acquaintance with the music of Brahms led to a broadening of his technique which is reflected in his subsequent song-groups: *Three Odes of Anacreon* (1869–78, *1880*), *A Garland of Shakespearean and Other Old-Fashioned Songs* (1873–81, *1874*) and the *Four Sonnets* of Shakespeare (1873–82, *1887*). As their title implies, the *Garland* songs were written in mock-archaic style, and he may well have been inspired in this by Sullivan's incidental music to *The Tempest* and *The Merchant of Venice*. As well as three Shakespearean texts, all with Parry's own fanciful titles – 'Love's perjuries = 'On a day – alack the day!', 'A spring song' = 'It was a lover' and 'A sea dirge' = 'Full fathom five' – he sets the anonymous 'The merry bird sits in the tree', Samuel Daniel's 'Love is a sickness, full of woe' and Skelton's 'Merry Margaret'. This conscious delving into the Great Treasure Chest of 16th- and 17th-century English lyrics foreshadows one of Parry's preoccupations in *English Lyrics*, though in his later 'old-fashioned' settings he usually avoids any Wardour-street archaisms, wisely leaving such period-piecery to the defter hands of Edward German and the like. The *Four Sonnets*, settings of Shakespeare's sonnets 29, 87, 18 and 30, are a more serious undertaking. Like Sterndale Bennett's sets of songs op. 23 and op. 35, they were published with both English and German texts. But whereas Sterndale Bennett set his songs to English texts, getting Carl Klingemann to translate them into German, Parry set the sonnets in a German translation by Friedrich Bodenstedt and then adapted the Shakespearean originals to his music afterwards – a curious Alice in Wonderland procedure! Setting the sonnet-form to music of course presented special problems. There was no question, with the rigorous through-written 14-line unit, of adapting the ballad form of song. Each sonnet had to have its own formal solution. The most attractive of the four, 'When in disgrace' ('Wenn ich, von Gott'), is also the simplest. Here he solves the structural problem by casting it into a loose but recognisable ternary unit with coda: A (lines 1–4), B (lines 5–8), A+Coda (lines 9–14). Musically the restless syncopations of the opening sweep the music onwards through the first two sections, to reach a resolution with the sudden move from minor to major mode at the words 'Haply I think on thee'. Here Parry produces a firm chordal texture, in his most noble, diatonic manner, and allows himself for the first time some word repetition and a majestic sequence (bars 39–46) (Ex. 1.1).

Ex. 1.1

Following Shakespeare's words, which use imagery of the lark arising at break of day from sullen earth as it 'sings hymns at Heaven's gate', the music maintains its buoyant mood to the end. The emphatic repetition of the final line is perhaps meritricious, but nonetheless this is an impressive song.

Almost all of Parry's energies in the field of solo song after the *Four Sonnets* were channelled into the twelve sets of *English Lyrics*. A notable exception which deserves mention is 'The soldier's tent' (1900, *1901*) for baritone and orchestra, written for the Birmingham Festival of 1902. (It was performed there the day before Elgar's *The Dream of Gerontius* received its first, disastrously ill-rehearsed performance.) Parry's choice of text was most unusual: a 'Roumanian folk-song' from the collection of *The Bard of the Dimbovitza* by Hélène Vacaresco, in the English translation by Alma Stretell and Carmen Sylva which Bax later utilised for a song-cycle [see Chapter 11]. Parry describes it as a 'scena' and it is conceived on a large scale. The poem describes a situation similar to that in Shakespeare's *Richard III*, where Richard sleeps in his tent before the Battle of Bosworth, his dreams filled with phantoms from his past. Here a nameless soldier is assailed by questions from dream-spirits whom he answers with courage and confidence. The dichotomy of the situation is realised in two musics, a lullaby-like texture for the phantoms and a soldierly *marziale* for his answers: 'I have my sword', he says, 'I have the fight' and, finally, 'I have Death.' But the vocal writing lacks strong ideas and dramatic contrast. The most imaginative writing is in the orchestral prelude and postlude where Parry evokes the nocturnal land-scape of the poem's opening lines: 'Across the mountains the mist hath drawn a cov'ring of bridal white.' But there is little sense of drama, and one can see why Parry never succeeded in writing an opera.

It is that remarkable collection of songs, the *English Lyrics*, which ultimately justifies Parry's claim as a major songwriter. They were published in twelve sets: ten during his lifetime (the first in 1885, the tenth in 1918), the remaining two posthumously in 1920. Altogether there are 74 songs, most of them arranged in groups of five, six and seven; Set I has just four, Set XI eight. They are a unique achievement. No other major British song-composer has produced so substantial a collection. Though there is no theme to the sets, each has its own distinctive character. Set II is devoted to poems by Shakespeare, Set IX to poems by Mary Coleridge; Sets III and VII are mainly devoted to Elizabethan and Jacobean poetry, Sets IV and VIII to 19th-century poetry. Sets I, V, IX and X are appropriate for a female singer, Sets II and VI for a male. Set XI is specifically designated for low or mezzo voice. They cover a wide range of mood and emotion, from 'light conceits of lovers' ('On a time the amorous Silvy') to songs of earnest philosophical idealism ('Whence'), taking in lullabies ('A Welsh lullaby') and ballads ('Proud Maisie'), landscapes ('Nightfall in winter') and poems of a personal (perhaps autobiographical) nature ('Looking backward'). Regarded as a whole, they show all the High Seriousness in art that Parry stood for. The songs are *serious* – earnest, high-minded even. Perhaps too much so. What is lacking is irony and satire; 'Love is a bable' is the nearest he ever came to this, which is a pity, for that song is extremely effective. What is also in short supply is a sense of humour. There are twinkles of humour in 'A stray nymph of Dian' and 'One silent night of late' but he is unable to let his hair down in the way that Stanford could. The nearest he comes to writing a humorous song is 'When icicles hang by the wall' (II.5) where he evokes a convivial winter scene, even managing to slip in a sly allusion to a popular song at one point. With perhaps the exception of Set XI, the weakest in terms of quality, each set contains at least one gem. Set IX is particularly consistent in invention. Above all, the *English Lyrics* show a wide and discriminating literary taste. Parry chooses not only the obvious English lyrical poets, but also many fine minor writers whose ideas appealed to him and whose poetry he found 'apt for music'.

It is easy to form the impression that Parry's choice of poet for the *English Lyrics* was mainly from the 16th and 17th centuries: that is to say, 'dead poets'. But a quick tally will show that whilst he set twenty poets from the 16th and 17th centuries, he set 37 poems by his contemporaries. (The other nineteen are from the early 19th century.) It must be said that his choice of contemporary poets was singular. Unlike Somervell, he was unable or unwilling to tackle either Browning or Tennyson, nor does he attempt other major Victorian lyric poets, such as Arnold, Bridges, Patmore or Swinburne. The omission of Robert Bridges, whom he set and indeed collaborated with on several occasions in choral works, is particularly surprising, for his stylish lyrics were to attract many song-composers of the next generation. He does set Christina Rossetti (once, but memorably) and George Meredith, but for the rest his chosen contemporaries are minor, little-known writers: Julian Sturgis, Langdon Mitchell, Mary Coleridge, A. P. Graves and Julia Chatterton. Coleridge, Sturgis and Mitchell inspired some of Parry's best songs. Mary Coleridge (1861–1907), the great-great-niece of Samuel Taylor Coleridge, was a family friend. She published a novel, *The Seven Sleepers of Ephesus* (1893), praised by R. L. Stevenson, and a collection of essays, *Non Sequitur* (1900), but is mainly known for her poetry which she collected together in *Poems Old and New* published just before her early death. Several composers as well as Parry were attracted to her poetry – Stanford in his immortal partsong 'The bluebird', Roger Quilter in his *Two September Songs* – but no-one set her more sympathetically than Parry. Julian Sturgis (1848–1904), brother of the Howard Sturgis who wrote the cult novels *Tim* and *Belchamber*, was born in Boston, Massachusetts, but brought at the age of seven months to England, where he lived for the rest of his life. He was a contemporary of Parry at Eton and remained a lifelong friend. As well as *A Book of Songs* (1894), from which the poems that Parry sets are taken, he wrote the opera librettos for Goring Thomas's *Nadeshda* (1885), Sullivan's *Ivanhoe* (1891) and Stanford's *Much Ado About Nothing* (1901). Langdon Elwyn Mitchell (1862–1935) was an American author known primarily for his theatrical work: *Becky Sharp* (his adaptation of Thackeray's *Vanity Fair*) was premiered in 1899, and *The New York Idea* in 1906. The four poems Parry sets are taken from his 1894 collection, *Poems*.

Parry's literary judgement was by no means faultless. One cannot agree with Graves when he 'safely affirmed' that 'his choice of words was impeccable' or that 'He never set a bad poem to music' (1926, II: 163). 'A girl to her glass' (V.6) and 'One golden thread' (XI.1) are feeble verse in any poet's book. But taken as a whole, Parry's choice was astute, and if all the poems he set in *English Lyrics* were brought together under one cover, they would make an impressive anthology.

'To Parry the words were everything', wrote his son-in-law, the singer Harry Plunket Greene (Graves, 1926, II: 170). Much has been written about the special quality of Parry's word-setting, almost, indeed, at the expense of the quality of the songs themselves:

> His melody . . . follows both the sense and the accentuation of the words with a fidelity that no English writer before him had ever approached . . . in the scrupulous observance of the verbal rhythm . . . he is, as ever, a model to composers (R. O. Morris, quoted in Graves, 1926, II: 166).

> In all these songs we recognise Parry's wonderful skill in accentuation, a skill that had not been so fully manifested in English music since the days of Henry Lawes (Fuller-Maitland, 1934: 19).

> . . . subtle phrasing, finely sculpted declamation and melody free of clichés – principles which Parry pioneered and which have distinguished English solo song in its finest periods (Banfield, 1985: 138).

Examples of this aspect of Parry's craft, found throughout the *English Lyrics*, can been seen in the following contrasting examples: a light ballad, 'Proud Maisie' (V.2), a personal lyric, 'Through the ivory gate' (III.5), and a sombre landscape, 'Dirge in woods' (VIII.4) (Ex. 1.2). As will be seen, it is not simply a matter of 'just note and accent' – such a basic requirement of the craft should be the *sine qua non* of every serious song-composer – but of creative imagination in the setting of the words, not necessarily taking the obvious route, but the imaginative, often unexpected one.

Ex. 1.2(a)

Ex. 1.2(b)

Ex. 1.2(c)

Parry's craft of setting English words was a personal one, which evolved through honing and experience as much as from example. His song-forms, however, are clearly modelled on those of German *Lieder,* notably varied strophic form and '*durchkomponiert*'. The latter he had used as early as his setting of Lord Francis Hervey's 'Angel hosts, sweet love, befriend thee'. Many examples of through-composed songs in *English Lyrics* are, as one would expect, settings of sonnets, such as those of Shakespeare (II.3 and VII.4) and Keats's 'Bright Star' (IV.6), but he also uses it in lighter songs, such as Sturgis's 'A stray nymph of Dian' (V.1). Geoffrey Bush states that his songs are 'generally through-composed rather than strophic' (1979: Introduction) but this is by no means the case. Admittedly only a few songs use a simple basic strophic method (A A1 A2) – e.g. 'At the hour the long day ends' (VI.5) and 'Marian' (VIII.3) – but the majority are strophically based. In poems of three stanzas he frequently adopts Schubert's plan of *Stolle – Stolle – Abgesang* (A(ab) A(ab) B(cb)). That is to say, the first two stanzas are to identical (strophic) or lightly varied (varied strophic) music, whilst the third stanza begins with new material but ends with a reprise of the first stanza's concluding music. Examples included 'A lover's garland', 'When comes my Gwen' and 'And yet I love her'. He also adapts this idea for two-stanza poems: A(ab) B(cb) – e.g. 'Under the greenwood tree', 'My true love hath my heart' (I.1) and 'Weep you no more' (IV.4). In four-stanza poems he often uses a ternary structure: A A B A – e.g. in Byron's 'When we two parted' (IV.3) and Mitchell's 'From a city window' (X.5).

Fuller-Maitland has drawn attention to Parry's fondness for 'feminine cadences' in his songs, even when there is only a single syllable to be set

(1934: 16). This is observable from his first published song, 'Why does azure deck the sky' where, on more than twenty occasions, important syllables are set to two notes of different pitch. Fuller-Maitland goes on to say that Parry was 'seldom again' to continue this 'singular mannerism', but it is surprising how often it occurs in the *English Lyrics*, particularly in the earlier sets (e.g. I.1 and II.2). Did he pick up this mannerism from Mendelssohn? It goes hand in hand with the use of 'feminine upbeats', another Mendelssohnian trait, which can be observed at the beginning of 'And yet I love her till I die' (VI.2), for example. The impression is often given that Parry adhered strictly to the Cranmerian doctrine of 'to every syllable a note', eschewing such florid word-setting techniques as melisma, but there are several places in his songs where he makes memorable use of melisma for expressive purposes, notably in 'A Welsh lullaby' (V.7), 'A lover's garland' (VI.4) and 'The maiden' (IX.6) (Ex. 1.3). Parry's writing for the piano is

Ex. 1.3(a)

Ex. 1.3(b)

Ex. 1.3(c)

frequently criticised for being awkward, unidiomatic or orchestrally conceived. But though his piano-writing is angular, lacking the natural fluency of Stanford or Somervell, it is always perfectly playable. His accompaniments are occasionally overloaded with notes, usually as a result of his doubling outer parts in octaves, or sometimes of doubling chords in octaves. Such writing naturally detracts from the vocal line. Three such examples are 'And yet I love her till I die', 'Bright Star' and 'The witches' wood' (IX.3). Sometimes one feels that Parry as thinking in terms of the orchestra rather than the keyboard. This is noticeable in 'big' songs such as 'Whence?' (VIII.1) and those two 'eschatological' songs in Set XII, 'When the sun's great orb' and 'O world, O life, O time'; it is even to be found in his setting of Shakespeare's 'Blow, blow thou winter wind' (II.4). But fortunately such overwriting is not the norm. That he could avoid such clutter and still sound like Parry is proved by those two early gems, 'Take, O take those lips away' (II.2) and 'Willow, willow, willow' (I.4).

At their best, there is in Parry's songs a wonderful interplay between voice and accompaniment. Take, for example, the way he 'clears' the piano out of the way to allow the voice to predominate at crucial places in a song (Exs. 1.2(b), (c), and 1.4). Another trait of the Parry song is the way in which a forceful piano introduction is abruptly halted to leave a pause (often a full bar's rest) before the singer enters (Ex.1.5). (Other instances occur in 'When comes my Gwen' (VI.1), bars 1–3, and 'One silent night of late' (X.6), bars 1–3).

Ex. 1.4

Ex. 1.5

It would be invidious to attempt to 'grade' or 'short-list' the 74 songs that make up *English Lyrics*. In the end, such an exercise would be a matter of personal choice. But certain songs stand out from the rest as being either well nigh perfect or especially personal expressions in song that only Parry could have written. For those unfamiliar with his songs, and, perhaps, daunted by their number, I pick out some gems, songs which merit special attention, whilst giving a general description of each set. (Further information can be found in Dibble (*1992*) or Pilkington (*1997*).)

Set I (1881–5, *1885*). In this short opening volume, Parry sets four poets: Sidney, Shelley, Scott and Anon. – aka-Shakespeare. 'My true love hath my heart' is of interest for the way in which Parry uses the poem's refrain to bind together the two through-composed strophes. 'Where shall the lover rest' is praised by Fuller-Maitland, who compares it with Stanford's 'La belle dame sans merci' and says it 'overshadows the other songs'. But this Brahmsian-inspired song 'protests too much' and would be more effective in the orchestral version that it so obviously calls for. The setting of Desdemona's 'Willow-song' proves that Parry could write a deft, uncluttered piano accompaniment. Of particular note is its final, exquisitely elongated refrain. The finest of the four is 'Good night' (Shelley). This early song shows Schumann's influence, particularly in the piano-friendly accompaniment. Notice the oblique opening, which veers to the subdominant, and the soaring vocal line of this ecstatic love-song.

Set II (1874–85, *1886*). Here is an all-Shakespeare set of five songs: four song-lyrics from the plays and a sonnet. The sonnet setting, 'No longer mourn for me' (Sonnet 71) shows Parry at his most Brahmsian, but in full control of sonnet-form. 'Blow, blow thou winter wind' anticipates Quilter's more famous setting with its minor/major dichotomy between verse and burden. It is more bluster, however, than blow, and suffers a banal conclusion. 'O mistress mine' opens with a Parry hallmark: a forceful piano introduction that comes to a sudden halt and a pause before the singer enters. This introductory idea – arpeggio figures unpeeling outwards in both hands – is used to link the two through-composed verses of the text. It is Parry at his most lightly delicate: no wonder it is so popular with singers. 'Take, O take those lips away' is a little gem, again very Schumannesque in the way the voice ends 'out-of-key', on the flattened sixth degree of the scale, leaving the piano to take over and make the resolution. As with 'Willow, willow, willow', the accompaniment is minimal but essentially pianistic, the words spaciously set. 'When icicles hang by the wall' is one of the few songs by Parry which reveals a sense of fun. Owls, rustic drones, convivial winter evenings round the fire are all evoked: he even manages in the second verse to tuck in a quotation from what Fuller-Maitland calls 'a modern convivial song' – 'For he's a jolly good fellow!' For all its varied word-painting, the song works extremely well and is one of the best settings of this familiar lyric.

Set III (*1895*). There was a long gap before the third set of *English Lyrics*, then the fourth set came close on its heels. (It will be noticed that the *English Lyrics* tended to make their appearances in pairs.) Here he sets for the first time a contemporary poem, Julian Sturgis's 'Through the ivory gate'; the other five songs are settings of Lovelace (2), Suckling (1), William Walsh (1) and Thomas Beddoes (1). Sturgis was to furnish Parry with lyrics for nine songs in *English Lyrics* – more than any other poet – and in 'Through the ivory gate' Parry created one of his finest, most original songs. The poem describes how a dead friend comes to the poet in a dream, telling him consolingly that friendship survives death; 'When I awoke, he'd gone . . .'. It is a serenely beautiful song, every nuance of the text caught by Parry, with wonderful give-and-take between voice and accompaniment (Ex. 1.6). Notice the way in which he carries the words through over the new piano figure. This is quite different from the traditional 'voice-with-piano-accompaniment' method of, say, 'Blow, blow thou winter wind', something he had learned from German *Lieder* and new to English song. The four 17th-century settings are very similar in style and method: somewhat too cosy and comfortable to be truly expressive, whilst the Beddoes setting is rather ballad-like, no match for the later 'Dream pedlary' (XII.5).

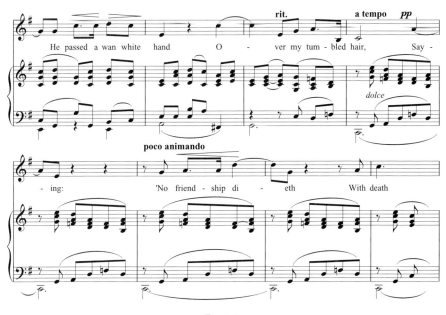

Ex. 1.6

Set IV (1885–96, *1896*). Except for 'Weep you no more', Parry restricts his choice in these six songs to 19th-century poets, including two Americans, Ralph Waldo Emerson and Langdon Elwyn Mitchell. Four of Mitchell's poems were set by Parry in *English Lyrics*, two of which, 'Nightfall in winter' (VIII.2) and 'From a city window', are amongst his finest songs. Neither of the American settings here, however, is very distinguished. The remaining songs are to poems by Byron (2) and Keats. 'When we two parted' (Byron) is particularly attractive, revealing Parry's ability to make use of silence and pause. He sets the four verses in ternary shape (A A B A). 'There be none of Beauty's daughters' is less successful, though Dibble prefers it, praising the 'expansive' interpretation of the text. The setting of Keats's sonnet 'Bright star' dates from 1885 but was revised for publication in 1896. It shows Parry's confident handling of sonnet-form, which he encapsulates in a shapely through-composed structure. The accompaniment, however, is thick and fussy. The remaining song, 'Weep you no more' (Anon., text taken from Dowland's *Third Book of Ayres*, 1603) is one of Parry's most attractive 'Treasury' settings. His use of tonality – strophe 1: G minor/strophe 2: G major, rejoining the first strophe's music for the refrain – perfectly mirrors the mood of the poem, and this is reflected too in the well-varied accompanimental figures. It does everything one would hope for with the setting of an 'old' lyric and is worthy to stand beside Quilter's more famous version. (Quilter would have admired the way Parry raises the word 'softly' by a note at the climax of verse 2.)

Set V (1876–1901, *1902*). These seven songs were written over a period of years, 'Love and laughter' in 1876, 'Crabbed age and youth' in 1882, 'Lay a garland' in 1888; 'Proud Maisie' is also early. Parry has collected together a very mixed bag of poets, from Shakespeare and Beaumont and Fletcher through Scott to Sturgis (2), Arthur Gray Butler and a translation from the Welsh by Edmund Jones. The Sturgis settings do not compare with 'Through the ivory gate': they are lighter poems, which Parry treats appropriately. 'A stray nymph of Dian', a fey little poem, is set in quasi-Elizabethan style, the two stanzas through-composed. There is a neat touch at the words 'But I stood gazing there' which is set unaccompanied, after which the piano 'marks time' whilst the nymph gazes. 'A girl to her glass' suffers from a very feeble text and an unfortunate echo, in its opening bars, of the popular song 'Just a song at twilight', which lingers and cannot be eradicated. In the setting of Walter Scott's ballad 'Proud Maisie' (from *The Heart of Midlothian*, 1818) the dialogue between Maisie and the robin is neatly reflected in the dialogue between voice and piano, producing an attractively irregular flow to the music, and also in the handling of tonalities: F major represents 'Proud Maisie', D minor and B-flat major (with E-flat major inflections) the robin. Parry uses a simple ritornello device – a written-out ornamental turn – to unify the song (Ex. 1.7), first heard on the piano but taken up by the voice at 'rarely'. Note the neat way in which it is taken into the piano bass at the end of the song, and the sly 'cuckoo' at the final cadence. It is a song that shows Parry at his most subtly inventive and attractive. Shakespeare's 'Crabbed age and youth', with its continuous use of antiphonal phrases, is a problematic poem to set, as Parry himself realised – see his letter to Dannreuther, 1882, quoted in Banfield (1985: 23). But this nondescript, workmanlike setting is redeemed by an imaginative coda – 'a masterpiece of prolongation', as Colles describes it (1945: 59). In 'Lay a garland on my hearse' (Beaumont and Fletcher), Parry seems unsure of himself: he clearly intended to write a miniature, but a bigger song is striving to burst out. The bass line has ostinato-like character and Purcell's 'Dido's lament' seems to be lurking somewhere in the wings. It does not match Warlock's more direct setting. Reverend Arthur Gray Butler (1831–1909), the author of 'Love and laughter', was an old acquaintance of Parry, Dean and tutor at Oriel College, Oxford, 1875–97, and author of plays and poetry, including *The Tragedy of Charles I*, from which this poem is taken. In 1882, Parry had toyed with the idea of writing an opera based on a libretto by Butler (see Dibble,

1992: 225): perhaps it is just as well he did not, if the present verse is anything to go by – a whimsical poem resulting in a whimsical song. 'A Welsh lullaby' (translated from the Welsh of 'Ceirog' (John Ceirog Hughes) by Edmund Jones) is an unusual song for Parry and shows how successful he could be when he broke away from his own, self-imposed conventions. There is little text to set and thus Parry is freed to make the music do more of the work. The lullaby mood is established with a long-held note over gently rippling semiquavers. The opening injunction, 'Sleep', is a godsend and Parry makes full use of it! He uses melisma – uncharacteristic but most welcome – on various key words in the text ('baby' and 'sleeping' in verse 2) and he is not afraid to halt his usually busy harmonic movement. The whole of the first verse and beginning of the second are set over a tonic-dominant drone, the music only moving flatwards (appropriately at 'torn') at the approach to the words 'Low in the grave I'll lie'. It is one of his best songs, similar in mood and texture to Elgar's 'A shepherd's song' but unaccountably far less well-known.

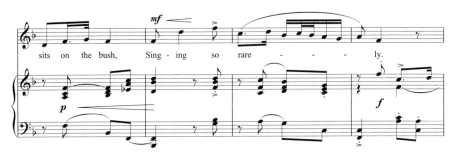

Ex. 1.7

Set VI (*1903*). This contains six songs, a 'male' songbook to complement the 'female' Set V. The poetry selected is singular in that only one poem has an attributable original: Shakespeare's 'Under the greenwood tree'. Of the other five, two are translations from the Greek (by A. P. Graves), one is from the Welsh (Edmund Jones again, this time from the Welsh of 'Mynydogg' (Richard Davies)) and two are by 'Anon.' Set V had concluded with 'A Welsh lullaby' and Set VI opens with another Welsh translation. 'When comes my Gwen' was written as a Christmas box for his younger daughter, Gwen, and her husband, the baritone Harry Plunket Greene. The five stanzas are set as three strophes (1, 2/3, 4/5), the first two verses strophic with different music for the short final verse. Before the final strophe there is an unexpected modulation into D major before a return to E-flat major, and this ending transforms what had been an ordinary song. Though owing much to the ballad, it has ardour and panache. 'And yet I love her till I die' sets the lyric 'There is a lady sweet and kind' from Thomas Ford's *Musicke of Sundrie Kindes* (1607): a poem Warlock was to make his own with three different settings. With its melancholy, lovelorn phrases, and shapely melody, it is the prototype of dozens of later Elizabethan settings, though Parry almost spoils the delicate vocal line with thickly overloaded piano accompaniment (octave-doubled triads and a heavy, low bass line). In 'Love is a bable' (Anon., early 17th century), Parry shows a side of his personality rarely seen. This lively and imaginative piece, a true scherzo song, is justly popular with baritones. Notice how he captures the wry humour of the final 'cadence lines' of each stanza. He structures the four verses in a ternary pattern: A B C A1. 'A lover's garland' is a translation from the Greek by A. P. Graves (1846–1931), the Irish poet and father of Robert Graves. (Colles remarks that the words 'seem to have travelled via Ireland and brought a rare Irish fragrance to the melody' (1945: 60)). It contains some neat hemiola play, the occasional hint of Mixolydian mode at the flattened-7th cadential chords and nice use of melisma at the cadences. This was a favourite song of Plunket Greene. The remaining two songs are less interesting. 'At the hour the long day ends', another translation from the Greek by Graves, is somewhat nondescript, the two stanzas set in a simple strophic manner. He treats the two stanzas of 'Under the greenwood tree' in a more subtle way, the verses set to different musical ideas, but joining together at the refrain – A(ab)-B(cb). The piano's canonic introduction returns as a ritornello between the strophes, with the imitation points swapped round. The accompaniment has a somewhat orchestral quality.

Set VII (*1907*). Of these six songs, all but one (Sturgis's 'Sleep') are settings of Elizabethan and Jacobean poetry: three light-hearted songs, one (Shakespeare's Sonnet 109) turbulently earnest. The Jonson, Heywood and Herrick settings are disappointing; the Shakespeare sonnet suffers from an orchestrally-conceived piano texture and the Sturgis setting from a thick, Brahmsian accompaniment. The most attractive of the set is 'On a time the amorous Silvy', a coy dialogue song. The amorous dalliance between Silvy and her shepherd swain is captured imaginatively in the singer's final cadence (Ex. 1.8).

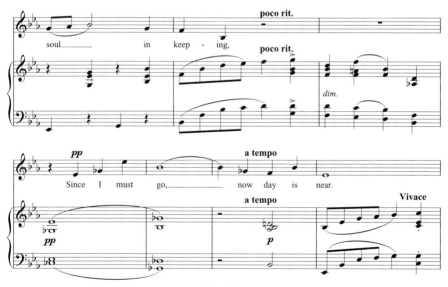

Ex. 1.8

Set VIII (c.1904–6, *1907*). This was published together with Set VII, but whereas Set VII mainly comprises 'old lyrics', Set VIII abandons old for new: three by Sturgis, two by Meredith and one by Mitchell. The set contains some of Parry's most individual songs, but the three songs to Sturgis's poetry (Nos. 1, 5 and 6) are disappointing. 'Whence?', with its praise of 'the prophets of days to be', would have appealed to Parry's political idealism, as expressed in choral works such as *Voces Clamantium* and *The Vision of Life*, but there is too much puff and bluster to make a solo song and too much orchestrally-conceived writing to make an effective piano part. Parry was clearly experimenting with tonality to see how far he could push the bounds of lyrical possibility. The music shifts continually from the home D major, through B-flat major, B minor, G major, A-flat major and F major, all in a matter of bars, ending with an exotic dominant 9th on E before finally cadencing back into D major. He expressed all this so much more succinctly (and memorably) in 'Jerusalem' (1916). In 'Looking backward', the theme of lost childhood happiness gives the song a strong personal, indeed autobiographical, flavour, despite the mawkish sentimentality of the poem. 'Grapes', an invocation to Bacchus, is a poor song; Parry was never at ease in convivial songs of this type. Of the two Meredith settings, 'Marian' is a jolly, lilting song, as strophically simple as Parry could ever be, whilst 'Dirge in woods', one of his few descriptive songs, contains some of his finest word-setting. The melancholy landscape of the pinewood is caught in the uncertain tonality, which gravitates from the initial G major to E minor. In the second verse, Parry begins to work the ritornello figure over-conscientiously, but saves the situation just in time. The song ends with an imaginative passage. The singer sings the words 'And we go,/And we drop like the fruits of the tree' over dissonant piano chords poised over a pedal B; the piano's opening ritornello then magically joins the vocal line at 'Even we', followed by a cadence into E minor which subtly turns back to G major (Ex. 1.9).

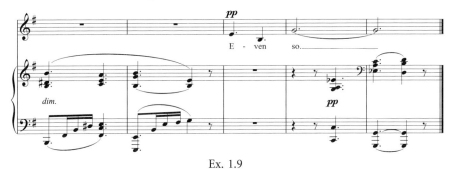

Ex. 1.9

Fine as it is, 'Dirge in woods' cannot compare with the other descriptive song in the set, 'Nightfall in winter' (Mitchell). This portrait of a still, bleak winter landscape is one of the most atmospheric of all Parry's songs. The accompaniment is characterised by a lame halting figure, as though of footsteps limping through the snow (Ex. 1.10). The bleak landscape is evoked in the way the voice doubles the piano's bass line as the music moves from E minor to the remote key of E-flat minor and a dull, insistent low E-flat pedal at the words 'And clouds come Bearing the gloom'. The piano subtly paints the text, yet maintains the flow of the music: note how the figure ♩ ♪♪ ♩ ♪♪ binds the song together, whilst the muddy chords, which so often one feels are an aural mistake in Parry's piano parts, are here used for expressive purposes. This is one of Parry's songs from which future generations of English song-composers were to learn their trade.

Ex. 1.10

Set IX (1908, *1909*). Parry dedicated Set IX to Arthur Duke Coleridge, father of Mary Coleridge (q.v.), seven of whose poems are set here. Parry was a friend of the family and these songs are in some ways a memorial tribute to Mary Coleridge, whose premature death (from appendicitis) had taken place the previous year. Her poetry is typically *fin de siècle* in its unpretentious way, slightly fey and wan for late 20th-century tastes perhaps, but polished, lyrical and emotionally committed. She may not be England's answer to Emily Dickinson, but she had a genuine talent, acknowledged by such discerning critics as Edward Thomas and Walter de la Mare. Set IX has a special place amongst the sets of *English Lyrics* in that it comprises a substantial number of settings by just one poet. In this it is virtually a song-cycle – certainly as close as Parry ever came to writing one – and it makes its best impact when the songs are sung in sequence. Sadly the sequence has the quality of the Curate's Egg – good only in parts. The set is framed by two 'big' songs: 'Three aspects' and 'There'. 'Three aspects' shows Parry in his *nobilemente e pomposo* vein. He reflects the 'three aspects' of life in three different musics. But the piano-writing is thick and cluttered and the overall impression one of pretentious bombast. 'There' is another of Parry's 'eschatological' songs in which he attempts to encapsulate the Great Truths in a statement of faith: 'What shall we find after Death?' But Parry's musical invention cannot quite keep up with his ideals. 'Whether I live', with its syncopated vocal line and pulsing piano chords, is a pedestrian ballad with echoes of the drawing-room – where, indeed, it became popular. 'The witches' wood' suffers from heavy-fisted piano-writing and music manacled to its text, changing with every changing poetic image; it is one of Parry's most Brahmsian-indebted songs. (It sounds at the outset as if we are starting out on a Brahmsian ballade.) The finest songs are the least pretentious. 'A fairy town' –

Parry's title: the original was 'St. Andrew's' – is the best of the set, imaginatively unified. The singer's line is modelled on a carillon figure (Ex. 1.11(a)) whilst the piano's drone-based opening figure acts as a ritornello between verses. Music for the entire song is derived from the carillon, as it peals its way through a wide range of keys (B minor/B major/E-flat major) and textures, until, in the poem's final couplet, it is treated as an ostinato with a long, descending melisma on the words 'downward go' (Ex. 1.11(b)).

Exs. 1.11(a)

Ex. 1.11(b)

As always, Parry's word-setting is immaculate – take, for example, the following (Ex. 1.11(c)):

Ex. 1.11(c)

'Armida's garden' begins like a slow waltz whose onward flow is held up by some magical pauses. At the end the singer is left hanging onto an out-of-key note (flattened submediant) which is taken over and resolved by the piano, just as in 'Take, O take those lips away' written a quarter of a century earlier (Ex. 1.12). 'The maiden' is a mere trifle but deftly crafted, with an effective triplet arpeggiated figure across the hands in the piano accompaniment. Parry allows himself the unusual luxury of a long melisma (including a turn, *à la* 'Proud Maisie') on the words 'singing' and 'shined'.

Set X (1909, *1918*). This was the last set that Parry himself prepared for publication. It was written expressly for and dedicated to Agnes Nichols, the wife of the composer/conductor, Hamilton Harty, and the soprano soloist in many of Parry's larger works, who gave its first performance in November,

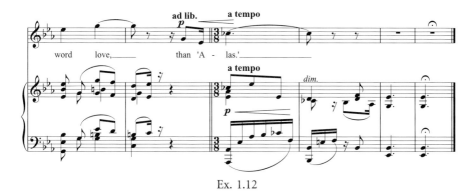

Ex. 1.12

1909; publication was delayed, however, until 1918. By then Parry had replaced the original first song (a recasting of an early Shelley setting, 'O world, O life, O time', later included in Set XII) with Christina Rossetti's 'My heart is like a singing bird'. Unlike Set IX, the songs are to a wide mix of poets, from Herrick via Alan Cunningham and Rossetti to Parry's favourite Mitchell and Sturgis; they are very mixed in quality. 'My heart is like a singing bird' is one of his most dramatic songs and one of his best known today. This setting of Christina Rossetti's poem, 'A Birthday', is carried through with great panache. 'From a city window' is arguably Parry's finest song. Mitchell's poem describes a man listening to sounds of people passing below his city window, 'on errands bitter or sweet/Whither I cannot know'. As with 'Nightfall in winter', the poem must have evoked a strong personal response in Parry who, as his biographer, Jeremy Dibble, reminds us, spent many lonely evenings in his Kensington Square house when forced to stay in London to carry out his administrative duties at the RCM. The song has a rich but disturbing atmosphere and an inventive form, which follows the direction hinted at by the words, but in a far more subtle, flexible way than in 'The witches' wood'. The 'hurrying, restless feet below' are conjured up in the restless, disjointed accompaniment (the *tierces alternées* very reminiscent of Elgar) (Ex. 1.13(a)). In contrast, the central section of this ternary-shaped song has a tranquil quality, with Parry using rich chords where the poet describes the bird that 'troubles the night', so rousing happy memories (Ex. 1.13(b)).

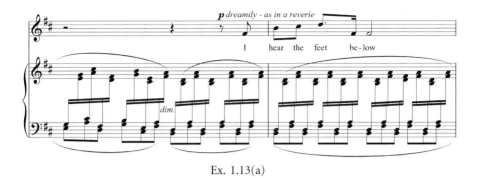

Ex. 1.13(a)

Ex. 1.13(b)

The other Mitchell setting, 'The child and the twilight' is another matter: the poem trite, fey doggerel to which Parry is unable to react with any conviction. Who, one wonders, were such verses written for? Grown-ups acting out childish emotions? The result is embarrassing in the same way that Quilter's contemporary *Four Child Songs* (1914) are. 'A moment of farewell' suffers from a poor poem too. Parry's setting is 'worthy', nothing more, but what could he do with such words as these?

> O bird flying far to the Ocean,
> O bird flying far to the Sea,
> I ask for one buoyant emotion,
> One thrill of thy rapture for me.

'Gone were but the winter cold' (Cunningham) sounds a plaintive note, but the move from slow 3/4 to quick 4/4 for the final verse does not resolve the song convincingly. Far more attractive and memorable is the final Herrick setting, 'One silent night of late', describing a visit by Cupid to the poet's household. It is full of invention and craftsmanship, the music, as in 'From a city window', following the course and contours suggested by the words in both vocal line and accompaniment. It has neat timing and a satisfying balance between voice and piano. Notice the Neapolitan 6th on 'knocking' –

'Who's that', said I, 'knocks there, And troubles thus the sleeping?' – and the lovely, final drooping sequence on 'dying' (Ex. 1.14). The underlying rhythmic figure ♪ | ♩. ♪♪♪ ♩ is almost overdone, but Parry astutely varies it by displacing the accents. It is a memorable song whose appropriately light, airy texture is maintained throughout.

Ex. 1.14(a)

Ex. 1.14(b)

Set XI (1910–18, *1920*). Parry, it seems, had intended to bring out two more sets of *English Lyrics*, and Sets XI and XII were published at the request of his executors, edited by Emily Daymond, Plunket Greene and Charles Wood. Of the 15 songs, only half-a-dozen had been specifically earmarked by Parry for publication; they are inevitably a rather mixed bag. Set XI is, in some ways, the weakest of the twelve. It comprises four settings of A. P. Graves (original poetry this time), and one each of Sturgis, Julia Chatterton and Massinger. The author of 'What part of dread eternity' is 'unknown', but was probably Parry himself. 'The faithful lover' (Graves) is of interest because its text 'seems to parallel almost exactly the hopeless battle Parry fought for [his wife] Maude's love.' (Dibble, 1992: 501). Indeed, the theme of several of the songs is lost or unattainable love. Perhaps Parry found them too 'pertinently autobiographical' to publish during his lifetime.

Set XII (1870s–1918, *1920*). It is appropriate that this final volume symbolically represents the entire spectrum of Parry's songwriting career: two of the songs, Herrick's 'To blossoms' and Shelley's 'O world, O life, O time', date from the 1870s; Julia Chatterton's 'The sound of hidden music' was written on what transpired to be his final birthday, 27 February 1918, and was the last song he wrote. Poetically it begins and ends with Julia Chatterton – one of the many minor women poets supplying text for songwriters at the time – and takes in poets from three different centuries: Lodge, Herrick, Shelley, Beddoes and Parry's friend, Harry Warner. The Warner setting, 'When the sun's great orb', probably dates from the war years and is dedicated to Miss Alice Elieson, the poet's wife. It is an extraordinary song, showing Parry at his best and worst. Warner's cataclysmic vision inspired Parry to his most adventurous writing, both harmonically and texturally; for example, the continually moving tonality (cf. 'Whence?'), the ostinato figure under the words 'Then will the mighty thunders clash', and the Wagnerian declamation to portray Armageddon with the singer assailing the heights with top A-flats and As. It is, in effect, a small operatic scena and needs the orchestral accompaniment to which it aspires to do it justice (and not only at the 'Judgement Day' trumpets). The Lodge and Beddoes settings are particularly fine. 'Rosaline' (Lodge) seems to date from the early 1880s, which makes it contemporary with Sets I and II. It is one of Parry's most exuberant, full-blooded and youthful songs – 'Heigh ho, would she were mine' – with a strong swinging tune. Lodge's long stanzas with their double refrains (one halfway through, one at the end of each verse) are handled with a delightful asymmetry. 'Dream pedlary' (Beddoes), which probably dates from the war years, is a setting of Beddoes's well-loved poem 'If there were dreams to sell'. Like John Ireland, Parry sets only two of Beddoes's five stanzas, which he deploys in characteristic fashion (A(ab)-B(cb)), the two verses joining in the same music for the final refrain. With its subtle word-painting and light, airy textures, it is one of Parry's most attractive songs.

Considered as a whole, the *English Lyrics* are a remarkable achievement, one of the milestones in the history of English song. They display Parry's limitations as a songwriter as well as his virtues, and this is possibly the reason why the songs have not achieved the universal acclaim from performers, listeners and critics as were those of, say, Dowland or Purcell or Warlock or Britten. What are Parry's limitations? Several have already been alluded to in passing in the comments on individual songs, and they can be summarised as follows. Firstly, though his songs are lyrical, justifying that overall title of 'English Lyrics', they are not always strikingly *memorable*. Parry had – like Finzi after him – the remarkable ability to write an unmemorable tune. Although he was able to come up with a resoundingly popular tune when required for a public occasion – works like 'Jerusalem', 'Repton' and 'I was glad' prove this beyond question – all too often he seems to have forgotten that part of the attraction of the solo song is the memorability of its vocal line. There are, of course, exceptions – 'O mistress mine', 'Take, O take those lips away', 'And yet I love her till I die' and 'When comes my Gwen' to name four – but these comprise only a fraction of the 74 *English Lyrics*. So often his songs flow past in a delightfully lyrical way but do not register in the memory. That art-songs with memorable tunes *can* be written in our generally anti-lyrical age is demonstrated by song-composers such as Quilter, Warlock and Britten.

Parry's songs are often too predictable – 'too comfortable', as Arthur Jacobs has said (1960: 156), lacking 'energy, surprise and irony'. Take, for instance, the 17th-century settings of Lovelace, Suckling and Walsh in Set III. 'To Althea, from prison' and 'To Lucasta, on going to the wars' show exquisite word-setting, but in mood are far too complaisant for their harrowing subject-matter. 'Why so pale and wan?' lacks the biting irony that Suckling demands and the shock ending – 'The devil take her' – is too demure: there is little of the devil in it. This shortcoming is reflected in the unadventurousness of his technique, in texture, harmony and melody, compared with his contemporaries. He lacks the dash and energy of Stanford, the drama of Somervell, the sheer love of sensuous harmonies and textures of Delius or Elgar. His harmonic resources are limited, a diatonic idiom which is loth to admit chromaticism: excellent for expressing noble sentiments but inadequate in situations of emotional tension. Despite his obvious love and knowledge of his poets, one feels that in some cases Parry is not completely engaged in the poem's meaning, so that though the *words* of the poem are set to perfection, its *spirit* has eluded capture. He is unwilling at times to wear his heart on his sleeve. This is what Banfield means when he writes that 'the overall impression is that Parry set his texts as studies in controlled lyricism rather than as compulsive responses to poetry.' (1985: 23).

Parry's attitude to music, as expressed in his books, lectures and articles, is one of 'High Seriousness': he takes for music the same high ground that Matthew Arnold takes for literature. It is a typical Victorian stance – or rather, a *persona* that the Victorians liked to present to the World and Posterity. But, as we now know, beneath his stiff upper lip, the Victorian Englishman could be playful and even downright vulgar. In a few works, e.g. the 'Shulbrede Tunes', Parry does relax a little, but in his songs, his earnestness is unbending. His aim was for High Art: the English *Lied*. So we have those songs where he tries vainly to capture concepts of Destiny and The Meaning of Life, such as 'Whence?', 'There' and 'When the sun's great orb': worthy, but not really the matter for song. When he does essay a frivolous or light-hearted song, the result is often coy and sentimental, as in 'On a time the amorous Silvy' and 'A stray nymph of Dian', or embarrassingly mawkish, as 'The child and the twilight'. In the *English Lyrics*, the nearest Parry gets to letting down his hair and unbuttoning his jacket is 'When icicles hang by the wall', in which good humour and a sense of fun peep through the kaleidoscope of musical images. But for all his determination to establish High Art Song, Parry does not always avoid the meretriciousness and sentimentality that he deplored in the popular Royalty ballads of his day. Songs such as 'When lovers meet again' and 'A girl to her glass' achieve the sentimentality of the drawing-room ballad without achieving the popular appeal and panache of the genre.

In his *English Lyrics* Parry's aim was to establish his own Golden Treasury of English Song. It was his deep love of English literature and his admiration for the German *Lieder* tradition that fired his imagination. He wanted to demonstrate that sympathetic, seriously considered musical setting could also enrich the wealth and heritage of English poetry. The breadth of range and eclecticism of his choice of poets and poetry is in itself an achievement. He was not afraid to choose poetry which many would have felt to be 'too perfect' or 'complete in itself' to need the addition of music, poems such as Keats's 'Bright star' or the Shakespeare sonnets. And he was quite prepared to choose poems by minor or obscure poets – for example, Sturgis and Mitchell – when he felt that they were 'apt-for-music'. Very importantly, he used song (as he did his choral works) to express and charter his own intensely felt feelings and spiritual and political beliefs: sometimes successfully, sometimes not, but always with commendably serious intention. In their different ways, songs such as 'Through the ivory gate', 'Three aspects', 'From a city window' and 'When the sun's great orb' all demonstrate this ideal. In these songs he dared to shoot arrows at the moon, knowing full well that he would not reach it (let alone hit it), but determined that the attempt should be made. In his *English Lyrics*, Parry set out for his successors the English way to serious art-song: a path which could be avoided or skirted but never ignored. For this he will always be admired and revered. Those demurely reticent, dove-grey volumes will always remain a touchstone for serious English song-composers.

2

Charles Villiers Stanford (1852–1924)

> In London here the streets are grey, and grey the sky above;
> I wish I were in Ireland to see the skies I love –
> Pearl cloud, buff cloud, the colour of a dove.
>
> All day I travel English streets, but in my dreams I tread
> The far Glencullen road and see the soft sky overheard,
> Grey clouds, white clouds, the wind has shepherded.
>
> W. M. Letts: 'Irish Skies'

Like those of his colleague Parry, Stanford's solo songs span his entire composing career, from *Eight Songs from 'The Spanish Gypsy'*, his op. 1 of 1878, to *Six Songs from 'The Glens of Antrim'*, op. 174, written in the early 1920s. Excluding unison settings, arrangements of traditional Irish tunes, settings of foreign texts and songs with chorus, they number almost 200: a very large output for a composer who was by no means a specialist songwriter. They show an enormous range, from the large-scale narrative ballad such as 'La belle dame sans merci' to a setting of Herrick's 'To carnations', an exquisite miniature only 13 bars long; from the serio-heroic 'Prospice' to the brilliant satirical spoofs of the final 'Nonsense Rhymes'. In discussing Stanford, it is inevitable that comparison will be made again and again with Parry. This is because, between them, they did so much to develop serious songwriting in English; and in doing so, they complemented each other.

In his choice of poetry Stanford was more wide-ranging than Parry, setting nearly fifty different poets, and mixing major writers such as Shakespeare and Jonson with minor ones such as Edmond Holmes, Cecily Fox Smith and George Jessop. It is instructive to compare the poets he set with those of Parry. At one extreme he was attracted to lighter verse, humorous or descriptive: the limericks of Lear or the verses of Moira O'Neill and Winifred Letts. They gave scope to the witty side of the man; one can hardly imagine Parry being attracted to these poets. At the other extreme, however, he was more willing than Parry to tackle the great writers of his time: Tennyson, Browning, Whitman and Bridges. The literary tastes of the two composers did occasionally coincide, particularly when choosing 16th- and 17th-century lyrics for setting. Even their choice of titles is similar: compare Parry's *A Garland of Shakespearean and Other Old Fashioned Songs* (1874) and Stanford's *Three Ditties of the Olden Times* (1877). But whereas Parry, in his twelve books of *English Lyrics*, seems to be marking out the kind of English poem suitable for musical setting, Stanford's major preoccupation was to present in lyrical form a musical portrait of his native Ireland. Taken together, his settings of Moira O'Neill, Winifred Letts, Charles Graves and John Stevenson give us a series of musical portraits of Irish life and landscapes.

Like other British composers of his day, Stanford benefited from his training abroad and his immersion in the German classics. Though, like Parry, his style is harmonically closer to Brahms, in songwriting techniques it is Schubert whose shoulder he is looking over. This can be seen in his fondness for sudden Schubertian switches of mode from minor to major and vice versa. His study of the German classics gave him a technique and a confidence that was at once the making of him and his undoing. He had a technical facility which he sometimes used in lieu of inspiration, so that amongst his many fine songs he also managed to write an 'amazing number of bad songs' (Boughton, 1913: 65). To read his essay 'The composition of music' (*Interludes, Records and Reflections,* 1922: 50), you might be led to think that he was giving advice on making a teapot rather than composing music. This emphasis on craftsmanship is probably why Stanford's musical voice is difficult to detect or define; there is a strange anonymity in his music, which acts as a mask to his musical personality. At the heart of his technique is his love of Irish folksong, and this, mixed with his knowledge and absorption of German *Lieder* writers, Schubert, Schumann and Brahms, and with his love and knowledge of English poetry, gives him a quite different perspective on songwriting to his contemporaries. Though he could fall into the misty sentimentality of the English drawing-room ballad, there is enough fresh air blowing from the West and the East to disperse it.

This cross-fertilisation of Irish melody and English and Anglo-Irish poetry gives his songs their freshness and suppleness. Like Parry, Stanford developed a technique that could cater for the special requirements of an English song tradition. If it was Parry who defined in his songs an appropriate way to set words, it was Stanford who found a method (less cumbrous, more fluent than Parry) to match voice and accompaniment. He himself summarised his own practice in the advice he gave to students (1922: 65):

> The accompaniment, that is everything which includes the bass, should be in most cases texture and suggestiveness, and not fixed detail of sufficient importance to interfere with the voice. Over-elaboration will kill the main theme [i.e. the vocal line], or at best, quarrel with it in a way sufficient to hide its purport. Support is what is needed, and support only. Accompaniment is only a secondary matter, however important it may be! In a few songs, the main idea is in the accompaniment and the comment in the voice. In most, the main idea is in the voice and the comment, or what is called 'atmosphere', in the accompaniment.

He goes on to cite as examples of these two types Schubert's 'Der Leiermann' and 'Die Junge Nonne'. Stanford's accompaniments certainly have a variety, strength of purpose and character compared with Parry's, and they sometimes take on a crucial structural role in the development of motives (see Banfield,

1985: 38). What Stanford lacks is the sureness and inevitability of Parry's word-setting. At times he can be surprisingly insensitive in this area. Take, for example, his setting of 'Come away, death' (No. 2 of *The Clown's Songs from Shakespeare*, op. 65, (1896) (Ex. 2.1). But if he errs in such details, his vocal lines are always singable and varied. He is able with ease to adopt 'patter-song' technique – that quick syllabic setting of text normally the preserve of the comic song – as in 'The fair' and 'Little Peter Morrisey'. Closely akin to this is the delightful 'conversational' style of Irish songs such as 'Grandeur'. At the other extreme is the spaciousness of his settings of 'noble' verse, mixing arioso declamation with shaped melodies in the finest of his large-scale songs, 'Prospice', 'To the soul' and 'Crossing the bar'. Between the two comes his ability, when the poem requires it, to write a shapely, lyrical melody, as in 'A soft day' and 'The fairy lough'.

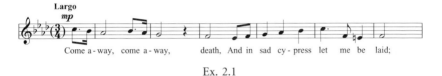

Ex. 2.1

Banfield (1985: 32) has drawn attention to Stanford's 'curiously emasculated style'. One noticeable weakness in Stanford's songs (a weakness he shares with Parry) is his limited harmonic palette. Compared with his contemporaries Elgar and Delius, or, indeed, with many of his pupils, Howells, Bridge and Ireland, his harmonic range is narrow; he seems to be reluctant to let himself go at big moments, and puts a restraint on his emotions. This is symbolised in his music both in the way in which he holds back from making a strong modulation and in his restricted use of sequence. Whereas Elgar will wear his heart on his sleeve, Stanford retains a stiff upper lip.

Stanford's opus list begins with a substantial vocal work which, though long out-of-print, requires comment. *Eight Songs from 'The Spanish Gypsy'* was published between 1877 and 1878; the music is undated but some of the songs were written by 1875. George Eliot is not usually regarded as a poet, but she wrote some fine poems, notably the blank verse 'O may I join the choir invisible' (1867) and the sonnet sequence 'Brother and Sister' (1869). *The Spanish Gypsy* (1864–5, revised 1867) is a long narrative poem interspersed with songs. From these Stanford selected eight to form a songbook, placing the originals in the following order: 4, 5, 6, 3, 8, 9, 2 and 1. (For fuller details, see Pilkington, 1997: 47–50.) Fuller-Maitland (1934: 14) says that Stanford's attempts to give Spanish colouring to the accompaniments are not completely successful. Indeed, it is difficult to detect any Spanish colouring at all: the songs might have been more interesting if they had. One of the best of the group is the second song, 'Sweet springtime', with its neatly appropriate imitative writing at the words 'Little shadows danced' (Ex. 2.2). Except for some careless word-setting they are technically adept, but lack any fine frenzy of inspiration; yet in this op. 1

Ex. 2.2

Stanford made a mark for himself as a songwriter to be watched. He was certainly not afraid to tackle the major poets of his day, and over the next thirty years made settings of Tennyson, Browning, Whitman and Bridges. His *Three Songs to poems by Robert Bridges*, op. 43 (1891, *1897*) are some of the earliest – and finest – solo setting of Bridges' verse. The texts are from *Shorter Poems of Robert Bridges*, Book III (1880), Nos. 17, 8 and 16, lyrics in squarely-stanza-ed verse and formally 'poetic' language, so typical of the poet. The third song, '"Say, O say!" saith the music' (= 'Song: I love my ladies eyes') presents a triangular situation: 'my lady' – the poet – and 'you', the reader/listener. The third verse is unusual in that the first and fifth lines are extended by 'tropes' inserted into the stanza pattern. In the second of these, '"Stray, O stray!" saith the music', the music does just that (Ex. 2.3). It is a song in which Stanford is at his most Schubertian – indeed, it could have been written by that earlier Schubert admirer, Arthur Sullivan.

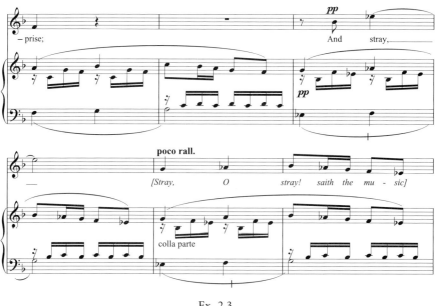

Ex. 2.3

In 1903 Stanford made settings of poems by his contemporary and friend, Edmond Holmes (1850–1936), taken from his sonnet sequence *The Triumph of Love*, which had just been published. They show Stanford in serious mood. Unfortunately the poetry is pompous and sombre, full of high-sounding sentiments; he needed better quality verse, such as Whitman's 'To the soul' or Tennyson's 'Crossing the bar', when essaying this particular mood. The gentler, less portentous songs are the best. 'Like as the thrush in winter' (Sonnet 48), a harmonically attractive song, ends appropriately thrush-like with a repetition of the words 'Sing on!', whilst 'I think that we were children [long ago]' (Sonnet 5), a delightful song, captures the childlike innocence of the poem, with the quiet chiming of Christmas bells on the piano skilfully developed as the song progresses. Stanford's choice of the sonnet-form was a cue for through-composed songs, and he skilfully manages to make musical sense of this musically intractable verse-form. He is not averse to adapting the poem to suit his own purpose on occasions, as, for example, in the second song 'Like as the thrush in winter', where he creates a refrain by ending with lines heard earlier in the song.

Songs of Faith, op. 97 (1906, *1908*) were published in two sets each of three songs, the first to poems by Tennyson ('Strong son of God', 'God and the universe' and 'Faith'), and the second to poems by Walt Whitman ('To the soul', 'Tears' and 'Joy, shipmate, joy'). All are substantial poems on religious themes and Stanford gives them a correspondingly serious character; he might well have borrowed a Brahmsian title for them, 'Six Serious Songs'. There is something of the German composer's heroic mood in the setting of Whitman's 'To the soul', the same poem that Vaughan Williams was to use the following year in *Toward the unknown region* (1907). Stanford's setting is big in conception to match the poem. The piano's off-the-beat marching tread leaves the singer exposed and obliged to lead throughout. Particularly Brahmsian are the upward chromatic sequences in the bass at the words 'Till, when the ties loosen' (Ex. 2.4(a)). The music begins in B-flat major, moves to the tonic minor for the second verse, only to return to a blazing tonic major at the words 'Then we burst forth' (Ex. 2.4(b)). The song is firmly of its time, but nonetheless fine for that and certainly not a period piece.

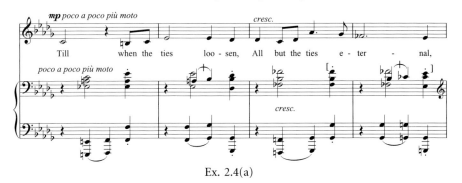

Ex. 2.4(a)

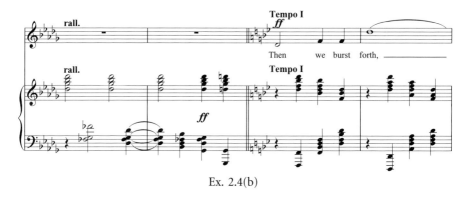

Ex. 2.4(b)

Admirable as these songs are, Stanford's major contribution to English song is his six 'Irish' song-cycles: in actual fact, five Irish cycles and one Scottish one. These were written between 1900 and 1920 and consist of 37 songs altogether – a substantial portion of his vocal output:

Title	Poet	No. of songs	Date written/*published*
An Irish Idyll, op. 77	Moira O'Neill	6	(1901), *1901*
Cushendall, op. 118	John Stevenson	7	1910, *1910*
A Fire of Turf, op. 139	Winifred Letts	7	1913, *1913*
A Sheaf of Songs from Leinster, op. 140	Winifred Letts	6	1913, *1914–16*
Songs of a Roving Celt, op. 157	Murdoch Maclean	5	1918, *1919*
Six Songs from the Glens of Antrim, op. 174	Moira O'Neill	6	1920, *1920*

The Irish songs reflect the one fixed point of Stanford's life: his attachment to Ireland. Yet, paradoxically, he uprooted himself from Ireland early in his career, when he went as a student to Cambridge at the age of 18, and he never returned there to live. What is more, his own home life was far removed from the peasant conditions portrayed in his songs. As Stephen Banfield has pointed out, 'his songs about the Irish countryside were written in comfortable Kensington' (1985: 32). Like so many self-imposed expatriates, he enjoyed his country from a safe distance, and the Irish cycles are typical Songs of an Exile, in which the composer dreams of an Ireland seen through rose-tinted pince-nez. Even so, Stanford had a genuine love and appreciation of Irish folk-music. Indeed, he made nearly 150 arrangements of traditional Irish tunes. But commitment and love are useless in the face of inferior poetry; the dialect poems of Moira O'Neill, Winifred Letts and John Stevenson have not worn well. One wonders whether they were acceptable in their own day: shallow sentiments, condescending attitudes and sentimental emotion. There was a vogue at the turn of the century for songs about 'The Land of Erin', just as there were for songs about 'Merry England', 'Glorious Devon' and the like. But Stanford's Irish cycles are too important a part of his creativity to be ignored, and are certainly of more worth than some critics have led us to believe. I have chosen two, perhaps the finest, for detailed consideration (*An Irish Idyll* and *A Sheaf of Songs from Leinster*), and refer briefly to some outstanding songs from the other collections.

The texts of *An Irish Idyll* come from *Songs of the Glens of Antrim* by Moira O'Neill (1865–1955). These songs of an Irish exile (in her case, in Canada) must have had a special appeal to Stanford. The poetry is attractive in form if superficial in content and is at its best when not breaking out into dialect. A poem such as 'Johneen', a mawkishly sentimental picture of doting parents drinking the health of their small son, grates on the sensibility. The six songs are basically strophic in form. O'Neill's long, loping stanzas give Stanford

Ex. 2.5(a)

Ex. 2.5(b)

plenty of opportunity for extended strophes and the poetic refrains scope for musical ones. In 'Cuttin' rushes', he divides the long, eight-line stanzas in half, but sets them strophically. In 'Corrymeela' the stanzas are set to alternating strophes of different music and in different keys, with the odd stanzas in F minor with F minor refrains, and the even stanzas in A-flat major with F major refrains: in each case, the verses are in 6/8, the refrains in 4/4. In the final verse he introduces a rippling semiquaver accompaniment in 4/4, adapting music of the second strophe to the 4/4 metre and rising through F-sharp minor and D major to the final broadened out refrain to give the song a satisfactory shape. Two songs in the set are particularly noteworthy. 'The fairy lough' is a memorable song because it has memorable ideas. Its gentle, tranquil mood is evoked by an impressionistic use of harmonics, reminding us that, for all his Irishness, Stanford was also the composer of 'The blue bird'. He juxtaposes two chords, D major and 1st inversion F major, which shifts the tonal focus on the music towards C major, before neatly turning back to D major. It is this tonal ambiguity which imbues the song with its dreamy, berceuse-like atmosphere (Ex. 2.5(a)). The accompaniment is neat and uncluttered, never obtruding into the path of the singer, yet deftly able to highlight phrases through word-painting (Ex. 2.5(b)). It is one of Stanford's most popular songs and deservedly so. 'A broken song' is the most original of the set, the dialogue of bold questions and hesitant answers brilliantly paced, with sensitive choice of chords, a balance of sounds and silences and varied textures.

Ex. 2.6

It is the forerunner of a whole genre of English dialogue-songs, of Butterworth's 'Is my team ploughing', Bridge's 'Journey's end' and Britten's 'At the railway station, Upwey'. Particularly effective is the enigmatic ending, where the music appears to be heading for D-flat, but finally side-slips back into F minor (Ex. 2.6). Stanford does not call the work a song-cycle, rather modestly describing it as 'An Irish Idyll in Six Miniatures'. He does not avail himself of thematic cross-reference, but in the unity of subject-matter and poet, the balance and contrast of songs and the 'cyclical' use of tonalities, which all centre around the key of F major/minor, *An Irish Idyll* is in all other ways a song-cycle: certainly more so than his George Eliot settings. It was also to set the pattern for his later Irish songs, for which he turned to the poetry of Winifred Letts and John Stevenson as well as Moira O'Neill.

Ex. 2.7

The texts of both *A Fire of Turf* and *A Sheaf of Songs from Leinster* are taken from *Songs of Leinster* (1913) by Winifred M. Letts (1882–1972). It is often difficult to differentiate O'Neill from Letts, for their subject-matter is so similar; roguish Irish children ('Johneen', O'Neill/'Thief of the world', Letts), damp Irish pastorals ('The fairy lough', O'Neill/'A soft day', Letts) and Irish exiles in England ('Corrymeela', O'Neill/'Irish skies', Letts) inhabit the poetry of both, in much the same lightly-versed English or *Punch*-Irish idioms. The seven poems in *A Fire of Turf*, all taken from the eponymous subsection in *Songs of Leinster*, are a mixture of pen-portraits and landscapes. The influence of Irish folk-music can be detected in some of Stanford's settings. 'The chapel on the hill', with its frequent plagal cadences, modal inflections and neat, unobtrusive accompaniment, could be one of Stanford's Irish folksong arrangements, whilst 'The fair' is a lively patter-song in the 'We're off to the fair' mode so popular at the time (indeed, a close cousin to his popular folksong arrangement, 'Trottin' to the fair'). Very effective is the way he allows the piano to complete the cadence to each verse, leaving the vocal line 'in the air' (Ex. 2.7). *A Sheaf of songs from Leinster* also contains patter-songs, 'Thief of the world' and 'The bold unbiddable child', both *à la jig* and both concerned with lively, unruly children, a girl and boy respectively. Quite different is 'Little Peter Morrisey', a touching portrait of a penniless urchin from the slums, neglected by his drunken parents. Stanford marks the song 'To be sung like a recitation'; the story is touchingly told, skilfully skirting the sentimental, though maybe not the condescending (Ex. 2.8).

Ex. 2.8

Between these child portraits comes the best known song of the set, 'A soft day'. 'Soft' in this Irish context means 'wet' and the music drips in sympathy in off-the-beat crotchets (Ex. 2.9). It has simplicity verging on the bland, certainly compared with his earlier landscape, 'The fairy lough', but it is brief and doesn't outstay its welcome, and there is a rightness in the way he treats the two stanzas to simple strophic variation. One feels that Ivor Gurney must have known and loved this song, for it seems to anticipate many of the ideas he was to use.

Ex. 2.9

The two framing songs, 'Grandeur' and 'Irish skies', are on a bigger scale. 'Grandeur' is a portrait of 'Poor Mary Byrne' as she lies on her deathbed, told with a nobility of understatement. The syllabic word-setting is well-suited to the Irish dialect of the poem, and the conversational style of declamation reminds one of Finzi's 'To Lizbie Browne', another fine female portrait (Ex. 2.10).

Ex. 2.10

The final song, 'Irish skies', is an exile's cry from the heart: the *Heimweh* of an Irish exile in London for his native Ireland. Here, as in 'Grandeur' and 'Little Peter Morrisey', Stanford is not afraid to show his heart; it sounds a strongly personal note which overrides any sentimentality.

Ex. 2.11(a)

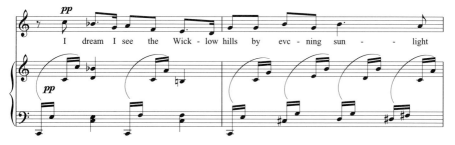

Ex. 2.11(b)

Ex. 2.11(c)

It also shows the skill with which Stanford 'works' his piano accompaniments, moulding and transforming them to fit new images and moods (Exs. 2.11(a), (b) and (c)). Again Stanford gives a unity to the songs without recourse to musical cross-reference, by tonality (the tonal centres of the six are E-flat major/ C major, F major, D-flat major, D minor/D major, D minor and C minor/C major) and subject-matter, offset by variety of mood and pace. With its two large-scale framing songs and emphasis on 'child songs', this is an even more satisfactory work than *An Irish Idyll.*

Songs of a Roving Celt, from the eponymous volume of poetry published in 1916 by Murdoch Maclean, belongs emotionally if not geographically to the Irish cycles. Indeed, the outstanding song of the set is 'The pibroch', in which two Scotsmen far from home hear the nostalgic sound of the pipes. It is a vividly graphic song in which the piano accompaniment acts as the pibroch, with bagpipe drone and pibroch tune (Ex. 2.12(a)). These create a background 'landscape' (and musical ritornello) for the singer, alternating with a simple chordal texture. Above this the singer has a driving rhythm which only relents at the song's unexpectedly slow, quiet ending (Ex. 2.12(b)).

Ex. 2.12(a)

It is one of Stanford's most original and inspired songs, showing what he could do when craftsmanship and inspiration met. However, some of Stanford's finest achievements are to be found in the individual songs written throughout his career. 'La belle dame sans merci' (1876, *1877*) is one of his earliest. Keats's poem is a daunting one to choose, mindful of the hallowed place it occupies in the canon of English literature.

The sil - ver dews of night are soft - ly fall - ing, The stars____

____ are on the hea - ther let us go.

Ex. 2.12(b)

Its 14 stanzas of narrative need to be focussed musically to avoid monotony but without detracting from its unity; Stanford solves this by structuring it as a set of vocal variations. As his theme he uses a simple, Aeolian-mode tune with an appropriate 'antique' air, very Brahmsian in its contours – indeed, it would fit into the op. 10 *Ballades* without difficulty. He tries gallantly to avoid monotony in his rhythmic treatment of Keats's short-lined quatrains, setting the theme to work in a variety of ways: in imitation, echo, and (when the pacing steed gets going) in canon by diminution. But the song's dour visage misses the magic and mystery of the poem and it needs a good singer to raise it from dullness. Schubert's 'Erlkönig' was clearly Stanford's model – he makes full use of Schubertian switches of mode from minor to major and back – but it lacks the intensity and terror of Schubert's masterpiece. It is, nevertheless, one of the finest examples of an English narrative song.

'Prospice' (1884, *1884*) is another big dramatic poem, in which Robert Browning expresses the personal pain he felt at the loss of his wife, Elizabeth Barrett. Stanford gives it an appropriately big, dramatic setting from the outset (Ex. 2.13). He divides Browning's unstanza-ed poem into four irregular sections, which he sets in varied strophic manner; the opening phrases of each are set aside from the rest, the first three underlined by a progression from E-flat major 6/3 to a dominant 7th with augmented 5th on D. The augmented 5th plays an important role throughout the song. The piano has an angular 6/8 running figure in octaves between the hands, which gives a tremendous drive to the 'Allegro con fuoco'. Over this the singer has a free declamation, the vocal line hovering obsessively round the minor third, G-B-flat, full of broken phrases which suggest that the narrator is gasping for breath. In the fourth strophe, at the words 'Then a light',

Ex. 2.13

a new musical idea appears. The tonality has already moved from G minor to G major (though with a strong pull towards E minor) and the song moves to its climax on the phrase 'And with God be the rest'; 'God' is clasped on a high F, after which the music cadences, via the ubiquitous augmented 5th, into G major. The ending is perhaps too easily achieved, but nevertheless, it is a passionate, romantic outpouring.

Stanford's setting of 'Crossing the bar' (1890, *1893*), Tennyson's famous valedictory poem, was composed soon after the poem's publication in *Demeter and other poems* (1889). Stanford sets the two stanzas semi-strophically, leaving the piano's accompanimental textures to reflect the text. The slow 3/4 Adagio falls into two parts: (a) a sarabande-like tread followed by (b) flowing triplets over gentle surging bass notes (Exs. 2.14(a) and (b)). The setting is noble if rather dry-eyed: restrained rather than emotionally committed.

Ex. 2.14(a)

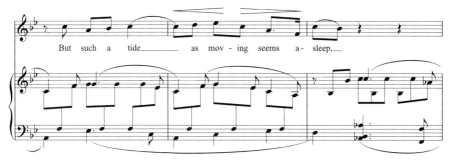

But such a tide_____ as mov - ing seems a - sleep,_____

Ex. 2.14(b)

But Stanford's songs would not be properly surveyed without reference to light conceits and trifles. 'To carnations', No. 3 of *Three Ditties of the Olden Times* (1877, *1877*) is a setting of one of Herrick's many poetic apostrophes to flowers. Stanford makes of the brief poem a musical epigram, a mere 13 bars long, with some deft three-bar phrasing (two bars text, one bar piano link) with a neat extension on the final phrase. 'A lullaby' (1882, *1884*), No. 2 of *Six Songs* op. 19, a setting of Dekker's famous lyric 'Golden slumbers kiss your eyes', is a delightful little lullaby, a gentle upward-rising scale on the piano acting as an ostinato which runs through the neatly-shaped vocal line (Ex. 2.15). The second of the two strophes is rounded off with a short coda, repeating the refrain line 'Rock them, rock them lullaby'.

Gold - en slum - bers kiss_ your eyes._

Ex. 2.15

In 'The monkey's carol' (*1921*) Stanford returns again to the poetry of Winifred Letts: here a poem about an organ-grinder's monkey asking (waif-like) for a Christmas gift. Stanford clearly had in mind Schubert's 'Der Leiermann' and he adopts and adapts the organ-grinder's accompaniment for his own purposes (Ex. 2.16(a)). The monkey is kept in his place, yet able to break into dance when required. Note the neat way in which the music modulates (voice-leading) from B major back to D major during the third verse (Ex. 2.16(b)). It is a childlike vision akin to that captured by Elgar in his *Starlight Express* songs. In its mixture of pathos, stark emotion and childlike humour, it is a delightful Christmas song. Last, but certainly not least in Stanford's song *oeuvre*, are the *Nonsense Rhymes*, settings of 14 limericks by Edward Lear, written for the amusement of his

Ex. 2.16(a)

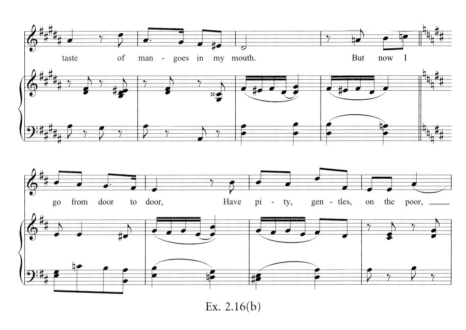

Ex. 2.16(b)

friends. The dates of composition are not known, nor were they published until 1960. The stratospheric opus numbers – 365–78 – are all part of the donnish humour. (In reality, Stanford's opus numbers reached just under 200.) The work's full title is 'Nonsense Rhymes by Edward Lear set to music by Karel Drofnatski', a composer who was evidently born at a town on the River Yeffil in the province of Retsniel. (Anyone with a retrogradable turn of mind will quickly decode this.) The settings comprise a series of baroquely elaborate spoofs, each targeting a different composer or style and incorporating wittily embedded quotation, all explained in elaborate after-notes to each song. For example, 'The Hardy Norse-Woman' (setting the limerick 'There was a young lady from Norway') refers to Grieg; 'The Compleat Virtuoso' ('There was an old man of the Isles') to 'Max von Beetelssohn'; 'The Absent Barber' ('There was an old man with a beard') to Handel (with help from Sir Henry Bishop); and 'The Aquiline Snub' ('There was an old man with a nose') to J. S. Bach (Ex. 2.17).

Ex. 2.17

There are also parodies of Brahms, Tchaikovsky and Wagner and an all-purpose
'Limerich Ohne Worte': 'a specimen pattern or model, to which any poem of
the Limerick type can be sung'. They are so much more amusing than the Irish
humours of 'Johneen' and the like. But . . .one feels that when one prefers
Stanford's pastiches to his serious songs, then something must be amiss: that
perhaps Stanford didn't take his songwriting very seriously and didn't aim very
high.

Banfield has pointed out (1985: 25) that Stanford's song output has not yet been
adequately assessed. Why is this? There are three possible reasons, all linked: its
vastness, its unevenness and its bewildering eclecticism. Few performers, and
only the most committed of listeners, know more than a dozen or so of
Stanford's 200 songs – and probably the same dozen. The songs included here
for comment represent the composer at his best; there are many indifferent or
plain dull songs – dull in their day and not brightened up since. Despite the
variety of the poetry he chose to set, ranging from Heine in the original to Irish
'folk' poets, from the High Seriousness of Whitman and Browning to the
'Aquiline Snubs' of the Lear parodies, the very eclecticism makes one question
Stanford's literary discrimination and ask whether he had any clear literary
touchstone.

    If one had to sum up Stanford's song output in one word, it would be
'Ireland'. Indeed, though many have deplored and belittled his Irish songs, they
do represent the composer at his most attractive and characteristic. There are, of
course, many songs that have no trace of the land of his birth in them – fine
songs too, such as 'Prospice' and 'To the soul'. But Ireland, its folksong, its

seasons and landscapes, its poets and its people, dominates his songs. His choice
of poetry lacks the High Serious ideals of Parry. He was happy to compose songs
of a light nature: good light music for which he chose good light verse. And, as
in the Lear settings, he was quite prepared to let his hair down. (One can hardly
imagine Parry writing 'The Aquiline Snub', even behind the pseudonym of
'Trebuh Yrrap'.) If Stanford's songs occasionally show a low voltage of
inspiration, they always have a technical security – that 'professionalism'
which he tried to instil into his pupils. And in some ways, it is the legacy
that he left to his pupils at the RCM that was to prove so important to 20th-
century English song. Amongst his pupils were at least 15 composers for whom
the composing of songs became a major part of their careers (see Banfield, 1985:
38), including seven of the major songwriters featured in this book: Frank
Bridge, Ivor Gurney, Gustav Holst, Herbert Howells, John Ireland, E. J. Moeran
and Vaughan Williams. Whether his teaching was inspirational or devitalising
seems to have varied from pupil to pupil; but as with so many teacher-pupil
relationships, it is often a matter of listening and learning and doing otherwise.
The simple fact was that Stanford taught them, and they went on to write fine
songs. Surely this must be more than mere coincidence.

3

Edward Elgar (1857–1934)

Speak, speak, music, and bring to me
  Fancies too fleet for me,
  Sweetness too sweet for me,
Wake, wake, voices, and sing to me,
  Sing to me tenderly; bid me rest.

Rest, Rest! ah I am fain of it!
Die, Hope! small was my gain of it!
  Song, take thy parable,
  Whisper that all is well,
  Say that there tarrieth
  Something more true than death,
Waiting to smile for me; bright and blest.

Thrill, string: echo and play for me
All that the poet, the priest cannot say for me;
Soar, voice, heavenwards, and pray for me,
  Wondering, wandering; bid me rest.

               A. C. Benson: 'The Song'

Elgar wrote solo songs throughout his composing career, the first, 'The language of flowers', in 1872 when he was 14 ('to my sister Lucy on her birthday'), the last, 'The woodland stream', in 1933, the year before he died. Banfield (1985: 440) lists 90, but some of these are missing, and some are arrangements, multi-voice or spoken voice (recitations). There are, even so, about 70 published songs, which indicates that Elgar was by no means uninterested in the medium. Yet no-one would claim that Elgar was a major songwriter. Why? How is it that a composer acknowledged as one of this country's finest symphonic composers and one of the major choral-writers of his day, is so disappointing as a writer of songs? Several reasons have been suggested: that the restrictions of the song medium did not give him scope for the expression of his ideas (Jacobs: 159); that his songs were an off-moment relaxation from work on the larger choral and orchestral canvases (Northcote: 93); whilst Banfield (1985: 18) suggests that Elgar was unwilling, afraid or 'too reticent' to show his personal feeling in the exposed medium of the solo song. One feels, too, that Elgar was restricted by the medium of accompaniment, the piano lacking the colour and range of the orchestra. He was never at ease when writing for the piano: his writing for the instrument is wooden, lacking fluency and imagination. Several of his songs cry out for orchestral depth and colour. There is another reason. Despite the fact that Elgar was highly literate and widely read, when it came to choosing texts to set to music, his poetic tastes were far from discriminating. Jerrold Northrop Moore's argument (1984(a)) that Elgar was so much 'bedevilled by a fine literary taste' that 'he felt it better to set the best second-rate poetry to music' is ingenuous. If true, then Elgar was doing himself no service, for you cannot make a silk purse out of a sow's ear. Of the 36 or so poets that Elgar chose to set, only a half-dozen can be considered writers of any rank. Instead, he prefers minor versifiers, such as Barry Pain, Roden Noel, Gilbert Parker, A. C. Benson, Felix Almond – and Mrs Elgar. Some of these are not even to be found in Q's comprehensive *Oxford Book of Victorian Verse* (1913) which omnivorously devours the smallest Victorian poetic minnow.

The poet to whom Elgar turned most frequently for his song-texts was his wife, Alice. He first set her words in 1888, 'The wind at dawn', when she was still Alice Roberts, and she features in *Sea-Pictures* ('In haven') as well as in 'The King's Way', his adaption of the trio section from his *Pomp and Circumstance March No.4.* The other poets that Elgar sets more than once – Alfred Noyes (8), Kipling (5), Gilbert Parker (3) and A. C. Benson (3: 4, if you count 'Land of hope and glory') – all indicate Elgar's very right-wing, 'Empire' affiliations and sympathies. But where are the major English lyricists: Shakespeare, Herbert, Herrick, Blake, Byron . . .? Tennyson and Yeats are each set once apiece, and his adored Shelley is represented by 'In moonlight', which is hardly a song in the usual sense. Elgar was persuaded to make a song out of the 'Canto Popolare' from *Alassio* (1904) and discovered that Shelley's lyric fitted the tune after a fashion: the result is a shotgun marriage, if ever there was one. (He did embark on a setting of Shelley's 'Ozymandias', but never completed it.)

The Shelley 'song' raises the question of Elgar's appreciation of poetry. How could anyone who genuinely loves poetry effect such a brutish marriage? Indeed, Elgar's handling of his texts in general shows lack of sensitivity. Even in such a hallowed masterpiece as *The Dream of Gerontius* he is not over-meticulous about 'just note and accent': take, for example, the Soul's 'I ever had believed . . .' (figs. 20–1) and the Angel's 'It is because then thou didst fear . . .' (fig. 24). Indeed, the Angel seems to have difficulty in pronouncing her Newman throughout. This lack of natural sympathy with his texts and cavalier attitude to word-setting blights many of Elgar's songs, as in 'In moving waters cool and bright' in 'The shepherd's song', and 'Tell me the stories that I am forgetting' in 'Pleading'. One of the worst instances occurs in his setting of Longfellow's 'Rondel', No. 6 of the *Seven Lieder*, where the words are simply pegged onto the tune. Even *Sea Pictures* is not immune from such criticism, as the very first song, 'Sea slumber-song', demonstrates (Ex. 3.1). I defy anyone to understand this passage when it is sung. Elgar has misconstrued what Noel has written, making nonsense of the sense. The key verb, 'dream', is tossed away too quickly and the phrase 'rocks and caves' has been cut off from *its* verb, 'veil'.

Ex. 3.1

In choosing such inferior poets, one might cynically claim that Elgar has done justice to their poems. Mediocre verse has, for the most part, resulted in mediocre songs, which rarely aspire higher to anything more distinguished than the drawing-room ballad. Many of his songs are, in Arthur Jacobs's words, of 'no particular distinction even within their own undistinguished class' (1960: 159). 'Is she not passing fair' has a certain rousing quality in its swinging 3/4, but songs such as 'Pleading' and 'The wind at dawn' too often rely on hammered chordal triplets, the hackneyed stock-in-trade of Parry's 'patent trade song'. The *Seven Lieder* falls into this category. These are all early songs, dating from the 1880s and 1890s; 1–3 and 5–7 had all been published previously and were brought together with No. 4 ('The poet's life') for the 1907 publication. 'Lieder' is a misnomer; that the publisher thought that they should aspire to the title is evident from the German translations. All are essentially in the ballad tradition. 'The poet's life' is particularly weak; 'A song of Autumn' drowns in its own morbid nostalgia; 'Through the long days' is nondescript; 'Rondel' has a delicate accompanimental idea but fails the poem in its shotgun word-setting; 'The shepherd's song' has an innocent pastoral charm, helped by a more than usually memorable vocal line, but Parry's 'A Welsh lullaby', similar in mood and texture, is much more original. The most interesting songs in the set are the first two. 'Like to the damask rose' – attributed by Elgar to Simon Wastell (1560–1631) but probably by Francis Quarles (1592–1644) – is a daunting poem to set. It is a morality on Man's Mortality, set out in long, 12-line stanzas – Elgar thankfully sets only two of a possible five stanzas. The first six lines of each are a series of similes about 'Life'

– 'Like as the damask rose you see,/Or like the blossom on the tree . . .' –
followed by a further six drawing out the moral of these similes – 'E'en such is
man: whose thread is spun,/Drawn out and cut, and so is done . . .'. Elgar sets it
as a full-blooded melodrama: we could be listening to the piano accompaniment to a silent film, with its sudden changes of mood and tempo. The setting
has been criticised for its exaggerated posturing. It is certainly over-the-top, in
the very best sense, but in this is only matching the 'morbid solemnity' of the
text. The most attractive song of the seven is 'Queen Mary's (lute) song', from
Tennyson's verse-drama *Queen Mary* (1875). Fauré-esque in its delicacy of
accompaniment, it is a charming light pastiche that Edward German would
have been proud of.

The two settings of poems by A. C. Benson of 1901 are far more characteristic.
Benson, one of the remarkable siblings of Edward White Benson (who was one
of Victoria's archbishops of Canterbury), was a housemaster at Eton when Elgar
made his settings. 1901 was, indeed, a truly Elgar-Benson year, for they also
collaborated on the *Coronation Ode* for Edward VII, a substantial work with a
powerful final chorus, which was later adapted, with new, more jingoistic texts,
into the solo song 'Land of hope and glory'. The *Two Songs* show the more
characteristic, reflective side of Benson's creativity. 'In the dawn' is a subtly
constructed love-song. The six verses are set in an unexpected tonal progression
that rises from C major, via E-flat major to the remote key of G-flat major,
before abruptly returning to the home key; each tonal centre evokes new
musical ideas:

A	A	B	B	C	A
C major		E-flat major		G-flat major	C major

In the first two verses the vocal line ends with an arching sequence taken up and
completed by the piano. But in the final verse, the sequence is drawn forward to
the third line, leading to a tranquil coda. 'Speak, music', from the collection *The
Professor and other poems* (1900) is an invocation to music. The poem (see
epigraph) consists of three irregular stanzas (like a short lyrical ode) of five,
seven and four lines each, with unusual triple rhymes ('bring to me . . ./ . . . sing
to me'), from which Elgar creates a ternary-shaped song, A1 B A2. The tonality
is ambiguous: ostensibly A major but veering constantly to its subdominant, D
major, in which key the middle verse is set. The reprising third verse, where four
lines have to accommodate the five lines of the opening stanza, is prolonged by
a coda, so that the music finally reaches (if somewhat reluctantly) the A major
'home'. This teasing tonal ambiguity is typical of Elgar. But perhaps the most
notable feature of the song is its metre: except for a single 9/8 bar, it is in 15/8
throughout. Elgar often uses this 'extra' beat for the piano to echo the voice
(Ex. 3.2). With its gentle tender melancholy, it is one of Elgar's most attractive
songs.

Ex. 3.2

Elgar's most characteristic, personal songs are those written in 1909–10, at the time he was working on his Violin Concerto and Second Symphony: three songs of a projected song-cycle to poems by Gilbert Parker, op. 59, and the *Two Songs*, op. 60. In both cases one senses the strain that the monochrome accompanimental medium has imposed on him. Both sets cry out for orchestral colouring and depth, and indeed Elgar furnished them both with orchestral accompaniments, in which form they received their first performances. The *Two Songs* are an oddity which only Elgar's jokey sense of humour could have conceived. The texts are supposedly folksongs from Eastern Europe, paraphrased by one 'Pietro d'Alba': i.e. White Peter (Rabbit), which was the name of his daughter Carice's pet rabbit. The joke is neatly rounded off at the end of the second song, which is signed with the place-name 'Leyrisch-Turasp, 1909' – an anagram of the German version of Peter Rabbit (= 'Petrus Has(e) Lyric'). Both songs are attractive – 'The torch' for its catchy melody, 'The river' with its 'Rustula' refrain. The orchestral conception, however, shows through in the piano accompaniments, with their *tremolando* rolls and orchestral textures. But this Eastern European joke evinced from Elgar a wildness and passion lacking in so many of his 'English' songs.

At the same time Elgar was composing these *Two Songs*, he began work on a song-cycle to poems by the Canadian-born writer Gilbert (later Sir Gilbert) Parker (1862–1932). He completed only three of the planned six, but allowed them to be published with their projected opus numbers, op. 59, Nos. 3, 5 and 6. (Nos. 1, 2 and 4 do not exist.) The incomplete 'cycle' was given its first performance in its orchestral version at the memorial concert for A. J. Jaeger ('Nimrod') on 24 January, 1910. 'O soft was the song' (59/3) translates least well to the piano, with its violinistic figurations (marked *quasi trem*) and *tremolando* rolls, but the words hardly help. More effective is 'Was it some golden star' (59/5), a stronger poem with its dreams of chivalric love expressed in a simple minor mode melody. But the finest in this truncated group is the final song, 'Twilight' (59/6). Here Elgar imbues Parker's mawkish verse musings on 'what might have been' with some of his finest elegiac music. Though not technically a chaconne, the song has a chaconne-like nobility: four chords drooping downwards, from tonic to dominant, beneath a tonic pedal-note intoned by the singer (Ex. 3.3(a)). It possesses some typical Elgarian features, notably a waywardness of tempo. Of the song's 34 bars, only 13 are *a tempo*: the music is continually being held back by *rits* and *ralls*. The closing cadence is particularly imaginative. After the singer's final 'Adieu', the music reaches the tonic (B) major, but then hesitates, making an unexpected modal cadence into G major before reaching its final rich B major (Ex. 3.3(b)). What is more, the orchestral original has in this instance been translated into excellent piano-writing. This is Elgar in his noblest elegiac mood, matching the elegy of *For the fallen*. It is arguably his most distinguished song for voice and piano.

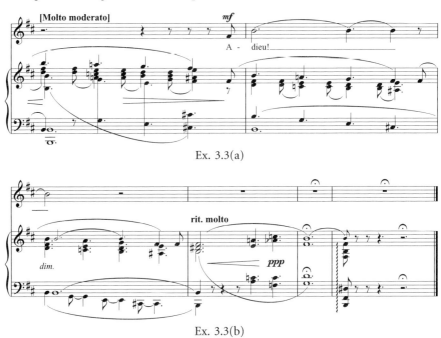

Ex. 3.3(a)

Ex. 3.3(b)

Another admirable song from the same year, though quite different in character, is 'A child asleep', dedicated to the baby son of Elgar's favourite mezzo-soprano, Muriel Foster, 'for his mother's singing'. Despite the slightly sentimental character of Elizabeth Barrett Browning's poem, it is a little gem of a cradle-song, with the true Elgarian stamp in its wayward vocal line and harmonies.

Childhood – scenes from, reminiscences of – always stimulated the best in Elgar. Some of his most attractive songs are those he wrote for the organ-grinder in Algernon Blackwood's fairy play *The Starlight Express* (1915). 'The blue-eyes fairy' is a light and charming waltz-song, but 'To the children', with its sudden changes of tempo and mood as it gathers up reminiscences from other parts of the play, is more profound – strangely moving and sad, and typically Elgar.

But without doubt, Elgar's supreme achievement as a songwriter is *Sea-Pictures* (1899, *1900*), his only completed orchestral song-cycle, and one of the landmarks of English Romantic Song. Scored for contralto solo accompanied by a full-size orchestra, the work was written in the summer of 1899 and first performed by Clara Butt at the Norwich Festival on 5 October, 1899, with Elgar conducting. It is a setting of five poems with sea themes, by a motley group of poets – Roden Noel, Alice Elgar, Elizabeth Barrett Browning, Richard Garnett and Adam Lindsay Gordon. One wonders where Elgar found some of his more obscure lyrics. Alice Elgar's 'In haven' needs no explanation – Elgar had set it two years earlier and it had already been published as 'Lute song' in *The Dome* (January 1898) – and Elizabeth Barrett Browning's poetry was as popular, if not more popular, with the Victorian public as her husband Robert's. Adam Lindsay Gordon – born in the Azores in 1833, bred in England, and domiciled in Australia from 1853 until his suicide in 1870 – was one of the pioneering Australian poets and his extrovert, outdoor bush-ballads were much admired in this country; Elgar had already set one of his poems, 'A song of Autumn' (*1892*). But to discover the poetry of Roden Noel (1834–94) and Richard Garnett (1835–1906) shows extremely wide-ranging tastes and reading. Could it be that the Elgars subscribed to the popular series of small poetry volumes, *The Canterbury Poets*, edited by William Sharp (aka 'Fiona Macleod') which were published in the late 1880s and 1890s? For the text of Noel's 'Sea slumber-song' was first published in *Poems by Roden Noel* as part of that series, whilst Garnett's 'Where corals lie' (originally obscurely published in *Io in Egypt and other poems* in 1859) and Gordon's 'The swimmer' both appear in the anthology *Sea Music* (1888). (It is rather coincidental that the six stanzas from the original thirteen of Gordon's poem which are included in *Sea Music* are the very same from which Elgar chose his 4½ stanzas for setting.)

Sea-Pictures is a true song-cycle, not so much by tonality – the key-centres of the five songs, E minor, C major, C major, B minor and D major, have no structural relevance – but by subject-matter, contrast, balance and cross-reference. Elgar has laid out his songs architecturally: three large-scale, complexly structured songs encompassing two shorter, strophic songs of much simpler character. The songs differ in character and vocal technique too: the two short ones 'voice-led', with clear-cut vocal melodies, whilst the other three are more symphonic, almost Wagnerian, employing the technique he was to use in *The Dream of Gerontius,* of pinning the vocal line onto a continuous orchestral texture. In all three it is the orchestra as much as the singer which supplies the musical interest. Because of the complexity of the bigger songs, it will be clearer to analyse them in conjunction with their texts.

The cycle begins with 'Sea slumber-song', a nocturnal sea-picture in short rhyming lines which Elgar moulds into two irregular strophes, each with three distinct sections (Fig. 1):

Fig. 1

Strophe 1	A1	Sea-birds are asleep, The world forgets to weep, Sea murmurs her soft slumber-song On the shadowy sand Of this elfin land;
	B1	'I, the Mother mild, Hush thee, O my child, Forget the voices wild!
	C1	Isled in elfin light Dream, the rocks and caves, Lulled by whispering waves, Veil their marbles bright, Foam glimmers faintly white Upon the shelly sand Of this elfin land;
Strophe 2	A2	Sea-sound, like violins, To slumber woos and wins, I murmur my soft slumber-song, Leave woes and wail and sins,
	B2	Ocean's shadowy might Breathes good-night,
	C2	Good-night!'

Each of the three subsections is characterised by important orchestral ideas, 'sea-motives' or 'aural sea-scapes' (Exs. 3.4(a), (b) and (c)). All three reappear later in the cycle: 'x' and 'y' in the third song, 'z' in the final song. In the short coda (C2), Elgar makes an excursion into C major before the final E minor cadence, neatly preparing us for the C major of the next song.

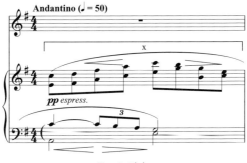

Ex. 3.4(a)

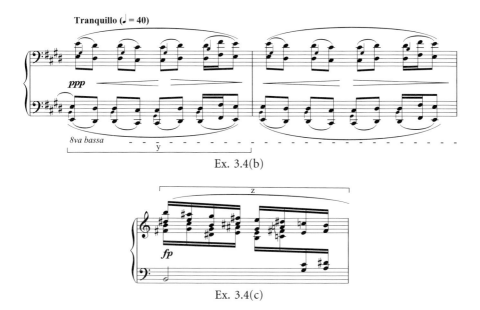

Ex. 3.4(b)

Ex. 3.4(c)

'In haven (Capri)' is the simplest of the set, a gentle love-song. Clearly for Elgar an autobiographically personal poem, it describes lovers, sure of the enduring haven of their love as they watch a sea storm. (So sure, in fact, that the storm outside is unnoticed in the music!) The poem is set out in three short, three-line stanzas, each concluding with a varied refrain, 'Love alone will stand/ last/stay'. Elgar scales down the orchestra to match the poem, which he sets in a simple strophic fashion.

In 'Sabbath morning at sea' Elgar more than justifies his use of orchestral accompaniment, achieving a nobility and spaciousness impossible in a voice/ piano format. It continues in the C major tonality of 'In haven'. From Elizabeth Barrett Browning's pious Victorian text, Elgar sets five (1, 3, 11, 12 and 13) of the original 13 stanzas, which he disposes in an A B C A C format, though with far more subtlety than this simplification would suggest (Fig. 2):

Fig. 2

Ritornello I

A1   (a)   The ship went on with solemn face:
                      To meet the darkness on the deep,
                      The solemn ship went onward.
      (b)   I bowed down weary in the place;
                      For parting tears and present sleep
                      Had weighed mine eyelids downward.

Ritornello I

B   (c)   The new sight, the new wondrous sight!
                      The water around me turbulent,
                      The skies, impassive o'er me.

(b)   Calm in a moonless, sunless light,
           As glorified even by the intent
              Of holding the day glory!

Ritornello II

C1   Love me, sweet friends, this sabbath day,
              The sea sings round me while ye roll
                 Afar the hymn, unaltered,
           And kneel, where once I knelt to pray,
              And bless me deeper in your soul
                 Because your voice has faltered.

Ritornello II

A2   And though this sabbath comes to me
              Without the stoled minister,
                 And chanting congregation,
           God's spirit shall give comfort. He
              Who brooded soft on waters drear,
                 Creator on creation.

Ritornello I

C2   He shall assist me to look higher,
              Where keep the saints, with harp and song,
Ritornello II   An endless sabbath morning,
           And, on that sea commixed with fire,
              Oft drop their eyelids raised too long
                 To the full Godhead's burning.

There are musics of quite different character again: 'A' is recitative-like (very
'Gerontian'); 'B' moves at a quicker tempo, with more dramatic vocal writing
over repeated triplets in the accompaniment; and 'C' is a melody (reminiscent
of one in *Cockaigne*) over throbbing triplets. It will be noticed how the first two
verses are linked by the same refrain (b) and by the 'sea-motive' 'y' from the
first song. The orchestra is given two *nobilmente* ritornellos: the first (I)
heralding verses 1 (A1) and 2 (B), the second (II) verse 3 (C1) (Exs. 3.5(a)
and (b)). These ritornellos dominate the sound-scape of the song more than
the vocal line (or, indeed, the text), but are deployed in a subtle, asymmetrical
manner, so that Ritornello II reappears before A2 and Ritornello I before C2 in
the final verse, where it continues in diminution in the accompaniment.

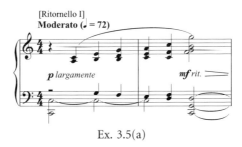

Ex. 3.5(a)

Ex. 3.5(b)

It is not until the words 'An endless sabbath morning' that Ritornello II returns (*cantabile e accelerando*), this time not only in the accompaniment but also taken up by the singer. This leads the music, via a sly reference at the words 'And, on that sea commixed with fire' to the main sea-motive 'x' from the first song, and to a bold confident climax.

The Garnett setting, 'Where corals lie', is the most popular song of the group and understandably so, with its delicate scoring and memorable vocal line underpinned by a gently jogging rhythm. Its tonality of B minor is always yearning towards D major; this the singer eventually achieves in the final verse, only for the orchestra to take the music into B major for the final cadence (Ex. 3.6). Elgar sets the four stanzas in ternary shape, A1 A2 B A3. The music of the third stanza, as we shall see, will echo in the central section of the following song. The words – a South Sea dream-fantasy – are frothy nonsense. Indeed, though one would never wish to lose the warmth of the human voice, the vocal line could easily be substituted by an orchestral instrument to produce a perfectly acceptable orchestral miniature – a 'Chanson de soir' perhaps?

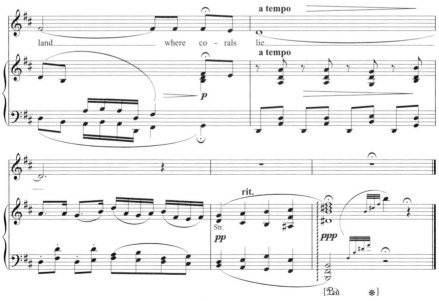

Ex. 3.6

The final song employs extracts from Gordon's long narrative poem, 'The swimmer', which graphically describes a swimmer struggling against a rough sea; it is the most complex and symphonic in structure. Once again, as in the second song, the music picks up the tonality referred to but rejected at the end of the previous song, in this case D major; and again, as in the first song, there are three strongly contrasted ideas (A B C) in the main outer strophes, which this time are recapped in a different order (A C B). Once more there is a ritornello, heard at the very beginning but interrupted by the singer's opening recitative (A1) (Ex. 3.7). This not only acts as a framework to the song, but is taken up by the singer at three points during the setting ('Love! When we wandered here together', 'O brave white horses' and 'To gulphs foreshadow'd').

Ex. 3.7

Between these two large outer strophes there is a lengthy middle section, which acts as a mid-way 'haven', during which recollections of earlier themes from the song-cycle are skilfully woven into the texture: the third verse of 'Where corals lie' (at the words 'From the heights and hollows of fern and heather') and the 'C' section of 'Sea slumber-song' (the four lines that Elgar sets of Stanza 3). This central haven is reflected tonally too: out of the surge and storm of G minor/D major into the calm water of E minor/C major/G major. The song had opened with the downward sklitter of the sea-motive 'z' from the first song, and it is this that naturally bridges the central section back to the reprise of the opening recitative music. A simplified plan of the structure of this complex movement is given below (Fig. 3):

Fig. 3

'z' from 1st song: DM

Ritornello interrupted by

A1 (recitative)   With short, sharp, violent lights made vivid   Gm
                            To southward far as the sight can roam,
                        Only the swirl of the surges livid,
                            The seas that climb and the surfs that comb.
B1   Only the crag and the cliff to nor'ward,   DM
                        And the rocks receding, and reefs flung forward,
                        Waifs wrecked seaward and wasted shoreward,
                            On shallows sheeted with flaming foam.

C1	A grim, grey coast and a seaboard ghastly,	Dm (over
	And shores trod seldom by feet of men	dominant
	Where the batter'd hull and the broken mast lie,	pedal)
	They have lain embedded these long years ten.	
Ritornello	Love! when we wandered here together,	DM
	Hand in hand through the sparkling weather,	
D (= recollections	From the heights and hollows of fern and heather,	Em
from 4th movement	God surely loved us a little then.	
and 'z' from 1st		
movement)	The skies were fairer and shores were firmer –	CM
	The blue sea over the bright sand roll'd;	
	Babble and prattle, and ripple and murmur,	
	Sheen of silver and glamour of gold.	
A2 (recitative)	So, girt with tempest and wing'd with thunder	Gm
	And clad with lightning and shod with sleet,	
	And strong winds treading the swift waves under	
	The flying rollers with frothy feet.	
C2	One gleam like a bloodshot sword-blade swims on	Dm (over
	The sky-line, staining the green gulf crimson,	dominant
	A death-stroke fiercely dealt by a dim sun	pedal
	That strikes through his stormy winding sheet.	again)
Ritornello	O brave white horses! you gather and gallop,	DM
	The storm sprite loosens the gusty reins;	
B2	Now the stoutest ship were the frailest shallop	CM
	In your hollow backs, on your high-arched manes.	
	I would ride as never a man has ridden	DM
	In your sleepy, swirling surges hidden;	
Ritornello (incorp.	To gulphs foreshadow'd through strifes forbidden,	
'y' from 1st movement)	Where no light wearies and no love wanes.	
Ritornello		

As can be seen, it is symphonic in its complexity, focussing the listener's attention firmly on the orchestra. Whether anyone catches more than the odd phrase of Gordon's poem is another matter. In the reliance of the poem on the sound and fury of alliteration and assonance, perhaps the words are expendable, but we are certainly on the borderline here (and, indeed, in the other two 'big' songs of *Sea-Pictures*), between art-song as it is usually known and symphonic music with a vocalise. Nevertheless, it is a powerful song, bringing together, as Banfield has pointed out (1985: 18), the two sides of Elgar's musical personality, the outward, invigorating extrovert and the private, hypersensitive nostalgic.

Not even the most fervent Elgarian would lay high claims for Elgar as a songwriter. He seems to have had no desire, as Parry, to forge an English equivalent of the German *Lied*, but was content to accept the artistically meretriciousness of the popular ballad format. His best songs outsoar the cosiness of the salon, but even so there is no doubting their provenance. Despite his deep, scholarly interest in English literature – witness the erudite notes he made for his symphonic study *Falstaff* (*Musical Times* 1913) – he never translated this into action in his choice of poets for song-setting, being content with second-rate and minor writers. Nor was he fastidious about word-setting, which is the hallmark of every great songwriter. The exceptions only to go prove the rule, and in songs such as *Sea-Pictures* and the Benson and Parker settings, the real Elgar peeps through and we have real music.

4

Frederick Delius (1862–1934)

They are not long, the weeping and the laughter,
  Love and desire and hate:
I think they have no portion in us after
  We pass the gate.

They are not long, the days of wine and roses:
  Out of a misty dream
Our path emerges for a while, then closes
  Within a dream.

Ernest Dowson:
'Vitae summa brevis spem nos vetat incohare longam'

Delius is unique amongst British song-composers in that, though he wrote nearly 60 solo songs, less than 20 are to English texts. The remainder are settings of Norwegian, German, French and Danish poetry. Though these have been supplied with English translations, Delius set them in the original languages; they are therefore out of the terms of reference of our particular survey, though they will be referred to as a background to his English-text songs.

Like many aspiring composers, Delius began to write songs early in his career. His first known song, written in his late teens but since lost, was 'When other lips shall speak', to a poem by Alfred Bunn (c.1797–1860), Balfe's librettist for *The Bohemian Girl* (1843). His last work, a setting of W. E. Henley's 'A late lark', was completed, with the help of his amanuensis Eric Fenby, in 1929. Not unexpectedly, his preferred English poets were the romantic lyricists of his own, or a slightly earlier, period: Shelley, Tennyson, Dowson, Henley, Fiona Macleod; there is also an incomplete setting of Yeats's 'The lake isle of Innisfree'. The exception is *Four Old English Lyrics* where he makes an unexpected excursion into 16th/17th-century texts by Shakespeare, Jonson, Nashe and Herrick. But it was the richly nostalgic, *fin de siècle* verses of Dowson, Henley and Macleod that inspired him to his finest songs: 'songs of sunset' metaphorically if not literally.

Born in Bradford of German parents, working for two years farming oranges in Florida, receiving his musical training at Leipzig, spending as much time as he could in Norway, domiciled for most of his life in France, Delius was the most cosmopolitan English composer of his generation. This is reflected in the cosmopolitan choice of language for his songs. He reacted differently to the special character and inflection of each language he set, so that his Verlaine settings differ from the Björnsen or the Nietzsche settings, or from the Henley or Dowson. This is due not only to the different emotional characteristics of the language, but also to different song traditions, and this is demonstrated in the *Three Shelley Lyrics*, which are unashamedly derived from, and aiming at, the English Royalty Ballad tradition. However, apart from the Shelley songs and the *Maud* song-cycle, English texts and the English songwriting tradition did not concern him in the early years of his career. The years 1888–90 were devoted to Norwegian poetry and led to the best of his early songs: 'Cradle song' (Ibsen), 'Twilight fancies' and 'Young Venevil' (both to texts by Björnsen). Here the influence was his friend and early mentor, Edvard Grieg. Many of the songs were written for and dedicated to Grieg's wife, the soprano Nina Grieg, and some of the texts, including 'Twilight fancies', had been set by Grieg himself. Griegian features are noticeable in these songs, such as the frequent use of 'echoing' of the singer's final phrase by the piano. ('Young Venevil' is full of such echoes.) More fundamental is Delius's adoption of Grieg's 'woof and weave' method of setting melodies, which the Norwegian composer had pioneered in his Norwegian folksong-settings, op. 17, and perfected in his op. 66, whereby a diatonic (modal) melody is given a richly-chromatic piano accompaniment. This can be heard in 'Twilight fancies' (Ex. 4.1).

Ex. 4.1

The technique is used in one of his later English songs, 'I-Brasil', whose vocal line, almost entirely modal-diatonic, could almost be a Scottish folk-tune. But this is exceptional, for more typically in the later, post-1900 songs, Delius's technique develops into something more radical. Compared with 'The nightingale has a lyre of gold' or 'Cynara', an early song such as 'Young Venevil' has a naïve simplicity. In the former, the melodic lines are not an independent entity (like a folksong) but one strand (albeit the most important strand) in a surrounding web of harmony: the strand that is attached to the words. In such songs, the vocal lines cannot exist outside their harmonic context. Just as seals out of water look clumsy and awkward, so Delius's vocal lines, taken out of their harmonic context, sound clumsy and angular – and are often awkward to sing. Yet, in their native elements, both are perfectly at home; Delius's vocal lines swim and glide gracefully and naturally when supported and underpinned by their richly subtle surrounding harmonies (Ex. 4.2).

As quick a growth to meet de - cay, As you, or a - ny - thing.

Ex. 4.2

In the best of the later songs, such as 'To daffodils' and 'A late lark', he moves smoothly between these two techniques to suit the context, chromatic vocal lines being reserved to create emotional tension, the more modal, folk-like vocal lines to express serener, calmer sentiments.

In his mature songs, a poem suggests not so much a *tune* as a *mood* to Delius. As A. K. Holland observed, 'The justification of his songs frequently lies not in the words so much as in the emotional echoes to which they give rise' (1951: 10). This results in some problems for both listener and performer. Delius's matching of vocal line and words is not always satisfactory. Eric Fenby once observed that Delius, in writing for the voice, 'had neither feeling for line nor feeling for words' (1936: 71). Compared with Quilter and Warlock, Delius was not particularly sensitive to the musical rhythms of his texts. Warlock himself pointed out that, whereas in the melodies of the great songwriters to alter a note would spoil the melody, in Delius's case this is not always true. The notes of his vocal lines are almost inconsequent: any note from the accompanying chord would have done equally well in the context (1923: 142–3). This is because the melodic/harmonic function of his accompaniments is of far more significance than the shape of the vocal line. In his best songs one remembers both vocal line and accompaniment as a unity; in his less successful ones, such as 'The nightingale', it is the accompaniment that lingers in the memory after the vocal line has evaporated.

Though written at the same time as the *Three Shelley Lyrics* and the 12 Norwegian songs, the five *Settings from Tennyson's 'Maud'* for tenor and orchestra (1891, *1990*) are of less significance. This is a pity, for they are the nearest Delius came to writing a song-cycle. They form a poetically connected sequence and pre-date Somervell's great *Maud* song-cycle by seven years. The vocal lines lack distinction and the musical momentum is full of what Fenby calls 'amiable commonplaces' (Holland: 53). Delius himself was clearly dissatisfied with them, for when Peter Warlock mooted the possibility of a performance during the 1929 Delius Festival, he rejected the idea. They remained in manuscript until 1990, when they were published by the Delius Trust (Collected Edition vol. 16). Many years later (1913) Delius made a unison song-setting of Tennyson's 'What does little birdie say'. The poem (from the sequence *Sea-dreams*, 1860) is one of Tennyson's most embarrassing efforts; its namby-pamby tweeness puts even Ambrose Philips in the shade:

> What does little birdie say
> In his nest at break of day . . .

Delius's equally gooey setting matches the text perfectly.

The *Three Shelley Lyrics* (1891, *1892*) were amongst the composer's first song publications. They show Delius writing English songs in the only English tradition that he was aware of, the drawing-room ballad, and they reflect all that was basically wrong with that tradition: vocal melodies which are mere pegs on which to hang texts; piano accompaniments which rely on hackneyed figurations and harmonies; above all, sentimentality of conception in which emotions are falsified and sent melodramatically 'over-the-top'. Certainly this is so with the first and last songs of the set, 'Indian love-song' and 'To the queen of my heart'. Shelley's lyrics verge on the sentimental; if not perhaps 'over-the-top', they display a 'fevered brow'. 'Indian love-song' ('I arise from dreams of thee') – later to receive a fine setting by Quilter – suffers from flaccid rhythms and nondescript ideas. In the third verse, Delius tries to stoke up the momentum by breaking into that stock cliché, hammered triplets. The tempo changes from the original *Allegretto tranquillo* to *Allegro molto con molta passione* (!) followed by *accelerando e cresc.* with the voice rising trumpet-like to a top B-flat. The only thing that saves it from disaster is the subtlety of the accompanying harmonies of the opening and the end. It is hard to believe that 'To the queen of my heart' (a text which may not be by Shelley) is by Delius. It is a regular pot-boiler, though again the chromatic harmonies are too sophisticated for the ballad genre. The opening vocal line could come straight from Teresa del Riego or a musical comedy of the period, going dutifully 'down the fifths' in the third phrase. Again we have hammered triplets leading to a *fortissimo* climax on a top A-sharp, and the rhythmic writing, especially in the vocal part, is atrophied and lifeless. The best of the three – which is reflected in its popularity – is 'Love's philosophy'. Here Delius seems to be finding a way out of the drawing-room with a more subtle invention. He avoids an obvious strophic approach to the two verses, which are through-composed in binary fashion (verse 1 moving from G major to B major, verse 2 from B minor back to G major). Instead, he unifies the music by means of the piano accompaniment: rippling semiquavers that, though not easy to play, are as pianistically effective as anything he was to write. At the end of the song, by repeating the final line of the poem, slowing the music down and underpinning the repetitions with chromatic harmonies, the music loses momentum. Nevertheless, this is full-blooded music, Delius at his most youthful, romantic, uninhibited: indeed, a Delius whom we shall rarely encounter again. If the song lacks the fleetness and gossamer of Quilter's famous setting, it is certainly a worthy alternative.

For the next 15 years Delius neglected English song-texts for French (Verlaine), Danish (Jacobsen, Drachmann and Holstein) and German

(Nietzsche). It was not until 1907 that he returned to English poetry and then to a contemporary poet, Ernest Dowson (1867–1900) who matched his music far more closely than Shelley or Tennyson, and to a format, solo voice with orchestra, which enabled him to express his special genius more effectively than did the monochrome medium of voice and piano. He had used orchestral accompaniment in the *Maud* settings, but these were his first essay in the medium: *Cynara* is a work of maturity. Indeed, in length and conception, it is Delius's most important English solo song.

Cynara (pronounced 'Sèe-na-ra', with an accent on the first syllable) was originally composed in 1907, the same year as *Songs of Sunset* (also to texts by Dowson), but remained in MS and unperformed until 1929 when Delius completed it with Fenby's help for performance at the Delius Festival of that year. 'Cynara', or 'Non sum qualis eram bonae sub regno Cynarae', to give it its full original title (taken from Horace's Odes, IV, I, 3), is perhaps Dowson's most famous poem. Indeed, some of the lines are so familiar – 'I have been faithful to thee, Cynara! in my fashion' – 'Gone with the wind' – 'I cried for madder music and for strange wine' – that on reading it one feels that one has stumbled into a dictionary of quotations. It captures the decadence and *ennui* of a lover constantly craving new sensations, yet unable to forget his old love. The poem is set out in four six-line stanzas rhyming A B A C B C, with two self-rhyming refrains at lines 4 and 6, which Delius ignores; instead, he leaves the words to carry the refrains alone. Though he charts the nuances of the four stanzas with subtle changes of tonality, tempo and metre, he cuts sometimes across their boundaries: e.g. in verse 2 there is a long gap between the lines three and four, and at the end of the third verse the music runs impetuously into the first line of the final stanza. The work is framed by a long slow introduction and a short coda. The introduction establishes the work's underlying tonality, E major, heavily coloured by the C-sharp minor of the opening bar, so that the added sixth (C-sharp) becomes an integral part of the tonic chord. At bar 7 a solo violin introduces the first important motive, a downward looping theme, 'a', which is immediately answered in the bass (bass clarinet/bassoon) by an upward chromatic idea, 'b'. These are 'framing' ideas, which reappear in the coda to bring the music to its cyclic conclusion. There are two other important motives: a downward motive embracing an octave (tone/minor 7th), 'c', first heard in bar 28 (= 'Cynara's shadow') and an upward, yearning figure, 'd', heard on violins/oboe/English horn over throbbing horns, at the beginning of the second verse (bar 56 onwards) (Exs. 4.3(a), (b) and (c)). In the final verse, the three main motives ('a', 'b' and 'c') are drawn together and the work ends with a telescoped reprise of the opening music, cadencing almost inevitably onto an added sixth chord on E major. A tabulation of the song's structure alongside the text is given in Fig. 1.

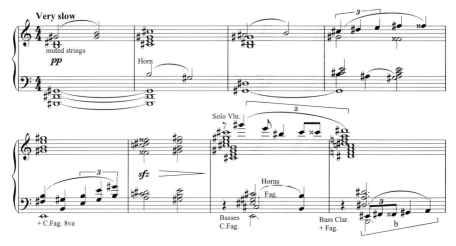

Ex. 4.3(a)

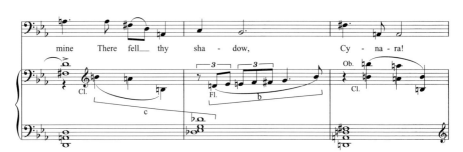

Ex. 4.3(b)

Ex. 4.3(c)

Fig.1

Introduction (23 bars) motives 'a' (solo vln, b.7) and 'b' (b.cl., b.8)		(C#M)EM→ E-flat M
(24–55) New motive 'c' (Clarinet, b.28) in combination with 'b'	Last night, ah, yesternight, betwixt her lips and mine There fell thy shadow, Cynara! thy breath was shed Upon my soul between the kisses and wine; And I was desolate and sick of an old passion, Yea, I was desolate and bowed my head: I have been faithful to thee, Cynara! in my fashion.	E-flat M, 4/4
(56–100) 'Yearning' figure 'd' over pulsing chords. NB. long break (5 bars) between lines 3 and 4	All night upon my heart I felt her warm heart beat, Night-long within mine arms in love and sleep she lay; Surely the kisses of her bought red mouth were sweet; But I was desolate and sick of an old passion, When I awoke and found the dawn was gray: I have been faithful to thee, Cynara! in my fashion.	3/2, quicker pulse (minim= previous crotchet)
(101–138) Dance-like (waltz- based) section (*vide* line 3). 'c' returns	I have forgot much, Cynara! gone with the wind, Flung roses, roses riotously with the throng, Dancing, to put thy pale, lost lilies out of mind; But I was desolate and sick of an old passion, Yea, all the time, because the dance was long: I have been faithful to thee, Cynara! in my fashion.	3/4, 'somewhat quicker'
(139–177)	I cried for madder music and for stronger wine, But when the feast is finished and the lamps expire, Then falls thy shadow, Cynara! the night is thine; And I am desolate and sick of an old passion, Yea hungry for the lips of my desire: I have been faithful to thee, Cynara! in my fashion.	Quicker/*forte* Very slow (3/4→4/4)
(178–end) Coda (9 bars): motives 'a', 'b' and 'c' drawn together		

Emphasis in the above comments has been on the orchestral structure of the piece. It is the orchestra which 'carries' the music; the baritone soloist, in fact, has a free *arioso* line, very similar to the solo part in *Sea Drift*, written a few years earlier. The soloist stands like a lone human figure in the rich orchestral landscape, adding little to the structure of the piece. He even manages, as we have observed, to avoid taking up any musical refrains where Dowson has supplied them, though the poet's obsessive reiteration of his old love's name, Cynara, does supply at least a rhythmic ritornello to the singer.

Cynara was originally intended to be part of *Songs of Sunset*. Another Dowson setting, of the poem 'Vitae summa brevis spem nos vetat incohare longam' ('They are not long, the weeping and the laughter') was written as a solo song in 1906, but incorporated later as the closing section of *Songs of Sunset* (II/5). The solo version was not published until 1987. Epitomising as it does Delius's philosophy of life, it is a welcome addition to the small Delian oeuvre.

Though sometimes linked with the English *fin-de-siècle* writers, W. E. Henley (1849–1903) was a sturdier and altogether more down-to-earth poet than Dowson. His poetry has attracted many songwriters, including Quilter and Butterworth, but he has never been set more memorably than by Delius in *A Late Lark*. Coincidentally, the two Delius settings of his poetry are inspired by bird-song: 'The nightingale has a lyre of gold' and 'A late lark', both of which come from the sequence *Echoes* in his 1888 collection, *A Book of Verses*. 'The nightingale' (1910, *1915*) is an unsatisfactory song, its tonality inconsequential and its mood ambiguous to the point of contrariness. In the brief, two-quatrain poem, Henley gives us the reason why he prefers the blackbird's song to those of the nightingale and lark: 'For his song is all of the joy of life'. Though one does not ask or expect a songwriter to 'catch at every particular epithet or metaphor' – 'To underline a poem word by word is the work of a misguided schoolmaster' (Warlock) – the indeterminate, lethargic bird-calls over a languid Chopinesque waltz hardly set the mood of the poem; nor do the aimless, chromatic meanderings of the vocal line evoke the childlike joy of Henley's words. The sudden quickening of tempo and texture at the beginning of the second verse is too abrupt and too brief to be convincing. The coda is by far the most effective part of the song, combining as it does the piano's introduction with the singer's final line. That is what Delius should have been aiming at all along, but it is too late to rescue the song.

'The nightingale' was published in 1915, the same year as 'I-Brasil', which is one of his most perfect songs. 'I-Brasil' is the Hesperides of Old Celtic mythology: the Land of Eternal Youth, Bax's 'Garden of Fand', located in the Atlantic Ocean 'where the last stars touch the sea'. Fiona Macleod's poem consists of two verses with two varied refrains:

> Old and gray . . . Come away! come away!
> Night and day . . . Far away, far away.

In Delius's strophic setting these refrains are memorably observed and acknowledged. Appropriate to the Scots lineage of the poem, he imbues the setting with a folk-like character. The piano underlines the sweet-sad mood with a solemn, Strathspey-style accompaniment full of Scotch snap rhythms, whilst the singer's modally inflected line is clear-cut, yet essentially Delius (Ex. 4.4(a)). Nothing could be more Delian than the ending, the singer echoing the final refrain

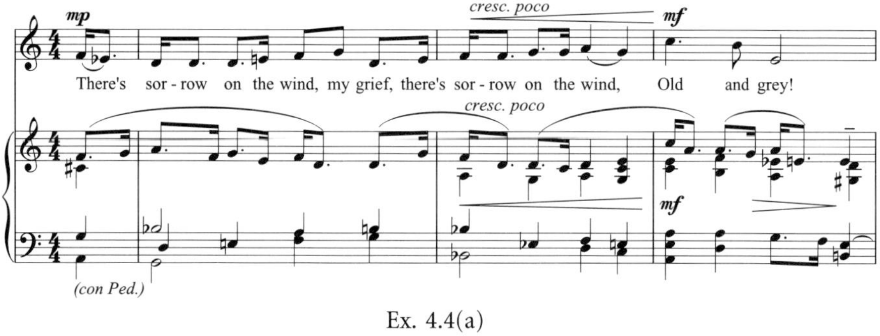

Ex. 4.4(a)

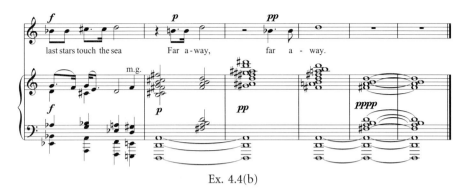

last stars touch the sea   Far a-way,   far a - way.

Ex. 4.4(b)

into the distance as I-Brasil is reached on that hallmark Delian chord, the added sixth (Ex. 4.4(b)).

In the year in which 'The nightingale' and 'I-Brasil' were published, Delius made the uncharacteristic choice of setting to music three early English lyrics: Nashe's 'Spring, the sweet spring', Jonson's 'So white, so soft, so sweet is she' ('Have you seen but a white lily grow') and Herrick's 'To daffodils'. In the following year he added a setting of that well-thumbed Shakespeare lyric, 'It was a lover and his lass' and the four were published together as *Four Old English Lyrics* (1919). Hitherto Delius had shown no interest in Elizabethan literature or in the current Tudor music revival: there is certainly nothing mock-Tudor about these four songs. But though he had 'jettisoned the ballad style' (Jacobs: 160) of his early Shelley settings, he had not found a satisfactory alternative. Not surprisingly, the two quieter songs are the most effective; the more extrovert songs fail to take wing, basically because they are over-cluttered with notes and harmonies. Indeed, 'It was a lover and his lass' is arguably the worst setting of this famous lyric by a major composer. The vocal line is extremely awkward in places and sounds as though the composer were setting a language foreign to him. (It is reminiscent of the eccentric accentuation of English in Stravinsky's *Three Shakespeare Songs* (1953).) Did Delius understand the purpose of the refrain 'Hey nonino'? It is set to such a sour, chromatic tune. (One feels that Delius did not particularly like the poem.) 'Spring, the sweet spring' is more effective, though its heavily-noted piano part, with its strong, unsubtle emphasis of the metre, requires a deft pianist to avoid grounding it entirely. The way in which Delius structures the poem is interesting. He completely ignores the neatly terraced stanzas, giving new music for each of the three verses. He even avoids musical matching in the famous 'bird-calls' refrain. But the song, with its headlong impetuosity, certainly captures the bustle of spring.

More attractive and characteristic are the two gentler songs. 'So white, so soft, so sweet is she' is an exquisite love-song. The rhythm of the piano's opening bars acts as a ritornello to hold the song together, enabling the singer to range freely, and the vocal line is modally contoured (though more chromatic in the second verse) over a rich, chromatically-harmonised accompaniment. In the second verse, the vocal line rises over neat semi-sequential phrases to a fine climax on the words of the song's title (Ex. 4.5).

Ex. 4.5

Compare this to the over-heated climaxes of the earlier Shelley songs! The
piano rounds off the setting with two pithy solo bars. Herrick's 'To daffodils',
with its sweet-sour musings on the fleetingness of beauty and life, is a text
perfectly attuned to Delius's philosophy. It is the finest of the set, for though
the piano establishes the mood, it is the singer who is in command. The vocal
line is a neat mixture of diatonic modality and chromaticism, whilst the
accompaniment consists mainly of richly harmonised chords with light
decorative arabesques echoing the vocal phrases. Note the way in which
Delius tackles the phrase 'As quick a growth to meet decay' – the knife
suddenly plunged in at the crucial final word (see Ex. 4.2). This is followed by
a procession of chromatic chords, so characteristic of the composer: 'We die/
As your hours do'. It is a chiaroscuro of colours, light and shade dappling
through the texture and helping to emphasise the bittersweet sentiments of the
poem. All is summed up in the piano's final cadence: a quiet C minor chord
with a flattened 7th added, followed by an even quieter C major chord with an
added 2nd (Ex. 4.6).

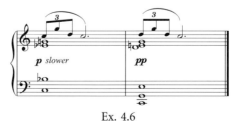

Ex. 4.6

A *Late Lark*, for tenor and orchestra, was Delius's final solo song and is his masterpiece in the genre, capturing Henley's poem definitively in terms that are pure Delius. It was composed between 1924 and 1929 (one of the works which Fenby helped complete), given its first performance during the 1929 Delius Festival and published in 1931. Henley's valedictory poem, which dates from 1876, is a prayer for rest, in which the poet draws together the images of the singing lark and the setting sun in his final prayer for his soul. It is cast in three irregular stanzas, which Delius observes in his setting. Despite the apparent freedom of form, the piece is tightly structured. As with *Cynara*, it is the orchestra that bears the burden of musical unification, releasing the voice to soar above, free as a lark, so that the music sounds like inspired improvisation. There are three main musical motives, each linked to an image or mood in the poem:

'x', representing the lark itself: heard at the outset on the oboe and taken up in succession by the singer (at the words 'from the quiet skies') and in diminution by the solo violin. This short bird-song motive is heard in a variety of adaptations throughout the song (Ex. 4.7(a));
'y', the 'serenity' ('sunset') motive: a long lyrical descending phrase, again first heard on the oboe at fig. [1](Ex. 4.7(b));
'z', representing night/death, which appears late in the song at the words 'And the darkening air/Thrills with the sense of the triumphing night' (Ex. 4.7(c)).

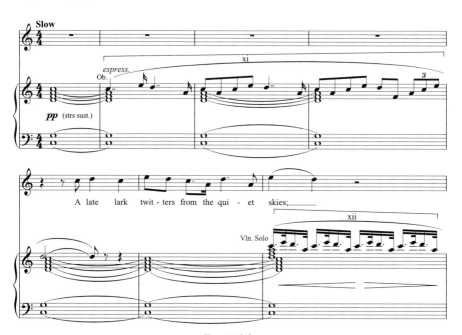

Ex. 4.7(a)

Ex. 4.7(b)

Ex. 4.7(c)

Broadly speaking, the work is a ternary structure, with the second verse (3/4, A little quicker) forming the central section and the return of the opening chord and the lark motive (2 bars before fig. [5]) as the reprise. But in Delius nothing is classically regular. The motives 'x' and 'y' thread their way through the entire work, but it is the falling thirds of the Night/Death motive, 'z', that concludes the song, cushioned on Delius's favourite added sixth chord. Notice the effective way in which Delius detaches the final word 'Death', making us wait until the 'z' motive has made its final appearance before it is heard (Ex. 4.7(d)).

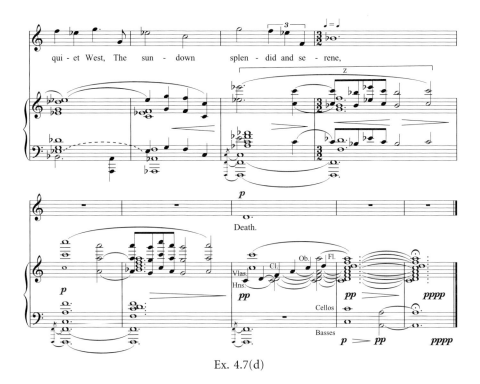

qui - et West, The sun - down splen - did and se - rene,

Death.

Ex. 4.7(d)

Fig. 2

Introduction: motive 'x' (= lark)		CM, 4/4, Slow
'x' (violin solo)	A late lark twitters from the quiet skies; And from the west, Where the sun, his day's work ended, Lingers as in content,	
fig. [1] motive 'y' (= sunset)	There falls on the old, gray city An influence luminous and serene, A shining peace.	DM-BM
fig. [2]	The smoke ascends In a rosy-and-golden haze. The spires	BM, 3/4, 'a little quicker'
fig. [3] 'y'	Shine, and are changed. In the valley Shadows rise. The lark sings on. The sun, Closing his benediction,	DM, 4/4
fig. [4] new idea, 'z' (violins)	Sinks, and the darkening air Thrills with the sense of the triumphing night – Night with her train of stars And her great gift of sleep.	6/4 AM
opening music returns		At [5] abrupt transition to Cm for final verse

	So be my passing!	
	My task accomplished and the long day done,	
	My wages taken, and in my heart	
'x'	Some late lark singing,	DM
'y'	Let me be gathered to the quiet west,	E-flat M
'z'	The sundown splendid and serene,	FM
	Death.	FM (with added 6th)

Both *Cynara* and *A Late Lark* were published in piano reduction versions (the first by Philip Heseltine, the other by Eric Fenby), but in no way can these be used for performance, for both works rely intrinsically on the rich orchestral colouring of the accompaniment.

Delius's contribution to English song is, as Banfield has pointed out, 'peripheral' (1985: 107). But his influence as a composer on a whole generation of English songwriters was enormous, and quite out of proportion to his own modest song output. Quilter, Ireland, Bridge, Grainger, Bax, Gibbs, Orr, Moeran, Warlock: all were indebted to his novel harmonic methods. Without Delius, none would have written their songs in quite the same way. Like Elgar, Delius was more at home working on a large canvas; songwriting played a relatively small part in his large output, and his English songs a small part of that small part. But that handful of songs is no negligible achievement.

5

Arthur Somervell (1863–1937)

A voice by the cedar tree
In the meadow under the Hall!
She is singing an air that is known to me,
A passionate ballad gallant and gay,
A martial song like a trumpet's call!
Singing alone in the morning of life,
In the happy morning of life and of May.

Alfred Tennyson: *Maud*

Parry, in his article in *The Century Guild Hobby Horse* (see Chapter 1), spoke gloomily of the state of English songwriting at the time he was writing, in the late 1880s. But after berating 'the makers of the patent trade-song', he ended on a more optimistic note:

> But strange to say, while things are almost at their worst, hopeful signs of a change begin to show themselves . . . there are most encouraging evidences of very young rising composers. It is really surprising to see how they come on. A few have already made their appearance who show to an extraordinary degree the delicate quickness of perception, and the instinct for rounding off and completing the musical presentation of a first-rate poetical lyric such as is among the rarest of gifts – while those who have a healthy feeling for declamation of their own language, and are capable of being inspired by genuine poetry, and doing things which are musically interesting and refined, look quite a promising troop (Parry 1888: 69–70).

As an example of a 'genuine English Musical Song' by one of this promising troop, he chose 'Marie at the window' by his pupil, the 25-year-old Arthur Somervell, and this was printed, in neat Century Guild script, immediately after the article. Such public recognition from the leading British composer of his day must have been greatly encouraging for the young Somervell. Parry was perceptive: Somervell did indeed possess the virtues he listed. What is more, he had one of the key assets of a successful songwriter, a genuine, deep affection for literature resulting from wide reading. This is reflected in his broad, not to say eclectic choice of poets, who range from anonymous 16th-century writers to his own contemporaries, from Browning and Tennyson at their most serious to the lighter verses of Harry Graham. Unusual for his time, he chose to set 18th-century poets: Thomas Percy, Isaac Bickerstaffe and Thomas Dibdin as well as

nearly a dozen settings of Burns, including a songbook. He also turned to North
American poets for his texts: J. R. Lowell, Eugene Field, Edgar Allan Poe and
Gilbert Parker. Though he did occasionally select minor writers, broadly
speaking his literary choice was bold and discriminating. Most importantly,
he was not afraid to tackle major poems by the leading poets of his day. No-one
has set the mature Tennyson and Browning more successfully than Somervell,
and he holds the distinction of being the first (and one of the finest) to chronicle
the travails of Housman's *A Shropshire Lad*.

In all his work, Somervell was served by a sound technique learned from his
years of study at the Hochschule in Berlin (1883–5), his pupillage under Stanford
at the RCM (1885–7) and his later private tuition with Parry. His idiom is
sturdily diatonic, with hardly any trace of modality, and chromaticism reserved
for emotionally tense moments. Even when compared with Parry and Stanford,
his is a conservative musical style, closer to Mendelssohn and Schumann than to
Brahms. (Is there a more Schumannesque song in the English repertoire than
'She came to the village church' in *Maud*?) He certainly did not imbibe, as did
his close contemporaries, Elgar and Delius, any obvious Wagnerian influence.
Indeed, in some songs it is the strong English lyrical voice of Sullivan that one
hears as much as anyone. His music is conventional and undemonstrative, but
can be eloquent and dramatic when required. His musical personality, however,
is not a striking one, which makes him a difficult composer to identify with the
innocent ear. It is as though he were deliberately being self-effacing and
cultivating an anonymous idiom.

Ex. 5.1

There are, however, some identifiable fingerprints: the downward drop of a perfect 5th, at the phrases 'sat by a pillar *alone*' in *Maud* and 'the *cherry now*' in *A Shropshire Lad* is already evident in that early song admired by Parry, 'Marie at the window' (Ex. 5.1). He is also fond of secondary 7ths in conjunction with strongly motivated sequential passages descending through a cycle of 5ths, particularly in penultimate phrases of musical paragraphs: most famously perhaps in 'Young love lies sleeping' (*Love in Springtime*).

Not unexpectedly, the earliest songs show him at his most conventional. *Six Songs by Robert Burns* (1885, *1886*) are nearer Sullivan than Parry or Stanford. Beyond the occasional Scotch snap there is no discernible Scottish element. They show craftsmanlike composition, with a good balance between voice and piano. He learned early the device of the piano picking up and echoing the singer's final phrase, to give a seamless passage from verse to verse. This is a songbook rather than a song-cycle: there is no attempt to unify the songs either by key or by motivic cross-reference, though the descending vocal line of the final song, 'Out over the Forth', could be seen to have a kinship with the tune of the first, 'Mary Morison'. But the songs are carefully placed for variety of pace and mood, and though they can be sung separately, are most effective in their given order. Despite its homage to the opening song of Schubert's *Winterreise*, 'Mary Morison' has a captivating tune, its square syllabic word-setting compensated by the freer cadences. 'Go fetch to me a pint of wine' begins as a drinking-song (*con fuoco*) but ends as a farewell to the Bonnie Lassie. These songs deserve to be heard occasionally. Several of Somervell's songs and song-sets are aimed at amateur and young performers, which reminds us that from 1901 he earned his living as Inspector of Music for the Board of Education, and was knighted in 1929 for his public services. *Four Songs of Innocence* (*1899*: a fifth was added in 1894) falls into this category; they are dedicated to 'Dolly and Gwen', the daughters of Hubert Parry. Innocent and innocuous, they are technically undemanding. Somervell was to continue this vein later with *Singing Time* (*1899*), songs for small children, *The Twins' Tune Book* (*1911*: for his own twin sons, Ronald and Hubert) and *Higgledy Piggledy* (*1931*), twelve songs for small children to poems by Harry Graham (1874–1936). But Somervell's outstanding contribution to English song is his five song-cycles. Four of these, *Maud*, *A Shropshire Lad*, *James Lee's Wife* and *A Broken Arc* are narrative cycles, in the *Liederkreis* tradition of Beethoven's *An die ferne Geliebte* and Schubert's *Die Schöne Müllerin* and *Die Winterreise*. Sullivan had made an earnest attempt to establish an English equivalent of this German innovation in the song-cycle he wrote to Tennyson's specially written libretto, *The Window* (1866, *1870*). He chose the right poet, but unfortunately the wrong poem. It was left to Somervell to find that suitable text in *Maud* (*1898*).

Tennyson's narrative sequence *Maud* sprang from the germ of a single lyric, 'Oh! that 'twere possible', written in 1833–4 and published by Lord Northampton in his anthology *The Tribute* in 1837. This appears considerably altered and revised as poem IV of Part II in the subsequent sequence. *Maud* was written in 1854 and published the following year, at the height of the Crimean

War, whose shadow lies across much of the imagery and, indeed, narrative. The story told can be summarised as follows: the narrator's father commits suicide (in 'the dreadful hollow') after failed speculations, leaving his family in ruin. The situation is enviously contrasted with the wealth and good living of his father's old friend, the 'Old Lord of Hall'. The narrator gradually develops love for the Lord's daughter, Maud, and despite the scorn of her brother and the rivalry of a 'new-made lord', he succeeds in winning her love. There follows a fatal encounter with her brother – again, at 'the dreadful hollow' – which leads to a duel and the brother's death. The narrator flees abroad, but the blighting of his hopes has driven him to madness. In the final poem of the sequence, his hopes reawaken; he reaffirms his will to live and vows to place himself at the service of his country. The narrative is told, not in retrospect, but as it happens. This gives the drama an immediacy but presents problems. The narrator is unstable, raving at times, and the poems reflect this. How can there be a consistent narrative in the circumstances? Certainly one senses that the optimism of the final poem is itself only a phase, another delusion; but only a sequel – *Maud Revisited* – could tell us that. It could be argued that *Maud* was Tennyson's best song-cycle libretto – though, of course, without his knowing it. Certainly compared with the flaccid, namby-pamby character of *The Window*, *Maud* has guts, real drama, real characters and real emotions. Its drawback, which Somervell recognised, was that it was too long.

Somervell's 'shooting-script' for the song-cycle contains only a small portion of Tennyson's monodrama. What he does is to fillet the poem, cutting out narrative too factually bare to set to music. In doing so, he makes what is already an enigmatic story even more so. (For example, he omits information about the father's suicide.) But a rambling, garrulous poem such as *Maud* will always pose problems for the songwriter, and in omitting such Tennysonian doggerel as the opening of I.19 ('Her brother is coming back tonight,/Breaking up my dream of delight'), one feels that Somervell is doing the poet a literary service. Even in the poems he does set he is forced to omit stanzas. All in all he uses barely a third of Tennyson's original, omitting fifteen poems and reducing all but two. He does, however, keep to Tennyson's original order, except in one instance: songs Nos. 11 and 12 are reversed. One of the great attractions of Tennyson's poem-sequence is the great variety of structure of the individual poems, both in length and verse pattern. He rarely keeps to parallel stanza-shapes, even within individual poems. This gives the composer immense flexibility for his song-shapes and inspired Somervell to some of his most original music.

Maud is scored for baritone and piano and consists of 12 or 13 songs, according to whether you use the 1898 or 1907 edition. 'Maud has a garden', the extra song, though written at the same time as the rest, was omitted by Somervell from the original publication. (Could the reason have been the rather explicit sexual imagery of the poem? Or perhaps he was superstitious of *13* songs? In *1907* the thirteenth song became 'Epilogue', thus avoiding the unlucky number! In the comments that follow, references are made to the full,

1907 version.) The virtues of *Maud* (like those of the girl herself) are too many to enumerate in detail; the comments that follow identify some of the highlights. Firstly, there is Somervell's immaculate sense of timing. This is partly the result of his skilfully adapted libretto, with its careful choice of poems and stanzas from those poems, but is due in equal degree to the musical pacing. The cycle begins in an almost leisurely way with a suitably melodramatic prelude, 'I hate the dreadful hollow', which seems to suggest that there is plenty of time for the drama to unfold. The portrait of Maud is built up brush-stroke by brush-stroke in songs 2–5, and the narrator's growing love for her in songs 6–9, ending with a waltz-song 'Come into the garden, Maud', which expresses his complete infatuation. There follows a sudden change of mood: two angst-ridden songs, 10 and 11, then an oasis of repose in song 12, 'O that 'twere possible' – a miniature gem, short and clear-cut as a diamond – before the long 'envoi' of song 13. The varied song-shapes range from the short, one-strophe structures of songs 3 and 12, through strophic and ternary-based structures of songs 4–8, to the long, through-composed arioso structures of 1, 9, 11 and 13. Though there is no clear-cut tonal centre, there is a discernible tonal progression, from the D minor/F major of the early songs to the B-flat minor 'achieving' B-flat major of the final song. The tonality of the songs hovers around flat keys, F major/B-flat major, not straying far either flatwards or sharpwise, so that the B major tonality of song 12 stands out. This reinforces its 'oasis'-like role in the sequence, and the side-slip down a semitone for the final song is consequently dramatic. The musical cross-references are subtle and some of them long-term. The sequence of spiky flattened 9ths and the consequent descending roulade of notes in song 1 returns in song 11 at the key word 'mad'. The *agitato* passage in song 11 echoes the end of song 8, and the flowing 9/8 idea from Maud's 'Battle-song' in song 2 is recollected at the reference to 'battles to come' in the final song. This song acts as the cycle's 'recollection' point. In keeping with the narrator's sad, nostalgic farewell, we have references back to earlier songs, not only to song 2, but also, at the words 'And it was but a dream', to song 12.

Maud was the first successful English song-cycle and remains one of the masterpieces of English song. Somervell chose a poet and poems entirely suited to his genius, and his aristocratic, conservative musical style is a perfect match for Tennyson's poem. Singers love it, audiences love it, yet it suffers unaccountable neglect in the concert-hall. If it had been written by a German composer, it would be a repertoire work; as it is, a live performance is a rare treat.

Somervell's *Songcycle from 'A Shropshire Lad'* (1904), again for baritone and piano, boasts the distinction of being the first Housman song-cycle; it may even be the first Housman setting. (In 1903, just seven years after Housman published his poem sequence, a composer named Ettrick wrote to the poet asking permission to use a poem, but nothing more is known either of him, or his setting or even the poem he chose.) Unlike Tennyson's *Maud*, Housman's *Lad* does not tell a coherent narrative; it does, however, hint at a sequence of events and there is a story lurking, tantalisingly out of reach, below the surface. Housman's poetic language is quite different from Tennyson's, full of classical restraint and irony and couched in short, pithy, epigrammatic stanzas free of voluptuous poetical language. Housman never used a long, Latin-based word where a short Anglo-Saxon one would do – how different from the rambling, histrionic language of *Maud*! Somervell's music reflects this; it is more lyrical and contained, less melodramatic – some would say too unperturbed and placid. Out of Housman's sequence of 63 poems, Somervell chose ten, Nos. 2, 13, 14, 21, 22, 35, 36, 49, 40 and 23. It is significant that, except for the last two songs, he keeps to the poet's original order. Like *Maud*, *A Shropshire Lad* is a true song-cycle in the balance, order and mutual dependability of the songs. He again follows a hallowed tradition of the German *Liederkreis* in subtle use of thematic cross-reference. For example, the music of the first song, 'The cherry tree' (= 'Loveliest of trees') is quoted note-for-note in the penultimate song, 'Into my heart an air that kills', transposed down a semitone and at a slower tempo. It begins in the piano part, whilst the voice intones the words on one note, as though drained of feeling (Ex. 5.2).

Ex. 5.2

Only in the second stanza does the singer recapture the melody, coming, as it were, out of his numbed daze. Followed as it is by the valedictory poem 'The lads in their hundreds', the effect is poignantly moving. At the same time, this reprise justifies the extreme, strophic simplicity of the first song, which sounds simplistic and bland on its initial acquaintance. Again Somervell deploys a variety of song-forms, from the simple strophic setting of 'When I was one-and-twenty' – here the strophic simplicity of the poem demands it, though note the telling change he makes in the last two lines – and the ternary patterns of 'On the idle hill of summer' and 'Think no more, lad', to the more sophisticated structures of 'In summertime on Bredon' and 'The street sounds to the soldiers' tread.' His use of 'penillion' technique in the latter is a stroke of genius. Above the music of a military march on the piano, the singer-narrator describes the passing troop of soldiers, the music fading away as the soldiers pass into the distance. His repetition of the final phrase, 'I wish you well', is for once forgivable, because poetically appropriate. Equally fine is 'White in the moon', where Somervell applies harmonies and textures in a far more romantic way than usual.

Many writers and singers regard Somervell's song-cycle highly. Banfield observes that Housman's poetry 'released Somervell's memorable gift for flowing and effortless melody' (1985: 52); Arthur Jacobs thought that Housman's verse 'has perhaps never been set better. The restraint of Somervell suits the poet much better than does Vaughan Williams's "over-emotional" treatment in *On Wenlock Edge*' (1960: 158). But I cannot help feeling that the settings are *too* restrained: simple-minded rather than simple, not so much flowing and effortless as bland. Though his vocal lines capture the outward mood of the poems, they do not, as in Butterworth's even simpler settings, express the hidden meaning behind the poet's thought, the unspoken 'words-between-the-lines'. One would never understand from Somervell's cycle that the Lad's problem was the 'Love that dare not speak its name'. It is as though he were taking Alfred Douglas's phrase literally, ensuring that the name is never spelt out. Somervell's idiom, unadorned, diatonic and heavily indebted to his mentors, Parry and Stanford, is firmly rooted in the 19th century in a way that Housman's verse never is. Even so, this, the first major setting of *A Shropshire Lad*, is a considerable achievement and was to set a standard, indeed model, for later works. He chose the poems which later composers were to turn to again and again: 'Loveliest of trees', 'When I was one-and-twenty', 'Bredon Hill', 'The street sounds to the soldiers' tread', 'Think no more lad', 'The lads in their hundreds'. It is interesting to note that Butterworth's first cycle begins with the same two poems ('Loveliest of trees' and 'When I was one-and-twenty') and that he adopts the irregular compound metre and folk-like setting of Somervell's 'The lads in their hundreds' as well as the 'ternary pie' of 'Think no more, lad'. John Ireland may unconsciously have taken a cue from Somervell in his setting of 'The street sounds to the soldiers' tread' (= 'The encounter'): both composers feature a military march in their accompaniments which fades into the distance as the song reaches its end. Tennyson's *Maud* had suited Somervell's aristocratic musical idiom perfectly; with Housman's *A Shropshire Lad* he had chosen a poet who called for a quite different approach and tone-of-voice. In their various ways, Butterworth, Vaughan Williams and Ireland were the composers who best matched the dark, ironic, troubled foreboding of Housman's Lad (Hold, 2000).

Somervell's last two narrative song-cycles are both to poetry by Robert Browning (1812–89): *James Lee's Wife* (1906, *1907*), for contralto and piano, and *A Broken Arc* (*1923*), for baritone and piano. For the song-composer, Browning poses problems, and in this matter it is instructive to compare him with his contemporary, Tennyson. Browning had a far greater interest in, and knowledge of music – as witness such musically inspired poems as 'A Toccata of Galuppi's', 'Abt Vogler', 'Master Hugues of Saxe-Gotha' and 'Charles Avison'. Yet when it came to writing words for musical setting, Tennyson had a natural aptitude that eluded Browning. Browning's language is rough-edged, clogged with consonants and deliberately colloquial and low-key, all of which can militate against its suitability for musical setting. Take for example one of the 'Cavalier Tunes':

King Charles, and who'll do him right now?
King Charles, and who's ripe for fight not?
Give a rouse: here's, in hell's despite now,
King Charles!

To whom used my boy George quaff else,
By the old fool's side that begot him?
For whom did he cheer and laugh else,
While Noll's damned troopers shot him?
                              Robert Browning: 'Give a rouse'

Maude Valérie White managed to set this to music, and it is possible for a singer
to get round the rough consonants, though only just. But Browning's poetry has
its own special attractions; it is serious, modern in tone and subject-matter,
direct and conversational in idiom, with a deliberate avoidance of the 'poetic'
diction used by Tennyson and his followers, and if the composer chooses his
poems carefully, they can be inspirational. This is what Somervell managed to
achieve in his two Browning song-cycles.

James Lee's Wife is the long narrative poem that opens Browning's *Dramatis
Personae* (1864). Its theme is the breakdown of marriage, told through the
words of the wife and set in coastal Brittany. Somervell selected stanzas from
five of the original nine poems (1, 2, 3, 5 and 7). By omitting the final two
poems, he alters the outcome of the story, lending a quasi-religious, optimistic
conclusion, as opposed to Browning's enigmatic yet more tragic ending. The
idea is very promising, but eventually disappointing. It lacks the colourful
dramatic vitality of *Maud* or the pastoral lyricism of *A Shropshire Lad*. But the
fact that it is one of the few British song-cycles of its period specifically written
from a woman's viewpoint should recommend it to mezzo-sopranos and
contraltos as a companion-piece to Elgar's *Sea Pictures*. Originally scored
with orchestral accompaniment (1906), it was published in piano score
arranged by Somervell himself in 1907; he later made a version for piano
quintet (1919).

A Broken Arc, for baritone and piano, is of greater interest; indeed, Banfield
considers it Somervell's best cycle and 'The worst of it' Somervell's best song
(1985: 60–1). The work is curious in that, though it seems to be narrating a
story, it is all an illusion. What Somervell has done is make up his libretto from
eight different poems, an anthology diversely selected from *The Two Poets of
Crosie* (song 1), *Dramatic Romances and Lyrics* (songs 2 and 4), *Men and
Women* (3 and 6), *Dramatis Personae* (5), 'Easter Day' (7) and *Pippa Passes* (8).
Something, however, *seems* to be narrated, namely a triangular love affair. Songs
1–4 paint portraits of various aspects of the hero's love; songs 5 and 6 narrate
her betrayal of him for his childhood friend; songs 7 and 8 present an
affirmative ending. But the narrative element is inevitably extremely tenuous,
even more so than in *A Shropshire Lad*. Somervell's music, however, convinces
us that there is a unified story being told through the subtlety of its construction
and cross-referencing. This can be appreciated in the thematic links between
songs 5, 6 and 7, but even more subtly in such details as the rich shimmering

chordal alternations which form the accompaniments of the two outer songs and the Quilterian cadential 9ths of songs 1 and 4. Somervell's sensitivity to his texts and his ability to analogise music to texts is evident throughout. Note the way he treats the two stanzas of Browning's famous poem, 'Meeting at night'. In the first verse, the poet describes the nocturnal scene as he beaches his boat, the piano accompaniment capturing the sea-surge and rippling wavelets. In the second verse, as the human elements come to the fore, the music supplies the drama of the tryst with rapid modulations, using the little vocal phrase associated with the words 'And the startled little waves' from the previous verse (Ex. 5.3).

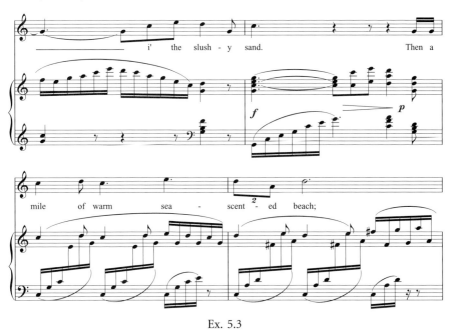

Ex. 5.3

The next song, 'My star', sets an unusual poem in one long stanza of two distinct halves, the first of short lines, the second long lines. (The 'star' described is the poet's beloved.) When the star 'that dartles the red and the blue' suddenly 'stops like a bird', the music does likewise. He neatly ties the two halves of the stanza together with the same refraining music. The most impressive songs are the sequence of three (5–7) beginning with 'The worst of it', in which the poet describes how his love has betrayed him. Somervell uses only three stanzas (1, 5 and 19) of Browning's 19-stanza poem, setting them out in three irregular strophes. It opens with a recitative-like idea, an upward chromatic figure ('a') leading from E-flat minor to a sustained, spread dominant chord ('b') on a tonic bass in G-flat major, over which the singer picks up the same chromatic figure (Ex. 5.4(a)). This idea is then repeated in a progression from G-flat major to B-flat minor.

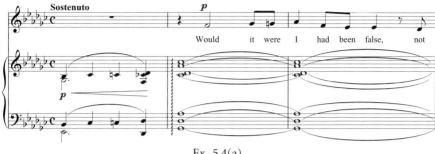

Ex. 5.4(a)

These motives form the basis of the entire song, infusing both vocal line and accompaniment. The first strophe ends with a modal cadence into E-flat minor from which the chromatic figure returns (bar 15) to herald the second strophe, where the poet asks his love about her unfaithfulness – 'What will God say?' Beginning reposefully (G-flat major), the music rises through intertwining contrapuntal lines of voice and piano to an anguished climax and a spread minor 9th chord ('c') (Ex. 5.4(b)). (Here perhaps we ourselves need to re-insert the two lines of Browning's stanza which Somervell omitted:

> Should you forfeit heaven for a snapt gold ring
> And a promise broken, were it just or meet?)

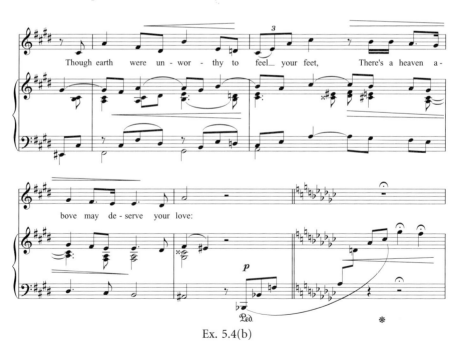

Ex. 5.4(b)

The final strophe develops and expands 'a' and 'b', ending as verse 1 with the modal cadence followed by a coda which develops and 'explains' the minor 9th arpeggio 'c', before cadencing onto an implacable E-flat minor. It is a song of unutterable sadness, made more poignant by the dichotomy between the rays of G-flat major sunshine breaking out of the bleak E-flat minor. This tonal base is suddenly broken at the beginning of 'After', when the music moves from E-flat minor to B minor. After broken bare octave phrases (echoes from the previous song), it moves into a *marcia funebre* tread, with a noble, elegiac quality similar to Gurney's setting of Masefield's 'The chief centurions'. In this poem the poet describes the aftermath of the duel between the poet and his boyhood friend, in which the latter has been killed. (Shades of *Maud*! The preparations for the duel had been described by Browning in the prequel, 'Before'; the death takes place between the two poems 'off-stage', as it were, in the manner of a Greek tragedy.) Somervell follows the shape of Browning's poem whose main section is framed by two couplets. Angular octaves herald these couplets which are set in a recitative-like manner, whilst the main body of the song is the funeral march ('d'). Later the voice develops motives from the previous song (cf. 5: 20–24 with 6: 30–32: 'Ha, what avails death, to erase/His offence, my disgrace?'). At the sudden break after these words, the narrator recollects happy childhood days, 'I would we were boys as of old/In the field, by the fold', in a broad lyrical melody (Ex. 5.5).

Ex. 5.5

This is, in fact, a quotation from Somervell's choral setting of Wordsworth's *Intimations of Immortality* (1907), which also refers to happy childhood days – a rare example of Somervell indulging in self-quotation. But the happiness is fleetingly brief: we are soon back to the bleak, broken octaves of the beginning. The ending is startling in its rawness of emotion. After the words 'I stand here now, he lies in his place' and a final reference to the chromatic figure 'a' comes the peremptory final line, 'Cover his face', which Somervell asks to be uttered 'with a shudder'. A fragmentary reference to the funeral march, bleak, 3rd-less B minor chords, and this harrowing song is finished. In the penultimate song, 'From "Easter Day"', the narrator seeks consolation from God. There are fleeting reminiscences from the two previous songs (the leaning appoggiaturas as well as a version of the arpeggiated chord 'c') before, at the words 'Only let me go on, go on,/still hoping', the music of the funeral march returns, now transformed into a consoling major version. This ending is perhaps too grandiose for modern ears, as poet and composer strive for the sunset of 'the Better Land!' The final song in the cycle is a setting of what is perhaps Browning's most famous poem, 'The Year's at the spring', which reinforces the sentiments of the previous song: 'God's in his heaven – /All's right with the world!' It is possibly too short to be convincing, especially after the painful doubts expressed so forcefully only two songs previously.

Though not possessing the unity or inevitability of *Maud* or *A Shropshire Lad*, *A Broken Arc* is a major achievement and its neglect is hard to understand. Quite apart from its dramatic and lyric qualities, it has great technical assurance – not something possessed by many British songwriters of the time – with splendidly pianistic accompaniments and imaginative, singable vocal lines.

These four song-cycles hold an unusual place in English song, where the non-narrative cycle, with a libretto consisting of an anthology of mood pictures by one or several poets is far more common: witness Quilter's *To Julia*, Gurney's *Lights Out*, Vaughan Williams's *Songs of Travel*, Elgar's *Sea Pictures* or the Irish cycles of Stanford. Indeed, Somervell himself does just that in his remaining song-cycle, *Love in Springtime* (1901). Though he calls it a song-cycle, it is really no more than a songbook whose seven songs, to poems by four different poets – Christina Rossetti (3), Charles Kingsley (2), and one each by Tennyson and 'E. S.' [?Ethel Speare] – are loosely connected by the theme of Spring. Tennyson's 'The city child' dreams of flowers of the countryside, the adult questioner's F major tonality answered by the child's A-flat major. 'The night-bird', another question-and-answer text, has a barcarolle-like accompaniment to match Kingsley's text; it is a neat little ditty with some characteristically ravishing third-phrase sequences. The most successful songs are those to texts by Christina Rossetti. 'Underneath the growing grass' is an epigrammatic one-pager: grave thoughts in a nutshell. The gem of the set is 'Young love lies sleeping', which has always been and remains the most popular, deservedly so, for it shows all the grace and subtlety of Somervell's art. He sets only three of the original eight stanzas (1, 3 and 8) of this pastoral idyll and uses them in a subtle mixture of strophic and ternary structure: A(aaba) A(aaba) B(cdba). The first two verses are set strophically, fully appropriate to the quasi-refrain of their opening lines, 'Young Love lies sleeping'/'Young Love lies dreaming'. This melody, set over a rippling accompaniment, has a Sullivan-like grace, the third phrase characteristically deploying secondary 7ths in sequence. In the third verse, with the entreaty 'Draw close the curtains', he begins with a new idea, the music sinking sequentially through F major and E-flat major, and at the words 'With faded fingers sere' the music makes an unexpected modulation into G major, in which key the piano quietly recaps the original melody across the singer's sustained cadence note. Then, with a magical flick of the wand, he recalls the music of the original strophe from the halfway sequences (Ex. 5.6). Finally, he adds a short coda to the song by repeating the opening and final line of the first stanza. The effect is musically satisfying, even if he does have to rewrite Rossetti's poem in the process.

Ex. 5.6

In addition to these extended works, several of Somervell's separate solo songs are worthy of exploration. Geoffrey Bush (1988: 283) has commented on Somervell's gift for writing lullabies, something clearly linked with his interest in writing music for children. One of his most enduringly popular songs is 'Shepherd's cradle-song' (*1890*) whose anonymous text 'from the German' is perhaps by the composer himself. It has a delightfully catchy tune over an expertly written accompaniment. Admirable is the effortless way in which he deals with the five-line stanza, strophe and stanza fitting like hand and glove, and the neat, brief excursion into the tonic minor when calm and peace are put at risk by the 'sheep-dog, fierce and wild' (Ex. 5.7). It is a fine example of what Garry Humphreys (*1976*) has called the inevitability of Somervell's songs: music which 'grows from the words and takes its shape from the metre'.

Ex. 5.7

'Orpheus with his lute', a late publication (No. 2 of *Three New Old Songs* (*1927*)) is a tender, vernal setting of Fletcher/Shakespeare's famous lyric. The unexpected opening – F major tonality for what quickly becomes an A major song – is balanced by an unexpected reference to a flattened 7th chord at the end. An unusual song in his output is 'On a summer morning' (*1899*), to an indifferent poem by Ethel Speare (a lady whose poetry he set on at least five occasions: she is probably the 'E. S.' of the final song in *Love in Springtime*). Somervell describes the song as 'set to music *in Volksweise*'; he has clearly modelled the tune on folksong and given it an accompaniment of appropriate simplicity (Ex. 5.8): shades of 'Linden lea'! – but it was published in 1899, three years before Vaughan Williams's epoch-making song.

Ex. 5.8

Arthur Somervell is an unaccountably neglected song-composer. Championed by Parry when a young man, acknowledged as one of the leading English songwriters by his thirties, assured of a place in the history of English music for his pioneering song-cycles, yet today he is rarely heard and rarely performed. Why this neglect? One reason may be that, for all his virtues, his musical personality lacks definition; it is as though he were being deliberately self-effacing, unwilling or unable to come into the spotlight, quite the opposite of songwriters like Quilter or Gurney, Warlock or Vaughan Williams, whose fingerprints are recognisable on almost every song they wrote. Very rarely does he indulge in self-revelation: the quotation from his choral work *Intimations of Immortality* in his song-cycle *A Broken Arc*, at the reference to past childhood happiness, is a rare exception. His songs too often reveal him as the Master of the Expected. There is a blandness about them; they lack that unexpected twist or dramatic surprise. Behind too many of his melodies there seems to lurk a hymn-tune: delightfully apt for the 'Shepherd's cradle-song', but not for *A Shropshire Lad*. When he does have a surprise up his sleeve, as in the way he repeats the final line of 'The street sounds to the soldiers' tread', long after we have thought the singer had concluded the song, or in the monotone reprise of 'Loveliest of trees' in 'Into my heart an air that kills', his songs take on a new dimension. And when he loosens his harmony from conventional rules and notions, he can be wonderfully effective, and nowhere more so than in 'White in the moon', a romantic conception with appropriately romantic textures and harmonies. However, compared with his close contemporaries Elgar and Delius, his idiom is conservative and old-fashioned. He was a legatee of the 19th century at its most mild and unexperimental, and his style remained untouched by 20th-century ideas. But Time has a wicked habit of jettisoning artistic avant-garde experimenters. In the end, it is what the music says and not how new it was in its day that matters. Perhaps, now that the 20th century has reached its end, amends will be made for this neglect, and Somervell's innate worth be recognised. His achievements were great. In his major vocal works he was willing and able to tackle important subjects using a large canvas. With *Maud, A Shropshire Lad* and *A Broken Arc* he achieved something that his predecessors had not managed: he created a genuine, home-grown English song-cycle, vocal music to match the size and seriousness of the instrumental sonata, orchestral symphony and choral oratorio. In his song-cycles he showed that his imagination and technique were more than adequate, able to range in mood from the intimately lyrical to the dramatic, and to integrate songs over a wide time-scale through subtle cross-reference and allusion.

6

Ralph Vaughan Williams (1872–1958)

> Bright is the ring of words
>   When the right man rings them,
> Fair the fall of songs
>   When the singer sings them.
> Still they are carolled and said –
>   On wings they are carried –
> After the singer is dead
>   And the maker buried.
>
> Robert Louis Stevenson:
> *Songs of Travel*

Ralph Vaughan Williams's songs span his long career, the first written when he was ten and the last when he was 85. There were, however, two substantial songless periods, the first during the 1914–18 War when he was on active service, and the second between 1927 and the mid 1950s. This second, long hiatus coincided with one of the most important periods of his composing career, which would suggest that song-composition was not of prime import- ance to him; but then in old age he returned to his early love, with the *Four Last Songs* and *Ten Blake Songs*. Nevertheless, the majority of the songs were written in the earlier years, before the outbreak of the First World War, a war that effectively split his career in two. It is significant that the first performance of the *Four Hymns*, commissioned for the 1914 Three Choirs Festival at Worcester, had to be cancelled because of the outbreak of war, and the work was not heard until 1920.

Vaughan Williams's style underwent radical changes over his long composing life, changes that are reflected in his solo songs:

1. Early songs, up to 1903–4: written before his 'hands-on' encounter with English folksongs.
2. 1904–14: songs reflecting his discovery of folksongs and his editing of *The English Hymnal*.
3. 1920–7: the post-war phase of his career with radical rethinking of his style, demonstrated in such major works as the *Pastoral Symphony, Flos Campi* and *Sancta Civitas*.
4. 1950–5: the final phase represented by works such as *Three Shakespeare Songs* and the *Ninth Symphony*.

His songs are set to a wide range of poets: chronologically from the 14th century (Chaucer) to 20th century, including poets younger than himself (Shove, O'Sullivan, and his second wife, Ursula). As well as popular authors from the well-thumbed anthologies, he turned to out-of-the-way names, such as Thomas Vaux, Jeremy Taylor and William Barnes. Women poets inspired several of his finest works: Christina Rossetti, Fredegond Shove and Ursula Vaughan Williams. But the writers who inspired him to his finest achievements were Dante Gabriel Rossetti, Robert Louis Stevenson and A. E. Housman: an extraordinary collection of bedfellows, revealing the composer's 'capacity for empathy' (Banfield 1985: 78).

Vaughan Williams has often been quoted as having disliked writing for the piano. He himself was an indifferent keyboard-player: his favourite performing instruments were the violin and viola. It is, then, not surprising, though rather unusual, that more than half of his major song opuses have accompaniments for instruments other than the piano: *On Wenlock Edge*, *Four Hymns*, *Merciless Beauty*, *Along the Field* and the *Ten Blake Songs*. His piano accompaniments are often very effective – witness 'The water-mill' and 'The new ghost'. Nevertheless, one feels that he was constrained by this traditional vocal relationship and recognised that other accompanimental textures were more suitable to his aims. There is little doubt that for Vaughan Williams, song was melody first and foremost, the singer rather than the accompanist the first priority.

The first song that Vaughan Williams wrote seems to have been 'Here I come creeping' (1882), to a poem by Sarah Roberts Boyle: the first to be published, 'Wishes' (*1893*). During this period he also set poetry by Coleridge, Tennyson and Browning, but the first song of importance is 'How can the tree but wither' (Thomas Vaux). Though not published until 1934, it had been written some 40 years earlier and the composer obviously had special affection for it. He was justified in this, for if it does date back to 1896, then it is a remarkable achievement. In its deliberate attempt to recreate the Elizabethan Ayre, it looks forward not only to Warlock, but even more to Finzi in his setting of 'Fear no more the heat of the sun' or to Britten in his 'Second lute-song' from *Gloriana*. The author of the poem, Thomas Vaux of Harrowden (1510–56), was one of those earnest early Tudor poets dubbed by C. S. Lewis as 'Drabs'. The poem, which Charles Wood had set a few years earlier (the third of *Four Songs* (*1892*)), is full of fatalistic sentiments, typical of the poet. (It will be remembered that it was Vaux who supplied Shakespeare's grave-digger with his 'grave'-song in *Hamlet*.) It consists of three long-lined stanzas, each with a two-line refrain, which are treated by the composer as A A B, with the same refrain music for each verse. The singer joins the piano's bass for the second half of the refrain, adding an appropriately 'grave' texture to the sound. Harmonically the music is 'penny plain', as in the contemporary *Three Elizabethan Part-songs*. The vocal line is in the Aeolian mode with a 'rogue' Phrygian D-flat to add to the melancholy. Much of the song is in four contrapuntal strands, with the vocal line, in keeping with its Elizabethan Ayre character, one of these strands, though the *prima parte*; the whole setting suggests a consort song accompaniment

(Ex. 6.1). This, with the deliberate archaisms – English cadences, hemiola rhythms, etc. – give it a strong period flavour.

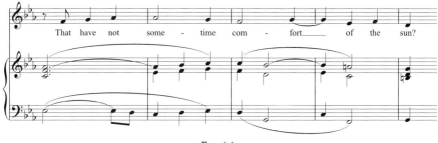

Ex. 6.1

More important to Vaughan Williams's subsequent development are two settings of the Dorset poet, William Barnes (1801–86), 'Blackmwore by the Stour' and 'Linden lea' (1901, *1902*). He gave them both the subtitle 'A Dorset Song'; indeed, Barnes himself called 'Blackmwore by the Stour' 'A Dorset Folk-Song'. But they were written in 1901, two years before the composer had heard Charles Pottifer sing 'Bushes and briars', an occasion which was to change the course of his life. Here, then, we have 'pre-folksong' folksongs. The four verses of 'Blackmwore by the Stour' are set strophically to a mock folk-tune which fits Barnes's mock folk-words perfectly. But far more attractive, as singers and audiences alike have proved, is 'Linden lea'. Again Vaughan Williams has matched the folk-like poetry with folk-like music, but only short examination of the tune, with its arty modulations, will show that it is no more a genuine folk-tune than Britten's 'The ploughboy'. They are rare English examples of what the Germans call *Volkstümliches Lied*. (Another example is Somervell's 'On a summer morning': see p. 100.) 'Linden lea' is nonetheless extremely effective and deserves its continued popularity. Importantly, it leads us to the brink of what was to be a crucial turning-point in Vaughan Williams's career – his discovery of *true* folksong. The other still-performed song of this period, *Orpheus with his lute* (1902, *1903*: he made another setting of the same poem 20 years later, No. 3 of *Three Shakespeare Songs* 1925) is a disappointment. With its strains of the Victorian parlour-song and Sullivan, it could be by any competent late 19th-century songwriter. It certainly doesn't sound like Vaughan Williams.

Vaughan Williams's emergence as a major songwriter came with two important works written, it would appear, simultaneously. They are settings of poems of quite different character by two contrasting poets: *The House of Life*, by Dante Gabriel Rossetti, and *Songs of Travel*, by Robert Louis Stevenson. Both were conceived as song-groups: songbooks if not song-cycles.

The House of Life (1903, *1904*) is a sequence of six sonnets by Rossetti, taken from the sequence of 101 sonnets of the same title that Rossetti wrote and published over a long period of time. Sixteen, including the 'Willow-wood' sequence, appeared in *The Fortnightly Review* in March 1869; a halfway house of

50, plus the pendant of eleven songs, in *Poems* of 1870; the complete 'building' of 101 in *Ballads and Sonnets* of 1881. They form a record of his love for his dead wife, Lizzie Siddal, and his infatuation with Jane Morris, the wife of his friend William Morris. Themes of love and death, aspiration and foreboding and, through it all, the ideals of art and beauty are expressed in highly sensuous terms: a sensuousness considered obscene at the time. In the previous year Vaughan Williams had set the mini sonnet sequence *Willow-wood* (sonnets 49–52) as a cantata for baritone and orchestra, with an optional chorus of women's voices. But the willowy gloom of these poems gave him little opportunity for contrast; and gloominess was never Vaughan Williams's *forte*. He found a much better balance of emotions in the sequence of six sonnets which form his song-cycle *The House of Life* (the final order number of Rossetti's sequence in brackets): 'Lovesight' (4), 'Silent noon' (19), 'Love's minstrels' (= 'Passion and worship') (9), 'Heart's haven' (22), 'Death-in-love' (48) and 'Love's last gift' (59).

The sonnet-form always presents the songwriter with a problem. Its rigid shape (14 lines long, falling into octave and sestet), its regular (iambic pentameter) line-length and its lack – indeed, proscription – of any form of refrain are all basically antipathetic to music. The composer either has to through-set the poem, or impose on it his own repetitive patterns. In *The House of Life* sonnets there is a further problem; Rossetti was a painter as well as poet, and inevitably his poems are full of visual imagery, which can prove difficult for music to make an entrée. Nevertheless, several other composers as well as Vaughan Williams have been attracted to Rossetti's sequence.

Ex. 6.2

The work is conceived on a large canvas, as revealed in the first song, 'Lovesight', with its long introduction and coda. The introduction consists of a sequence of three distinct ideas, disconnected both thematically and tonally: (i) a rising sequence of notes in 3/4, treated sequentially ('x'); (ii) a downward sequence of chords in common time ('y'); and (iii) a wavering quaver figure which turns out to be the accompaniment of the ensuing song (Ex. 6.2). These ideas only make sense as the cycle unfolds – clearly a piece of 'backwards planning' by the composer – for (i) and (ii) are to be key motto themes, representing, in Banfield's words (1985: 78), the 'tenderness of love' ('x') and 'death-in-love' ('y'). The 'tenderness in love' theme is first articulated by the singer to the words 'When do I see thee most, beloved one?' Another important theme – 'attained spirituality' – is to emerge later ('z'). The final song draws these three themes together, finally fusing 'y' and 'z' at the words 'Take my last gift; thy heart hath sung my praise' (Ex. 6.3).

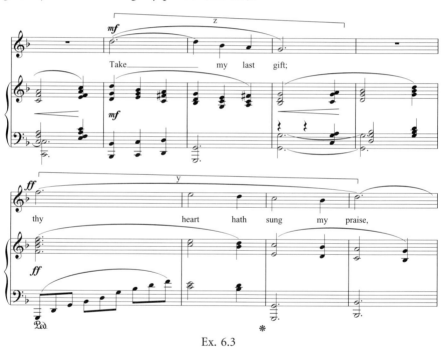

Ex. 6.3

In these songs Vaughan Williams has still to find his own voice. There are many references to and (to use his own phrase) 'cribbings' from other composers. Somervell's *Maud* certainly influenced the cyclic shape. 'Heart's haven' takes a backward look to his 19th-century predecessors. And we hear echoes of Brahms (the middle section of 'Silent noon' is a crib from the E-flat major Intermezzo, op. 117/1), Schumann (the 'heraldic' motto) and Wagner ('Death-in-love' – 'the most blatant Wagnerism to be found in Vaughan Williams' (Banfield, 1985: 82)). There are, however, signs of things to come, notably the theme 'z' which opens and dominates the final song, 'Love's last gift': a theme which will recur throughout Vaughan Williams's music, perhaps most familiarly in his great hymn-tune, 'Sine nomine' (see Ex. 6.3).

The most impressive songs are 'Silent noon' and 'Love's minstrels', the second and third in the sequence. 'Silent noon' has always been the most popular of the songs; indeed, this is the *only* song from *The House of Life* that is widely known, and it was performed and published ahead of the main cycle. With its richly romantic idiom, capturing the hazy tranquillity of a summer's day in sensuous music, it deserves its popularity. It is interesting to see how Vaughan Williams deals with sonnet-form in this song by fitting it with a ternary (A B A) shape. 'A' (lines 1–4) consists of irregular throbbing chords underpinning a tranquil vocal line. Then, following an unexpected but characteristic lurch from B-flat major to G major, comes the long middle ('B') section (lines 5–10), with a new idea introduced as the poet describes the surrounding landscape – 'golden kingcup fields' and the notorious 'cow parsley' (subject of a famous rebuke by *The Times* critic after its first performance) evoking the 'visible silence'. After what sounds like a reference to 'Drink to me only' in the accompaniment, there is another unexpected modulation, this time to a static *pianissimo* F major chord, above which the singer's quasi recitative, 'Deep in the sun-search'd growths the dragonfly/Hangs like a blue thread loosen'd from the sky', leads (via 'x') to a reprise of the 'A' material for the last four lines (Ex. 6.4).

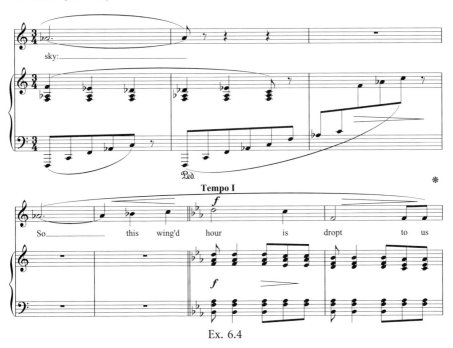

Ex. 6.4

For all its attractiveness, 'Silent noon' is still embedded in the sounds of the previous century and not characteristic of the way Vaughan Williams was to develop. In 'Love's minstrels', however, we hear the composer deliberately exploring new territory. It may not be a successful exploration, but its originality makes it worthy of detailed consideration nevertheless. The opening prelude, with its 'gesture' of unrelated triads (throbbing D major, spread F minor/D major, B-flat minor – note the mediant relationships, so characteristic of the composer) is one that will echo throughout Vaughan Williams's mature career (Ex. 6.5).

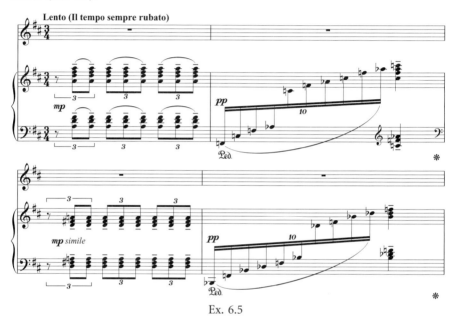

Ex. 6.5

Rossetti's own title for this poem was 'Passion and worship' and the sonnet tells of lovers being serenaded by rival minstrels: the oboe, which symbolises Love's passion, and the harp, symbolising Love's worship (typically 'coloured' by the painter-poet as flame-winged and white-winged). These are evoked in the textures of the song, a haunting single-line fragment in a Dorian-coloured mode for the spirit of the 'hautboy' (which serves both voice and accompaniment) and throbbing chords and arpeggios for the harpist. The melodic lines are indebted to both plainchant and folksong, and the textures are extremely economic – in some places two parts counterpointing, in some places just a single line. The singer takes over from the piano's single-line 'oboe' strand with a monody, and the first six lines of the sonnet have minimal accompaniment, giving 'a new feeling for space and silence' (Banfield, 1985: 81). The entire song has a feeling of tenuousness: of things not, or only just, hanging together. Gradually, as the song progresses, these ideas coalesce and give the music formal meaning. 'Love's minstrels' looks forward not only to the songs of Vaughan

Williams's early maturity, but also to the vocal music of the 1920s, when he was experimenting with accompanying instruments other than the piano (the string trio of the Chaucer Roundels, the solo violin of the second Housman cycle, the unaccompanied settings of Seumas O'Sullivan) and the late Blake settings, where he used a solo oboe to support the voice.

The history of *Songs of Travel* is a complex one. Vaughan Williams composed 'Whither must I wander' in 1901, at the same time as 'Linden lea' and 'Blackmwore by the Stour', and it was published, like them, in *The Vocalist* in 1902. This encounter with Robert Louis Stevenson's verse must have whetted the composer's appetite, for, after completing *The House of Life*, he turned from the hot-house, sensuous verses of Rossetti to the extrovert, open-air song-lyrics of Stevenson, completing a further eight songs to form a song-cycle. In this form they were performed by Walter Creighton and Hamilton Harty in December, 1904. However, Vaughan Williams was persuaded by his publishers to issue them in two separate volumes. Volume 1, published in 1904, brings together the 'outdoor', extrovert songs: 'The vagabond', 'Bright is the ring of words' and 'The roadside fire' (= 'I will bring you brooches'); Volume 2, published in 1907, is a more lyrical sequence of love-songs: 'Let beauty awake', 'Youth and love', 'In dreams unhappy' and 'The infinite shining heavens'. Why the publishers insisted on this division is unclear. By axing the cycle in half, they destroyed the work's original variety. Discovered amongst Vaughan Williams's manuscripts after his death was a ninth Stevenson setting, 'I have trod the upward and downward slope', clearly intended as a short epilogue to the cycle. Whether this was written at the same time as the others (as Kennedy suggests) or later (1952, as Banfield surmises) is not clear. It was not, however, until 1960 that the complete cycle of nine songs was published in the order that we have now come to accept; and this was given its first performance in a BBC broadcast on 21 May 1960 by Hervey Alan and Frederick Stone. (The relics of the earlier publication can still be seen in the final version, where the original numbering of the volume 2 sequence of 1907 has been left, most confusingly, at the head of each song.)

There could be no more contrast between the hot-house atmosphere of Rossetti's sonnets and the outdoor fresh air of Stevenson's *Songs of Travel*. The fact that Vaughan Williams could turn from one extreme to the other is indicative of his great gift for empathy, not only in the realms of atmosphere and imagery, but also in questions of poetic form. With Rossetti, Vaughan Williams was faced with the 'narrow confined cell' of the sonnet-form – something he had to expand and give as much variety to in his music as possible. With Stevenson, on the other hand, he has been presented with *song-lyrics*, words deliberately written with music in mind. In at least two cases Stevenson, following the practice of his fellow-countryman Robert Burns, wrote his words with a melody in his ear. 'The vagabond' is 'To an air of Schubert' (which one he doesn't state);'Whither must I wander' (= 'Home no more home to me') 'To the tune of Wandering Willie'. All of the poems have what the song-composer delights in – a wide variety of metres, stanza-shapes and line-length, from the eight-line mixture of trochees and dactyls of 'The vagabond' to the simple 'traditional' quatrains of 'The infinite shining heavens'. In between is the novel, almost Hardy-esque stanza-form of 'Let beauty awake' and the alternating long and short stanzas of 'In dreams unhappy'.

The images of the poet as wanderer were part and parcel of the Romantic mood of the 19th century. For musicians, Stevenson's verse would immediately have referred back to the great wayfaring song-cycles of Schubert, *Die schöne Müllerin* and *Winterreise*. As in *The House of Life*, Vaughan Williams uses a wide variety of musical styles, ranging from the extreme, uncharacteristic chromaticism of 'In dreams' (an experiment he thankfully did not repeat) to the modality of 'Whither must I wander', from the neat 'English' style of 'The roadside fire' to the mystical Vaughan Williams of 'The infinite shining heavens', and from the soaring romantic vocal line of 'Let beauty awake' to the sturdy diatonicism of 'Bright is the ring of words'. This is, perhaps, the most disconcerting aspect of the cycle; it is as though the composer were trying to imitate Stevenson's 'sedulous ape'. He carefully ties up the cycle by references back in some of the songs. Indeed, a song such as 'Youth and love' is not intelligible without knowledge of its references to 'The vagabond' and 'The roadside fire', whilst the final song acts almost as a catalogue of what has gone before, and can only be understood after the other eight have been heard. More subtle is the way that the tramping feet of the Wayfarer in the first song are transferred into the 'jogtrot' – caravan, canary and all – of the third song. Taken as a whole, however, the quality is uneven, and certain songs stand out above the rest. 'The vagabond' has deservedly earned its popularity. Here we have an early sighting of the composer's characteristic use of mediant relationships, the song-phrases rising through sequences of minor thirds (C minor to E-flat minor in verse 1; E minor→G minor→B-flat minor and finally A minor→C minor in verse 3). (It should be pointed out that the repeat of the second stanza after the third is Stevenson's own doing, and not meretricious fancy of the composer.) Vaughan Williams's ability to create memorable tunes and textures is again evident in 'The roadside fire', the finest of the many settings of this famous lyric. Some commentators have criticised the accompaniment of this song: 'merely awkward instead of delicate' (Day, 1961: 89), 'Marred by the poorest accompaniment of the nine' (Kennedy, 1964/1980: 80). This criticism is difficult to understand, for when played as Vaughan Williams has written it, it works perfectly. The transformation of the song from jogtrot to the dreamy arpeggios in the final verse is extremely effective and the return to the earlier texture at the end is magical (Ex. 6.6). He achieves a similar effect at the final cadence of 'The infinite shining heavens' where, after a detour through flattened areas of a modal E-flat, the music moves, at the words 'a star had come down to me', through a sequence of increasingly rich chords (spreading outwards in treble and bass) to reach D major (Ex. 6.7).

Ex. 6.6

Ex. 6.7

'Whither must I wander', though the first song to be written, is in some ways the most prophetic, with its simple folk-like melody set in a correspondingly strophic manner. It is instructive to look at the effortless way his melody encompasses Stevenson's long-lined stanzas (basically an AABA shape = ab ac dd ac). 'Bright is the ring of words' opens with an idea that was to become the composer's calling card (Ex. 6.8).

Ex. 6.8

(He had already used it in the final song of *The House of Life*.) The sturdily confident idiom of the opening has disappeared by the end of the verse, to give us a gentler second verse: the same tune but with pianissimo harp-like spread chords and a valedictory conclusion that makes a perfectly satisfactory ending to the cycle. Why, then, did he feel the need to write an extra song? 'I have trod the upward and the downward slope' is both unnecessary and redundant, and its cross-quotations from earlier songs naïve and self-conscious – it sounds more of an 'Afterthought' than 'Epilogue'.

Between *Songs of Travel* and his next major solo vocal work, *On Wenlock Edge*, three important events had happened in Vaughan Williams's life: he had discovered and begun collecting English folksongs; he had been appointed music editor of *The English Hymnal*; and he had been to Paris to study with Ravel. There is no trace of *The English Hymnal* in *On Wenlock Edge*, but folksongs and Ravel did have an impact. He wrote *On Wenlock Edge* during 1908–9, immediately after his return from Paris. Ravel's influence on the work is not over obvious; you certainly would not think that he had been, in his own words, 'having tea with Debussy', unless you count such superficial elements as the use of whole-tone scales and the impressionistic bell-sounds in 'Bredon hill', which may have been suggested by Ravel's *La vallée des cloches*. Much more important is the general freeing of technique and the way in which Vaughan Williams allows his imagination to roam widely in his exploration of the traditional piano quintet texture, creating effects that no English composer had dared to at that point. The impact of his study of English folksong is much stronger, and is evident in both the contours of melodic lines (for example, the 'ghost's phrases in 'Is my team ploughing?', in 'Oh, when I was in love with you' and in the final verse of 'Clun') and the modal harmonies which imbue much of the piece. Elsewhere, however, the feeling is romantic, earthy and spiritual by

turns. This is emphasised by the accompaniment of the solo tenor voice by
string quartet and piano, which is used vividly to portray pictorial and dramatic
elements, at times threatening to usurp the role of the singer. Indeed, the work
is theatrical in places, a series of operatic scenes rather than a song-cycle.

The composer set six of Housman's poems (Nos. 31, 32, 27, 18, 21 and 50
from the original sequence), clearly too short a sequence to outline any
narrative, as Somervell's earlier cycle had done, but acting as the Lad's reflections
on life, love and death. An unusual feature is the relative size of the six settings.
Three substantial songs – 'On Wenlock Edge', 'Is my team ploughing' and
'Bredon Hill' – encompass two very short ones – 'From far, from eve and
morning' and 'Oh, when I was in love with you' – with 'Clun' acting as a
postlude. 'On Wenlock Edge' begins with a graphic portrayal of the windswept
trees in Housman's first stanza, and this turbulence continues in the background
for the rest of the song. At times the composer almost breaks the back of his five-
some accompaniment; one feels that he would have liked a full orchestra to do
his word-painting justice. (In fact, he did make an orchestral version, first
performed on 24 January 1924.) 'From far, from eve and morning' is one of his
finest achievements. After the elaborate accompaniment of the opening song, he
turns to utmost simplicity: wide-spreading piano chords underpin a vocal line
that never strays far from its home note (B-natural) (Ex. 6.9).

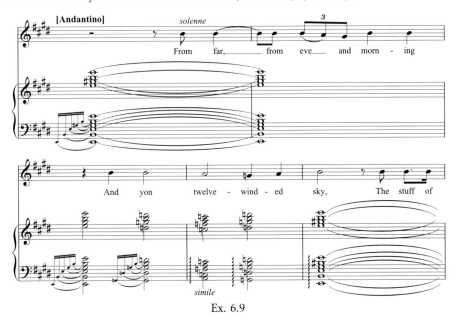

Ex. 6.9

In 'Is my team ploughing?', Vaughan Williams, more than any other composer,
marks the difference between the two poetic voices; this is not an interior
conversation between self and conscience, but a dialogue between two distinct
people. Over a remote, timeless chord of D minor, the ghost sings a gentle,

folk-like melody, mainly stepwise in movement, Dorian in mode. The living friend answers in a tortured wail, a vocal line full of tritonal and chromatic intervals (Ex. 6.10).

Ex. 6.10(a)

Ex. 6.10(b)

Vaughan Williams, as we have seen, deliberately omitted stanzas 3 and 4 (see Introduction, p. 12). 'Oh, when I was in love with you' takes up the same key (D minor). Lightweight in tone, epigrammatic in its brevity, with a melody that could be an authentic folksong, it acts as a much-needed respite between the intense emotions of songs 3 and 5. 'Bredon Hill' is the most substantial, pictorial and ambitious song in the cycle. In the accompaniment, the composer uses a compendium of bell effects: the hazy bells of a summer morning, alternating unrelated 7th chords played *pianissimo* between strings and piano (verses 1 and 2); more animated bell-sounds for piano alone (verses 3 and 4); bleak 'winter bells' (verse 5); a reiterated pedal G for 'the one bell only' (verse 6); and frenetic, almost deafening bell-rings in the final verse. 'Clun' – a setting of the poem, 'In valleys, of springs of rivers' – acts as a quiet, consoling epilogue to the cycle, creating a mood of peace and serenity which Vaughan Williams was to recapture in several later works, such as the Tallis Fantasia and the 5th Symphony.

Since it was first performed, *On Wenlock Edge* has provoked extremes of praise and censure, most notably in the famous verbal duel between Edwin Evans (pro) and Ernest Newman (anti) in the columns of *The Musical Times* in June and September, 1918. In a particularly vituperative essay, Newman criticises the music on several counts: that it does not mate happily with the prosody of the poems (he compares Vaughan Williams's settings unfavourably with Butterworth's in this respect); that the composer lacks a fine ear for the niceties of English poetic rhythm; that he is too inclined to turn lyricism into melodrama or pictorialism; and that he generally fastens upon the obvious externals of a poem at the expense of its meaning. It would seem from Newman's tirade that there is very little going for Vaughan Williams's song-cycle! On the contrary, whatever the critics have said, it remains, with Butterworth's, the most popular of all the major Housman settings. It is a true song-cycle – for to take any song out of its context only diminishes it – and in its spacious, almost symphonic matching of texts and themes it is in all senses a major work. Whatever reservations one may have about the over-dramatic treatment of Housman's verses in the first, third and fifth songs, by the time the hushed tread of root-position chords reach their A major home in the final song, we realise that we have experienced something quite magical. What is strange is that Vaughan Williams chose to set Housman in the first place. Why should the poet's irony and cynicism have appealed to this stoically optimistic composer? It is yet another example of Vaughan Williams's wide range of subject-matter and his ability to empathise with a wide range of emotions.

Up to this point, Vaughan Williams's songs have a secular air to them; their subject-matter is love, art, the countryside and the joys and tribulations of living. The next two works mark a step that was to be crucial in his progress as a composer: the exploration of religious and spiritual texts. Though confessedly agnostic, worship, and particularly the place of music in worship, was a vital part of Vaughan Williams's nature, and from now on his choice of 'librettists', for operas and choral works as well as songs, included religious poets and writers. He was particularly attracted to the religious divines of the 17th century, George Herbert, Isaac Watts, Richard Crashaw and Jeremy Taylor, and these are the writers to whom he turned for texts for the *Five Mystical Songs* (1905–11, *1911*) and the *Four Hymns* (1913–14, *1920*). These two works form a closely-bonded pair, and not only in their choice of poets; both were commissioned for Worcester Three Choirs Festivals, 1911 and 1914 respectively, and both are examples of Vaughan Williams's conscious attempt to break away from the traditional voice-and-piano format. So much so, indeed, that the *Five Mystical Songs* can only be regarded as solo songs by proxy, as it were. The composer's preferred scoring was for baritone solo, chorus and orchestra. The chorus is marked 'optional' and is used sparingly (typically as a background shadow to the soloist, 'humming and aahing'), but its part is crucial. The alternative version for baritone and piano sounds wan, gutted and filleted (as indeed it is). This is particularly so in the final joyful 'Antiphon', 'Let all the world in every corner sing', with its 'bell-ring, cymbal-clashing mood of celebration' (Kennedy, 1977: 4). The settings range from the hymn-like character of 'The call' and the simple profundity of 'I got me flowers', to the large-scale central song, 'Love bade me welcome'. This, with its gently floating accompaniment of parallel open triads, looked forwards not only to Vaughan Williams's own later music, but also to the 'mystical' Warlock of the *Corpus Christi Carol* and 'Balulalow' (Ex. 6.11).

Love   bade me wel - come;   yet my soul drew   back,___   Guil - ty of dust   and sin.

Ex. 6.11

In *Four Hymns*, the tenor soloist is accompanied by piano with viola obbligato, a combination that Brahms had used in his late set of songs, op. 91. Certainly there is no question of the viola being 'optional' here; it acts as a descanting companion to the voice, adding a reflective commentary on the text. These songs show an increased maturity and individuality, as the composer finds techniques suitable to his own musical thinking: the free declamation of the Jeremy Taylor setting, 'Lord! come away!'; the flexible modality of Watts's 'Who is this fair one', with the Phrygian G-flat and 'Dorian' D-natural both naturally accommodated within the F minor tonality; and the serene, liquid floating triads in the penultimate Crashaw setting, 'Come Love, come Lord'. Here at last we have a complete song-cycle that sounds like no other composer. Gone are the disconcerting cribbings and 'sedulous apings' that mar the unity of his previous song-cycles. The composer has gained full self-assurance.

Four Hymns, in hindsight, marks a broad paragraph in Vaughan Williams's composing career. Its premiere had to be cancelled due to the outbreak of war and it was not heard until May 1920. During the four war years Vaughan Williams's time and energies were devoted to other things. It was not until 1921 that he turned again to songwriting with a group of songs, *Merciless Beauty* (*1922*), which explore more radical territory than hitherto. These settings of three roundels by Chaucer are written for high voice, with alternative accompaniments: string trio (two violins and cello), or piano. The trio version should be insisted on, not only because of the contrapuntal nature of the accompaniment, but also because of the essentially chamber-consort-like atmosphere that the composer aspires to. (The piano version sounds exactly what it is: a literal short-score transcription of the string trio.) Stylistically the music shows Vaughan Williams at his most simple, almost naïve. It is close in texture and ideas to the *Suite of Six Short Pieces* for piano written in the same year. There is a gentle archaic austerity in the songs that gives them a 'wild-flower freshness' (Kennedy, 1964/1980: 178). On another level, Vaughan Williams is clearly trying to solve a basic problem of songwriting. In the *Songs of Travel* Stevenson's verse had furnished the composer with a variety of lyrical shapes to which Vaughan Williams had responded naturally. In *The House of Life*, he had been confronted with a rigid, essentially *poetic* form, the sonnet, which he had adapted ('destroyed', in Tippett's notorious phrase) in order to find an appropriate musical shape. In *Merciless Beauty* he was confronted (or rather, he confronted himself) with a form even more rigid than the sonnet. But here, instead of 'destroying' the poetic form, he matches his music with it.

It was Chaucer who introduced the rondel form into England from France. There are several variants of the basic rondel/rondeau shape. In the French examples of Deschamps and Machaut, it was a form in which one or more lines occur amongst other lines three times, with as many as fourteen or as few as seven lines altogether, but, crucially, only two rhymes. Chaucer's version of the form, as these three rondels demonstrate, is an idiosyncratic one; it follows neither that used by Machaut or Charles D'Orléans nor that of later rondeleers such as Austin Dobson. Instead it comprises of a very close-knit scheme in which seven of the 13 lines are refraining lines. Take the first of the rondels set by Vaughan Williams, 'Your eyën two'. The rhyme-refrain scheme is given at the side, the capital letters denoting the repeated refrain; the text is the slightly modernised version used by the composer:

Your eyën two will slay me suddenly:	A
I may the beauty of them not sustene,	B
So woundeth it throughout my hertë kene	B
And by your word will helen hastily	a
My hertës woundë, while that it is green,	b
Your eyën two will slay me suddenly;	A
I may the beauty of them not sustene.	B
Upon my troth I say you faithfully,	a
That ye be of my life and death the queen,	b
For with my death the truthë shall be seen:	b
Your eyën two will slay me suddenly:	A
I may the beauty of them not sustene,	B
So woundeth it throughout my hertë kene.	B

This complex interweaving of refrains and rhymes, even more strict than the villanelle and ballade, gives the poetry (and the poet's thoughts) a noble, ritual quality. Vaughan Williams matches the refraining patterns in his vocal line as nearly as possible without being pedantic. So, the music to lines 1 and 2 is heard again in lines 6 and 7, and 11 and 12, and the third line is repeated at the end. Some may think that the composer has woven a rigid web for himself, but he compensates for his 'pre-destined' vocal line – most beautiful in itself – with variety elsewhere. The three poems, each one on the subject of unrequited love, all have variety in themselves, ranging from the sad, wounded tones of 'Your eyën two' to the humour and colloquial language of 'Since I from love', and Vaughan Williams has given the three diversity in tempo, metre and texture. So the first is in 5/4 metre throughout, relieved by the occasional crotchet triplet, which gives a flexibility and flow to the music. 'So hath your beauty' begins with a long recitative-like section before moving into a 4/4 'cortège'-like accompaniment, whilst the final song, 'Since I from love', has continually changing metres (3/4, 2/4, 4/4). It is the string trio that supplies the variety and variations to the recurring refrains, and in doing so sets up a crucial working-partnership with the voice. (For some perceptive comments on these songs, see Dent, 1925: 231–5.)

Despite the relatively modest size of the songs, Vaughan Williams's achievement is considerable; in other circumstances it could have had far greater repercussions, not only to song-composers but also to 'song-poets'. For the principle that he demonstrates is that it is possible in the 20th century to revive the 17th-century ideal of poetry and music fusing together formally, where the poem can suggest the form of the music. As it is, *Merciless Beauty* has been a voice crying in the wilderness, dismissed by some (Day, 1961: 178) as 'quaint', ignored or overlooked by others. Sadly Vaughan Williams himself did not follow up this radical experiment.

The other songs from the 1920s form a mixed group, in choice of poet, accompaniment and musical quality. Steuart Wilson introduced three of the new song-groups in a historically important concert on 27 March 1925: *Two Poems by Seumas O'Sullivan* (1925, *1925*), *Four Poems by Fredegond Shove* (1925, *1925*) and *Three Songs from Shakespeare* (1925, *1926*). The Shakespeare settings, though pleasant and simple, are not important. The Shove settings show both Vaughan Williams's strengths and weaknesses. Fredegond Shove (1889–1949) – the surname is pronounced as in 'grove', not 'halfpenny' – was the wife of G. F. Shove, Reader in Economics at Cambridge, and daughter of another Cambridge don, F. W. Maitland, who had married Florence Fisher, the sister of Vaughan Williams's wife Adeline. She was a poet in the 'Georgian' mould, of modest if real skills, though one must wonder if family ties had not influenced Vaughan Williams in his choice. One of the poems he chose, 'Motion and stillness', is quite unsuitable for musical setting; Vaughan Williams's treatment is glum and unmemorable. 'Four nights' has more clarity of purpose, its four verses mapping out the four seasons, but still fails to elicit a strong musical response. The remaining two are far more successful, if in quite different ways. Of the four, 'The new ghost' reflects Vaughan Williams's preoccupations in his larger-scaled works of the period, particularly *A Pastoral Symphony* and *The Shepherds of the Delectable Mountains*, and looks forward both in subject-matter and method to a later small-scale masterpiece, *Valiant-for-Truth* (1940). The poem describes the Soul leaving the human body for its maker. Adjacent minor triads (C minor/B minor/D minor) dominate the song's tonal progress and the spirit of the song's 'free-rhythmed declamation' is reinforced by the composer's direction in the final bars: 'There need not be exact correspondence between the time of voice and pianoforte here'. 'The water mill' has proved to be the most popular of the set, a Dutch painting in music, of a mill and its inhabitants, human and feline and inanimate. Word-painting abounds, and Vaughan Williams skilfully adapts the well-tried 'mill-wheel'/'spinning-wheel' figuration to his own idiom (Ex. 6.12). Later, at the reference to 'the clock inside the house', this is further adapted to clock-chiming imagery. Filled with this profusion of ostinatos, the song has a dreamily mesmeric effect.

There is a mill, an an-cient one, Brown with rain, and dry with sun, The mil-ler's

[*pp sempre*]

Ex. 6.12

The two Seumas O'Sullivan settings, 'The twilight people' and 'A piper', are interesting as examples of Vaughan Williams's attitude to piano accompaniment. At the end of each song, he has appended the following note: 'this song may also be sung without accompaniment', which suggests that the vocal lines are, as in a folksong, self-sufficient – indeed, they are – and that the accompaniments are no more than an added-on extra – which they are. The accompaniments are hardly idiomatic to the instrument. That of the first song is minimal, written entirely in the treble clef, the lowest note the G below middle C (i.e. the lowest note of the violin), as though intended to mimic a violin; whilst that oft-set poem, 'A piper', with its drone bass and pipe-like tune, would appear to want to be scored for a pipe over 'the open 5ths of a fiddle or hurdy-gurdy' (Banfield, 1985: 330). All this underlines the tenuousness of the piano's role.

A similar lack of direction is reflected in the other two works of the period. In *Three Poems by Walt Whitman* (*1925*) Vaughan Williams returns to one of his first poetic loves, whom he had set chorally and in vocal duet, but never in solo song. Though recognisably the Vaughan Williams of the time, they lack definition and clarity, and rely too much on the use of ostinato figures in the piano accompaniment. In 1927 he returned again to the poetry of A. E. Housman, but the contrast between *Along the Field* (as it came to be known) and *On Wenlock Edge* could hardly be greater. Only four of the nine poems which he set are taken from *A Shropshire Lad* (1896), the remaining five from Housman's more recent *Last Poems* (1922). The scoring too is quite different; instead of the luxurious texture of piano and string quartet, Vaughan Williams has opted for a solo violin. This paring down of accompanimental resources has already been observed in the Chaucer *Rondels* and the O'Sullivan settings, but here is taken to an almost monk-like extreme of abstinence. In place of the port-and-brandy of *On Wenlock Edge* we have cold spring water. Vaughan Williams had as his models not only the *Four Songs for Voice and Violin* (1916–17) by his friend Gustav Holst, but also his own folksong arrangements, 'Searching for lambs' and 'The lawyer', written two years before *Along the Field*. The fact that the compass of the solo violin reaches no lower than G below middle C and therefore cannot form a true bass with the tenor soloist (with the consequent lack of depth and weight) and that it is essentially a melodic instrument means that it has perforce to act as a descant to the voice. But Vaughan Williams uses it with great imagination, turning what could have been inhibiting restriction into creative breadth. The accompaniments range from the simple descants of the first and last songs, 'We'll to the woods no more' and 'With rue my heart is laden', to the folklike accompaniments, with drone basses and multiple stoppings, of 'Good-bye' and 'Fancy's knell'. The violin sometimes shares melodic material with the voice (as in the first song), sometimes has quite different music (as in 'In the morning' and 'The sigh that heaves the grasses'). In the mysterious 'The half-moon westers low', the violin plays a series of major thirds (hence suggesting the whole-tone scale) whilst the singer has, by contrast, an extremely chromatic line, thus giving the song a nebulous feeling which is not resolved by the final cadence (Ex. 6.13). At the first performance of seven of the songs, the *Musical Times* critic remarked that 'The composer has aimed at giving the poet the first place, obscuring the verbal effect as little as possible', qualifying his praise with the rider 'Unless one is a poetry lover these songs may appear rather bare.' But bareness and austerity was exactly what Vaughan Williams was seeking, and if he does not capture the inner turmoil of the 'Lad', as he had done in *On Wenlock Edge*, he underlines the fatalism of the poems more tellingly.

Ex. 6.13

The history of the songs is interesting. Vaughan Williams originally set nine poems. Seven of these were performed by Joan Elwes and Marie Wilson in their recital on 24 October 1927 (the one reviewed by the *Musical Times* referred to above). For some reason Vaughan Williams withheld publication until 1954, when they were revised and published under the title *Along the Field*. Only eight survived the revision; 'The soldier' was rejected. 1927–1954: it is an interesting fact that this period, a complete 'generation', was to be a time when Vaughan Williams remained mute as far as solo song was concerned. Did the revision of the Housman songs stimulate his final short, Indian Summer of song? For it was very soon after this that he returned to the medium, with the setting of 'Menelaus', the first of the four songs to poems by his second wife, Ursula, which were published after his death as *Four Last Songs* (*1960*). Thus we have this unexpected late harvest of solo songs, all written when the composer was in his eighties, a time of life when most songwriters have called it a day and retired to bed.

Four Last Songs are, according to the published score, fragments of two projected song-cycles. Certainly they do not form a readily discernible sequence. Two of the songs, 'Procris' (1958) and 'Menelaus' (1954), are oblique commentaries on Greek myths and legends; the other two, 'Tired' (1956) and 'Hands, eyes and heart' (?1956) are personal love-songs. In these settings Vaughan Williams indulges once more, and for the last time, in the harmonic luxury of a piano. And the songs, particularly the 'Greek' pair, reflect the style of his last works (notably the *Three Shakespeare Songs* for unaccompanied chorus, and the Ninth Symphony) in their disembodied atmosphere, created by strangely altered modes (a minor mode with a flattened fifth in 'Procris', and augmented 5th chords with a 7th in 'Menelaus'). Features of the earlier Vaughan Williams can be detected in the characteristic progression through the mediants, which is such a strong feature of 'Procris'. The other two songs owe their uniquely intimate, personal quality to the relationship between poet and composer. 'Hands, eyes and heart' is a woman's prayer for her loved one, each invocation, in turn to hands, eyes and heart, set off by tender vocal lines. 'Tired', the most attractive of the set, is a gentle lullaby, whose rocking accompaniment pivots over a series of root-position chords (B-flat minor/G-flat major/E-flat minor). In the final cadence, Vaughan Williams seems, as Michael Kennedy has pointed out (1964/1980: 368), to make a reference back to 'Linden lea': in this, one of his final songs, turning back the clock of his song-career to where it began (Ex. 6.14(a) and (b)).

Ex. 6.14(a)

Ex. 6.14(b) part 1

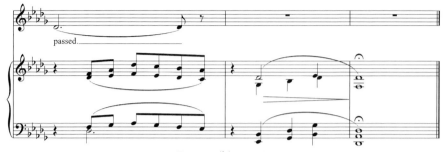

Ex. 6.14(b) part 2

From a poetic or sentimental point of view, these would fittingly have been Vaughan Williams's 'Last Songs', but as chance would have it, he was to add a postscript, the result of an unexpected commission. One of Vaughan Williams's finest orchestral works, *Job: a masque for dancing* (1930), had been inspired by William Blake, but Blake the artist rather than Blake the poet. Indeed, Vaughan Williams said that he preferred the artist to the poet, and when, in late 1957, he was approached to make settings of Blake's poetry for a short film, *The Vision of William Blake*, he was at first unenthusiastic. However, he agreed to consider the poems on condition that he was not expected to set 'that horrible little lamb – a poem I hate!' He wrote nine of the songs very quickly (in four days), then one morning announced that he had woken in the night with 'a tune for that beastly little lamb, and it's rather a good tune!' The poems are scored for the unusual combination of voice and solo oboe, and in this eschewing of the harmonic resources of the piano, the composer has restricted himself as he had in *Along the Field*. But at least in the Housman settings he had the opportunity for producing chords and drones; with the oboe he had no such luxury. The result is songs with an austerity unique to Vaughan Williams and English song. All ten poems are taken from *Songs of Innocence and Experience* (1789–93) with the exception of 'Eternity', which was published posthumously, and they include many of Blake's most famous poems, such as 'Infant joy', 'The piper', 'London' and 'Ah! sunflower', as well as 'The lamb'. The songs – one of Vaughan Williams's last completed works – were first performed in a BBC broadcast by their dedicatees, Wilfred Brown and Janet Craxton, on 8 October 1958, six weeks after the composer's death. The film, which was first shown two days later, used only eight of the settings, omitting 'A poison tree' and 'The piper'.

Despite the unusually sparse texture, Vaughan Williams managed to create some very effective settings, ranging from the austere and passionate 'Ah! sunflower' and 'A poison tree' to the pastoral simplicity of 'The piper', 'The shepherd' and 'Infant joy', from the spare, powerful style of 'London' to the 'calm gaze' of the final song, 'Eternity'. The oboe is silent in three of the settings, 'London', 'The shepherd' and 'The divine image', but Vaughan Williams obtains maximum variety from the instrument when it is deployed, interweaving it with the voice as a pastoral background as in 'The lamb', as a lilting dialogue in 'The piper' or as a sad counterpoint in 'A poison tree'. Particularly effective in its simplicity is 'The divine image'. The unaccompanied voice has a strong hymn-like tune in 4/4 in the Dorian mode for the opening verses, which changes to a lilting 3/4 metre and a major mode for the final verse. The whole sequence is 'a masterpiece of economy and precision' (Ottaway, 1980: XIX 577). Thus, at the age of 85, without need for the luxury of harmony, relying on his natural melodic gifts, Vaughan Williams completed his songwriting career. In the context of this great composer's creative life, songwriting may have played only a small part, but it was an important part nevertheless. Even the songs of his which are neglected or little known show the impress of his musical personality and deserve exploration and revival, whilst works such as *Songs of Travel* and *On Wenlock Edge* remain amongst the most loved masterpieces of English Romantic Song:

> Still they are carolled and said –
>   On wings they are carried –
> After the singer is dead
>   And the maker buried.

7

Gustav Holst (1874–1934)

> On Betelgeuse
> the gold leaves hang in golden aisles
> for twice a hundred million miles,
> and twice a hundred million years
> they golden hang, and nothing stirs,
>   on Betelgeuse.
>
> Space is a wind that does
> not blow on Betelgeuse,
> and time – oh time – is a bird,
> whose wings have never stirred
> the golden avenues
> of leaves on Betelgeuse.
>
>   Humbert Wolfe: 'Betelgeuse'

Though his orchestral music is best known, most of Holst's music is text-based. Of the 192 works listed in Imogen Holst's catalogue of her father's music, only 54 are instrumental, the rest settings of text. Yet for a composer who spent so much of his career setting words to music, he wrote relatively few solo songs. Seventy-two are mentioned by Imogen Holst, published and in manuscript (Holst, 1974), but barely a quarter are of importance. Holst's interest in songwriting appears at best to have been lukewarm. He does not seem to have had a compelling desire to write songs and he certainly did not show continuous interest in the medium as did Parry, Stanford, Somervell or even Vaughan Williams. Furthermore, he made no serious attempt to write a song-cycle, as Vaughan Williams did with his Rossetti, Stevenson and Housman settings. His early opuses, the *Six Songs*, op. 15, for baritone and piano and the *Six Songs*, op. 16, for soprano and piano, are no more than collections of individual songs grouped together to suit a particular voice and set to a motley collection of poets. There are only three works which deserve serious attention, written over a span of twenty years and drawing on an eclectic range of texts: the *Nine Hymns from the Rig Veda*, op. 24, the *Four Songs for voice and violin*, op. 35, and the *Twelve Songs to poems by Humbert Wolfe*, op. 48. But these three are important enough both in their own right and historically to ensure Holst a place in the history of English song.

On his own admission, his early songs were 'a peg of words on which to hang a tune' (Mellers, 1947: 146). The poets he chose for setting are eclectic and predictable: Tennyson, Kingsley, Hardy, Bridges, Breton, Hume, Sidney, Blake and Anon., all represented by well-anthologised lyrics. Here, one feels, is a man who hasn't a deep interest in, nor a wide knowledge of poetry, but has taken poems from the first books he can find on his bookshelf. (It is significant that most of the Hardy and Kingsley texts are taken from their novels.) The songs are pot-boilers on the outlook for a publisher and aimed at the royalty-ballad market. 'Lovely kind and kindly loving' (Breton) from the op. 16 set, is a case in point. It is not a particularly good example of the genre, and failed to find a publisher when it was written in 1903. Why then did Holst allow it to be published in 1923, the year he wrote his 'radically modern' *Fugal Concerto,* and by which time he had produced such original masterpieces as *The Planets* and *A Hymn of Jesus*? Two of the songs from these two sets, however, are of passing interest and still find their place in recital programmes. 'The sergeant's song' (1903, *1903*) sets the song-lyric Hardy included in his novel *The Trumpet Major* and is geared to the 'Rollicum-Rorum', 'Glorious Devon' (here read 'Dorset') end of the publishing market. Though it doesn't compare with Finzi's masterly setting in *Earth and Air and Rain,* it has some nice touches, as, for example, in the way he gives different music to the alternating stanzas, A B A B. A is a jolly, modally-tinged march-tune which would not have been out of place in one of his works for military band; B is more roving in its tonality, taking the music from A minor to F-sharp major, then abruptly slipping back to the home key for the original refrain. 'Weep you no more' (1903, *1907*), a setting of the familiar anonymous 16th-century text, gives us a distant glimpse of the mature Holst. The high, celesta-like arpeggiated chords, though clearly marked with late Romantic labels of dominant and secondary 7th, have a static, mesmeric quality which remind us, in Merlin-like hindsight, that this is the composer-to-be of 'Venus' and 'Neptune'.

In 1899 Holst began studying Sanskrit literature in order to make his own translations into English. Over the next ten years he prepared texts for several works, notably the opera *Savitri* (1908) and the many settings of the Hindu sacred verses called *Rig Veda,* which were scored for a variety of combinations, ranging from solo voice and piano to mixed chorus and orchestra. The *Hymns from the Rig Veda,* op. 24 (1907–8, *1920*), written a mere four years after 'The sergeant's song', show remarkable progress. They are original in conception, unique in English, or even European, solo song, taking the forms of invocations to elemental forces and moral powers: to the Dawn, the Sky, Faith, etc. In his final version, Holst has set nine of these prose-poems in three groups of three: Set I: 'Ushas' (Dawn), 'Varuna I' (Sky) and 'Maruts' (Stormclouds); Set II: 'Indra' (God of Storm and Battle), 'Varuna II' (the Water) and 'Song of the frogs'; Set III: 'Vac' (Speech), 'Creation' and 'Faith'. A tenth hymn, 'Ratri' (Night), was never published. The settings lack stylistic unification – occasional cross-references like the deep pedal C's of 'Varuna I' and 'Creation' are more likely coincidental than intentional – and they vary considerably in quality. 'Maruts', whose galloping accompaniment is borrowed from a much earlier Kingsley setting, 'The day of the Lord' (c.1897), is more conventional in conception, the trampling hooves more suited to the Wolf's Glen than the Indian plains. 'Indra', with its heavily marching 3/4 bass, is in Holst's *nobilimente* style ('Noblest of songs for the noblest of Gods'), again more pertinent to a European than Asiatic context. But most of the songs show a determination to experiment, to break new ground and to forge a new language. Most importantly, they are a conscious attempt by Holst to find a style of declamation suited to the English language and a new relationship between voice and accompaniment, whilst at the same time retaining the mystical quality of the Sanskrit originals, which he does by the use of unusual modes, metres and accompanimental ideas. In 'Ushas', he uses mesmeric repetition of a chant-like fragment over a series of static chords. There is a similar device in 'Vac': a fluid, chant-like line with rich, sustained piano chords of irregular duration beneath. In 'Faith' – in spite of the tour-de-force of its piano accompaniment, whose arpeggiated chords spiral down four octaves from the top of the piano – the words and spirit of the setting are closer to a Christian sacred song than a Hindu chant. (Indeed, it would not sound out-of-place in a church service.) In 'Varuna II' he experiments with the whole-tone scale, the voice descending the scale from upper to lower C, with quietly throbbing crotchet chords in the accompaniment. The use of the accompanying instrument is particularly interesting. Often there are no conventional piano introductions: the voice comes straight in. One cannot, perhaps, expect light relief in a sequence of hymns, but Holst does manage to leaven the solemn-serious atmosphere in 'Song of the frogs'. The grotesque words – in which the frogs Aristophanically celebrate finding their voices with the onset of the rain – are set to a 7/4 (4+3) metre, in the dancing scherzo mood that we are often to encounter in Holst's later works. The refrain, 'Brothers rise and join the throng', is particularly characteristic with its Phrygian 2nd invading the traditional minor mode (Ex. 7.1).

Ex. 7.1

The outstanding songs are 'Varuna I' and 'Creation'. 'Varuna I' is an early glimpse of the mature Holst, looking forward, indeed, to 'Betelgeuse' in the Humbert Wolfe settings. The accompaniment qualifies as a forerunner of 1980s minimalism: two hollowed-out (bare 5th) chords (E-flat and C) in the right-hand over a deep pedal drone C in the left-hand. The singer has an unusually inflected mode: two repeated phrases, balancing each other, but using quite different gamuts, the first pivoted on C, the second on B-flat. These two phrases are 'underpinned' – hardly 'accompanied' – by two pairs of chords: (i) bare 5ths on E-flat and C, and (ii) a G-flat major chord alternating with the tritone B-flat/F-flat, all suspended over a deep, impassive pedal-drone C (Ex. 7.2). The coda to the song effectively brings the second phrase into the tonality of the first.

Ex. 7.2

'Creation' complements 'Varuna I' in its use of a long-sustained and deep pedal C. The austere philosophy of the text – 'Then, Life was not! Non-life was not!' – clearly appealed to Holst and was to find its echo in later works, notably Wolfe's remote star-poem, 'Betelgeuse'. The song falls into two distinct parts. It begins with unaccompanied singer, the words set in irregular 7/4 metre in a strange mode which, like that of 'Varuna I', splits into two gamut segments, here pivoted round the opening G (Ex. 7.3(a)). The note C clearly has tonic implications, as the piano's *pianissimo* entry on low C's reveals. The symbolism – one note for both singer and piano – could not have been made more manifest: 'One! One alone! Calm and self-existing.' (Ex. 7.3(b)).

Ex. 7.3(a)

Ex. 7.3(b)

When 'fierce glowing Desire' is mentioned, the music's character changes radically, textures (rapid arpeggios), swift modulations and dissonant harmonies matching the change. Starting from the same tune and mode, the vocal line increases in tension, rising higher and higher until it achieves its climax at the words 'Whence cometh creation?', before falling back, to a quiet D-flat based chant over the pedal C.

Most of the songs are strophic in outline, ranging from simple strophic of 'Maruts', 'Song of the frogs' and 'Faith', to more complex strophic variations of 'Ushas', 'Varuna I' and 'Vac'. 'Indra' and 'Varuna II' have ternary structures. Only 'Creation' has a freer, through-composed form, though, as has been shown, the second part of its bipartite structure develops ideas heard in the first.

A problem that confronts both performers and listeners in the *Rig Veda* hymns is that of the texts themselves. Though Holst must be applauded for taking the trouble to make his own translations, it has to be said that his literary talents are unimpressive. The *Rig Veda* texts (like those he supplied for himself for *A Hymn of Jesus*) are irritatingly pretentious or naïve by turn. They are full of Wardour-Street archaisms – '-eths' and 'haths' – obsolete words and needless inversion, and read like a cross between sub-Bible and sub-Whitman (a very dangerous poet to try to imitate). Take the following random samples:

> 'Oh let us not be yielded up to Death to be destroyèd,
> To be destroyèd in thy wrath . . .' [Varuna I]

> 'We would fain welcome you fitly . . .' ['Maruts']

> 'He the Proud One whose eye controlleth all things,
> He alone doth know it,
> Or perchance even He knoweth it not!' ['Creation']

'Varuna II' opens with:

> ''Fore mine eyes,
> Yawning and hungry,
> Looms the grave . . .'

Who, hearing this sung, will understand that opening line? ('Four'? 'Fore'? 'For'? . . .) Far more importantly, there is little feeling for the spirit of the originals. They may be *literal* translations – but who cares? They certainly don't feel or sound literal. Holst's oft-expressed desire was to find 'the peculiar genius of our language' (Short, 1990: 443), but what is the point of taking such infinite care about word-setting when the words are trash? There is little doubt that the quality of the music – which is admirable – is hampered by the weakness of the texts, and this shortcoming will always be a deterrent to potential admirers.

The decade which separated the *Rig Veda* hymns from Holst's next songs, the *Four Songs for voice and violin*, op. 35 (1916–17, *1920*), coincided with his growing preoccupation with English folksong. He began arranging folksongs in 1906: *Folk Songs from Hampshire* were composed between 1906 and 1908; *A Somerset Rhapsody*, 1906–7; the folksong-imbued *Second Suite in F* for military band in 1911; and the unaccompanied *Six Choral Folksongs* in 1916, the same year in which he began work on *Four Songs*. Wilfrid Mellers has said of the third of the *Four Songs* that it is 'perhaps as close as Holst came to folksong' (1947: 147). The texts are taken from *A Mediaeval Anthology* (1915) edited by Mary Segar, the source for several of his carol-settings. 'Austerity' is a word that inevitably crops up in reference to these songs. They are like a glass of cold water – or rather, four glasses of cold water – amongst the homely cups of tea of English song of the period. The idea of using a solo violin to accompany the voice came to the composer one summer evening in 1916 when he happened to go into Thaxted church and heard one of his Morley College pupils, Christine Ratcliffe, playing her violin to which she improvised a wordless song. In their turn, Holst's songs were to have a strong influence on Vaughan Williams, whose Housman settings, *Along the Field*, for the same combination, were composed some ten years later.

The lack of a harmonic instrument means that the songs have to rely on contrapuntal textures, with a strong emphasis on the melodic line. In all four, Holst uses modally based melodies, in keeping with the medieval provenance of the texts: Nos. 1 and 3 Aeolian, Nos. 2 and 4 Phrygian, though, as will be seen, freely altered with chromatics. It is instructive to note how he achieves variety of texture and setting within these severe, self-imposed restrictions. In 'Jesu sweet, now will I sing', he eschews irregular metres for a general *senza misura*. The violin is *colla voce* throughout, and as the irregularities of the vocal line are not precisely noted, either in note-length or rests, the violinist has a demanding task. The first three verses are treated strophically, making an unexpected move from minor to major in the final verse: something Vaughan Williams may have subconsciously remembered in the penultimate setting, 'The divine image', of his *Ten Blake Songs*. The violin's contribution is a simple seven-crotchet ostinato before, between and after the verses, and support and punctuation whilst the singer sings. 'My soul has nought but fire and ice' is a perfect epigram, eight bars long. The violin accompaniment is minimal, basically three two-part chords which are summarised in the final cadence (Ex. 7.4). The Phrygian mode/mood is firmly established by the recurrent E-flat.

Ex. 7.4

Above this the singer has a flexible declamation, the E-flat here reserved for two important words: 'And my body *earth* and wood' and 'that *we* may do his will'. It is formidable in its simplicity. (Cold water, nonetheless.) 'I sing of a maiden', setting the first two verses of a familiar, oft-set text, begins with the singer heard unaccompanied for the first 12 bars. The opening verse is an introductory *Allegretto* preamble, before the singer embarks on the narrative proper at a slightly slower *Andante* tempo with new melodic material. When the violin enters, on a high A, there is an unexpected move from the initial Aeolian A minor towards C-sharp minor. Then, in a pretty painting of the text, the violin gradually descends, 'As dew in April/That falleth on flower', down to its lowest C-natural (Ex. 7.5).

Ex. 7.5

The song ends with both voice and violin approaching each other from different directions, to disappear into the tonic A. The song is a marvellous example of Holst's economy and subtlety. Taking the three-bar phrases as units (= two lines of poetry; each verse is a quatrain), the song's structure can be tabulated thus:

v.1 ab v.2 cd v.3 cd v.4 aa v.5 bd

'My leman is so true' uses another Phrygian-mode melody. Here we have note-for-note writing between singer and violin, the violin playing in almost continuous crotchets. The three verses are set in traditional Bar form, AAB. As in the first song, the violin supplies a ritornello that acts as prelude, interlude before verse 2 and coda to the song (Ex. 7.6). It will be noticed that it echoes the singer's cadence notes of the second song, but its role is even more integral.

Ex. 7.6

The singer has a flowing line with bars of continuous metrical change: 3/2, 5/4, 4/4, 3/4, 2/4. The opening strophe follows a traditional folksong structure: aaba. In the second verse, the singer picks up the cadence feature from the violin's ritornello – a further example of the give-and-take between the two lines that are such a feature of the settings. In the third verse, a new melody appears, though it sounds slightly familiar. Indeed, it is developed from the violin's ritornello, poised over a pedal E on the violin, before the song is wrapped up with the original strophe ending. Writing to his friend W. G. Whittaker in May 1917, Holst said that this song was the nearest he had yet achieved in his search for 'the (or *a*) musical idiom of the English language' and 'a tune at one with the words' (Holst, 1974: 127). Despite their modest scale, these songs are gem-hard, tough and durable as diamonds.

Twelve years separate the composition of *Four Songs* and his next, and final, song-set, the *Twelve Songs to poems by Humbert Wolfe,* op. 48 (1929, *1930*); they were his first songs with piano since the *Rig Veda* hymns. The 20-year silence, however, had not diminished his skill with the medium; indeed, one of the marvels of this swan-song is the effectiveness of the piano-writing, remarkable from someone who was not a particularly good pianist. Up to this point Holst had yet to prove that he was a dedicated song-composer. His songs lack breadth and variety; too many of them are remote or austere and uncommunicative. When he does try his hand at a jolly song, as in 'The sergeant's song', one feels that it is with bravado rather than conviction. Though he sets words immaculately, real involvement with his texts often seems to be lacking. It is as though his head were involved but not his heart. With the Wolfe settings, one feels, at last, that the two have come together and that he has been inspired. But what an unexpected poet to be inspired by!

Humbert Wolfe (1885–1940) was born in Milan of a German father and Italian mother, brought up in Bradford and educated at Oxford. By profession he was a civil servant – indeed, he was known as the 'Civil Service' poet – and ended an illustrious public career as Deputy Secretary at the Ministry of Employment (1938). (One of his publications was *Labour Supply and Regula-tions* (1923) – few other poets could cap that!) Out-of-hours, however, his avocation was poetry, and between the wars he published several volumes of verse which achieved considerable popularity. Holst came across a copy of one of these, *The Unknown Goddess*, in 1927 and wrote to Wolfe to say how much he liked it. Two years later he set twelve of Wolfe's poems – ten from *The Unknown Goddess* (1925), the remaining two, 'Now in these fairylands' and 'A little music', from *This Blind Rose* (1928) – which were performed by Dorothy Silk in February 1930, under the title *The Dream-city*. They were subsequently published as separate songs and it was not until 1970 that they were brought together as a sequence under the title *Twelve Humbert Wolfe Songs*. Holst never intended them as a song-cycle and after the first performance left the performing order to the players. The 1970 published edition follows that adopted by Peter Pears and Benjamin Britten in their historic recording (ARGO ZRG 512). If the songs are to be performed as a cycle this is as effective an order as any.

Wolfe was not a great poet; he is forgotten today and ironically would be completely ignored except for the fact that Holst set him to music. But he was at his best a fine poet, in his use of para-rhymes ('Envoi') and metrical experiments ('Rhyme') an original poet, and in his choice of subject-matter a contemporary one. What is more, he suited Holst: the two writers matched each other perfectly. Both were concerned with matters transcendental, both lovers of London, by day and by night ('The dream-city') and, importantly, Wolfe was a lover of music, as so many of his poems show. Though many of the poems chosen by Holst are written in Wolfe's favourite short-lined quatrains (which the composer inevitably gathers together into larger strophes), there is much metrical variation: the pithy couplets of dialogue of 'Journey's end', the intricate virtuoso handling of its own subject-matter in 'Rhyme', and the chiming refrain of 'Betelgeuse'. Holst treats them with a correspondingly wide variety of approach, from the terse speech-song of 'The thought' to the fecund invention of 'The floral bandit', and ranging in tone from stark austerity ('Betelgeuse') to spring-like joy ('Persephone'), from the child-like playfulness of 'Rhyme' to the sad dialogue of 'Journey's end'. The word-setting is immaculate, as one would expect from such an expert in this field. Above all, it is the lyricism of the settings which is so attractive. In choosing Wolfe, Holst may have inadvertently (though deservedly) perpetuated Wolfe's name. But in discovering Wolfe's poetry, Holst opened up a vein in his own creativity that he rarely explored. His rediscovery of lyricism, or rather discovery of a new lyricism, led, as we shall see, to one of the masterpieces of 20th-century English song.

Ex. 7.7(a)

Ex. 7.7(b)

Ex. 7.7(c)

The songs fall into three basic types: (i) love-songs (2–5), (ii) philosophical songs (7–10), interspersed by (iii) 'poems of fancy' (1, 6, 11 and 12). All settings are recognisably mature Holst in their use of quartal harmonies and neo-modal idiom (the latter far more advanced than the simple folksong modality of the *Four Songs*). He uses a far more chromatic gamut of notes in the vocal lines, which is reflected too in the accompaniments. Take, for example, the mode (a mixture of E major and F minor) which gives an out-of-the-worldly strangeness to 'Betelgeuse', the 'altered Lydian' of 'The thought' and the 'Phrygianality' of 'Persephone' (Exs. 7.7(a), (b) and (c)). He develops the technique, used as early as the *Rig Veda* songs, of creating modal gamuts that act as reflecting mirrors of each other, most noticeably in 'Journey's end', 'The thought' and 'Now in these fairylands', where the second verse is an almost direct inversion of the first (Ex. 7.8).

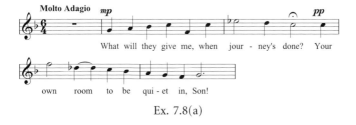

Ex. 7.8(a)

Ex. 7.8(b)(i)

Ex. 7.8(b)(ii)

Not every song is of the same high quality. In 'Envoi', the pianist's continual doubling of the vocal line is quite at odds with the discrete relationship of voice and accompaniment in the other songs. Its ending has a rhetoric more appropriate to Parry and Somervell than Holst, and it is one of the few songs in which he indulges in one of his musical vices – that stalking, crotchet-bass ostinato, so often used as an easy option, as the composer himself was the first to admit. 'Things lovelier' is almost a non-song in its minimality. The accompaniment, a sequence of inscrutable, rhythmically-inert chords, sits high in the treble clef throughout and smacks of undigested experimentation. In 'In the street of lost time' he again resorts to an over-familiar Holstian device, this time of contrary-motion chords, into which even the addition of chromatic notes cannot inject life. But the best songs – 'Persephone', 'The floral bandit', 'The dream-city', 'Journey's end', 'Rhyme' and 'Betelgeuse' – are outstanding.

Holst captures the filigree delicacy of Wolfe's 'Persephone' in quick arpeggiations over a Phrygian-mode gamut, which the singer (literally) reflects in the opening vocal line (see Ex. 7.7(c)). He has deliberately chosen the unusual time-signature of 8/4, each bar of which swallows half a stanza in one gulp, in order to give a broad sweep and urgency to the music. At the same time, he indulges in Hopkins-like 'sprung rhythm' within the eight-crotchet bar, with irregular stresses throughout. The effect is at once flexible and confining, giving the vocal line a curiously oriental flavour. 'The floral bandit' is one of Holst's most original songs. Following the cues and clues provided by the poet ('the small language of the rain' – 'Who is this lady? What is she?/the Sylvia all our swains adore?' – 'For buds at best are little green/keys on an old thin clavichord') Holst indulges in a witty orgy of musical quotations: '*Jardins sous la pluie*', 'Who is Sylvia?' and a Bachian three-part invention (two parts for the 'clavichord', the third for the singer), ending up, like the poem, with music broken off in mid-flight (Ex. 7.9).

the la - dy who for e - v'ry man breaks off her mu - sic in the mid - dle.

Ex. 7.9

Wielding a technical virtuosity worthy of Uranus the Magician, Holst somehow manages to make the song work, balancing all these quite disparate ideas. Its use of parody, toccata-like textures and ostinato gives the song a quite distinctive 20th-century sensibility. The composer has travelled a long way from the drawing-room ballads of his youth.

With its dream-like imagery of London and references to places dear to the composer's heart, the gardens of 'Kensington, Richmond Hill and Kew and Hampton', 'The dream-city' could have been written specially for Holst. Not unexpectedly it was the first of the songs to be written. In a gently-rocking 7/4, the Thames of Hammersmith laps against its banks, stilled only when the poet speaks of 'A silent square', whilst the singer unfolds the magic city landscape above. 'Journey's end' is a question and answer dialogue between a boy and his parent. One problem with such a poem is how to vary the inevitable to-and-fro, especially when short couplets are used, as here. Wolfe skilfully avoids symmetry by shortening the questions and extending the answers by enjambment. Holst extends this even more by varying the pitch and shape of the vocal lines, so that no verse/couplet is entirely repeated. A 'Venus'-like upward-rising scale binds accompaniment and vocal line, the singer catching on to the piano's rising figure each time for the Boy's questions, whilst the Father's replies (See Ex. 7.8) are answered in reflected vocal lines over sustained chords. The song inevitably begs comparison with the slightly earlier setting by Frank Bridge (see Chapter 9, pp. 182–3). The two songs could hardly be more different: Bridge's is taut, angst-ridden, extended; Holst's cool, almost coldly-detached, classically compact. Both are masterly; we are fortunate to have two such fine settings of the same 20th-century poem.

'Rhyme' is a poem that reflects its title in its virtuoso rhyming. The sheer verbal exuberance will easily carry the song-setter through such 'difficult' words as 'conjugate' and 'paradeigm' [*sic*]. A rippling accompaniment, pentatonic arpeggios which resolve onto 1st inversion triads, dance along with child-like innocence and the lilt of a nursery rhyme. The song has a ternary shape, with a central section for the middle stanzas 3 and 4 of semiquavers flowing against each other in contrary motion, before the reprise of the original texture in the final verse.

'Betelgeuse' is a fantasy-picture of that remote red star in the constellation of Orion. It reflects in song, once and for all time, Holst's lifelong preoccupation with Old Age, Solitude, Loneliness and Remoteness, which he explored so vividly in such orchestral works as 'Saturn' and 'Uranus' in *The Planets* and his orchestral masterpiece *Egdon Heath*. The music is built on two opposing tonalities a semitone apart: F and E. This can be heard clearly in the dominants and tonics of the piano accompaniment: F in the left-hand, E in the right-hand, which climb skywards in a series of ladder-like ostinatos (Ex. 7.7(a)). It is a cold, life-forsaken texture, which even the D-flat major chords that later punctuate it cannot alleviate. The only moment of warmth comes at the words 'nor ghost of evil or good/haunts the old multitude on Betelgeuse', when a 1st inversion chord of D-flat major is sustained, giving a strange but only temporary respite to the texture. Holst manages to avoid monotony yet preserve the still, mesmeric atmosphere by making subtle alterations to these ostinatos, which sometimes coincide with, sometimes avoid the beat, so that the basic feeling for the pulse is quickly lost. The singer, as in so many of Holst's songs, breaks effortlessly from arioso into recitative. The reiterated refrain 'On Betelgeuse' only adds to the mesmeric monotony. Imogen Holst has described how the audience at the first performance of 'Saturn' from *The Planets* suite 'felt they were growing older and older as the slow, relentless tread came nearer' (1974: 51). As we listen to 'Betelgeuse', we experience a similar feeling.

Wilfrid Mellers in his perceptive article on Holst (1947: 148) spoke in reference to the composer's vocal lines of their 'mournful frigidity'. This mournful frigidity – bleak austerity – lack of fun or humour – cerebral intellectualism – is a defining quality of Holst the composer. It shows him at his strongest and at his weakest. No-one can evoke the loneliness of a landscape or of the human spirit better than Holst. But, in the words of the Chorus from Britten's *The Rape of Lucretia*, 'Is this all?' In her biography of her father, Imogen Holst recounts a poignant anecdote on the occasion of the first, private performance of the Humbert Wolfe songs. The programme ended with Schubert's C major String Quintet, and hearing that warm, affectionate music, Holst suddenly realised:

> all that he had lost by clinging to his austerity. He had reached far into the distance, but he had missed the warmth of the Schubert Quintet, and it seemed as if that warmth might after all be the only thing worth having (Holst, 1951: 109).

In the Humbert Wolfe settings we see a thawing of this austerity, revealing a more genial side to Holst's personality. It is interesting to speculate which poets he might have gone on to set: perhaps not Walter de la Mare or Edward Thomas, but maybe Thomas Hardy? But it was not to be. In March 1932, within two years of the first performance of the songs, Holst was taken ill during a lecture-tour of America and was a semi-invalid for the remaining two years of his life, able to compose very little.

8

Roger Quilter (1877–1953)

Go, lovely rose –
Tell her that wastes her time and me,
    That now she knows,
When I resemble her to thee,
How sweet and fair she seems to be.

    Tell her that's young,
And shuns to have her graces spied,
    That hadst thou sprung
In deserts where no men abide,
Thou must have uncommended died.

    Small is the worth
Of beauty from the light retired:
    Bid her come forth,
Suffer herself to be desired,
And not blush so to be admired.

    Then die – that she
The common fate of all things rare
    May read in thee;
How small a part of time they share
That are so wondrous sweet and fair.

Edmund Waller: 'Go, lovely rose'

Roger Quilter seems to have realised from the outset of his career that songwriting was his natural métier. He made his London debut as a composer in 1900 with *Four Songs of the Sea*, performed at Crystal Palace by Denham Price. Song-composition was to occupy his attention throughout his life and he published new songs, latterly at more infrequent intervals, up to the time of his death in September 1953. His compositions for other media were occasional and for the most part unmemorable, though he is still possibly best known to the public for *A Children's Overture*, that skilfully-woven medley of nursery-tunes written as the overture to the children's play *Where the Rainbow Ends* (1911). His songs appealed to the leading singers of his day: Ada Crossley, Muriel Foster, Plunket Greene, John Coates, Mark Raphael; above all, to Gervase Elwes. It was Elwes who launched Quilter's career by persuading Boosey to publish 'Now sleeps the crimson petal', and from then until his own tragic death he was to introduce Quilter's finest songs, notably *To Julia* (which is dedicated to him) and the *Seven Elizabethan Lyrics*. Quilter himself would often accompany Elwes, and Scott Goddard recollected that:

> one of the lasting memories of concert-going during the first quarter of the twentieth century . . . will be the exquisite interpretations of his songs, the composer at the piano, by Gervase Elwes (1925: 216).

Quilter began his career when English song was at a particularly low ebb in its history. There was no vital tradition for serious song; popular songs and ballads dominated the market. Writing in 1887, in his preface to *Lyrics from Elizabethan Songbooks*, A. H. Bullen bewailed the fact that 'song-writing is now almost as completely a lost art as play-writing. Our poets who ought to make "music and sweet poetry agree", leave the writing of songs to meaner hands. Contrast the poor thin wretched stuff that one hears in drawing-rooms today with the rich full-throated songs of Campian and Dowland. O what a fall is there, my countrymen!' But whereas Parry, Stanford and Somervell consciously strove to establish a serious song-writing tradition based on the example of the German *Lied*, Quilter, like his close contemporary, Frank Bridge, seems to have accepted the sorry situation; he seized the dowdy song-ballad and decided to make a lady out of it. Thus Quilter's songs spring from the very source which Parry had so vitriolically castigated, the 'patent trade-song . . . whose sentiments is sodden with vulgarity and commonness, whose artistic insight is a long way below zero' (1888: 69). What he did was to raise the genre of the English drawing-room ballad to a serious art-form, by exquisite craftsmanship, sensibility and a discerning choice of poetry: not necessarily great literature, but texts with an aptness for musical setting. Though Quilter shared with Parry a high standard in his choice of poetry and always showed great care in word-setting, he realised that the poet was only one of the song-composer's considerations, and that the singer too deserved equal regard, if not indulgence. Therefore 'keeping the musical line', as he called it, was of paramount importance. It is indicative of Quilter's modest aims that, rather than attempt – like Parry – to forge a new tradition and court failure, he chose to build upon the living tradition of the ballad. This, despite its artistic shallowness, had a firm social foundation and a readily identifiable public. But the risks were enormous. That he could himself lapse back into the worst mannerisms of this tradition can be seen in an early song, 'June' (*1905*). The lyric is almost a parody of the 'Moon/June' cliché:

> Dark red roses in a honeyed wind swinging,
> Silk-soft holly-hock coloured like the moon;
> Larks high overhead lost in light, singing;
> That's the way of June.

But no-one can accuse the composer of failing to embody the spirit of the poem in his music – right down to the cliché repetition of the final lines (Ex. 8.1). This is, in fact, the ballad itself, no more, no less.

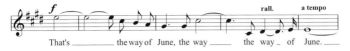

That's _____ the way of June, the way _____ the way _ of June. _____

Ex. 8.1

To see how far Quilter, when dealing with superior poetry, could outsoar such banalities, one has only to look at another song published in the same year, 'Come away, death' (Ex. 8.2). To the musically thin and shallow tradition of the drawing-room ballad, Quilter brought new depth and sensitivity. His achievement was to raise that tradition to a perfection and adventurousness that was never surpassed.

Come a-way, come a-way, death,   And in sad cy-press   let me be   laid; _____

Ex. 8.2

Clearly, however, there was more to Quilter's musical background than the Royalty Ballad. Despite the slightly dilettante air that he evinced, and indeed cultivated – a private income meant that he never had to earn a living – he had received thorough training in his craft. With Cyril Scott, Norman O'Neill, Balfour Gardiner and Percy Grainger, he was a student at Hoch's Conservatory in Frankfurt am Main, where he studied for four-and-a-half years with the eminent Russian professor of composition, Iwan Knorr (1853–1916). He found Knorr's academic teaching method tough and rigorous, but there is little doubt that his own fastidiousness in technical matters was the result of his studies in Frankfurt. Like so many British composers of his generation, he was introduced to songwriting through his acquaintance with German *Lieder*; his favourite songwriters were Schubert and Schumann (Raphael, 1953–4: 20). Their influence, with that of Grieg, one of the most popular song-composers in England at the turn of the century, laid the foundation of his own technique. (See the final song of *Songs of Sorrow*, 'In spring', for unmistakable Grieg influence.) But as well as 'a whiff of German sweetness', Frank Howes detected in his songs 'a very faint aroma of French perfume' (1966: 195). Quilter constantly reminds one of Gabriel Fauré, a composer he greatly admired (Banfield, 1985: 111); we also know that he possessed a copy of Duparc's songs in his library. This 'French Connection' was something very welcome in English song at the time. Of native songwriters, one of his favourites was Maude Valérie White (1855–1937) – a predilection shared curiously enough by Vaughan Williams – who made a modest attempt in her songs to raise the artistic level of the ballad by a more adventurous choice of text and an avoidance of stock musical ideas. It is significant that she later become an admirer of Quilter's own songs. From a harmonic point of view, a composer often thought of as an influence is Delius, but, according to Quilter himself, he knew almost nothing of the older composer's music until c.1908, by which time

he had already written his important early works, the *Three Shakespeare Songs,
To Julia, Seven Elizabethan Lyrics* and *Songs of Sorrow*. However, when he heard
early performances in this country of *Brigg Fair* and *Sea Drift*, he was 'so
overcome by the beauty both of the composition and the performance that I
could not resist writing enthusiastically to Delius, though I hardly knew him
then' (Warlock, ed. Foss, 1952: 155–6). His later songs, notably *Two September
Songs*, clearly show this enthusiasm.

'He tells me that he likes poetry even more than music – his preferences are
for Shakespeare, Shelley, Keats, Blake and Herrick', wrote a visitor (Brook, 1946:
88), and this is borne out by several other friends and acquaintances. But a
passionate love of poetry on the part of a composer can result in a literary
attitude to song-writing, with over-meticulous concern for 'just note and
accent', a fault noticeable in the songs of both Parry and Finzi. Quilter,
however, is not a 'poet's composer' in this sense, but a 'performer's composer'.
The 'musical line' dominates every poem he sets. As Mark Raphael has pointed
out, 'Correct verbal accents, phrasing and work-painting all had to fall in with
his idea of "keeping the line"' (1953–4: 20). Quilter's list of favourite poets
reflects his choice of song-text. Of the forty or so poets he sets, Shakespeare
ranks highest, with 19 settings, whilst Herrick is set eight times, Shelley seven
and Blake four. Poems by Shakespeare's contemporaries account for a dozen
more. His choice of his own contemporaries, however, is not so discerning.
Apart from Stevenson, Dowson, Henley and Mary Coleridge, they are for the
most part very minor, long-forgotten/'long-to-be-forgotten' talents. Tennyson,
the major lyricist of the Victorian period, is set only once, and then in a
bowdlerised form ('Now sleeps the crimson petal'), whilst the major lyric poets
of his own age, such as Hardy, Kipling, Yeats and Housman, are notable by their
absence. Some of the poems set are mere doggerel, which would make even
Patience Strong blush. One wonders how so great an admirer of our great lyrical
poets could even have *thought* of choosing the following, let alone actually
setting it to music and publishing it:

> Trollie lollie laughter!
> Swallows skim the sky;
> Nightingales come after,
> When the moon's up high.
>
> When the golden moon comes
> Over the trees,
> Soon, soon, soon comes
> Cupid o'er the leas . . .
>   Victor B. Neuberg: 'Trollie lollie laughter'

Quilter's own attempts at poetry – which he set in *Four Songs of the Sea*, 'Fairy
lullaby', 'April love' and, under the pseudonym 'Romney Marsh' (!), in 'Spring
voices' – do not rise to any greater heights of sentiment. When, however, he
kept to his named favourites, he was far more assured. The songs of Shakespeare
and the delicate love-lyrics of Herrick and his contemporaries inspired the best

in him. His music is a perfect match for the 'light conceits of lovers'. The limits
he set for his texts set the limits for his songs. They are short and lyrical; formal
and well mannered; personal and intimate: in Scott Goddard's aptly chosen
epithet, 'conversational'. Within these limits his reaction was sure. Only
occasionally does he fail, and the failure is usually the result of an over-reaction
to his text (a fault that impairs many of the songs of Ivor Gurney too). The last
two songs from *Three Pastoral Songs,* op. 22, are cases in point. Less frequently,
he makes the opposite mistake, choosing a text that is beyond his interpretative
ability. 'Fear no more the heat of the sun', from the second set of Shakespeare
songs, is a rare failure of this kind.

Despite the paramount importance to Quilter of the musical line, the detail of
his word-setting is both meticulous and imaginative. Devices such as word-
painting are rare, but have great impact when used (see bars 36–9 of 'By a
fountainside', op. 12, no. 6). His aim is not to follow slavishly the poetic shape
of his text but to complement text with appropriate musical shape: to transform
the 'music of poetry' into the 'music of music'. The vocal line of 'Fair house of
joy', op. 12, no. 7, demonstrates these points well and shows at the same time
how he can give new life to the most familiar lyric (Ex. 8.3).

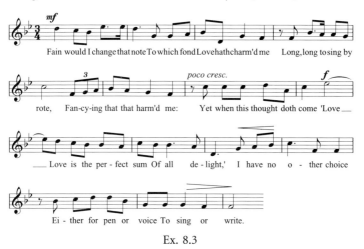

Ex. 8.3

Notice how the vocal line counterpoints the verse-structure – the first two lines
of the poem are 'counterpointed' into three bars of music, giving rise to
asymmetrical three-bar phrases – and how the middle lines of the stanza (bars
7–10) are set with great rhythmic flexibility. There is continuous interplay
between vocal line and basic poetic metre, so that out of the fifteen bars of the
strophe, only four duplicate a rhythmic pattern.

Scott Goddard, in a perceptive, though somewhat grudging, article on the
composer, described Quilter as 'the foremost living English example of the
singer's composer . . .He possesses, in as strong a degree as any songwriter, the
knowledge of the disposition of the human voice and the ability so to fashion

his works that the most is obtained from that instrument with the greatest facility' (1925: 216). He keeps within a traditional tonal idiom but with certain modal inflections, such as the flattened 7th already evident in his op. 1, *Songs of the Sea*, and the occasional use of the pentatonic mode. Diatonic, stepwise motion is by far the commonest type of interval in his melodic phrases. Octave leaps are usually reserved for climaxes (the beautiful opening octave in 'Brown is my love', op. 12, no. 5, is unusual) and sevenths, such as the drooping sevenths in 'Come away, death', op. 6, no. 1, very rare. The falling sixth, however, is a Quilterian hallmark, heard at its most familiar in 'To daisies', op. 8, no. 3. On the other hand, he avoids chromatic movement, and the examples in 'By a fountainside' (bar 19) and 'Drooping wings' (bars 17–18) are equally unusual. Awkward intervals, such as the tritone, and double leaps are carefully avoided. This smoothness of vocal line leads Quilter naturally to a syllabic style of writing. 'Autumn evening', op. 14, no.1, and 'Dream valley', op. 20, no. 1, are two characteristic examples of this style, where constant quaver motion is maintained in a deceptively casual way. This 'low profile' is certainly appropriate to the contours of most English lyric verse. It gives to Quilter's songs a rapt, dreamy quality, a facet that was to influence later composers, notably Peter Warlock. To listen to Warlock's 'My own country' beside 'Dream valley' reveals Warlock's debt to Quilter in this matter.

The relationship of vocal line and accompaniment shows Quilter's craftsmanship at its most masterly. Like other members of the 'Frankfurt gang', his music is harmonically conceived and dependent. It is somewhat surprising, therefore, that he achieved such success as a songwriter, a medium in which a strong, independent vocal line is of paramount importance. One has only to compare Quilter's songs with those of Cyril Scott to realise how skilfully he overcomes this problem. His vocal lines, despite their prominent solo function, are forever linked to their harmonic implications and can never be sung or listened to without reference to those implications. For example, the singer will often cadence onto the dominant note of the harmony. Warlock's observation that song is 'essentially unaccompanied tune' certainly cannot apply in Quilter's case. The role of the accompaniment is therefore crucial, but functions on several levels, as in any art-song. It not only 'feeds' the harmony to the vocal line, but also is so written as to give full prominence to that line. Rich discords, such as ninths and elevenths, so much a part of his idiom, are handled in such a way that they do not interfere with the singer's line. A comparison between Delius and Quilter in their respective settings of Shelley's 'Love's philosophy' is most illuminating (Exs. 8.4(a) and (b)). Delius, once he has set up a figurative pattern to accommodate his harmonies, is content to keep that pattern going throughout. With Quilter, the figuration is entirely flexible, allowing the voice prominence at all times. Delius's song sounds naïve and pianistically dull beside the subtle textures of Quilter's, in which voice and accompaniment are imaginatively entwined.

Ex. 8.4(a)

Ex. 8.4(b)

Rodney Bennett has commented that Quilter's piano accompaniments are 'the sort of thing that the voice can swim upon' (1926: 409). If he is kind to his singer, he is no less considerate to the pianist. Anyone who has accompanied his songs will tell you that they are a delight to play. Moreover, his textures are all his own, quintessentially Quilter. It is rare that he resorts to conventional mannerisms, such as pulsating chords, that baneful cliché of the drawing-room ballad that even so sensitive a composer as Elgar found hard to avoid in his song accompaniments.

As far as their overall shape is concerned, the majority of Quilter's songs are strophic. A few of the shorter ones – e.g. 'The maiden blush' and 'Julia's hair' from *To Julia*, and 'Damask roses' and 'Brown is my love' from *Seven Elizabethan Lyrics* – are through-set (often binary in form) but a longer through-composed song, such as 'By a fountainside' is unusual. Except for a few early songs, however, the variety within the strophic format is considerable, ranging from simple alterations (A1 B A2), as in 'How should I your true love know?', to more complex structures, such as 'Go, lovely rose'. These patterns are usually suggested by the texts themselves, though occasionally the composer superimposes a musical shape onto the verse. This can be seen in some of the final songs in the song sets, as in, for example, 'Cherry ripe', op. 8, no. 6, where he forces a *da capo* shape onto the text by repeating the opening strophe.

'Play the opening bars of almost any of his songs, and you are left in no doubt as to who wrote them', wrote Mark Raphael (1953–4: 20). The hallmarks of a Quilter song are as unmistakable as those of Fauré, Ravel, Warlock or Britten. So personal and familiar are they that one is forced to ask, when does the hallmark become a mere cliché, the fingerprint a tired mannerism? There is often a strong family likeness to his melodies. Compare, for instance, the following examples, from 'The jealous lover' and 'Who is Sylvia?' (Exs. 8.5(a) and (b)):

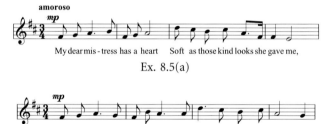

Ex. 8.5(a)

Ex. 8.5(b)

Compare, too, the openings of 'The fuschia tree', op. 25, no. 2, and 'Arab love-song', op. 25, no. 4, or 'Through the sunny garden', op. 18, no. 5 and 'Spring voices'. Some of his fingerprints – such as the extension or repetition of final vocal phrases – are characteristic of the drawing-room ballad as a whole, but many can be regarded as true Quilterisms. Amongst these are some characteristic cadences (Ex. 8.6 (a), (b), (c), (d) and (e)):

(*The Bracelet*, Opus 8 No 1)

Ex. 8.6(a)

loves   no   de - lay;

(*My Life's Delight*, Opus 12 No 2)

Ex. 8.6(b)

Dead   with   last   year's   Rose.

(*A Last Year's Rose*, Opus 14 No 3)

Ex. 8.6(c)

one ____   swal-low   come ____

(*Blossom Time*, Opus 15 No 3)

Ex. 8.6(d)

Love ____   do you hear me   sing?

(*Over the land is April*, Opus 26 No 2)

Ex. 8.6(e)

The latter is adumbrated as early as 'Moonlight', op. 1, no. 3 (see Ex. 8.8). A musical phrase that crops up in many different songs is illustrated in Ex. 8.7. It appears, of course, in 'To daisies', at the words 'The dull-eyed night', but can also be heard in 'Fair house of joy' (bar 5) and, in modified form, in 'Morning song', op. 24, no. 2 (bar 8) and in several other songs. 'Take, O take those lips away', op. 23, no. 4, is so full of such fingerprints that it verges on self-parody.

Ex. 8.7

Another characteristic is the unobtrusive way in which his vocal lines usually begin: in the middle register of the voice, never with long sustained notes, rarely on any chord except the tonic. The piano accompaniments, too, contain recurrent mannerisms. In strophic settings he will often raise the original keyboard *tessitura* to a higher octave in subsequent strophes (e.g. 'The night piece', op. 8, no. 4, 'Under the greenwood tree', op. 23, no. 2, etc.). His harmonic idiom is instantly recognisable, with careful spacing giving maximum sonority and sensuousness to his favourite chords of the 9th and 11th. In his harmonic movement, too, he shows clear predilections, as in the way he will repeat an initial phrase a minor third higher, noticeable as early as 'The sea-bird', op. 1, no. 2, and used to magical effect in 'The night piece'. Such hallmarks are so authentically Quilter that any variation from the norm – such as his use of imitative contrapuntal writing in the second set of Shakespeare songs, or the rare occasions when he begins the vocal line of a song on a chord other than the tonic, as in 'Brown is my love' (mediant) and 'Music and moonlight' (supertonic) – tends to stand out conspicuously. The recurrence of these features, from the earliest to the latest songs, underlines a curious feature of Quilter's songwriting career: his style and idiom hardly altered. An uninitiated listener confronted with 'Love's philosophy' (published 1905) and 'A song at parting' (published 1952) would not be likely to realise that almost fifty years separate them. As a composer, Quilter arrived on the musical scene virtually fully-fledged.

Though he lived to be 75, Roger Quilter wrote his finest songs before he was 40. The peak of his career was reached in the works written between 1905 and 1910, a period roughly corresponding to the reign of Edward VII. If Elgar was the symphonic master of the Edwardian age, then Quilter was its most typical and representative song-composer. The songs written in the two decades after 1910 show no important development, whilst those of his later years are little more than rehashes of old formulas. This presents the commentator with a difficult task, for instead of a gradual climb to maturity, or indeed a gentle arc, Quilter's career shows a sudden burst followed by a sad, slow decline. Purely for convenience, then, I have separated his songs into three chronological groups for discussion: the early songs, 1900–10; those written between 1910 and 1933; and the songs of his last twenty years.

Early songs: op. 1–14 (1900–10)

As has already been noted, the Quilter style is recognisable as early as 'Love's philosophy' (1905). It would be tidily convenient to be able to say that it is apparent from the outset, but this is not the case. His earliest acknowledged publication – *Four Songs of the Sea*, op. 1, *Four Songs of Mirza Schaffy*, op. 2, and the two Binyon settings, 'At close of day' and 'The answer' – are uncharacter-istic. (In 1897 he had published two songs, 'Come spring!' and 'The reign of the stars', both to his own words, under the pseudonym Ronald Quinton. Written on the title-page of his own copy is: 'On no account to be reprinted in any form under my name . . . Roger Quilter 1916'.) The *Four Songs of the Sea* (1900, *1901*) are settings of his own verses. The piano accompaniments lack the subtlety of later songs and the vocal writing is dull and unimaginative. The third song, 'Moonlight', for instance, is square-cut and stodgy, all three verses set to identical music. But the verse – insipid imitations of Mary Coleridge and R. L. Stevenson – is hardly the inspiration for a masterpiece (Ex. 8.8).

Under the sil - ver moon - light   Flutter the great white wings, —

Woo'd by the soft hight bree - zes   Tender with whis - per'd things.

Ex. 8.8

Echoes of Elgar's *Sea-Pictures* (1898) seem to be audible, but this is feeble stuff by comparison. Though boldly published as his op. 1, they are best regarded as juvenilia. (They were republished ten years later as *Three Songs of the Sea* with the original opening song omitted.) However, with the *Three Songs*, op. 3 (1899–1905, *1905*), his own authentic voice can be heard for the first time. 'Love's philosophy' is still one of his most popular songs, and justifiably so. For sheer technical prowess there was nothing in English song at that time to compare with it. Its voluptuous harmonies and passionately soaring vocal line are entirely in keeping with the sensuousness of Shelley's verse. The rippling, toccata-like piano figuration – reflecting the fountains, rivers and oceans of the poem – swirl around the *legato* phrases of the vocal line, which is buffeted and buoyed up like a boat (see Ex. 8.4(b)). The elongation of the vocal line and repetition of words at the end of the song are, in this instance, entirely appropriate. No less successful is the way in which Quilter matches the gentle, lyrical flow of Tennyson's words in 'Now sleeps the crimson petal' (1899). Flexible syllabic word-setting, together with a fluid vocal line, results in some irregular barrings, most unusual for the time. Like its companion, this song has achieved great popularity, and within its modest aims this is deserved, though one wishes that Quilter had set the poem as Tennyson had written it. By omitting the three central couplets, he not only ruins the subtlety of Tennyson's exquisite lyric but also misses the musical opportunities that the original verse-form gave. Nevertheless, the song holds an important place in the composer's output. Its syllabic style of word-setting, with its resulting flexible vocal line, was to find many echoes later, not only in his own songs (notably *To Julia*), but also in the songs of a composer such as Peter Warlock. The third song of the group, 'Fill a glass with golden wine', is vastly inferior. Quilter has misread Henley's poem. The heavy-footed accompaniment suggests a rumbustious drinking-song, which the words neither propose nor require. This foursquare, solid setting is oddly insensitive in spirit and detail, ignoring such crucial points as enjambment and forcing poem and music into a shotgun marriage.

Four Child Songs, op. 5 (*1914*), settings of poems from R. L. Stevenson's *A Child's Garden of Verses*, need not delay us. Admittedly there may be ironic overtones in Stevenson's poems, but the sentiments strike one, at best, as smug and self-satisfied, extremely patronising and supercilious:

> Little Indian, Sioux or Crow,
> Little frosty Eskimo,
> Little Turk or Japanee,
> O! don't you wish that you were me?
> No. 4: 'Foreign children'

Quilter sets them in a correspondingly twee, nursery-tea-side manner. One wonders for whom they were written. In comparison, the 'Christopher Robin' collaborations between A. A. Milne and Harold Fraser-Simpson assume proportions of genius.

Quilter's next work is quite a different matter. The *Three Shakespeare Songs*, op. 6, were the first fruits of his lifelong attraction to Shakespeare. Shakespeare's lyrics have been, and probably need to be, re-interpreted by each generation of English songwriters. Just as Arne and J. C. Smith represent the 18th century, Parry the late 19th century, Warlock and Finzi the inter-war years and Michael Tippett the 1960s, so Quilter gives us the authentic interpretation for the Edwardian era. Indeed, the whole Shakespeare series captures Quilter's career in a microcosm, for in spite of fine individual songs, none of the later sets achieves the perfection of op. 6. Furthermore, this is the only set where there is any attempt at overall unity. There is a clear relationship and contrast of tonality (in the original, low-voice version: C minor; E-flat major; C minor/major) and of character and mood, as well as certain thematic cross-references (e.g. the use of a 'Phrygian' cadence in modulations to the dominant key in the first and third songs). The poignancy of 'Come away, death' is well captured in the drooping 7th at the word 'cypress' (bar 5) (see Ex. 8.2) and in the 'Phrygian' cadence at 'fair cruel maid' (bar 9). By leaving the voice in the air and unresolved at the end of the first stanza, he breaks the squareness of the strophic setting, and at the same time underlines the pathos of the words. His extension of the final lines of the poem shows how he can take a conventional ballad formula and make a meaningful musical point (Ex. 8.9).

Ex. 8.9

Note how he builds up the climax: first, the long-held C, then higher to an E-flat, and finally a melismatic phrase which droops 'weepingly' down to the dominant. Shakespeare understood as well as any Elizabethan lyricist the special requirements of 'words-for-music' and would hardly have placed the word 'weep' at this point in the poem unless he expected the composer to do something with it. 'O mistress mine', despite some imaginative subtleties in phrasing, is the weakest of the set. The piano's introduction (repeated as an interlude between strophes) has no apparent connection with the vocal line, and the extension at the end of the second verse seems self-indulgent here. The repetition of the opening line of the poem at the end is quite unjustified, made worse by an excruciatingly sloppy cadence. This, however, was the song that inspired Peter Warlock to take up songwriting, resulting in his own exquisite setting of the same lyric, 'Sweet-and-twenty'. The text of 'Blow, blow thou winter wind' has always presented composers with a problem. Is the mood to be defiant or despairing, melancholy or jolly? (See Moore, 1953: 120–2, for an interesting discussion of Quilter's setting.) Quilter (perhaps wisely) leaves the interpretation to the singer. The mood veers like a weathercock to all four compass points. The piano's opening hammer-blows, ambiguous with their missing thirds, are followed by a *forte* entry by the singer on his top notes, a defiance immediately tempered by the descending vocal line (Ex. 8.10).

Ex. 8.10

Again, in the major-mode refrain, the irony of Jaques's words is well caught in a feigned jog-trot jollity (note the leisurely pace: crotchet = 88) and the abrupt way in which the singer is required to leave his final note (Ex. 8.11).

Ex. 8.11

The true function of the 'hollow' chords of the piano's introduction is then revealed. Uncommitted to either mode, they lead us naturally back from the major refrain to the minor tonality of the second verse. One outstanding virtue of the set is Quilter's avoidance of the pitfalls of archaism and pastiche. There is no hint of the Wardour-street idiom that prettifies such contemporary 'period-songs' as 'Granny's second minuet' and the like. He uses melisma (first song) and bare-5th chords (third song) for musical, not archaic, reasons. It is a trap that he does not entirely avoid in the second set, op. 23.

To Julia, op. 8 (1905, *1906*), is one of Quilter's most ambitious conceptions. Whereas op. 6 is an integrated song-group, this is a true song-cycle, wherein the whole is greater than the parts, delightful and effective as these may be out of context. The work consists of settings of six short poems addressed by the poet Herrick to his mistress Julia. It is unified by two mottoes, the main one representing 'Julia' and a subsidiary one which, because of the way it complements the 'Julia' motif, could perhaps be regarded as representing 'Herrick' (Exs. 8.12(a) and (b)).

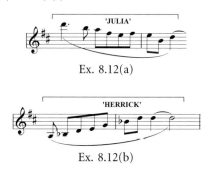

Ex. 8.12(a)

Ex. 8.12(b)

In addition, the very mention of Julia's name, motto or no, is invariably characterised by either a falling 3rd or 6th. An unusual feature is the insertion of two purely instrumental sections: a brief *Prelude,* and an even briefer *Interlude* between songs 5 and 6. Both are somewhat perfunctory and the cycle would function satisfactorily – indeed, benefit – without them. The sequence is well balanced and contrasted in tempo and character, brisk *allegro* songs (1, 4 and 6) complemented by gentler love-songs (2, 3 and 5). If the rippling piano textures of 'The bracelet' remind us of 'Love's philosophy', 'The maiden blush' and 'To daisies' are the quintessence of the composer's warm, romantic style fore-shadowed in 'Now sleeps the crimson petal'. But it is 'The night piece' and 'Julia's hair' that show Quilter at his most original. 'The night piece' is a deft scherzo, matching the nocturnal magic of Herrick's words, with accompani-ment and voice sharing equal honours. The form is subtly conceived. The first two verses are treated in varied strophic manner, with the 'Herrick' motif as prelude and interlude. In the third verse this motto is developed sequentially, moving almost obsessively through keys a minor third apart (E minor – G minor – B-flat minor) until, in a sudden blaze of light, we reach D-flat major – and 'Julia' (Ex. 8.13).

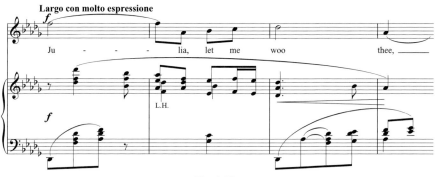

Ex. 8.13

'Julia's hair' is unique in Quilter's output: slow, almost static, a sensuous evocation of a lover's rapt contemplation. The opening vocal line – an adaptation of the 'Julia' motif – is accompanied, syllable by syllable, with 'frozen' 4/2 chords. The eventual resolution of these bittersweet sonorities onto a modal cadence at the words 'Have their reflected light; is magical (Ex. 8.14).

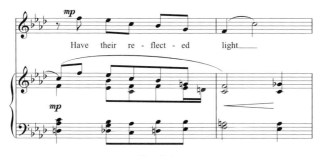

Ex. 8.14

If only Quilter could have sustained such imagination to the end. The final song, 'Cherry ripe', is a disappointment. The composer seems torn between public and poetic requirements and is (at the risk of a pun) unusually cavalier in his treatment of Herrick's verse. Instead of allowing the poem to suggest its own musical shape, as in the previous songs, he imposes a preconceived (*da capo*) form. The inevitable result is the most contrived and least integrated song in the cycle. Notwithstanding, *To Julia* is a masterly achievement of sustained, poetic lyricism. With its delicacy, balance and fragrance, and sheer facility of craftsmanship, it has qualities that English songs all too often lack. If it remind us of Quilter's debt to a composer like Fauré, it is none the worse for that.

The *Songs of Sorrow*, op. 10 (1907, *1908*), to four poems by Ernest Dowson, is Quilter's most personal work, the direct outcome of the depression left by an illness which he had recently suffered. (His original title was *Voices of Sorrow* (Banfield, 1985: 120).) There is a self-indulgent, almost melodramatic quality in these songs, though no-one can accuse the composer of failing to capture the overblown sentiments – the 'decaying roses' – of Dowson's poetry. The choice of text raises a problem. Though it is sensuously lyrical, Dowson's poetry is not particularly well suited to musical treatment. His long, sinuously convoluted sentences are a hazard to any songwriter. That Quilter mirrors these serpentine lines in his music is no reason for praise. The result is that both vocal line and piano accompaniment lack clear definition. There is no denying, however, the subtlety and strength of feeling of the songs – qualities that, in the hands of a sympathetic interpreter, would quite outweigh these criticisms. It is perhaps significant that the most effective song of the group, 'A land of silence', is also the simplest.

But how much more vital and imaginative he is when he chooses congenial texts, as in his op. 12. The *Seven Elizabethan Lyrics* ranks as one of his finest works. Though not so integrated as the previous sets, Quilter has clearly set out, in these delicate, pastoral love-lyrics, to achieve maximum diversity of mood and tonality. There is a neat balance of song-types, progressing from simple strophic settings in the first two songs and reaching greatest subtlety of form in the sixth song. The final song, 'Fair house of joy' (again in simple strophic form) acts as a jubilant coda. Of the seven songs, the fourth and sixth deserve special attention. Both show that, when handling stanzas of complex detail, he could work with fluency and skill. The gentle pastoral idiom of 'The faithless shepherdess' is captured in music as delicate as Meissen china. The 'archaisms' are slight but tasteful and the continual alteration of the basic metre between duple and triple gives the song a sprightliness in keeping with the text (Ex. 8.15).

Ex. 8.15

'By a fountainside', to the poem by Ben Jonson, is one of Quilter's finest inventions. Here he is at his most subtle, most gentle, most moving – most memorable (Ex. 8.16).

Ex. 8.16

The way in which he integrates the whole with the two motifs 'x' and 'y' is masterly. Sometimes they are divided between voice and piano (bars 23–5), whilst on another occasion the piano has the motifs with the voice singing a free descant above (bars 32–4).

Ex. 8.17

The harmonic figurations in the accompaniment show an exquisite refinement hardly matched by Fauré. Note, for example, how he echoes and re-echoes the vocal line (Ex. 8.17). The song is full of such felicities, yet Quilter skilfully manages to weld these into a cogent and beautifully-shaped statement.

The *Four Songs*, op. 14 (1909–10, *1910*), is an uneven group, in no way comparable to the preceding song-groups. The two Henley settings, 'A last year's rose' and 'Song of the blackbird', are routine stuff, the latter a naïve catalogue of bird-songs mentioned by the poet, whilst William Watson's 'April' is a trite waltz-song. But the first song, 'Autumn evening', is outstanding. The mood of Arthur Maquarie's modest elegy is eloquently caught in the piano's halting introduction and in the singer's melancholy, broken phrases in the final verse (Exs. 8.18(a) and (b)).

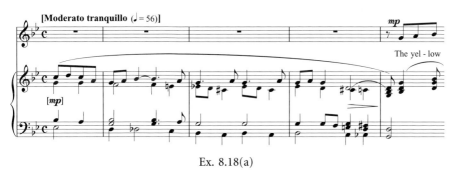

Ex. 8.18(a)

Ex. 8.18(b)

Op. 15–30 (1910–33)

The sad fact about Quilter's career is that, by the age of 32, he had reached what was to be the peak of his achievement. Despite a few individually fine songs written over the next twenty years, there is nothing to match opp. 6, 8 and 12. In many of the later songs he seems more concerned with the way of saying than with what is said. Hence he lavishes meticulous care on the most deplorable texts. Rather than explore new possibilities, he is content to re-work old formulas, and the vast majority of songs are re-visits to the rich veins he had already exploited.

Of the *Three Songs*, op. 15, the first, 'Cuckoo song' (Alfred Williams) (1913, *1913*) was written as a vehicle for the voice of Madame Melba, whilst the last, 'Blossom time' (1914, *1914*) was impeded before composition by the trite verses of Nora Hopper. (She had already supplied the lyric for 'June' and Quilter unfortunately returned to her yet again in 'Spring is at the door', op. 18, no. 4.)

However, the second song, 'Amaryllis at the fountain' (Anon. 16th century) (1914, *1914*), is a worthy pendant to the op. 12 set. One of Quilter's through-composed songs, it has a protean life all its own, constantly changing mood with the words: placid, pompous, stormy, fey, all in the space of 24 bars, yet – like 'By a fountainside' – firmly held together by its opening vocal motif. Brief as an epigram, it would make an excellent conclusion to a Quilter group in a recital.

Op. 18 is a ragbag of a collection which eventually took the form of two distinct song-groups (nos. 1–3, *Three Songs for Baritone or Tenor* and nos. 5 and 6, *Two September Songs*) with the remaining song, 'Spring is at the door', squeezed in between. The *Three Songs for Baritone or Tenor* are lightweight pieces. 'To wine and beauty' is a triple time re working of op. 3, no. 3 ('Fill a glass with golden wine'), with an identical modulation (to the dominant via the mediant) in its second phrase. But whereas, in the earlier setting, music seemed at variance with words, here the jaunty swing of the music is entirely in keeping with Rochester's sentiments. 'Where be you going?', setting a fugitive poem by Keats, is Quilter's contribution to the then popular genre of 'Devonshire' songs: it need not delay the singer. 'The jocund dance' is notable only as being the first of his Blake settings. The swinging tune and accompaniment – the music could well have strayed from an Edward German operetta – fit Blake's slight verses (from *Poetical Sketches*, 1783) in appropriate manner, though the rustic maiden, Kitty, is given a somewhat over-fulsome apostrophe at the end. The *Two September Songs* (*1916*), dedicated to Muriel Foster, are settings of Mary Coleridge; they appear as 'Chillingham I' and 'Chillingham II' in her *Collected Poems*. Though light in weight, they are, strangely enough, more adventurous harmonically than anything Quilter had previously written. Parallel 9ths, in the manner of Delius, are handled with great deftness. They are best heard in the first song, 'Through the sunny garden', where, as upward-drifting chords, they underline the words 'Far away and blue' (Ex. 8.19).

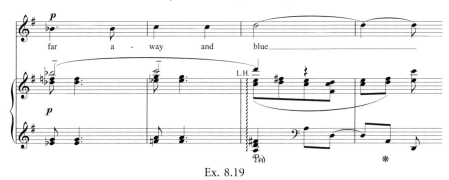

Ex. 8.19

'Dream valley', the first of *Three Songs of William Blake*, op. 20 (1916–17, *1917*), is considered to be one of his finest songs; Sydney Northcote goes so far as to describe it as a masterpiece (1966: 100). The gentle, melancholy poem – the title is Quilter's own – is treated to a simple syllabic setting. Unpretentious and delicately attractive, it effectively captures the dreamy atmosphere, though one would hesitate to make larger claims. Its two companions lack its delicate perfection. In 'The wild flower's song' he cushions the impact of Blake's final, epigrammatic line 'I met with scorn' by repeating the first verse afterwards. 'Daybreak' (Blake's own title is 'Morning') is more successful, capturing the urgency of the poet's dawn journey:

> To find the western path,
> Right through the gates of wrath
>   I urge my way . . .

Both songs, however, suffer from over-elaborate treatment of what are, after all, very simple poems.

A similar stricture can be levelled at 'Cherry valley' and 'I wish and I wish' from *Three Pastoral Songs*, op. 22 (Joseph Campbell) (1920, *1921*), highlighted in this case by painfully banal texts. The first song of the group, 'I will go with my father a-ploughing', is more effective in its unassuming way, though it lacks the urgency of Ivor Gurney's more familiar setting. These songs were originally scored for piano trio accompaniment, which perhaps accounts for the unusually elaborate textures in the solo piano version.

Some fifteen years separate the first set of Shakespeare songs from the second, but it is significant that Quilter's idiom remains fundamentally unchanged. Admittedly there is a conscious effort to leaven the normally chordal, arpeggiated textures with contrapuntal imitation, but this is confined to piano introductions and interludes and is hardly more than an historical nod. Unlike op. 6, *Five Shakespeare Songs*, op. 23 (1919–21, *1921*) was not conceived as a set. The second and third songs were, in fact, published separately in 1919, the latter as a duet for soprano and alto in its original form. In the first set he had skilfully managed to skirt the drawing-room (though, in the case of 'O mistress mine', only just). In several places in the second set, however, the drawing-room is all too close. In 'Under the greenwood tree', we can all but hear the teacups rattle. There's no sound from the greenwood; winter and rough weather are far away on the other side of the windowpane. Feste's curtain-song, 'Hey, ho, the wind and the rain' is given musical comedy treatment. The bitterness and irony of Shakespeare's words are ironed out into pleasant frippery. It is significant that Quilter omits Shakespeare's original verse 4: 'toss pots' and 'drunken heads' have no place in his refined version of Shakespeare's world. The lush harmonic ending to 'Take, O take those lips away' is mere prettification and no response to the poignancy of the words. The greatest disappointment, however, is the first song, 'Fear no more the heat of the sun'. It lacks the sense of doom and foreboding which the slow, sarabande-like tread gives to Gerald Finzi's fine setting, and fails to reach the heart of this great elegy. The song begins impressively enough, but is immediately spoilt when Quilter drops back into accompanimental cliché (Ex. 8.20).

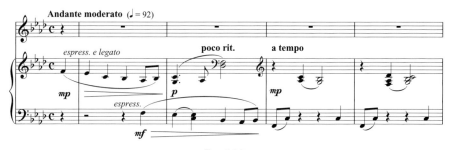

Ex. 8.20

Inspiration sags even more in the third verse – sweet, cloying 9ths and lush discords are no response to 'Fear no more the lightning flash/Nor the all-dreaded thunderstone' – and at the words, 'Fear no slander, censure rash', we again descend into the realms of musical comedy. As Scott Goddard wryly commented: 'Elegantly he paints the words each in skilfully chosen colours, constructing a kaleidoscope of harmonies, seen through which, life becomes all prettiness, even in its sadness (1925: 216) (Ex. 8.21).

Ex. 8.21

Only at the final lines of the Envoy is there a return of his usual sensitivity and imagination. But by then, of course, it is too late. In this instance, Quilter has chosen a substantial poem to set that has proved to be beyond his scope. How ironical it is that the most successful song of the set is the one that requires the lightest touch and, because of the over-familiarity of the lyric, was the one least likely to succeed. The attractiveness of 'It was a lover and his lass' is as much due to the freshness of response to this 'over-exposed' lyric as anything. Note in particular the deft way in which he phrases the poem (Ex. 8.22). This time the imitative opening is skilfully integrated into the body of the song.

Ex. 8.22

Though the set as a whole is a disappointment after op. 6, it has a certain period charm, akin to Frederick Austin's arrangements for *The Beggar's Opera* dating from the same year.

Five English Love Lyrics, op. 24, and *Six Songs*, op. 25, are no more than loose collections of solo songs written over a period of seven years (1921–8) and brought together for the convenience of publication. There are some fine individual songs, amongst which one must mention 'Morning song' (Thomas Heywood), op. 24, no. 2 (1922, *1922*), 'The time of roses' (Thomas Hood), op. 24, no. 5 (1928, *1928*) and 'Music, when soft voices die' (Shelley), op. 25, no. 5 (1926, *1927*). But two are particularly outstanding: 'Go, lovely rose' (Edmund Waller), op. 24, no. 3 (1922, *1923*) and 'Arab love-song' (Shelley), op. 25, no. 4 (1927, *1927*), and these deserve close attention. 'Go, lovely rose' shows what magic Quilter can achieve when he chooses a lyric that suits his particular genius. Though he has obviously taken note of the regularity of Waller's stanza pattern (see epigraph), he avoids a simple strophic setting. Instead, he allows the poem to suggest its own natural course. The result – though motivically unified – sounds like an extended, impassioned soliloquy. The irregular lengths of the five-line stanzas produce an asymmetry that he uses to musical advantage (Ex. 8.23(a)).

Ex. 8.23(a)

Note the subtle way in which he captures the inflections of the verse, and so achieves rhythmic variety. All is caught within a shapely musical line, rising to a climax on the fourth phrase, with a simple yet affecting coda on the fifth. At the same time the five component phrases themselves have a structural purpose in the song. The second verse begins strophically, then veers into the mediant key and runs, without break, into the third verse. In contrast to the *cantabile* character of the opening strophes, the words are here treated in a free, *parlando* fashion, the music fleetingly surfacing into new tonal regions (submediant major). Following the poet's hint, the composer then makes an enjambment of the last two stanzas, and it is with the opening words of the final stanza that the music reaches it impassioned climax (Ex. 8.23(b)). The flattened tonic 7th thrusts us into the subdominant and it is not until the final two lines of the poem that the music returns to the home key *and* makes the necessary recapitulation of the main thematic material (Ex. 8.23(c)). This is one of the magic moments of English song, and one has only to look closely to understand why. Notice how deftly musical and poetic considerations are counterpointed.

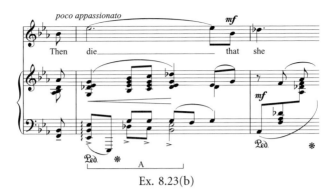

Ex. 8.23(b)

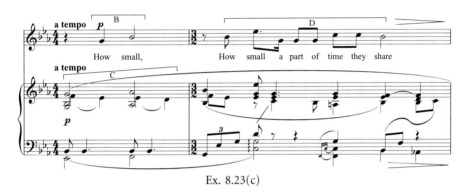

Ex. 8.23(c)

Motivically the final stanza recaps the first strophe. Phrase A, however, is in the piano bass, whilst the voice has a mixture of phrases B and D. The *tonal* recap comes with the fourth line of the verse, when motives B and C are heard simultaneously in voice and piano, followed by a variant of D, and the song ends with an augmented version of the original refrain-line. It is an example of consummate craftsmanship, a masterly balancing of ambiguities. 'Arab love-song', a setting of Shelley's poem, 'My faint spirit was sitting in the light/Of thy looks', has suffered unaccountable neglect.

Ex. 8.24

It is one of Quilter's most powerful, 'masculine' songs. Appropriate to the 'galloping hooves' of the 'barb', the shifting harmonies are suggested rather than sounded, whilst the voice rides, as it were, on the back of the accompaniment. Notice how he embeds subtle echoes, from voice to piano, within the fleeting texture (Ex. 8.24). There are few English songs that have the dash and buoyancy of this little gem. All is achieved with the greatest economy.

The *Two Songs* to poems by R. L. Stevenson, op. 26 (1922, *1922*), are, like the earlier Mary Coleridge settings, essentially light music, remarkable only for the extreme refinement of texture and idiom that Quilter was to cultivate in his later songs. The central section of 'In the highlands' is tonally and harmonically more adventurous than anything he had written. But why? The slight text hardly warrants it. 'Over the land is April' shows Quilter virtually rewriting Stevenson's lyric to fit his own preconceived musical scheme. The 'third stanza' – Stevenson wrote only two – is entirely Quilter's own invention.

With *Five Jacobean Lyrics*, op. 28 (1923–5, *1926*), dedicated to Mark Raphael, Quilter returns to the idea of an extended song-group, though, as with the second Shakespeare set, this larger concept came afterwards. 'The jealous lover' was written and published in 1923, the remaining songs in 1925, and all five published as a set in 1926. There is no attempt to unify the group thematically, and the fact that the first and last have the same tonality has no structural significance. Except for the second song, none has anything new or original to say. 'The jealous lover' (Rochester) is a cantabile love-song in triple time, the kind of song he was to essay again, more memorably, in 'Who is Silvia' from the third Shakespeare set. 'I dare not ask a kiss' is a nondescript Herrick setting, too brief to make an impact and inferior to his earlier Herrick settings in *To Julia*. His treatment of Lovelace's 'To Althea from prison' is a disaster. Poem and music are so much at odds with one another that one begins to wonder if the composer had accidentally set the wrong words. Why the tonal wanderings in the second verse? – the words don't suggest them. And how can the music of the opening verse possibly be recapped, virtually unchanged, in the final verse, where the words are of a quite different character? Thus it is that the key-line of the poem, 'Stone walls do not a prison make', is set with a nonchalance verging on the insensitive. A similar aberration occurs in 'The constant lover' (Suckling) where, once again, he superimposes a musical form onto the verse by repeating the opening strophe at the end, *da capo* fashion (cf. 'Cherry ripe' from *To Julia*). The most impressive song of the set is 'Why so pale and wan?' Rhythmically buoyant and alive, harmonically adventurous, abrupt and lyrical by turns, it captures admirably the distraught spirit of Suckling's poem. The most unexpected feature is the form. Having built up what seems to be a simple strophic structure, he then smashes it. Verse 3 is set in declamatory fashion, with an unexpectedly abrupt – though nonetheless effective – cadence (Ex. 8.25).

Ex. 8.25

A similar inconsistency affects the third set of Shakespeare songs (*Four Shakespeare Songs*, op. 30 (1926–33, *1933*)). 'Who is Silvia?' bears a close resemblance to 'The jealous lover' (see Ex. 8.5), though the result is more memorable, marred only by unnecessary repetition of the word 'garlands'. 'When daffodils begin to peer' emasculates Shakespeare's earthy lyric. (Did Quilter really know who Autolycus's 'aunts' were, I wonder? He treats them as family relatives rather than tumbling whores.) The same criticism must be levelled at 'Sigh no more, ladies'. Despite elaborate fluctuations of tempo, he misses the point of the lyric completely. Only in the third song, 'How should I your true love know?', does he have anything vital to say. This setting of Ophelia's song from *Hamlet* has a poignant beauty, made all the more moving by its unaffecting simplicity. The delicate piano accompaniment is leavened throughout by echo-phrases, and there is telling use of the 'Phrygian-2nd' in the middle verse (Ex. 8.26).

Ex. 8.26

This is a song that should be far better known and one of the few songs by Quilter that is entirely appropriate for a female singer. 'I arise from dreams of thee', op. 29 (1919, *1931*), is something of an exception in the composer's output. An extended setting of Shelley's poem and subtitled 'serenade', it is scored for tenor and orchestra – there is an effective transcription for voice and piano – and was first performed at the Harrogate Festival in 1929. It is one of his most ambitious concepts, yet at the same time one of his most personal. Here his sensuously chromatic harmonies are entirely in keeping with the dreamy quality of Shelley's verse. There is a wealth of accompanimental detail, from the quietly mysterious opening bars (Ex. 8.27) to the extended coda, with its wisps of bird-song (a clear homage to Delius). Wide-ranging in emotion, from the wearily lovesick to the impetuously-passionate, it deserves more than its handful of performances.

Ex. 8.27

Later songs (1933–53)

There is little more to relate. Quilter's career as a song-composer had virtually ended. If only he had understood this himself and refused to publish any more. Perhaps privately he did realise that his Muse had burnt out, for, significantly, none of his later songs is graced with an opus number with the exception of two Shakespeare settings, op. 32. There is no denying that the same masterly skill and craftsmanship are still often evident in these later songs. Some show interesting new features: a tendency to start the vocal line on a discord ('Drooping wings' and 'Daisies after rain') and a tonal adventurousness not noticeable in earlier works. But all this care is lavished on texts that, for the most part, are trite and banal. Such exquisite over-refinement is a sure sign of decadence: perfection of the means, but lack of substance; the medium without the message. Here we have the saddest thing: a craftsman with nothing to say.

Even when the poets of his choice do rise above the mediocre, the result is often disappointing. None of the later Shakespeare settings attain the quality of the earlier. They are like unmemorable encores given by an ageing singer on his farewell tour. 'Orpheus with his lute', the first of *Two Shakespeare Songs*, op. 32 (1938, *1939*) – which of all Shakespeare's lyrics calls for memorable musical ideas – dies from sheer dullness. Its companion, 'When icicles hang by the wall', slips disastrously into musical comedy routine when it reaches its refrain, with greasy Joan endlessly keeling the pot. 'Hark, hark, the lark' (*1946*) is a weak rehash of the rippling-toccata style which he had essayed so memorably once and for all in 'Love's philosophy' forty years previously, whilst 'Tell me, where is fancy bred?' (*1951*) is yet another triple-time *cantabile* song. Though he attempts to capture the mystery of 'Come unto these yellow sands' (*1951*) by sudden key-swings from tonic major to submediant major, the musical material is commonplace.

Of the remaining songs, which include the insipid 'Come Lady Day' (*1938*), the embarrassing jingoism of 'Freedom' (*1940*) and the Celtic doodlings of 'The walled-in garden' (*1952*), there is little to salvage. Occasionally the old Quilter magic flickers. 'Music and moonlight' (Shelley, 1935, *1947*), with its guitar-like accompaniment, is a graceful serenade and has a harmonic piquancy that is new. The 'out-of-key' start to the vocal line is a refreshing novelty (Ex. 8.28).

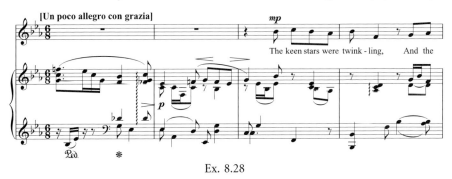

Ex. 8.28

And there is a poignancy about 'A song at parting' (Christina Rossetti, *1952*) that goes beyond the fact that it was to be his own epitaph. Ironically, the one work of these later years that seems to have real survival value is *The Arnold Book of Old Songs* (*1947*), his arrangements of old popular songs and folksongs, the best of which are worthy alternatives in recital programmes to the usual Grainger or Britten. But taken as a whole these last songs are a sad catalogue and they inevitably raise the question, for whom was he writing? By the mid-1930s the public for his songs had dwindled considerably. In the changed world of the 1930s and 1940s, Edwardian elegance had no place. In retrospect, looking at the songs that he wrote in the last twenty years of his life, one feels that, deep in his heart, Quilter realised this too.

C. W. Orr once remarked: 'It has been well said that whereas genius is always renewing itself, talent can only end by becoming self-repetitive.' That Quilter was a songwriter of great talent rather than genius is indisputable. His choice of text and subject-matter, as we have seen, was extremely limited. Yet he was himself fully aware of his limitations. Only on rare occasions did he attempt to set a substantial text – e.g. 'Fear no more the heat of the sun' – to which he was unable to do justice. The range of his song-types was also limited. All the basic patterns he used were already adumbrated in songs written before 1910: the *cantabile* vocal line over a rippling toccata-like accompaniment of 'Love's philosophy'; the sustained, *bel canto*, *andante* song (usually in triple time) of 'To daisies'; the playful *allegretto* with its bantering rhythm of 'The faithless shepherdess'; the short, through-composed lyric in binary form of 'Damask roses' and 'Brown is my love'; the melancholy *andante* (often in duple time) with syllabic word-setting of 'Now sleeps the crimson petal' and 'Autumn evening'. He increasingly relied on these song-types and many of his later songs are hardly more than re-workings of old formulas. Though he sought to raise the artistic level of the drawing-room song, he was perfectly prepared to accept the limitations of its scope. For example, voice and piano are restricted to traditional roles. Never are we given the pleasure of hearing the voice alone, unaccompanied. And, except for the prelude and interlude in *To Julia* – neither of which is particularly effective – the piano is never allowed to function independently, except for brief introductions, interludes and codas. Elsewhere it keeps to its role of underpinning the vocal line. Like a 'gentleman's gentleman', it never obtrudes.

But perhaps Quilter's greatest limitation was his lack of vision. There is nothing in his output to match the dark forebodings of Warlock's *The Curlew* or, at the other extreme, the exuberant high spirits of Warlock's 'sociable songs'. Nor is there a song with the dramatic sweep of Gurney's 'The folly of being comforted'. His aims were modest, his talent that of a Campion rather than a Dowland. The title of one of his later songs, 'The walled-in garden', could aptly serve as a metaphor to summarise his career. He was content to cultivate a small plot of ground: a garden with neatly-trimmed lawns and a variety of exquisitely fragrant flowers. (Interestingly, many of his songs are about, or refer to, flowers: 'Now sleeps the crimson petal', 'To daisies', 'Damask roses', 'A last year's rose', 'The wild flower's song', 'Go, lovely rose', 'The time of roses', 'Daisies after rain'.) One wishes at times that he would look over the wall and describe to us the countryside beyond. But he never does. It is revealing that, in his setting of Mary Coleridge's 'The valley and the hill', he omits one of the stanzas:

> O the red heather on the moss-wrought rock,
> And the fir-tree stiff and straight,
> The shaggy old sheep-dog barking at the flock,
> And the rotten old five-barred gate!

Shaggy sheep dogs and rotten old gates have no more place in his world than 'drunken heads' and 'doxies over the dale'. If his thoughts ever strayed outside his garden, it was to a 'dream valley' world, 'over the hills and far away'. Yet within this unpretentious garden-plot of song he was the supreme professional. He never miscalculates; his songs are always effective, a delight to sing and play. Moreover, they appeal not only to the experienced professional but also to the aspiring amateur and, from the other side of the concert platform, have achieved wide popularity with the listening public. Such a talent for popular communication should never be underestimated.

9

Frank Bridge (1879–1941)

'Tis but a week since down the glen
    The trampling horses came
– Half a hundred fighting men
    With all their spears aflame!
They laughed and clattered as they went,
    And round about their way
The blackbirds sang with one consent
    In the green leaves of May.

Never again shall I see them pass;
    They'll come victorious never;
Their spears are withered all as grass,
    Their laughter's laid for ever;
And where they clattered as they went,
    And where their hearts were gay,
The blackbirds sing with one consent
    In the green leaves of May.

Gerald Gould: 'Horsemen'

Frank Bridge as a songwriter presents a problem. Whereas most of the composers in this survey wrote songs throughout their working lives, Bridge wrote all his songs at the beginning of his career, before his decisive turn to 'modernism' in the 1920s, and songs were never a major part of his output. His songwriting spans less than a quarter of a century, from 1901–25. Of his 55 completed songs, 42 were written before 1914 and only five between 1920 and 1925. What is more, his songwriting during those twenty-five years was spasmodic: there are three gaps when he produced nothing at all (1908–12, 1914–17 and 1920–2). It would seem then that he was an unenthusiastic songwriter; not uncommitted, perhaps, but reluctant to place the medium high on his compositional priorities. Unlike Ireland, Vaughan Williams and Holst, he chose not to explore the possibilities of the solo song in a post-war context. The handful of songs he did write in the early 1920s – the three Tagore settings, 'Goldenhair' and 'Journey's end' – show fascinatingly what he could achieve using an advanced harmonic and textural idiom – so much so that one regrets his inability or reluctance to continue. He was by upbringing an instrumental musician, and an instrumental composer at heart; text-setting, one feels, cramped his style. In no way, then, do the songs represent his musical career in microcosm, as with Vaughan Williams or Ireland. Yet with all these reservations and qualifications, Bridge's harvest of songs is too rich and too high in quality to ignore.

From 1899–1903, Bridge was a student at the RCM where, like so many of his contemporaries, he studied composition with Stanford. Stanford's influence on his songs is not, however, particularly noticeable, except maybe in the importance that Bridge placed throughout his career on craftsmanship. From the start, Bridge's harmonic idiom was richer and more sensuous than Stanford's, his ear attuned to the popular idioms of the Victorian ballad. But if that is where his songs are rooted, when compared with the general run of popular ballads published at the turn-of-the-century, Bridge's songs are superior in technical refinement, richness of colour and harmony, and inspiration. Together with Quilter, he raised this humdrum, ossified art-form to a level that few would have thought possible. The songs from the period 1914–19 show a marked individuality. Though the smoke of the Victorian concert-room can still be detected, songs such as the three Mary Coleridge settings show a refinement and technical assurance closer to French songwriters such as Fauré and Debussy and well beyond that of their English counterparts. This radicality increases in the songs written after the First World War, with the influence of continental composers such as Schoenberg and Berg. ''Tis but a week' and 'What shall I your true love tell?' show an extremely dissonant, polytonal idiom, whilst the Tagore songs verge on atonality. In all his music Bridge possessed a professionalism beyond his peers, which made many of his British contemporaries appear little more than talented amateurs.

His choice of poetry for setting is, however, another matter. It seems haphazard, opportunist, lacking the literary discrimination of Ireland and Quilter or the dedication of Vaughan Williams and Butterworth. One senses that he didn't read poetry much or widely, and possibly only to find poems to set to music. His preference was for the light and gracefully-written, for poetry that set a clear, unambiguous mood and with little philosophical depth. It is noticeable that, unlike his distinguished contemporaries, Somervell, Quilter, Ireland, Butterworth, Gurney and Warlock, he did not attempt to write a song-cycle. The majority of settings are not of an English poet but of a German poet in English translation, Heine. There are nine complete Heine settings, almost every one to a different – often indifferent – translator: so we have Heine *apud* Kate Kroeker ('E'en as a lovely flower'), Francis Hueffer ('Rising when the dawn still faint is'), James Thomson ('BV') ('The violets blue') and Emma Lazarus ('All things that we clasp'). Other poets he favoured include Herrick, Shelley, Robert Bridges, Mary Coleridge and Rabindranath Tagore. Mary Coleridge and Tagore inspired some of his finest songs, though the difference between the gentle refined verses of the Victorian lady and the sensuous love-poems of the Bengali could hardly be greater. Many poets were set only once; they range chronologically from Shakespeare ('Blow, blow thou winter wind') to Rupert Brooke and Gerald Gould, taking in Keats, Landor, Tennyson, Arnold, Whitman, Yeats and Joyce. He also turned to more obscure writers, such as Thomas

Ashe (1836–89) and H. D. Lowry (1869–1906). Altogether, excluding Anon., he set twenty-six different poets: an enormous tally considering his relatively small output of songs. These facts only underline the feeling that Bridge's literary tastes were not strongly developed or focussed.

From a technical point of view, Bridge shows in his songs the same precision and professionalism to be found in his instrumental music. His word-setting is immaculate; he weighs and balances his texts, allows the words to breathe and goes to their dramatic core, nowhere more so than in the final songs. But though highly sensitive to 'just-note-and-accent', he never allows this to dominate his music, as is sometimes the case with Parry and Finzi. (In this respect he shows a close parallel with his pupil, Benjamin Britten.) By any standard his piano accompaniments are faultless; there is none of the awkwardness of Vaughan Williams or the limited keyboard technique of Finzi. Like Roger Quilter's, his accompaniments are idiomatic, fitting the fingers like a glove and supporting the voice, but at the same time they make full use of the piano's potential without distracting from the vocal line. This is discernible throughout his career, from an early song such as 'Go not, happy day' to the Tagore, Wolfe and Joyce settings of the 1920s.

There is, however, one aspect of his songwriting that does cause concern, namely the cavalier way in which he alters some of his texts by omission and/or repetition. This is a discourtesy that often occurs in songwriting, and something which poets have repeatedly complained about (*vide* Housman and Vaughan Williams's omission of stanzas from 'Is my team ploughing?') Even a composer particularly sensitive to poetry like Quilter occasionally repeats words and phrases, or even (as in 'Cherry ripe') whole stanzas. Bridge regularly rejigs his texts, usually for reasons of musical shape. In two of his best-known songs, 'Love went a-riding' and 'When you are old', he creates a ternary shape by repeating the poem's opening stanza at the end, much in the style of an 18th-century *da capo* aria. But whereas with the *da capo* aria the poet/librettist would have been aware that the composer intended to do this, neither Mary Coleridge nor W. B. Yeats would have expected or welcomed it. Such repetition can only alter the sense of the poem. (In the case of Yeats's setting, Bridge compounds the insult by ignoring the poet's own final stanza – a case of committing sins of repetition and omission at one and the same time: see Introduction, p. 12.) In acting in this way Bridge highlights the instrumental thinking of his songwriting, his desire to impose an abstract form onto his text. It is an attitude that has its virtues as well as its drawbacks; as a result his songs are concentrated, economical and formally satisfying.

In his study of Bridge's music (1976), Anthony Payne recognises four periods in the composer's career: the Early Years (c.1901–12), the Middle Period (c.1912–20), the Years of Transition (c.1920–5) and the Final Harvest (c.1925–41). All of Bridge's songs were written within the first three of these periods, and in commenting on them it will be convenient to demarcate them thus.

The early songs, 1901–12

These form a clear group, divided from the songs of the Middle Period by a 'song-silence' of four years between 1908 and 1912. Some of these early songs were published in *The Vocalist* magazine during 1905; others, including 'Blow, blow thou winter wind', 'Come to me in my dreams' and 'Fair daffodils', were not published until the following decade. Though many of these songs lack individuality, Bridge's personal voice can be heard in songs such as 'Come to me in my dreams' and 'Fair daffodils'. The dominant poet of the period is Heinrich Heine, whom Bridge sets in a wide variety of translations; the best know is 'E'en as a lovely flower' (transl. Kroeker) (1903, *1905*). This is the poem notoriously criticised by D. H. Lawrence in his pamphlet 'Pornography and obscenity' (1929) and equally notoriously set to music by Lord Berners in his *Lieder Album* (1913) as an apostrophe to a white pig. Whether or not Heine had porcine love in view, Bridge clearly hadn't, and he gives the poem full drawing-room ballad treatment, with richly syncopated chords (doubled between the hands) throbbing beneath a sustained vocal line. There are, however, more subtle touches. The harmonies are richer and the tonal palette more wide-ranging than found in any ballad, and rather than give the poem conventional strophic treatment, he through-composes the two stanzas of the poem. The first two lines are set *quasi* recitative and he repeats them at the end to give a framework to the song. 'The violets blue' (transl. James Thomson and originally published in *The City of Dreadful Night and Other Poems*, 1880) (1906, *1916*) is a true miniature – the Heine/Thomson poem is only five lines long – but Bridge almost bursts the confines of its 25 bars in the intensity of its emotion. It is a remarkable achievement, which makes one wonder why he could not have done something similar with 'All things we clasp' (transl. Emma Lazarus) (1907, *1916*). Here, for some reason, Bridge omits the first of Heine's two stanzas, but then proceeds to set the remaining quatrain twice. Perhaps he felt that the decapitated poem was too short to make a song about, even though, as we have observed, he managed to do so convincingly with 'The violets blue'.

The two early Keats settings are disappointing. 'The Devon maid' (1903, *1905*) is an early example of the 'Glorious Devon' genre of songs. The poem is one of Keats's least characteristic and the song equally uncharacteristic of Bridge. 'Adoration' (1905, *1918*), which rises step by step to a bombastic climax, relies for its interest on the rich harmonies of its accompaniment. Bridge's only Shakespeare setting, 'Blow, blow thou winter wind' (1903, *1916*), reflects Quilter's contemporaneous version in its use of minor mode/major mode contrast between verse and refrain, but lacks Quilter's memorability. Bridge, however, makes better sense of the awkward final line, 'This life is most jolly', than do most setters of this poem. The outstanding songs of this period are 'Go not, happy day', 'Fair daffodils', 'So perverse' and 'Come to me in my dreams'.

'Go not, happy day' (1903, *1905*), a setting of one of the lyrics from Tennyson's *Maud*, is, with 'Love went a-riding', Bridge's best-known song. The piano has a

delightfully irregular, windmill-like ostinato: sextuplets over two quavers, but in a
cross-rhythmic pattern (three groups of four semiquavers in the r.h. against four
quavers in the l.h.), over which the singer floats an insouciant melody (Ex. 9.1).

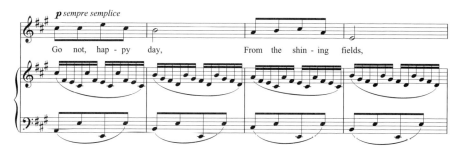

Ex. 9.1

Bridge casts the poem in ternary shape, the opening verse repeated at the end
(in this case a repeat sanctioned by the poet), and wisely he omits the four
strange lines about the 'Red Man' by his Cedar Tree. It is a song that never fails
to thrill, a superb example of Bridge balancing technique and imagination.
'Fair daffodils' (1905, *1919*), on the other hand, is an unjustly neglected song,
with a memorable and deftly written piano part. Herrick's two long stanzas are
set A(ab)/B(cb), the new music at the opening of the second strophe melding
back again into the concluding music of the first. There is an unexpected move
from the tonic, G major, up a tone to A major before the final lines. The singer,
however, ignores this and cadences back immediately into G major: unexpected
but most effective. Though there is some awkward word-setting, as, for
example, in the prolongation of unimportant words like 'And' and 'Or', the
song deserves to be better known. 'So perverse' (1905, *1905*) – Bridges set by
Bridge – is a curious little song that has invited extreme reaction, from 'Wryly
humorous' (Payne, 1976: 29) to 'triviality mindlessly courted . . .best forgotten'
(Banfield, 1985: 72). Robert Bridges' ironic triolet is set over a quiet jogtrotting
tonic-subdominant bass – as basic an idea as you'll find in an art-song: indeed,
it is almost a non-accompaniment. The artfulness comes in the way Bridge
keeps you waiting at the cadences, by elongating them well past their expected
expiry date: two bars of song, four bars of 'keep-you-waiting'. It is a trifle, but
neatly-turned nevertheless. 'Come to me in my dreams' (1906, *1918*) sets
Matthew Arnold's poem 'Longing' from his sequence 'Faded leaves', first
published in *Empedocles on Etna* (1852). This is one of Bridge's finest songs,
in which he magically transcends the sentimental naivety of the drawing-room
ballad tradition. The four verses are set as a ternary shape: A B1 B2 A (the
reprise of the first strophe again sanctioned by the poet). It is rich in ideas, but
how economically Bridge uses them! The piano introduces several important
motives that are used later on (Ex. 9.2). The chord marked * acts as a way-
marker to introduce verses 2 and 3, which are set to new music, more animated
and flowing.

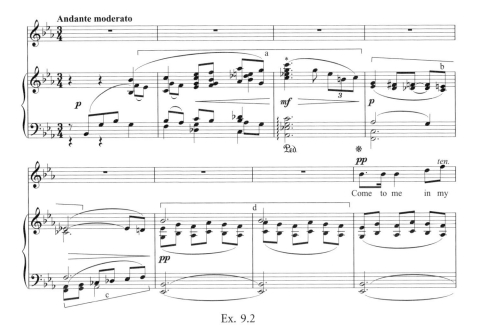

Ex. 9.2

Verse 3 sets out with this new material a semitone higher, reaching a climax at the words 'Come now, and let me dream it truth!' At this point the music comes to an abrupt half on a B minor chord, and a slower, recitative-like section – 'And part my hair, and kiss my brow,/And say – *My love, why suff'rest thou?*' – leads back to the original D-flat major tonality and the floating 6ths of (d) for the reprise of the opening strophe. Banfield (1985: 11– 12) picks out Matthew Arnold's poem for censure: 'This kind of verse, though not exactly bad, is impossible to make fresh' and cites Bridge's song as an illustration. Others will feel that Bridge has made of Arnold's 'faded leaves' a little masterpiece of desire and yearning.

Bridge's *Three Songs* for medium voice, viola and piano were composed between November 1906 and January 1907. Bridge himself took part in the first performance, surprisingly as a pianist rather than viola-player. Settings of three different poets, all three are slow and melancholy in nature, none moving beyond *Andante moderato* in tempo, as though Bridge was deliberately showing the traditional aspect of the viola obbligato's personality. The addition of a viola to the traditional singer-piano format inevitably puts a new slant on song-writing, with the viola inevitably acting as a concertante instrument. One of the features of the songs is the seemingly effortless way in which Bridge combines the three performers. It is instructive to see how he deploys the viola, differently in each song. In the first it shares material with the singer and piano, in the second has a ritornello and in the third duets with the singer. The weakest of the group is the third, a setting of Shelley's 'Music, when soft voices die', originally written with a cello obbligato. Against the duetting soloists, the piano has an arpeggiated sextuplet-semiquaver figure with augmented 5th chords. The text-setting however lacks any striking features and is marred by several textual misreadings. 'Where is it that our soul doth go?' is another Heine poem in translation by Kate Kroeker. It is a powerful musical response to a common-place versification. Bridge sets only the final verse of the three-verse poem and rearranges the pieces into an intricate musical jigsaw, held together by the viola's sad little ritornello. The most ambitious and most effective song is the first, 'Far, far from each other', setting verses from Matthew Arnold's poem 'Parting' (one of the 'Marguerite' poems from his *Switzerland* sequence). He again omits stanzas, choosing only verses 3, 4 and 6, which he sets as a ternary song. Note how he skilfully integrates the two main musical ideas. At the opening, the viola and piano have two counterpointing themes: viola (a), piano (b); on entering, the singer takes over (a), the viola (b) whilst the piano has only an accompanimental role (c) (Ex. 9.3). This is vocal chamber music of the highest quality.

Ex. 9.3

The middle-period songs, 1912–20

After a gap of four years, 1908–12, Bridge returned to songwriting in 1912 with a group of songs which, whilst continuing the style of the earlier songs, shows an added maturity and confidence, particularly in the two Mary Coleridge settings. He could still hark back to the Royalty Ballad, and both 'Isobel' (1912, *1913*) and 'O that it were so' (c.1912, *1913*) distinctly show their popular origins. Even so, both contain memorable moments: 'Isobel' (Digby Goddard-Fenwick) with the exquisite cadence of its ritornello (an A major chord over a B in the bass leading to a dominant 7th on C-sharp); 'O that it were so' (Landor) in the disarmingly conversational tone of its opening stanza. The Landor setting is an excellent example of Bridge's ability to pace a song. The poem consists of two three-line stanzas. Bridge sets the first in unadorned recitative-style, which takes up a mere ten bars, less than a quarter of the song. The second stanza, in which the music suddenly blazes out emotionally in full drawing-room ballad style, is expanded and elaborated, to take up the song's remaining 23 bars.

There is no such meretriciousness in 'Strew no more roses' (1913, *1917*), an adaptation of the final stanza of Matthew Arnold's poem 'The new sirens' (1849). Here again he makes a ternary pie out of the text by repeating the opening strophe, with slight variation, at the end. Yet that variation proves to be one of the highlights of the song. After the phrase 'O pale maidens!', instead of voice and piano continuing immediately onto the final line, the piano is heard alone, as though the singer were too speechless with sorrow to continue. The song shows Bridge's developing technical resources: rich chromatic harmonies veer back and forth from E minor tonic to E-flat major beneath a highly flexible vocal line (Ex. 9.4).

Ex. 9.4

The most important works from the pre-war period are the *Two Songs* to poems by Mary Coleridge (1914, *1916*). A well-contrasted pairing, they show how much more adventurous Bridge's harmonic and textural imagination was than that of his British contemporaries. 'Where she lies asleep' is one of the most beautiful lullabies in the English repertoire, a delicious berceuse which deserves to be as well known as Rachmaninov's 'To the children', with which it shares the same gentle, rapt mood. As Anthony Payne has observed (1976: 29–30), in its

warm, flowing lyricism it captures something of the lazy tenderness of the
contemporary orchestral tone poem, *Summer*. 'Love went a-riding' is a virtuoso
piece, a joyous ride on the back of Pegasus, who leaps tonal fences with
confident ease. It is indeed a war-horse for the pianist, requiring hands of steel,
yet the notes all lie under the fingers. One can only admire the sheer
craftsmanship of it: those three memorable opening chords (E-flat minor – D
major 7th – 2nd inversion of secondary 7th on G-sharp) which return to round
off the song (see Ex. 9.5); the way the music gallops along on open-string 5ths;
the reining back of the expected modulation (from G-flat major to E-flat) at the
end of the first verse; the veering to A major for the second verse and the
unexpected modulation to D minor; the high, rippling arpeggios at the word
'Stay here', another unexpected fence-leap at the words 'But Love said "No!"'
(dominant of D-flat major) and yet another at 'for the horse I ride has wings'
(dominant of F major) before the home straight of G-flat major is reached for
the reprise of the first strophe. It is the most exhilarating ride in English song,
and deservedly one of Bridge's most popular songs (Ex. 9.5).

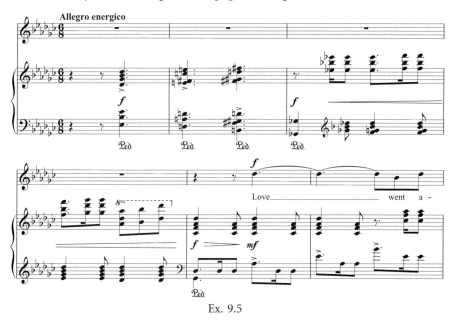

Ex. 9.5

After 'Love went a-riding' there is another gap in Bridge's songwriting,
between May 1914 and February 1917, after which he resumes again with
another Mary Coleridge setting, as though nothing had happened. 'Thy hand
in mine' (1917, *1917*) has a charmingly inoffensive poem from which Bridge
creates a song full of oblique harmonies, almost Fauréan in their subtlety. The
long strophe is so varied and inventive that Bridge can, and does, repeat it
virtually unaltered for the second verse. These late wartime/immediate post-war
songs (1917–19) show an increasing breadth of song-types, from vocal scherzos

to intimate lullabies, and a wider range (and more perceptive choice) of poets: Whitman and Francis Thompson, Irish writers such as Yeats, Stephens and Colum, and younger poets such as Gerald Gould (1885–1936) and Rupert Brooke (1887–1915). The songs also reveal an increasing harmonic sophistication. One senses that Bridge is at a creative crossroads, wondering which signpost to follow. Hence we have songs such as 'When you are old' which look backwards to his earlier romantic idiom, and others, such as 'What shall I your true love tell?' and ''Tis but a week', which look forward to the more dissonant, bitonal, and inevitably less popular Bridge idiom of the 1920s. 'So early in the morning, O' (1918, *1918*) is a setting of verses by the Irish poet, James Stephens. (Quilter was to set the same text some eight years later.) The words – 'deft, onomatopoeic doggerel' (Banfield, 1985: 344) – hardly matter; Bridge is concerned with writing a rapidly-paced scherzo. The effect is intoxicating, a tour-de-force of lightness and speed, with gossamer-light textures, a predominately high tessitura, astutely-placed rests and a careful balance between vocal line and accompaniment ending in a long, deft coda. Nevertheless, there are signs of things to come, in the parallel triadic harmony and, most notably, one of the first appearances in his songs of the characteristic bitonal 'Bridge' chord (bar 24 *et seq.*) (Ex. 9.6).

Ex. 9.6

'Mantle of blue' (1918, *1919*) sets Padraic Colum's 'O, men from the fields', a poem that has been a popular choice with several other composers, including Herbert Hughes, Arnold Bax and Edmund Rubbra. It is yet one more example in Bridge's growing list of lullabies, but this time a lullaby of a darker kind: we are left wondering whether we are witnessing a sleep or a death. (The poet himself didn't envisage a death.) The rocking accompaniment is poised over a tonic/dominant drone (D/A), the dominant note remaining as a pedal throughout the song until the final *tranquillo* bars.

'Blow out, you bugles' (1918, *1919*), a setting of one of Rupert Brooke's '1914' war-sonnets is unique in Bridge's output. It is a big song in every sense, virtually a solo cantata, with a long (27-bar) 'sinfonia' before a single word is heard, and orchestral in its conception. Indeed, in its first performance, at a Boosey patriotic concert the week after Armistice Day 1918, it was performed with string orchestra accompaniment. Even in its piano version there is an *ad lib.* part for solo trumpet, crucial to the song's dramatic conception. It has in its grandeur, nobility and its very subject-matter, an Elgarian quality, particularly close to

Elgar's Binyon settings, *The Spirit of England* (1915) written earlier in the war. At the same time, in its use of the 'Last Post', it can be seen to pre-echo later works of Bridge, such as the Piano Sonata and *Oration*. But it is a strange hybrid which doesn't really work in its piano version, trumpet or no trumpet. For once Bridge has fallen down on his technique, trying to cram an elephant into a matchbox. However, in its homage to the dead of the First World War, and its pre-echoes of later works, it has a crucial, symbolic place in Bridge's song-oeuvre.

'The last invocation' (1918, *1919*), a prayer at the close of life, is Bridge's only setting of Walt Whitman. It is based on a simple idea: a softly-treading chordal ostinato (mostly 2nd and 3rd inversions of 7th chords) in even crotchets, above which the singer floats a limpid vocal line, set to a Mixolydian D but pointedly introducing a C-sharp at the crucial word 'doors'. There is an almost Holstian feeling to the song, though Holst would certainly not have allowed himself the rich romantic climax on 'Strong is your hold O mortal flesh . . . O Love'. Equally simple and affecting is 'Into her keeping' (1919, *1919*). Bridge casts the song in ternary form which perfectly reflects the pattern of Henry Dawson Lowry's three brief stanzas. The outer strophes are set to 6/8 lullaby-like textures with ambiguous tonality – E-flat major poised obliquely over a pedal G – whilst the contrasting central strophe – *più mosso* in 4/8 – ranges through a variety of keys before returning home to the G-pedal E-flat major. As in 'Mantle of blue', there is ambiguity about the text: is the poet's love sleeping or dead? Clearly this enigmatic sentiment was one which appealed to Bridge.

There is no such ambiguity about Yeats's poem 'When you are old and grey', based on Ronsard's 'Quand vous serez bien vieille'. Here the poet asks his beloved to remember, when she is old, the days of her youth and how she was admired for her grace and beauty. Bridge chose to leave out Yeats's final stanza, which goes on to say 'Murmur, a little sadly, how Love fled', and in doing so substantially alters the meaning of the poem. Instead he effects his familiar ternary form by repeating the opening line of the first stanza with its original music at the end. Once more the mood is one of lullaby, and as in his earlier Mary Coleridge setting, 'Where she lies sleeping', he sets up a gently syncopated 12/8 ostinato on the piano through which the singer glides, the piano gently pre-echoing and commenting on the vocal line. And as in 'Into her keeping' and 'Come to me in my dreams', he breaks the hushed stillness in the central strophe. This change is signalled by a spread fortissimo chord, followed by a vigorous contrasting texture, after which he subtly slips back to the lullaby music in the final lines of the verse (cf. bars 34 *et seq.* with bars 13 *et seq.*) concluding the section with a most beautiful melismatic ornamentation of the final phrase (Ex. 9.7(a)). There are many other subtleties, such as the careful placing of 1st inversion chords (bars 13, 34, 42, 49) which act as waymarkers throughout the song, and the way in which he varies the cradle-rocking ostinato (a lesser composer would not have bothered). Note, too, how he manages, even in the pianissimo fade-out coda to the song, to effect a climax note, and that exquisite ending, where the music drifts away as into a dream (Ex. 9.7(b)). Despite the fact that, by omitting one of Yeats's stanzas, Bridge has not encompassed the full meaning of the original poem, he has nevertheless created one of the most beautiful love-songs in the repertoire.

Ex. 9.7(a)

Ex. 9.7(b)

The final songs of this immediate post-war period are two of his most original. For 'What shall I your true love tell?' (1919, *1919*) he chose a poem by the Lancastrian-born Catholic writer Francis Thompson (1859–1907). Its opening line refers to Ophelia's famous song in *Hamlet*, 'How should I your true love know'?, and like that lyric consists of a question-and-answer dialogue, here between a message-carrier and a dying maiden. In this it foreshadows his setting of Humbert Wolfe's dialogue-poem 'Journey's end' of 1925. Bridge differentiates question and answer, giving the questioner a bleak musical idea centred round a pedal G-sharp, and the maiden rich, spread chords. The tonality of both shows more subtle features than this would suggest. The key signature of four sharps implies E major/C-sharp minor, but the opening notes – E – F-sharp – D – G-sharp – confuse this, particularly the D-natural and the tritone interval that this makes with G-sharp, and the persistent use of G-sharp as a pedal. (Compare this with the pedal G in the ostensibly E-flat major of 'Into her keeping' written less than a month earlier.) Against this G-sharp the singer declaims a line with a prominent A-natural, which suggests a Phrygian modality (Ex. 9.8(a)). The maiden's answer clashes with the piano's B-sharp (3rd of the dominant 7th on G-sharp), after which the piano concludes the strophe with a contortedly chromatic version of the singer's phrase (Ex. 9.8(b)). As the song progresses through its questions and answers, the music grows agitated and florid, the dying girl's responses more and more breathless. It ends with the ambiguous E – F-sharp – D phrase from the introduction, tritoning onto bare G-sharp octaves, leaving the song unresolved and (we take it) the maiden dead. It is a most disturbing song; one of Bridge's best.

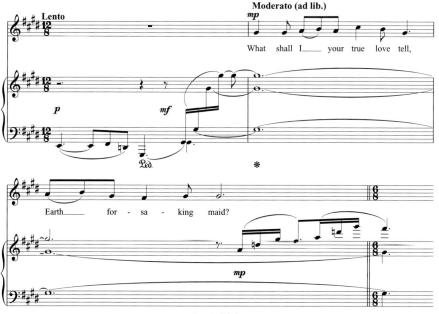

Ex. 9.8(a)

Ex. 9.8(b)

''Tis but a week' (1919, *1919*), written the day after the Thompson setting, is quite different in mood. Gerald Gould's poem (see epigraph) contrasts an army which has passed through the countryside a week previously (and, it is hinted, will never pass that way again) with the blackbirds which sang then and are still singing. Bridge's music emphasises the antithesis between the war-marching soldiers and their 'trampling horses' – another 'Pegasan' accompaniment of galloping hooves – with the blackbirds singing their (by implication) 'anti-war' songs – heralded by added 6th chords and roulades of notes of an almost Messiaen-like richness (Ex. 9.9(a) and (b)).

Ex. 9.9(a)

Ex. 9.9(b)

This contrast is underlined too in the music's two tonal centres: B minor for the warring humans, C major for the birds. Note the skilful way that Bridge corkscrews back to B minor (E-flat major/A-flat major/A major) using dominant 9ths and 11ths (Ex. 9.9 (c)).

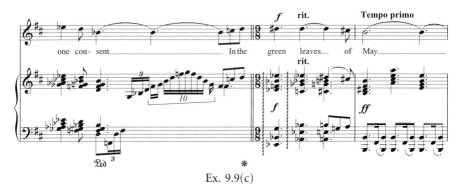

Ex. 9.9(c)

The years of transition, 1920–25

Another gap, of three years, lies between the Thompson and Gould settings and the first of the Tagore songs, during which time Bridge's style was beginning to undergo a great sea-change, signalled by that extraordinary work, the Piano Sonata (1922–5). Of his five last songs, the one least affected by these developments is 'Goldenhair' (1915, *1915*), a love-poem from James Joyce's collections of early romantic lyrics, *Chamber Music* (1907). The rippling semiquaver figuration of the accompaniment reminds us of his earlier piano pieces, and is almost Delian in its sensuous harmonic flow (cf. Delius's *Three Preludes* for piano of 1923). But the harmonies are spiced with more modern chordal formations, including chords based on the 4th (bars 33–4) and a typically bitonal 'Bridge' chord (bar 20). Over this the singer has a continuously evolving line which makes no reprise until the final cadence.

In January 1922 Bridge made a setting of a prose-poem, 'Day after day' (*1925*), by the Bengali poet, Rabindranath Tagore (1861–1945). More than two years later he added a second song, 'Speak to me, my love!' (1924, *1925*) and in June 1925 a third, 'Dweller in my deathless dreams' (*1926*), dedicated to John McCormack. All three are complex in texture and the second and third in particular seem to call out for orchestral treatment. (Bridge in fact made orchestral versions of the first two, which were published as *Two Songs* for mezzo-soprano and orchestra.) They are, nevertheless, perfectly pianistic, though requiring a highly skilled player. Stylistically they are the most advanced in idiom of all his songs. They are contrapuntally conceived, with rich bitonal harmonies and melodic lines in which whole-tone and chromatic modes interplay with normal diatonicism, and at times verge on an atonality not unlike that of the pre-12-note works of Schoenberg and Berg. All three match perfectly the sensuous, dream-like imagery of Tagore's texts.

In 'Day after day', the poet describes a scene between two coyly reticent lovers, the (?female) narrator and the mysterious visitor who 'only comes and goes away'. The text, despite its free-verse format, has a rondel-like shape to it, the phrase 'he only comes and goes away' returning like a refrain. Bridge reflects this in a formal structure of great sophistication. There are four basic ideas:

(a) a languid, downward-drifting chain of inverted 7th chords, which take on the function of a ritornello (bars 1–4);
(b) a vocal line strongly pentatonic in outline which is answered in the inner voice of the accompaniment, and a simple, rocking ostinato of 4th chords which is always associated with the poetic 'refrain' (bars 5–11);
(c) a more animated idea in which the piano's descant weaves a contrapuntal thread through the vocal line (11–16). This links back to the music of the opening ritornello (17–23) and the poetic refrain (25–30);
(d) another static idea, characterised by open 5ths in the bass and wavering figures across adjacent tones in quavers and triplet quavers (31–40).

Ex. 9.10(a)

Ex. 9.10(b)

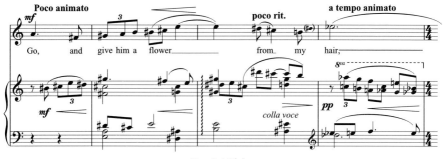

Ex. 9.10(c)

Ex. 9.10(d)

From this point on, these four ideas are reprised: (c), bars 40–5; (a), 46–52; (d), 53–60 – this section ending in a climax on a bitonal 'Bridge' chord (this time A-flat minor over G major); (b), the final refrain, after which the music fades away over the rocking 4th chords, leaving a single C-sharp to linger on. The richly complex relationship between music and text can be seen in Fig. 1:

Fig. 1

- (a) [piano introduction]
- (b) 'Day after day he comes and goes away'
- (c) 'Go, and give him a flower from my hair, my friend.'
- (a) 'If he asks who was it that sent it, I entreat you do not tell him my name.'
- (b) 'For he only comes and goes away . . .'
- (d) 'He sits on the dust under the tree.'
- (c) 'Spread there a seat with flowers and leaves, my friend.'
- (a) 'His eyes are sad, and they bring sadness to my heart.'
- (d) 'He does not speak what he has in mind;'
- (b) 'He only comes and goes away.'

Despite the complex structure, the result is clear and simple. One marvels at the way in which Bridge manages to restrict the vocal line to a compass of a minor 9th (E-flat–E-natural).

There is no such reticence in 'Speak to me, my love!', which begins as a deceptively simple waltz-song and rises to passionate climaxes. In the poem, a lover describes how he and his beloved will spend the night together. (Is his beloved there or is he dreaming of her? We do not know.) The opening waltz, the tune again on an inner (tenor) part as in the refrain of the first song, consists of a characteristic Bridge idea of an upward-rising scale motive, rising out of a unison and passing through a major 3rd to an augmented 5th. Above this is a simple spread-chord drone (A – E) which remains constant against the ever-changing harmonies beneath (Ex. 9.11(a)).

Ex. 9.11(a)

The musical texture is rich and full throughout, except in two brief passages, where the accompaniment is pared down to a single line ('When your words are ended, we will sit still and silent') and to nothing at all ('Only the trees will whisper in the dark'). Between these comes a short *Allegro con moto* section, one of the most striking and mysterious passages in all of Bridge's songs: *pianissimo* and full of chordal clusters (Ex. 9.11(b)), suggestive, perhaps, of the trees whispering in the dark.

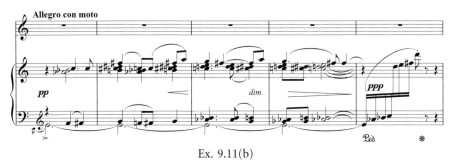

Ex. 9.11(b)

Bridge divides the text into three strophes, each freely based on the opening waltz idea (the second adapted to 4/4 metre). The song ends with a final *pianissimo* reference to the waltz, now shed of its drone accompaniment and cadencing inconclusively on the augmented 5th, with a plucked C major arpeggio beneath.

In 'Dweller in my deathless dreams' the poet describes another fantasised beloved, one whom he fashions in his dreams and catches in the net of his music. The opening piano idea could have been borrowed from that remarkable late piano piece 'Through the eaves' (No. 2 of *In Autumn*, 1924): an irregular (5-quaver) whole-tone-imbued ostinato figure descends from on high over an A-flat pedal-note. Like 'Speak to me, my love!', it is basically an ethereal waltz, but though the piano part is exceptionally elaborate – one could wish for 12 fingers in places – it is formally far simpler than the previous two songs: three strophes set out in Bridge's favourite ternary pattern, A1 B A2. All three are linked by a common refrain, consisting of rich, *Rosenkavalier*-like triads (Ex. 9.12). Even here, Bridge avoids obvious symmetry. The third verse begins its reprise a major 3rd lower than the first, whilst the refrain of the central strophe is down a tone. The song has a nocturnal glint and glister to it, and with its high 'divided string' octaves and rich harp-like arpeggios, it is the song that most calls out for orchestral treatment.

Ex. 9.12

'Journey's end' (1925, *1926*), written in November 1925, sets a poem from Humbert Wolfe's collection *The Unknown Goddess*, published in the same year; it is one of the Wolfe poems that Holst was to set four years later. Like 'What shall I your true love tell?', it is a dialogue-poem, in this case between parent (?father, ?mother) and a child. The mystery of who and what is one of the intriguing aspects of the poem. Banfield (1985: 339) suggests 'an innocent nursery scene of a mother and child playing together'. Pilkington (1993: 16) gives a darker reading: a mother is trying to give reassuring answers to her ill and feverish child. On a higher metaphysical plane, another reading could be: Man is asking the old Unanswerable Questions of His Maker. Wolfe's poem has a slightly self-righteous, prissy tone and, with its 'cool dormitory', an almost prep-school flavour. But out of this fairly ordinary lyric, Bridge creates a striking song, full of astringent harmonies (his favourite bitonal chords in evidence) and dramatic tension. It is more tonally rooted than the Tagore songs, as its key signature (two flats and definitely G minor) indicates, though the music constantly veers off towards other, often remote regions. Bridge makes structural use of the poem's question-and-answer convention. Note the skilful way in which he gradually builds up from innocent questions to the final fortissimo outburst. To begin with, the Son's questions do not move away from their G minor anchor and the Parent's answers return firmly home to G minor cadences. But as the questions grow more searching, the answers more frantic, the music moves further and further away from the home tonality and the harmonies grow more dissonant, to a point where the very music seems to pull itself apart (Ex. 9.13).

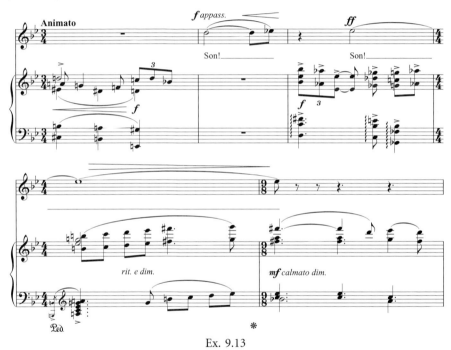

Ex. 9.13

But after this climax the music subsides abruptly to the calm, almost indifferent mood of the opening, and cadences onto a G minor chord, albeit an unresolved minor 7th. In its calm beginning, rise to frantic climax and return to opening calm, it reminds us of a similar musical journey taken by Charles Ives in the abstract dialogue of *The Unanswered Question*.

It is instructive to compare Bridge's song with Holst's setting of the same poem (*Twelve Songs*, 1929: see p. 135). Holst's song is cold and impersonal – 'curtly indifferent' (Pirie, 1974: iv); Bridge's is angry, dramatic, committed. It is difficult to believe that two such different interpretations could be made of the same text. But, in the illogical nature of things, both songs are masterpieces in their own right. It would have been interesting to know which one Wolfe himself preferred.

The song's title turned out to be prophetic, for, sadly, this really was Journey's End as far as Bridge the songwriter was concerned; most regrettably, for the post-war songs show qualities of craftsmanship and imagination unique in English song. His progress as a songwriter indicates something of the sea-change that took place in his composing career, especially in that crucial period immediately after the First World War. More perhaps than any other British composer who lived through and survived it, Bridge's creative career was affected by the Great War. To compare an early song, such as 'Go not, happy day', with a wartime song such as 'Blow out, you bugles', and then with his final song, 'Journey's end', illustrates this progress in a nutshell. (Alas! he was unable, or unwilling to carry his great songwriting skills through the 'Final Harvest' years of his career.) The Tagore and Wolfe settings hint at further possible developments within this masterly composer's technique, and one must share Anthony Payne's regret 'that Bridge did not turn his mind to writing an extended cycle in his mature style' (1976: 30). How we would wish to have a group of songs – even more, a song-cycle – contemporaneous with his final string quartets, *Enter Spring, There is a willow grows aslant a brook* and *Oration*!

10

John Ireland (1879–1962)

When vain desire at last and vain regret
Go hand in hand to death, and all is vain,
What shall assuage the unforgotten pain
And teach the unforgetful to forget?
Shall Peace be still a sunk stream long unmet,
Or may the soul at once in a green plain
Stoop through the spray of some sweet life-fountain
And cull the dew-drenched flowering amulet?

Ah! when the wan soul in that golden air
Between the scriptured petals softly blown
Peers breathless for the gift of grace unknown,
Ah! let none other alien spell so-e'er
But only the one Hope's one name be there,
Not less nor more, but even that word alone.

D. G. Rossetti: 'The One Hope'

In his survey of English song, *Byrd to Britten*, Sydney Northcote wrote: 'The significance of John Ireland in the history of English song can hardly be over-estimated' (1966: 107). Of the English songwriters who established themselves before the First World War, Ireland was one of the few who continued to make songwriting a major part of his creativity. After the war, Frank Bridge wrote very few songs, Vaughan Williams's output was intermittent (he was busy with large-scale works), Bax's main songwriting period was over by the mid-1920s, whilst Quilter's post-war songs show no significant development on those he wrote between 1905 and 1914. Ireland not only continued to write songs, but also developed and extended his range: his legacy of 87 songs represents one of the most important contributions to English Romantic Song. His range was wide, not only in choice of poet but in type of song. He could write 'tuneful' songs with a popular flavour and appeal without compromising musical quality. Such songs span his entire career, from 'Hope the hornblower' (1911) and 'Sea fever' (1913) through 'I have twelve oxen' (1918) and 'Great things' (1925), to the Elizabethan settings of 1938. In contrast, he could write songs of uncompromising seriousness, indeed grimness, such as the *Five Poems by Thomas Hardy* (1926), which can hardly be said to court popularity. He was also one of the most experimental English songwriters of his time, seeking to expand the medium in order to place it on a par of musical seriousness with his instrumental music. He did this not only through major song-cycles, *The Land of Lost Content* (1920–1) and the five Hardy songs, but also by experimenting with novel ways of combining words and music, in works such as *Marigold* (1913), *Earth's Call* (1918) and *We'll to the Woods No More* (1926–7).

It is hardly surprising that songwriting attracted John Ireland, for he came from a strong literary background. Both of his parents were writers, his father a notable newspaper editor in Manchester and his mother the biographer of Jane Welsh Carlyle. Books and literary conversation filled his childhood home, and writers such as Richard le Gallienne and William Watson visited the house. Ireland in later life enjoyed telling the story of the great American poet and essayist, Ralph Waldo Emerson, who 'came to visit us when I was very young and left his top hat in the hall. I took it and filled it with daisies for him' (Schafer, 1963: 26). In view of Ireland's subsequent devotion to setting poetry to music, this anecdote has an almost symbolic ring to it. His love and knowledge of literature is borne out by the habit he had of prefacing many of his instrumental works with quotations from poetry; indeed, many titles of his piano pieces, for example *Three Pastels*, have literary connotations. The poets he chose for setting to music indicate literary discernment and wide reading, a well-balanced choice of lyric poets from the 16th, 19th and 20th centuries. Nor was he afraid to express deeply felt emotion, choosing poets whose words and sentiments elicited a strong personal response. Many of the 16th-century poems he chooses to set are familiar texts: Sidney's 'My true love hath my heart', Samuel Daniel's 'Love is a sickness', Dekker's 'The merry month of May', though there is only one Shakespeare setting – the first of Autolycus's songs from *The Winter's Tale*, and that in his earliest song-publication, *Songs of a Wayfarer* – but in his final songbook, *Five XVIth Century Poems*, he sets unfamiliar lyrics by William Cornish, Thomas Howell, Nicholas Breton, Richard Edwardes and Anon. His choice of 19th- and 20th-century poets is highly personal: no Tennyson or Browning, but Beddoes, Emily Brontë, Dante Gabriel and Christina Rossetti, Mary Coleridge, Arthur Symons and Ernest Dowson; and as well as Housman, Hardy and Brooke, such relatively obscure poets as Harold Monro, Aldous Huxley and Sylvia Townsend Warner. The poets to whom he returned again and again were Housman (10 settings), Hardy (9), D. G. Rossetti (5) and Symons (5), and of these it was Hardy and Housman who drew from him his finest, most original music.

Like so many of the English songwriters who came to public attention in the decade before the First World War, Ireland was a pupil of Stanford, with whom he studied at the RCM from 1897 to 1901. Stanford's authoritarian style of teaching, resented by Ireland at the time but later acknowledged as beneficial, instilled in his pupil a strong sense of self-criticism and a sound technique. As far as songwriting is concerned, Ireland soon outsoared the conventional outlook of his teacher, who would certainly not have appreciated the original caste of mind shown in such works as *Earth's Call* or *We'll to the Woods No More*. But Stanford's more hearty songs, particularly the *Songs of the Sea* (1904), must have set the pattern for Ireland's three Masefield settings, 'Sea fever', 'Vagabond' and 'The bells of San Marie', with their direct appeal, tunefulness and uncomplicated accompaniments. From a harmonic and emotional viewpoint, Ireland's debt is far greater to Elgar. The two composers shared a similar lyrical quality and the same sharp, almost violent contrasts of mood, from ecstatic heights to *de profundis* gloom: the heart at one moment on the sleeve, the next hidden away from prying eyes. But, as with his close contemporary, Frank Bridge, he learnt much from listening to the new music from the continent, and in his own music one can detect the influence of Strauss, Debussy, Ravel and even early Stravinsky. He himself cited Ravel as one of the composers from whom he had learned most, notably the use of the whole-tone scale and the non-functional use of chords. But equally important – and symbolic as far as Ireland is concerned – are the influences from the further reaches of musical history. Like so many of his British contemporaries, he found a way out of the stifling tonal traditions of 19th-century music through the rediscovery of earlier traditions, particularly plainchant, with its modal and melodic flexibility. Folksong, though not eschewed, was of far less importance to him than to Vaughan Williams, Holst, Bax or Butterworth.

But in discussing Ireland's musical personality, one must go beyond music. He himself once commented that no-one would understand his music who had not read the works of Arthur Machen (Longmire, 1969: 20). The prose-writing of Machen (1863–1947), with its mystical feeling for the spirit of place, especially associated with ancient civilisations and pagan ritual, hovers, a winged epigraph, over all of Ireland's mature music, notably instrumental works such as *The Island Spell* (1912), *The Forgotten Rite* (1913) and *Mai Dun* (1921). If Machen had written poetry, then Ireland would surely have set it. But this mystical quality of strangeness and otherness, the feeling that 'Something lies beyond the scene', informs many of his finest songs, particularly the Hardy and Housman settings with their strong emphasis on the historical associations of place. Mention has already been made of the number of works that have locatingly descriptive titles. These titles are often taken from places that had significant personal associations for him: *Chelsea Reach, Soho Forenoons, Mai Dun, Sarnia*. He himself later said that his publishers had demanded them (Schafer: 33), implying that they were not important to him – slightly disingenuous considering the way he constantly prefaced his instrumental works with poetic quotations. No wonder the poetry of A. E. Housman with its emphasis on place and the poetry of place so attracted him. Linked with this is another important factor in Ireland's make-up, his response to Nature. Here again, it is more clearly stated in his piano-music: *April, Amberley Wild Brooks, Equinox* and the great *Sarnia* sequence, but is equally recognisable in songs such as *Earth's Call*, 'Spring sorrow' and 'The Lent lily'.

It will be apparent that Ireland was a very *personal* composer, a lyricist concerned with his own feelings rather than a dramatist exploring the conflicting relationships of several people. (It is hard to conceive of John Ireland writing an opera.) Indeed, there is a strong autobiographical element in all his music, whether he is setting words or not, though direct articulation of these ideas is rarely made explicit. (The date, 'February 22', which appears at the end of several of his words – the birthday of a close friend, Arthur Miller – gives us one telling, though never divulged, clue.) The autobiographical aspect in his music shows itself even more revealingly in the way in which he constantly resorts to self-quotation. His music, not least his songs, is a diary of his emotions, and in some respects his songs, from *Marigold* onwards, can be viewed not as individual pieces of music, but an extended piece embracing his entire career. One song leads to another, each one illuminating or expanding on its predecessor; all are connected by an intricate web of cross-references. Indeed, an unsympathetic critic might suggest that Ireland was writing the same song over and over again. In looking more closely at these self-quotations, it will be seen that they are not arbitrary, but are, in nearly every case, personal archetypal musical symbols. Banfield (1985: 163–9) has identified five of these recurrent symbols, which range from ecstasy through pain and sorrow to darkness and despair. Most of these will be instantly recognised by those acquainted with Ireland's music. Because they are essentially sound symbols, any verbal definition can only be tenuous and is therefore placed in inverted commas:

1. 'ecstasy': symbolising the timeless moment when the beauty of nature is captured by the individual, represented musically by murmuring alternation of chords, usually (though not always) adjacent triads: 'The Lent lily' (Ex. 10.1(a)), 'The trellis', 'Santa Chiara'. Banfield says that the technique is an old one, dating back to Wagner's *Waldweben* (1985: 164), but it is more likely that Ireland discovered it in Debussy or Ravel.
2. 'heat of passion': this, one of Ireland's most potent symbols, consists of chromatic chordal appoggiaturas, reminiscent of Strauss's *Rosenkavalier*, and appears in several songs where unrequited passion or 'inward and remembered happiness' is being described. It can be heard in 'The trellis', the Epilogue to *The Land of Lost Content* and, significantly, 'My true love hath my heart' (Ex. 10.1(b)).
3. 'frustration'/'denial': a chromatic line in octaves, usually in the middle of the texture, yearning like a lost soul. The most potent examples can be found in 'Youth's spring-tribute', 'Lad's-love' (Ex. 10.1(c)) and 'Santa Chiara'.
4. 'stoicism': there are at least two musical symbols for this very John Irelandish attribute – (i) quasi-liturgical modality, as in 'Santa Chiara' and 'Penumbra' (*Marigold*) (Ex. 10.1(d)), and (ii) a falling 5th in the bass, a motive that haunts his Housman song-cycle, *The Land of Lost Content*. It can be heard prominently in those two related songs, 'The vain desire' (*The Land of Lost Content*) (Ex. 10.1(e)) and 'The one hope', which Ireland himself linked by title.
5. 'dislocation and numbness': almost atonal in its use of whole-tones and ultra chromaticism. The best examples of this symbol can be heard in 'Spleen' (*Marigold*) (Ex. 10.1(f)).

Ex. 10.1(a)

Ex. 10.1(b)

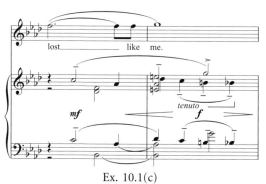

Ex. 10.1(c)

Ex. 10.1(d)

Ex. 10.1(e)

Ex. 10.1(f)

Peter Crossley-Holland (1954: 534) has discerned three main phases to Ireland's career:

1. 1903–20, when Ireland's personal style was developing from a relatively traditional harmonic idiom. It is the period when he encountered Machen's writing. As far as his songs are concerned, it covers his early popular successes, 'Sea fever' and 'Hope the hornblower', and his first individual work, *Marigold*, after which there is a gap in the war years before he returns to songwriting with settings of Rupert Brooke, Monro and Symons, and his first Housman songs.
2. 1921–9: the post-war years, which see his most productive phase of song-writing, a period of personal, bittersweet emotions framed by his two Housman song-cycles, *The Land of Lost Content* (1920–1) and *We'll to the Woods No More* (1926–7) and including his Thomas Hardy settings and mature settings of D. G. Rossetti and Arthur Symons.
3. 1930 onwards: a period of clarification of his style, during which time Ireland was mainly concerned with larger-scale, orchestral works. There is only a handful of songs: *Songs Sacred and Profane* (1929–31) and the *Five XVIth Century Poems* (1938). From 1945 to his death in 1962, Ireland wrote relatively little music and no songs.

Songs of a Wayfarer (1903–11, *1912*) was Ireland's first substantial work and contains his earliest surviving essay in the medium. The five songs are settings of poems by William Blake, James Vila Blake (no relation), Shakespeare, Rossetti and Dowson. The Mahlerian title suggests a companion-piece to Vaughan Williams's *Songs of Travel*, but the wayfaring element is tenuous and hardly more than a crude title to unify the set. The majority of songs were written between 1903 and 1905, but the final song, 'I will walk on the earth' (James Vila Blake) dates from 1911. This, as Ireland later confided to Geoffrey Bush, was a pot-boiler written to entice the publishers to accept the other songs of the set (Bush, 1981: Foreword) – something that he later regretted. The cycle is all the better for its omission. The songs have the virtues and drawbacks of their youthful provenance: a confident disdain for conventional harmonic proce-dures, as in the Dowson song, as well as some crude word-painting in the William Blake and Shakespeare settings. (Reference to linnet and lark imme-diately evoke trillings in the accompaniment.) As the first song he published, 'Memory' (Blake) has an almost emblematic significance; the final lines could be a summary of Ireland's pessimistic philosophy:

> And, when night comes, I'll go
> To places fit for woe,
> Walking along the darkened valley
> With silent Melancholy.

Indeed, the phrase 'the darkened valley' remained with him and he used it as the title of a fine piano piece some fifteen years later (1920). Ireland unfortunately makes a gabble of Shakespeare's text in his setting of 'When daffodils begin to peer'. In Act IV, scene 2 of *The Winter's Tale*, Autolycus sings six verses; the first three (those normally set by songwriters) follow the same verse structure, linked to each other by a varied refrain in the second line. There follows a short passage of dialogue before he continues with two more stanzas, which have a different verse structure (shorter lines 2 and 4 than before) and different matter ('But shall I go mourn for that my dear/' in verse 4 refers not to 'aunts' tumbling in the hay of verse 3, but to the intervening dialogue), whilst the sixth verse, 'Jog on, jog on, the footpath way', is a 'curtain-stanza' to conclude the scene, and has nothing to do with anything that has gone previously. That is to say, this is not one song but three. Inexplicably, Ireland sets verses 1–3, verse 4 and verse 6, which makes a nonsense of everything. 'English May' is important as Ireland's first of many settings of the poetry of Dante Gabriel Rossetti, as well as his first attempt to set a sonnet to music. The poem is a curious one, expressing as it does good wishes through negative statements; the poet wishes his beloved the good health of May – not this English May, but an Italian one. The sonnet is through-set, ending with an impressive rising figure in both voice and accompaniment (Ex. 10.2).

Ex. 10.2

The most original song in the set is 'I was not sorrowful' (Dowson), in which Ireland's individual idiom and rich harmonic style is clearly discernible. The *ennui* of Dowson's text is well caught in the piano's painful chords (r.h.) and dripping arpeggios (l.h.), and in the singer's opening monotone (Ex. 10.3). This texture is hypnotically maintained until the words 'until the evening came/And left me sorrowful', at which point the arpeggio breaks off to allow the words to stand out on their own.

Ex. 10.3

Ireland's versatility is shown in his next songs, all written with half an eye on the popular ballad-concert market. 'Hope the hornblower' (Newbolt) and 'When lights go rolling round the sky' (James Vila Blake), both published in 1911, owe something to Stanford's sturdily diatonic songs. The Newbolt setting is particularly successful, its memorable jog-trotting accompaniment buoying up the perky vocal line (Ex. 10.4).

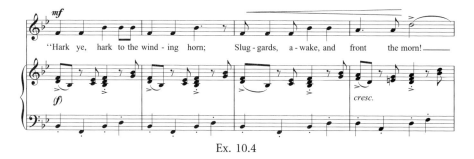

Ex. 10.4

The three verses are set strophically, the third beginning *minore*, à la Schubert, the tonality rising up, from B-flat through D and F, until it achieves its tonic, though with superimposed dominant harmonies. 'When lights go rolling round the sky' is less successful. It is marred by a rather pretentious poem (again by James Vila Blake, a versifier for whom Ireland had an inexplicable fondness, for he set him three times) with its mock-Tudor phraseology – 'certes' and 'cometh John' and 'ope mine eyes'. Ireland sets it in popular ballad style with jolly bouncing French rhythms, but, as with so many songs of its kind, it suffers from irritating jocosity.

'Sea fever' (Masefield) (1913, *1915*) was, and still remains, Ireland's most popular, if not most characteristic, song. It was first published as a tenor song but later the composer preferred it sung by a baritone, and as such it is a staple of the baritone repertoire. It has a classic song-shape: the three stanzas are set in varied strophic manner, each strophe of four phrases, the third of which goes 'down through the 5ths'. The voice has a flexible *quasi-recitative* line over a solid crotchet accompanimental tread, which is varied in the final verse with rich descending parallel motion chords. The closing chords are modally altered (flattened 7th and 2nd and a major tonic chord) to give a memorable cadence (Ex. 10.5).

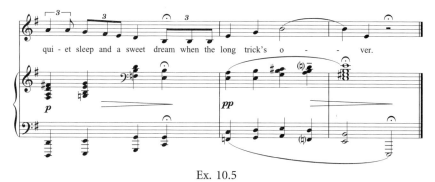

Ex. 10.5

However, the setting presents a problem in its interpretation of the poet's text (and always has: see Colles, 1928: 14). Masefield's title is 'Sea fever'; the words have a restlessness and urgency. Ireland's setting is sturdy and stoical rather than feverish. But Ireland's misinterpretation has not detracted from the song's popularity: which gives us something to ponder on. (See Introduction, p. 15.)

The most important solo vocal work that Ireland wrote before the First World War is *Marigold* (1913, *1917*). Subtitled 'Impression for voice and piano', it consists of three songs, two to poems by D. G. Rossetti, the other by Ernest Dowson. It is not a song-cycle in the usual sense, for the poems do not share the same poet or subject-matter, nor are they linked by narrative. They are, however, held together by the composer's vision of unity, which he achieves through the use of a motto theme and other cross-references. It is one of the most original vocal works of its time by a British composer, the music subtle and allusive and containing the composer's first important use of musical symbols. The three poems are a journey into darkness, moving from spring-like imagery, through frustration to dark despair – which could explain why the sequence has never earned the popularity it deserves.

'Youth's spring-tribute' is a setting of Sonnet 14 from Rossetti's long sequence, *The House of Life*, which Vaughan Williams quarried for his first song-cycle. With its celebration of love and springtime, the setting has a carefree innocence rarely encountered again in Ireland's songs. The gently rocking 7th chords, with their emphasis on the interval of a Perfect 4th, are reminiscent of the inverted 7th chords used by Quilter in 'Julia's hair' (q.v.), producing a similar serene, static feel to the music. This 4th interval is later transformed, at the words 'and through her bow'rs the wind's way', into the motto-motive which is to permeate the sequence (Ex. 10.6(a)) and is later transformed into what it always aspired to be, the 'ecstasy' motive (Ex. 10.6(b)). The song ends with the 'requited love' symbol, appropriately at the words 'for this is ev'n the hour of Love's sworn suit-service' (Ex. 10.6(c)).

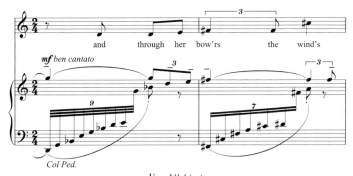

Ex. 10.6(a)

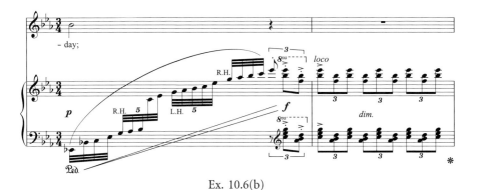

Ex. 10.6(b)

Ex. 10.6(c)

Symbols and motto appear throughout 'Penumbra', the setting of a mysteriously intense lyric by Rossetti. The song opens with the 'stoicism' symbol, like a brief wisp of plainchant (see Ex. 10.1(d)) which is picked up from the piano by the voice. There is a brief reference to the passion symbol, at the words 'All might rejoice in listening', and the song ends with the 'ecstasy'symbol ('when sea and wind are one'). But it is the motto theme that dominates, threading its way through the song in a variety of guises, and emerging in the final verse over a rippling accompaniment, prompted by the poem's sea imagery. The cycle ends with a tortured interpretation of Verlaine's 'Spleen' in Dowson's English version. The piano presents a very chromatic idea of an almost Schoenbergian atonality (= the 'dislocation and numbness' symbol) which obsesses the song, giving rise to its elusive harmonic style and tonal ambiguity (see Ex. 10.1(f)). At the end of the poem there is a glimpse of hope, when the poet, tired of all else in life, finds solace in his beloved. In the piano coda, there is a reference back to the first song, giving it (and the cycle) some repose, though the discord (albeit a mild one) in the final cadence leaves an ultimate question mark. *Marigold* has a self-searching, almost expressionistic intensity rare in English song; something one would expect from Schoenberg or one of his pupils rather than a British composer. It looks forward to the *angst* of Warlock's *Saudades* and *The Curlew* written half a decade later.

Four years separate *Marigold* and 'Sea fever' from Ireland's next songs, during which time a world war was ravaging Europe. Perhaps not unexpectedly, several of the songs that he wrote when he took up his pen again reflect that war. *Songs of a Great War* (1916, *1917*) suffers from weak, sentimental verse (by Eric Thirkell Cooper), but in the *Two Songs to Poems by Rupert Brooke* he chooses two of the most famous poems inspired by that war, 'The soldier' ('If I should die, think only this of me') and 'Blow out, you bugles'. In their patriotic sentiments and bluster, both songs now sound dated. It is interesting to observe how Ireland manages in the first song to fit the irregular stanzas of the sonnet-form into strophic form – an octave into a sestet won't go, but Ireland contrives to achieve it. Both songs show the composer's use of self-quotation, though in this case quotation stored up for the future, for the ideas that he uses in bars 14–15 (and 32–33) of the first song and bars 44–45 of the second were resurrected as the 'big tune' of his *Epic March* of 1942. Neither of these settings compare in musical quality with his other Brooke setting, 'Spring sorrow' (1918, *1918*) composed in the following year. This unpretentious song, in a folk-like idiom reminiscent of 'Linden lea', captures perfectly Brooke's sad little love-poem. There is an Irish flavour to the tune; the accompaniment is basically diatonic, with modal touches (an effective flattening of the leading note) at the cadences, but the doubling of the vocal line by the piano is unnecessary and detracts from the song's integrity.

The outstanding vocal work of this period is *Earth's Call* (1918, *1918*). Subtitled 'a Sylvan Rhapsody', it is a spacious setting of a sonnet by Harold Monro, with extended passages for piano alone. Indeed, it is almost a piano piece with a vocal obbligato. Ireland gives the piece a ternary structure, the outer sections dominated by the oscillating 'ecstasy' symbol, a perfect analogue to the spring scene depicted by Monro (Ex. 10.7(a)).

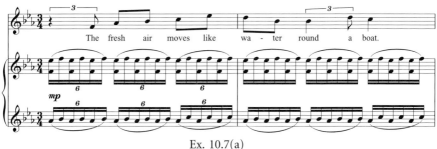

Ex. 10.7(a)

As the poet describes the scene, the music rises to an ecstatic climax: 'Look! Look!'; then, at the words 'They've gone', changes tempo (*Meno mosso*) and character (solemn chords) as he asks, 'What are the great trees calling?' This leads to an extended section in 3/4 as the poet and his companion lie on a bank listening 'till we understand/Each through the other, every natural sound'. At this point the piano has a long (18-bar) cadenza-like interlude. Beginning *ppp mistico*, it rises gradually (*incalzando*) to a *fff* climax, at which point the oscillating figure from the beginning returns, this time complete with calling cuckoos which the singer refers to in the last words he sings (Ex. 10.7(b)).

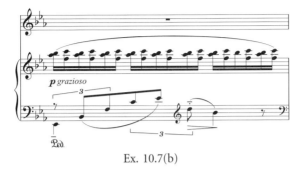

Ex. 10.7(b)

Whether Monro's unpretentious sonnet deserves such elaborate treatment is a matter of conjecture; but clearly its nature mysticism touched a chord in Ireland. In its spacious treatment of a relatively short text, and the prominence given to the piano, it has more of the character of a scena than a solo song. Indeed, in its modest way, it looks forward to the canticles and solo cantatas of later English song-composers.

The decade after the First World War was to prove Ireland's most prolific in songwriting terms. The years 1918–22 were particularly fecund, including his first Housman cycle, *The Land of Lost Content*, and the little songbook *Mother and Child*, as well as several fine single songs. *Mother and Child* (1918, *1918*) comprises settings of eight poems about children from Christina Rossetti's *Sing-Song: A Nursery Book* (1873). They are all very short, mostly a page long, much like Peter Warlock's slightly later *Candlelight* (1923), though lacking their memorability. Ireland dedicated them to his sister who had recently given birth to her first child. But who were they written *for*? They are too difficult (and adult) for children to sing, and not the sort of music children would readily listen to; nor would Christina Rossetti's verses appeal to most adults. Perhaps this is the reason why they are so little known or performed.

Several of the single songs of the period are Ireland *in modo populo*. 'The bells of San Marie' (1918, *1919*), is a rather dull sequel to 'Sea fever', whose poet (Masefield) and salt-sea imagery it shares; 'If there were dreams to sell' (1918, *1918*) is even more dull, not a patch on Parry's or William Busch's settings of Beddoes's famous lyric; whilst 'Vagabond' (1922, *1922*) inevitably calls for comparison with Vaughan Williams's eponymous Song of Travel – and there is half a nod towards the end of the strophe to 'Linden lea' – but the colloquial idiom used by Masefield in his poem sounds very dated. More widely appealing is 'I have twelve oxen' (Anon. 16thC) (1918, *1919*), one of Ireland's most successful ventures into earlier poetry. It is extrovert, tuneful and immediately memorable, with a strangely sensuous quality about it absent from Warlock's later setting. Like so many late medieval lyrics, the poem has an enigmatic quality: does the singer really have 48 oxen (12 brown, 12 white, 12 black, 12 red)? – or is he just chatting up the 'little pretty boy'? – or is it just nonsense? 'The sacred flame' ('Thy hand in mine'), one of two Mary Coleridge settings from 1918 (it was also set at the same period by Frank Bridge) is notable for the echoes in its accompaniment of his symphonic poem, *The Forgotten Rite* (1913). There is a strong bi-modal feeling to the opening, the B-flat tonality in the r.h. countered by D-flats and G-flats in the bass (Ex. 10.8). Debussy's 'Prière', the second of his Villon Ballades, seems to hover over the words 'We two will kneel before the shrine'.

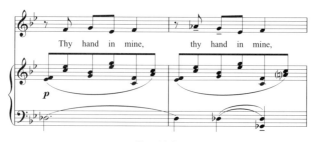

Ex. 10.8

The *Three Songs* to poems by Arthur Symons show a darker side to Ireland's personality. Except for the fact that they are all by the same author, the three poems are unrelated – indeed, the songs were originally published separately – but Ireland draws them together autobiographically, as it were, by the use of his musical symbols. 'The adoration' (1918, *1919*) sets an enigmatic little poem about the Magi's gifts, of myrrh, frankincense and gold – all of which, in this version of the story, are rejected – and is pervaded by the liturgical symbol of 'stoicism'. 'The rat', (1918, *1919*), which symbolises unappeased desire gnawing at the poet's heart, is appropriately represented by the 'frustration' symbol. The bitter poem has resulted in an uneasy song, with a continual tonal tug-of-war between the ostensible home key of B minor and the remote key of E-flat major. 'Rest' (1919, *1920*) brings a calmer mood, resignation if not peace, with the flame of passion suddenly rekindling at the words 'Summer murmuring'. The most attractive of his Symons settings is 'Santa Chiara' (1925, *1925*). The poem's subtitle, 'Palm Sunday: Naples', hints at the poem's meaning. The poet asks for a palm to be carried for him, as he himself is unable to, having lost his faith. The song is almost a summary, an epitome, of Ireland's use of musical symbols; there is a different one for each verse, beginning with a quasi-liturgical, almost plainchant idea ('Because it is the day of Palms,/Carry a palm for me'), followed in verse 2 by the swaying chords of the 'ecstasy' symbol ('The sea is blue from here to Sorrento') and in the third and final verse the chromatic 'frustration/denial' symbol ('I have grown tired of all these things'). All are held together by the vocal line, strophically based but flexible to the nuances of the changing situations.

The unease of the Symons settings is counterbalanced by the *Two Songs*, 'The trellis' and 'My true love hath my heart', composed in 1920. These are two of

Ireland's happiest songs, written just before he embarked on the dark journey into the Land of Lost Content. Though settings of poems of quite different authors from different centuries, they are companion works, sharing many musical ideas. The novelist, Aldous Huxley (1894–1963), wrote and published a fair amount of poetry in his undergraduate days. 'The trellis' appeared in *Oxford Poetry 1918* and Ireland made his setting in 1920, before Huxley had made his name as an *enfant terrible* novelist. The poem is one of serene contentment, love fulfilled for a change, with the two lovers hidden from prying eyes behind a thick-flowered trellis. Not unexpectedly, it is the 'ecstasy' and 'requited passion' symbols which dominate. The song opens with the cool murmur of adjacent triads, an idea that he was to return to in the opening song of *The Land of Lost Content*, 'The Lent lily' where, again, flowers are the subject of song. Between the last words of the opening stanza, 'And we lie rosily bow'r'd' and the first line of the second, 'Through the long afternoon' Ireland wordlessly fills in the amorous scene in the piano's intervening music with a heartfelt outburst of the 'passion' symbol (see Ex. 10.1(b)). 'The trellis' is a perfect matching of poem and music, and clearly had special significance for the composer, for not only does he quote passages in future songs, but also in later instrumental works (cf. the Cello Sonata (1923), first movement, 11 bars after fig. 3 (*tranquillo*), with bars 34–6 in 'The trellis'). In 'My true love hath my heart', the passion symbol becomes explicit. It not only opens the songs but also becomes its main ritornello, reaching a massive augmentation at the final cadence. However, the song is marred by opaque, clotted accompanimental textures – a recurrent flaw in some of Ireland's mature songs.

As a songwriter Ireland discovered Housman's poetry relatively late, in 1917. Perhaps he was daunted by the already classic examples of Somervell, Vaughan Williams and Butterworth. Two separate settings in 1917 and 1919 act as a prelude to the two major cycles of the 1920s. The title of 'The heart's desire' (1917, *1917*) is taken from the first stanza of the poem 'March'; Ireland, however, does not set this or the second stanza, but begins his song with stanza 3. The melody is as folk-like as Ireland ever attempted, a mixolydian mode on D-flat, the music hovering around the dominant A-flat on which note the vocal line begins and ends, whilst each verse is set to a folk-like A A B A pattern. 'Hawthorn time' (1919, *1919*) is less attractive, its nostalgic atmosphere evoked in lazy, somewhat aimless harmonies. It is a setting of Housman's ''Tis time, I think, by Wenlock town' – the title is Ireland's own – and it was from this poem that he was to take the title and epigraph for the piano postlude to his last Housman songs, *We'll to the Woods No More*: 'Spring will not wait the loiterer's time/Who keeps so long away', though this epilogue makes no reference to the earlier song.

A year later Ireland began work on a cycle of six poems from *A Shropshire Lad* for tenor and piano, *The Land of Lost Content* (1920–1, *1921*). Here he found at last the right poems to express his edgy pessimism and dark ecstasies. The title is taken from a poem (XL in Housman's sequence) which he does not set and, following the custom of the time, he gives the songs his own titles, mostly taken from the text of the poems – 'The Lent lily' is, unusually, Housman's own: the majority of the poems in *A Shropshire Lad* are title-less. It is a true tenor cycle, with a predominantly high tessitura – unlike so many English 'tenor' songs, which are really for high baritone – and this feature flavours the entire work. The six songs which form the cycle are subtly integrated, notably by the recurrent cadential figure of a falling 5th (the 'stoicism' symbol) which pervades the entire work. The cycle begins in a 'celebration of transience' with 'The Lent lily', but in the subsequent songs it becomes clear that 'happiness is in the past' (Banfield, 1985: 172–3).

Many would agree with Sidney Northcote that 'The Lent lily' is one of Ireland's finest songs. Above a piano accompaniment of flowing and eddying 3rds within a metre oscillating between 3/4 and 2/4, the singer sings a gentle, Dorian-inflected vocal line. The first three verses are set strophically and, following Housman's unusual enjambment between stanzas 3 and 4, the composer runs the last two verses together, the eddying 3rds reaching a richly dissonant climax at the words 'spring's array' (Ex. 10.9).

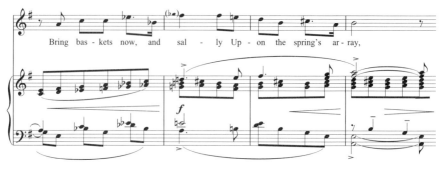

Ex. 10.9

One criticism of the song – a valid one – is that Ireland interprets the joyful words in too melancholy a manner – something he had done earlier, as we have seen, with Masefield's 'Sea fever'. It is as though he were forcing upon this song the fatalistic mood of the later settings. Singers will always have a problem giving the opening phrase, ''Tis Spring: come out to ramble', any vernal conviction. 'Lad's-love' (= 'Look not in my eyes') had already been memorably set by Butterworth, but Ireland emphasises the frustrated, homoerotic under-tones of the poem better than anyone. This is a sensuous, passionate song whose vocal line is always yearning upwards. This is noticeable from the very opening line and even at cadences: something unusual in English song, where cadences tend to fall, but entirely effective in this context (see Ex. 10.1(c)). 'Goal and wicket' (= 'Twice a week, the winter thorough') shares the footballing imagery of 'Is my team ploughing?', linked on this occasion with cricket to form a winter/summer contrast. Ireland sets the poem strophically, with complex harmonies over an energetic, striding bass, and underlines the poem's ironic unease with a disturbing pattern of tonalities. It is impossible to predict where the pianist's opening ritornello is going to halt: it starts with a D minor 7th chord, and then goes through B-flat minor 7th, A major and F minor 7th before reaching a chord of F-sharp minor 7th. E minor – the home key according to the key signature – is not properly reached until the verse's cadence. The song ends with a tonal version of the striding bass line, which rumbles on to the final, surprisingly defiant cadence: a pre-echo of the *basso ostinato* of the fifth song.

'The vain desire' (= 'If truth in hearts that perish') is a poem that has had little attraction for composers. Ireland sets the four short stanzas as two musical strophes (1/2; 3/4). The tonality veers constantly between E-flat major and A minor – i.e. tonalities a tritone apart – with the 'motto' motive of the falling 5th prominent both in the vocal line and the piano bass. The piano's ritornello, which appears between the strophes and as a postlude, is the emotional heart of the entire cycle, reflecting not only the tritonal relationship of the basic tonalities but also incorporating the falling 5th motto (see Ex. 10.1(e)). The singer's cadential phrase should be noted, as Ireland brings it back at the end of the cycle. 'The vain desire' is one of the bleakest songs in the repertoire, the more so since it is so subdued in tone. In 'The encounter' (= 'The street sounds to the soldiers' tread') Ireland, following Somervell's example, uses penillion technique, giving the piano self-contained material – a robust, insistent march-like idea – above which the singer declaims an equally robust line, sometimes doubling, sometimes in descant with the piano's r.h. Ireland makes effective use of bitonality throughout. The singer has a modal line (G major/D minor, with no accidentals and no F); the pianist a very chromatic (almost Hindemithian) tune over a striding four-note ostinato, F-G-A-B, with ambiguous tonality, outlining as it does the tritone. Somehow the composer manages to guide the song into C major for the final cadence. This song is one of Ireland's most original inventions. The 'Epilogue' (= 'You smile upon your friend today': another seldom-set lyric) acts as a short, quiet coda, all passion spent. The two stanzas are set as a binary unit (verse 1: D-flat major to B-flat major; verse 2: back to D-flat major) which has the effect of one long, through-composed strophe. Between stanzas, after the words 'happy the lover', the 'heat of passion' symbol suddenly blossoms out, referring us back inevitably to his earlier songs, 'My true love hath my heart' and 'The trellis'. In keeping with its epilogal function, the song echoes ideas from earlier songs in the cycle – the flowing 3rds of 'The Lent lily', the ubiquitous falling 5th – and the singer concludes with exactly the same cadence as 'The vain desire'.

The Land of Lost Content is not for the faint-hearted: its bleak fatalism is not likely to attract a large popular audience. Yet, as Alec Robertson has pointed out, it 'catches the lonely, frustrated, and often bitter mood of the poems' better than any other work (1956). Certainly no songs have captured the homoerotic undertones of Housman's verse more effectively.

We'll to the Woods No More (1926–7, *1928*) is subtitled 'a cycle for voice and piano by A. E. Housman and John Ireland' – a generous touch which Housman probably would not have appreciated. The work is unique in that, though there are three parts to it, only two are songs: the epilogue is for piano alone. The two poems set, 'We'll to the woods no more' and 'In boyhood', are from Housman's second, though not final, collection, *Last Poems* (1922); it reveals if anything more dark psychological wrestling than its 26-year-old predecessor. The work, though short, fully qualifies to be a song-cycle, with musical cross-references and a D tonality binding it together. There are echoes from earlier works as well as pre-echoes of works to come; it is clearly another work with strong autobiographical meaning, as the by now familiar birthday dedication ('To Arthur, for February 22nd 1927') indicates. (The words 'In memory of the darkest days' are written on the MS.) 'We'll to the woods no more' – a translation of a French pastoral poem – is the prefatory poem to *Last Poems*. There are two main musical ideas: a cortège-like 5/4 tread and an idea made up from ambiguous (unrelated) major 3rds, the sort of harmonic piquancy which Alan Rawsthorne was to make his own (Ex. 10.10). It ends on an unresolved discord: a B-flat hanging over a D

Ex. 10.10(a)

Ex. 10.10(b)

minor bass. 'In boyhood' retains the D minor tonality with ideas (e.g. the 'stoicism' symbol of dropping 5ths) which hark back to the earlier cycle. The style is conversational and the word-setting syllabic, quite different in style from the subtler rhythmic setting of the first song. The cycle ends with 'Spring will not wait', in which the singer takes no part – as though emotions were by now 'past words'. It is headed by two lines from Housman's poem 'March' which Ireland had set, as 'Hawthorn time', eight years earlier. The music is more affable, in D major, with sprightly French rhythms which refer back to the song 'Friendship in misfortune' (1926) and the E-flat piano *Prelude* (1924), and forward to the *Piano Concerto* (1930). But clouds gather for the conclusion, which recaps the music of the two previous songs: the ambiguous 3rds and unresolved B-flat from the first song and the dropping 5ths from the second (Ex. 10.11).

Ex. 10.11

It is an experimental, nonce form, but is it successful? The two songs alone do not make a satisfactory unit, but does the piano epilogue resolve this? It is instructive to note that Ireland allowed the piano epilogue to be published subsequently as a separate piano solo.

Ireland's first setting of Thomas Hardy's poetry, 'Great things', was made in January 1925, though not published until ten years later. Hardy's tribute to Cider, Dance and Love is given an extrovert setting with not a little hint of the music-hall. It is worthy to stand beside Warlock's drinking-songs, covering as it does one of the few drinks – Cider – that Warlock had left unsung. In the same year he set three more Hardy poems, 'Summer schemes', 'Her song' and 'Weathers', all taken from *Late Lyrics and Earlier* (1922), which were published as a group, *Songs to Poems by Thomas Hardy* (*1927*) and dedicated to John Goss. Less brashly extrovert than 'Great things' and more relaxed than the cycle which was to follow, it is one of Ireland's most appealing vocal works. The two long stanzas of 'Summer schemes' – a song also memorably set by Finzi – are given two different, reflecting tonalities: A-flat major modulating through to A major in the first verse, and A major back to A-flat major for the second, both using the same basic strophic material. Ireland's musical symbols play a prominent part: the rippling 'ecstasy' symbol emerges in the first verse at the sharpwards modulation when the 'little fifers' 'Flood the plain/with quavers, minims, shakes and trills', and when the words turn questioning and the music darkens – 'but who shall say/ What may not chance before that day!' – we hear the ominous 'stoical' falling 5th and a fleeting allusion to 'The vain desire' (Exs. 10.12(a) and (b)).

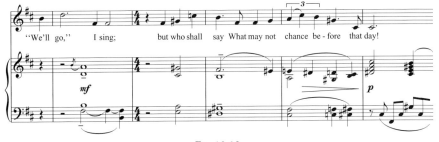

Ex. 10.12

'Her song' is one of Hardy's teasingly ambiguous poems. The 'her' of the poem is thought to represent the ghost of Hardy's first wife, Emma, and from the way she speaks the lady in question certainly seems to inhabit a different world. Ireland gives the words a simple, folk-like melody, but one capable of great flexibility (Ex. 10.13(a)) – notice the rhythmic and melodic alterations which he makes at the end of the final verse (Ex. 10.13(b)).

Ex. 10.13(a)

Ex. 10.13(b)

It is one of Ireland's finest songs, poignant and moving, all the more so because he himself is not personally, emotionally involved. 'Weathers' is an idiosyncratic setting of this popular anthology poem, the first, spring-like verse in the major, the second, wintry verse in the minor, both with ambiguous minor cadences in the piano righted by the singer's 'And so do I'.

The poems for *Five Poems by Thomas Hardy* (1926, *1927*) are taken from *Late Lyrics and Earlier* (songs 3 and 5) and the recently published (1925) *Human Shows, Far Phantasies, Songs, and Trifles* (songs 1, 2 and 4). This is a true song-cycle, as distinct from the previous songbook, on the theme of love, or perhaps in this case, 'un-love'. Hardy's bleak vision is matched by Ireland's equally bleak music. The very title is cheerless: no colourful descriptive name, as in the Housman cycles, but a mere factual record of what has been set. Nor does he use titles for the individual songs, either Hardy's or his own, but simple numbers. The choice of poetry is unusual, poems of Hardy's not often, if ever, set by other composers. All are equal-stanzaed, but treated to free, through-composed musical shapes, declamatory in character with elaborate accompaniments. 'Beckon to me to come' (a setting of Hardy's 'Lover to mistress') begins with a simple 3/4 pattern which gradually sours, ending on an unresolved discord. The imagery of the poem is perfectly captured musically in the 'beckoning' figure in the piano's introduction (Ex. 10.14).

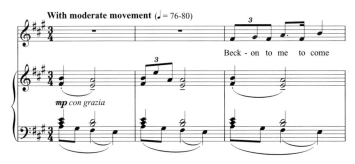

Ex. 10.14

Both 'In my sane moments' (= 'Come not; yet come!') and 'It was what you bore with you, woman' (= 'Without, not within her') are held together by rhythmic ideas on the piano: the former has an insistent chordal idea over a drone and, again, ends bleakly, with a D-flat minor/D minor cadence – the adjacent semitonal triads which Vaughan Williams so often used for his most desolate music – whilst the latter has a rippling accompaniment produced by the piano r.h.'s six quavers against the l.h.'s four quavers, above which the singer floats a free arioso line. The fourth song, 'The tragedy of that moment' (= 'That moment'), is a strange but nonetheless effective little piece: a *Marcia funebre* tread with a drum-like tag-rhythm over three chords, all united by a common pedal A: a hollow, 3rd-less D, F major and G-sharp minor, the latter, of course, creating a sharp discord with the pedal-note (Ex. 10.15). The piano, in sympathy, as it were, with the profundity of the mood, is confined to the bass clef throughout. The final song, 'Dear, think not that they will forget you' (= 'Her temple') begins with a recollection of the first song and ends with a reference to the stalking chords of the fourth song before cadencing onto a D-flat major chord with added 2nd and 6th. After the minor mode melodies and minor triad chords, it does (with the poem) finally achieve some consolation.

Five Poems could be by no composer but Ireland: it is a sombre masterpiece of 20th-century English song. Particularly noteworthy are the ease with which Ireland sets Hardy's none-too-easy-to-set words and the wonderful balance between vocal line and accompaniment.

Ex. 10.15

The bleak vision of the Hardy cycle was followed by *Three Songs* (1926, *1928*) to dark, brooding poems on the theme of friendship, a subject dear to Ireland's heart. The unity of poetic theme and musical cross-references within the group give the songs a cyclic feel, despite each being to a different poet. Emily Brontë's 'Love and friendship' compares love and friendship with two different thorny plants, the rose briar and the holly tree. For the first time in his songs, Ireland uses mixed metres (3/4 and 2/4) and dance-like French rhythms, something already familiar in his piano music and here adopted in an extremely effective way. There is some telling word-painting at 'scorn' (verse 2), when chromatic thirds descend in semiquavers through held notes (Ex. 10.16).

Ex. 10.16

It is interesting to see how he counterpoints the verse form and the musical form, the first of the two strophes being recapped in the middle of the second verse: a seemingly odd mismatch, yet justified by the sense of the poem. The text of 'Friendship in misfortune' is attributed to 'Anon.', though it could well be by Ireland himself. If 'Love and friendship' is concerned with briar rose and holly, the floral emblem of 'Friendship in misfortune' is the ivy. Again, there is some pertinent word-painting, as at the word 'blight', where the two conflicting tonalities of the song, D minor and D-flat major, are heard together. At the end, the song struggles from the D major tonality, onto which the singer has cadenced, back to the 'proper' key of D-flat major for the final added-note chord (Ex. 10.17).

doub - ly   bright.

Ex. 10.17

'The one hope' (D. G. Rossetti) is an extraordinary song, almost entirely autobiographical in that it quotes from several earlier works: 'The trellis' (bars 40–5), 'The vain desire' (opening bars), the Piano Sonatina (7–13) and the Cello Sonata (53–5), as well as referring back to the first song in its final cadence. The reference to 'The vain desire' is perhaps inevitable, as it was from Rossetti's poem that Ireland took the title for this Housman setting. The meaning of Rossetti's poem, the last sonnet from his sequence *The House of Life*, (see epigraph) is enigmatic. What is 'the one hope'? Rossetti told Alice Boyd that the poem referred to 'the longing for accomplishment of individual desires after death' (Pilkington, 1989: 74). The song shows Ireland's ability, one he shared with Elgar, to draw an eclectic, seemingly unrelated array of ideas into unity through sheer force of musical personality. Texturally it ranges from stark, '4th-y' harmonies, doubled between the hands, almost like some gritty organum, to the lush, Straussian harmonies of the 'passion' symbol ('Ah! when the wan soul in that golden air'), and encompasses the hypnotic wavering of the 'ecstasy' motive ('And cull the dew-drenched flowering amulet'), a long 13-bar section over an ominous A-flat pedal ('Shall Peace be still a sunk stream long unmet') and a strange harmonic passage where diminished 7ths (l.h.) break away in contrary motion from half-related 2nd-inversion chords (r.h.) ('Breathless for the gift of grace unknown'). What is equally impressive is the confident way in which he handles voice and accompaniment, with plenty of pauses and silences in the piano part to allow the words to be heard. Somehow he manages both to make musical sense of it all and to wrap the short cycle up with a 're-think' of the final cadence of the first song. This is a spacious, highly subtle and (despite the *angst*) beautiful song, which casts an illuminating light on Rossetti's obscurely veiled text.

   Ireland turned again to old, faithful poets, Rossetti and Symons, for the *Two Songs* (1928, *1919*), though neither is as memorably original as the 'Friendship' trilogy. In 'Tryst' ('In Fountain Court') Symons describes a peaceful June afternoon: a tryst at which both he and the afternoon seem to be waiting, symbolised by 'a drowsy tune', a simple quaver ostinato, which murmurs through the texture. In 'During music', Rossetti describes the effect that music has on him: though the art is as strange to him as Egyptian hieroglyphics, to hear it played stirs and moves him. Ireland symbolises this with an arpeggiated figure (r.h.), which runs as an ostinato throughout most of the song over rich chords (l.h.). There is, however, a feeling of routineness in the two settings, as though inspiration were flagging. Both suffer from elaborate, harmonically clotted textures and, particularly 'Tryst', rely too easily on the old symbolic gestures, now wearing thin.

One feels in these songs that Ireland is running out of steam, that he has worked this rich seam as far as he can and needs to find new territory to quarry. But to do this he needed to find new poets to stimulate his imagination. Rossetti, Symons, Housman, Hardy: they all share a similar dark, brooding quality and inevitably suggest the same old musical responses. What Ireland does in the songs of his final decade of songwriting is to go to new poetic sources, all unusual, as it turned out. Certainly the choice of female poets in *Songs Sacred and Profane* (1929–31, *1934*) is unexpected in a composer of strongly bachelor existence and legendary misogyny. Five of the six poems are by contemporary women poets: two by Alice Meynell (1847–1922), a Catholic convert and apologist who narrowly missed the Laureateship after Tennyson's death, and Sylvia Townsend Warner (1893–1978), author of the novels *Lolly Willowes* (1926) and that neglected master-piece, *The Corner that Held Them* (1948) and, in her younger days, one of the editors of *Tudor Church Music*. The remaining poem is by W. B. Yeats. It is an unusual anthology, and the poems make strange bedfellows. The title is a little misleading for the songs are mostly 'Profane'; the 'Sacred' element is marginal and, where present, sardonic. The Warner poems present the age-old musico-poetic problem of how the composer can deal with poetic irony, when the poet says one thing but means another. It was a problem which taxed Schumann when he set Heine, Vaughan Williams and Butterworth when they set Housman, and nearly every 20th-century song-composer aspiring to set 20th-century poetry. Even so, it is the wryly ironic Warner songs rather than the more staid Meynell settings which succeed. 'The advent' (Meynell) is a meditation on Christ's birth in which the liturgical motive drifts through the texture as it does in his earlier Symons setting, 'Santa Chiara'. The change of mode at the end, from D minor to D major, seems perfunctory, and the word-setting has a cramped feeling to it. 'My fair' (Meynell) is again spoiled by overcrowded word-setting as well as by an over-written piano accompaniment – much too elaborate for the simple love-poem it accompanies. 'Hymn for a child' (Warner) is a description of the 12-year-old Jesus speaking in the temple, wryly Sacred, verging on the Profane. Its 'ruthless rhymes' would have tickled Ira Gershwin, and indeed the poem is strongly reminiscent of Sportin' Life's 'It ain't necessarily so':

All the scribes and sages
Quit their dog-eared pages . . .
Speaking without bias
He reviewed Elias:
Said the dogs did well
Eating Jezebel . . .

Ireland smoothly counteracts this by emphasising the childlike aspect of the situation, with an innocent ostinato rhythm for the vocal line over a simple chordal-crotchet accompaniment. The other two Warner settings are equally ironical and in them Ireland demonstrates a new astringent, pared down style. They were written within a week of each other and, with their shared G tonality, make a nice pairing. 'The soldier's return' is rather enigmatic until you realise that the soldier in question is dead and has returned as a ghost. His presence is depicted in march-like staccato chords and ghostly fragments of tune, and described by the singer in a blunt, folk-like vocal line. 'The scapegoat' is another satirical song: the scapegoat here is happy, for he has been released from the burden of carrying other people's sins. Again, the accompaniment has a regular rhythmic tread; the neat word-setting is through-set like its predecessor, though ending with a short reprise of the opening music and a bitonal, impertinent cadence worthy of Poulenc (Ex. 10.18).

Ex. 10.18

Indeed, in the Townsend Warner songs one feels that Ireland has been opening his ears to the new, anti-romantic music from the continent to see if he could replenish his own, increasingly middle-aged idiom with new ideas. Even so, the gem of the set is not the satirical Warner songs or the more staid Meynell songs, but the setting of Yeats's beautiful re-composition of an old Irish love-song, 'The salley gardens'. Here is Ireland at his most simple and affecting, in a straightforward strophic setting whose repeated strophes are full of subtlety and variety. His characteristic alternating 3/4 and 2/4 metre allows for flexibility of word-setting; notice, for example, how he lingers over 'little snow-white feet' (Ex. 10.19).

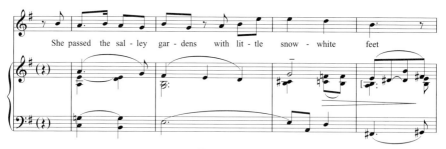

Ex. 10.19

Tonally the song veers between E minor and G major, lending the music a bittersweet quality. (In technique and atmosphere, it is similar to his setting of Hardy's 'Her song'.) It is a worthy alternative to Ivor Gurney's setting of the same poem and Britten's familiar folksong arrangement.

Between *Songs Sacred and Profane* and the *Five XVIth Century Poems* (1938, *1938*) the only song Ireland wrote was 'Tutto è sciolto' (c.1931, *1933*), his contribution to *The Joyce Book* (1933). Joyce's title refers to the aria 'All is lost now,/By all hope and joy am I forsaken./Nevermore can love awaken . . .', from Bellini's opera, *La Sonnambula*, and in his poem he remembers a lost love:

> A birdless heaven, sea-dusk, one lone star
> Piercing the west,
> As thou, fond heart, love's time, so faint, so far,
> Rememberest.

Ireland avoids the temptation, which a later 20th-century composer might succumb to, to refer to Bellini's music in his setting. Instead, we have a song of charming, unaffected simplicity, lyrical and improvisatory, with clear echoes of popular music: the sort of song one associates with Poulenc. Yet the fingerprints of Ireland are there in the mixture of chromatic 3rds, the fleeting plainchant of the opening motive, the way the music is structured over a cycle of falling 5ths, the rich harmonic language and the mixture of duple and triple metres (Ex. 10.20(a)).

Ex. 10.20(a)

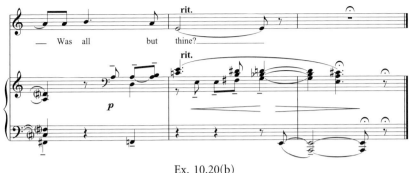

Ex. 10.20(b)

Everything is spare and transparent, used with the greatest economy. Notice the way the opening idea is neatly recalled at the end (Ex. 10.20(b)). It is one of the most memorable of the 'tilly' of 13 songs which makes up *The Joyce Book* and deserves to be more often performed. After the Joyce setting there comes another gap in Ireland's songwriting, this time of seven years, before his final set of songs, *Five XVIth Century Poems*. In this songbook, Ireland finally yielded to the English song-composer's traditional source of lyrics, the treasure-chest of 16th-century (or, as he insisted, XVIth Century) lyrics. Here Ireland is trying on Peter Warlock's cap and wearing Elizabethan motley. (Indeed the songbook might well have been called 'Five Songs of Springtime' in homage to Warlock.) It is significant that all the songs are in major keys – unusual for a composer so fond of the minor mode. Though some motives interlink the songs – a rising octave in the vocal line at cadences and the use of sequential patterns down the thirds – each song can stand independently. Most are pithily epigrammatic, short and to the point. 'A thanksgiving' sets the early Tudor text, 'Pleasure it is/ To hear, iwis,/The birdes sing', attributed to William Cornish, and is an exultant song, with neat little imitative points embedded in the texture. No more than a preludial flourish, though useful for that, it shows a craftsman at ease with his songwriting. 'All in a garden green' (Howell, c.1568) is another short song, setting two stanzas of 'fourteeners' describing spring's gifts of fruit, flowers and love. 'An aside' (Anon. temp. Henry VIII) is a light-hearted patter-song with a tune that would not be out-of-place in a musical comedy; it is a rare example in his songs of Ireland's impish sense of humour. Again, as its title indicates, it is a brief ditty, of three verses and a short coda. The curiously titled 'A report song' (Nicolas Breton) refers to the echo-like repetition of words at the end of the first line of each verse. (The poem is taken from *England's Helicon* (1600) where its full title reads, 'A Report Song in an dreame, between a Sheepheard and his Nimph'.) Its accompaniment, in a bouncy 6/8 reminiscent of Warlock's 'Robin Goodfellow', has a similar extrovert mood to Ireland's earlier setting of Hardy's 'Weathers'. The final song, 'The sweet season' (Richard Edwardes), is by far the longest of the five, set out in three large strophes. It is tonally restless, with very flexible word-setting over a brisk, march-like accompaniment and an unexpectedly subdued ending. In its praise of the month of May, it refers us back to

'English May' from his first songbook, *Songs of a Wayfarer*, appropriately bringing his songwriting full-circle. For with these songs, Ireland's songwriting career came to an abrupt halt: sadly, for one feels that he still had new poetry to set, new songs to sing. These last two songbooks and the Joyce setting seem to have heralded a new lease of life, a further exploration of the possibilities of wedding words and music, a new economy of expression and a greater transparency of textures.

Unlike so many of his songwriting contemporaries, Ireland continued after the First World War to expand his activity in this field and hone his technique. He delved more and more deeply (perhaps too deeply) into his personal 'well of loneliness', an exploration perfectly summed up in *The Land of Lost Content* and his setting of Rossetti's 'The one hope'. His songs form a spiritual diary; the autobiographical element present in all his music is particularly noticeable in those songs where his feelings are articulated through the words of the poets with whom he felt a special empathy: Housman, D. G. Rossetti, Symons and Hardy. In this he is 'the compleat romantic song-composer'. Peter Pears has referred to Ireland's 'edgy pessimistic nature', saying how perfectly it matched Housman's poetry; the phrase could sum up Ireland's musical personality too. Though he could write a rousing ballad – 'Hope the hornblower' – or a hearty convivial song – 'Great things' – these are, one feels, Ireland hiding behind a mask, desperately concealing his true feelings. In a perceptive analysis of Ireland's character written in the early 1920s, Gerald Cumberland described Ireland's music as bearing

> the imprint of a reserved, a difficult and a self-distrusting psychology. There is in it a beauty that is only half revealed, even only half guessed at. It is music that is spiritually shy. Over it is an immense reserve, a reserve that makes even the style a little crabbed and forbidding (1923: 55).

Even in his serenest songs, such as 'The trellis', one feels a sadness lurking in the wings. There is a bittersweetness about all his best music. His two large-scale Housman and Hardy cycles have a bleak fatalism, which not only matches that of his poets, but expresses his own lonely outlook on life. That he could express this through the art of song so powerfully is his great achievement. As a songwriter, Ireland has never been given his due, but his place in English song is of fundamental significance.

11

Arnold Bax (1883–1953)

Nor right, nor left, nor any road I see a comrade face,
Nor word to lift the heart in me I hear in any place;
They leave me, who pass by me, to my loneliness and care
Without a house to draw my steps nor a hearth that I might share.

Ocón! before our people knew the scatt'ring of the dearth,
Before they saw potatoes rot and melt black in the earth,
I might have stood in Connacht, on the top of Cruchmaelinn,
And all around me I would see the hundreds of my kin.

Padraic Colum: 'A rann of exile'

Of the composers discussed so far, Arnold Bax was surely the one whose talents marked him out to be a songwriter. For as well as being one of the leading composers of his generation, he was also a gifted poet, whose work was regularly published between 1908 and 1923. Indeed, during the period when he lived in Dublin (1911–13), he was as highly regarded as a writer as a composer. In other circumstances he might well have followed the example of his younger brother, Clifford (1886–1962), who had a distinguished career as playwright, poet and editor. But in the end the call of music was stronger and more urgent. After the mid 1920s he seems to have abandoned any literary ambitions, though his autobiography, *Farewell my Youth* (1943), remains one of the best-written, most readable works of its kind by a musician. With this dual creative interest in words and music, it might be assumed that song-writing would have a special appeal to Bax. Indeed, as with so many composers, his first composition was a song – it does not survive but, according to his sister, it was called 'Butterflies all white' – and his early career is rich in song-settings. Of the 140 or so songs listed by Banfield (1985: 415), 67 were written before he was 30. Thereafter his song output gradually diminished and in the last 25 years of his life he wrote virtually nothing. This was a pattern shared by many of the English Romantic songwriters under study, e.g. Vaughan Williams, Holst, Quilter and Bridge. But whereas a composer like Quilter produced his best work before he was 30, Bax's later songs are, on the whole, his best. Despite his impressive output of songs, however, he is disappointing as a songwriter. There are several gems, but much else is flawed, encumbered with overwritten piano accompaniments and awkwardly written vocal lines. This is the main reason why, for all their other virtues, Bax's songs have never been performed as regularly as those of his immediate songwriting contemporaries.

His songwriting career falls into four discernible phases:

1. Early songs (up to c.1905) written when he was still a student at the RAM, settings of an eclectic range of poets, including Breton, Browning, Dyer, Shelley, Wordsworth and his own brother Clifford.
2. 1904–1908, devoted to the settings of 'Fiona Macleod'.
3. 1907–1911: settings, in the original German, of Rückert and Dehmel.
4. 1911– : settings of contemporary Irish poets ('AE', Campbell, Colum and Stephens) and of Hardy and Housman.

Several of the songs – arrangements of French and English folksongs, of English lute-songs, and the songs to foreign texts – are outside our remit.

Bax's early music was strongly influenced by the rich chromaticism of Liszt, Wagner and Strauss, and this is apparent in the songs of the period – the passion of 'Thy dark eyes to mine', from *A Celtic Song Cycle* (1905) has a truly Wagnerian drive to it. But he was also open to a wide array of other influences, all very healthy for a questing young composer, and one senses his acquaintance with the music of composers as diverse as Debussy, Ravel, Rachmaninov, Scriabin and even early Stravinsky, and from this country, Elgar and Delius. But the most important and long-lasting element in the formation of his artistic personality came not from music but literature. In 1902 he read W. B. Yeats's narrative drama, *The Wandering of Oisin*, and this led to an almost religious conversion: 'The Celt within me,' he was later to way, 'stood revealed' (Bax, 1943). He made extended visits to the west of Ireland and immersed himself in all things Irish: the countryside, its people, its language, its legends, its literature, and, to a lesser extent, its folk-music. (The influence of Irish folk-music was of less importance to Bax than to E. J. Moeran.) From 1911–13 he lived in Dublin, participating in the literary life of the city in the period which the poet George Russell ('AE') described as its 'Golden Age'. He numbered among his friends W. B. Yeats, Padraic Colum, 'AE' and James Stephens, and he himself began writing poetry, novels, stories and plays, which he published under the pseudonym 'Dermot O'Byrne'. For the next ten years, author Dermot O'Byrne shared a dual artistic life with composer Arnold Bax, though it was not until 1943, when his autobiography *Farewell, my Youth* was published, that the majority of people realised this. As well as appearing in literary magazines, be brought out three books of poems: *Sea-foam and Firelight* (1909), *A Dublin Ballad and Other Poems* (1918) and *Love Poems of a Musician* (1923). Not unexpectedly, he set his own poetry to music, though (as with Ivor Gurney) not as often as one would have hoped or expected. (A sample of Bax the poet can be found in the discussion on his song, 'When we are lost', p. 218.) This preoccupation with Irish culture seems strange to us: here was a fairly wealthy middle-class Englishman with no Celtic roots (either Irish, Scots or Welsh) who becomes, by proxy as it were, a fully-fledged member of an intensely nationalist group of Irish writers, an honorary member of 'Celtic-dom'. As we have seen, Stanford, born and bred in Ireland, created in his songs the music of an Irishman in Exile: a land-of-his-birth which he never seems to have wished to visit except in his music. Bax, born in Streatham, adopted Ireland as his spiritual home and in his music expressed the soul and spirit of Celtic nationalism as no other composer, certainly no Irish-born composer of the time, was able. In his poem 'In Memory of W. B. Yeats', W. H. Auden said of Yeats 'Mad Ireland hurt you into poetry'. 'Mad Ireland hurt you into music' might well be the epitaph for Arnold Bax. He retained his love for the country and continued to visit it to his very last; indeed, he died whilst on a visit there. As far as Bax's songs are concerned, the period of 'Celtic' influence dates from 1903, when he set his first Irish poet, Moira O'Neill ('The grand match'), and lasts until 1926, with his setting of James Stephens's 'Out and away'.

As has already been mentioned, Bax's songs, and particularly the early ones, pose a problem, with their overwritten piano accompaniments, awkwardly written vocal lines and (surprisingly for a poet) occasional insensitivity to word-setting. Over-elaborate accompaniments are to be found in many of the early songs. In some of them – 'Spring rain', 'Magnificat', 'Glamour' and 'When we are lost' – cascades of notes 'smother rather than illuminate the singer's message' (Jacobs, 1960: 169). The piano part of 'Spring rain' is a veritable Raindrop Prelude, enjoyable in itself, but rendering the vocal line redundant. Similarly, 'The fairies' has far too portentous an accompaniment for so simple a poem, and once again the piano part is more interesting than the vocal. (The fairies and will-o'-the-wisps of Allingham's poem have clearly led him astray.) Banfield has suggested that there is an orchestral conception at the heart of Bax's piano writing: that his songs are tone poems for piano and voice rather than songs in the traditional mould (1983: 666). This does not mean that his piano parts are conceived in quasi-orchestral terms, for the writing is, as always with Bax, perfectly conceived for the instrument, perfectly idiomatic. It is, rather, a matter of over-elaboration of ideas for the job in hand, not only in the complex textures, but also in a finicality in harmony and melody. He cannot leave well alone, but constantly ornaments straightforward melodic and harmonic ideas with added-notes and appoggiaturas. The problem is not so much the use of chromaticism – in a song such as 'In the morning', he shows that he can use chromatic inflections most imaginatively to illuminate the text he is setting – but so often his chromatic additions to the harmony and inflections to the vocal line are meretricious. ('There's chromaticism, and there's chromaticism', as Mrs Bailey would have said. It is the 'and there's chromaticism' of which Bax is so often guilty.) If, however, his piano accompaniments sometimes require the virtuosity of a Medtner or Rachmaninov to do them justice, they are essentially pianistic in conception; he was himself a fine pianist. His writing for voice, however, shows less understanding. His fondness for chromatic inflection often leads to ungrateful vocal lines. Take, for example, the last verse of 'Thy dark eyes to mine', from *A Celtic Song Cycle*. Often this chromaticism has no apparent textual reason and merely disfigures what is basically a simple diatonic tune. This can be seen in his best-known song, 'The white peace' (Ex. 11.1).

Ex. 11.1

Why the chromatic alteration at the word 'plain'? If it were 'pain' (as, indeed, it is in verse 2) one could understand. Here, however, an attractive vocal phrase is disfigured, a wart on its nose. There are several other examples: in 'Eire', 'A lullaby' (at the words 'all about your bed') and 'Magnificat'. Again, in his early songs, Bax has a habit of doubling piano and voice, an annoying practice and one which apprentice songwriters are urged to avoid, as it weakens the impact of the vocal line. The opening song from *A Celtic Song Cycle*, 'Eilidh my fawn', is marred by this solecism and it is particularly noticeable in 'Magnificat (1906, *1907*), a song which probably marks the lowest ebb in his songwriting career. This setting of the familiar verses from St. Luke's gospel was written for a family Christmas in 1906. The words, with their ineradicable memories of the Anglican Evening Service, are a strange choice for a solo song by any songwriter, let alone the secularly-minded Bax, but it would seem that he was inspired by a Pre-Raphaelite painting, as the song's subtitle, 'After a Picture by D. G. Rossetti', indicates. This uncomfortable mixture of sacred and secular informs the entire piece; take, for instance, the opening vocal line (Ex. 11.2). The vocal writing is contortedly chromatic throughout and the piano accompaniment thick and turgid, a short-score for an orchestral piece manqué. The song ends with one of the most appalling cadences in the repertoire. Surprisingly, this was one of the first of Bax's works to be published.

Ex. 11.2

Perhaps I have highlighted these faults too strongly. Bax, even in the most technically-flawed of his early songs, possesses many virtues which his contemporaries lacked, notably a spaciousness of conception – he allows his poems to *breathe* – and a desire to harness an advanced harmonic idiom to the art of English song. But what needs to be emphasised is that he was not a natural songwriter. One has only to compare the awkwardness of these early songs with the grace and adroitness of the early songs of Quilter and Gurney to appreciate the difference in natural talent. Bax learned the art of song-writing by experience. The songs that he wrote after the First World War are by far his best.

Not all of these early songs are flawed. One of the finest is 'The enchanted fiddle', published in the *Album of Seven Songs* of 1919, but dating back in its original form to 1906. The song has a unique history. It began as a setting of Yeats's 'The fiddler of Dooney'. In 1918, after it had already been engraved for publication, Bax changed the words on the proofs, substituting a new poem, 'The enchanted fiddle', which he attributed to 'Anon.' but which is almost certainly by Bax himself. (Two pages from this amended proof are reproduced in Foreman, 1979: 19–20.) Why did he make this alteration? Possibly for the same reason that Peter Warlock adapted his early setting of Yeats's 'The cloths of heaven' to Arthur Symons's 'The sick heart'. Yeats disliked many of the settings of his poetry, but having no musical skills himself, appointed a censor to inspect all future settings prior to publication. Bax probably felt such interference unacceptable, especially as the censor was as unmusical as Yeats, so rather than risk unnecessary humiliation, he put on his poetic cap and rewrote. In some ways this was regrettable, for he never attempted to set Yeats again, and thus we lost what could have been one of the great artistic collaborations of the period: between the leading Irish poet and the leading 'Celtic' composer.

Ex. 11.3

The resulting song, however, is a fine one. Bax's poem, despite being so contrived, is a brilliant piece of contrafactum; notice, for example, the way the words 'The folk coming up to pray' in stanza 2 fit perfectly the religious-solemn chords and melismatic vocal line of Yeats's original 'They read in their books of prayer', and how, in the final stanza, he manages to match the word 'dance' with Yeats's to the same dancing melisma (Ex. 11.3). What is more, the words (whether by Yeats or Bax) are set to a delightfully appropriate jig-like tune, simple, folk-like and unpretentious, looking forward to those original accompaniments to his *Five Irish Songs*.

Because it is an example of contrafactum, 'The enchanted fiddle' is not strictly an example of Bax setting his own poetry to music; rather, it is Bax the poet setting words to the music of Bax the composer. He did, however, set his own texts in the more conventional way on at least three occasions, all anonymously: 'When we are lost' (1905, *1979*) and 'Glamour' (1921, *1979*), under the pseudonym 'Dermot O'Byrne', and 'Lullaby' ('Slumber song') (1910, *1920*) under the pseudonym 'Sheila MacCarthy'. His poem for 'When we are lost' is strongly influenced in feeling and imagery by the poetry of 'Fiona Macleod'; it was written in the same year as *A Celtic Song Cycle*, when Bax was at the height of his Macleod phase, and takes the poetic form of the Swinburnian Roundel. (There was a great vogue amongst certain British and American poets at this time for such old 'French' forms, the Roundel, the Ballade, the Villanelle and the Triolet, notably Swinburne, Austin Dobson, Andrew Lang, W. E. Henley and 'Fiona Macleod' himself under his/her real name, William Sharp):

> When we are lost within the dust and sand
> Of desert years, who then shall count the cost
> Of two lives chained at Destiny's command,
>   When we are lost?
>
> The shadow of fear our winding path has crossed,
> The cloudy waves surge onward to the land.
> Time's thundering storms sweep down with ice and frost,
>
> To chill the songs of love. Can it be planned
> That we must follow shadows and be tossed
> Hither and thither by fate's relentless hand,
>   When we are lost?

A modest little poem with a tiny sentiment tucked into a fragile poetic form, it calls for a simple, unaffected setting. Instead it receives a thunderous virtuoso piano part, crying out for orchestral clothing, working its motives to death and leaving little for the voice to do. Words and music are here at odds – schizophrenically so, as they are the work of the same person.

'A lullaby' had a remarkably quick conception: the poem was written on 21 March 1910 and set to music the very next day. When it was published in 1920 (as No. 2 of *Three Songs*, with two of his Housman settings, 'Far in a western brookland' and 'When I was one-and-twenty') it was re-titled 'Slumber-song'.

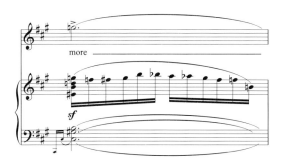

Ex. 11.5(b)

Ex. 11.6(a)

Ex. 11.6(b)

The finest song of the cycle is also the best known. 'A Celtic lullaby' is a cradle-song, tense rather than soothing, and treated with characteristic sophistication. Though the strophic outline of the four stanzas can be discerned, Bax has deliberately blurred it. In the opening bars he presents us with two important ideas: a horn-call (a) followed by a sequence of rich chromatic chords (b) (Ex. 11.7). These opening bars of the piano part seem to bode ill, with what sounds like one of Bax's meretricious chromatic alterations (see *in Ex. 11.7), for when the singer enters we hear it in its 'natural' version, to the sweet crooning words, 'Lennavanmo, lennavanmo'. In the subsequent verses this 'soodling' refrain is ornamented and developed in both voice and accompaniment (Ex. 11.8). It could be argued that the chromatic alteration is

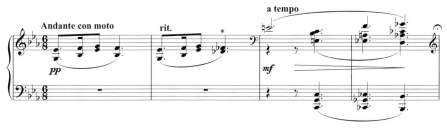

Ex. 11.7

musically 'justified' by repetition, when the singer takes it up in the third verse (see Ex. 11.8(c)), but there is no poetic justification: the words hardly call for such *angst*. Whether such sophisticated treatment of what, after all, is a simple lullaby is justified, is a matter of opinion, but Bax's setting carries conviction.

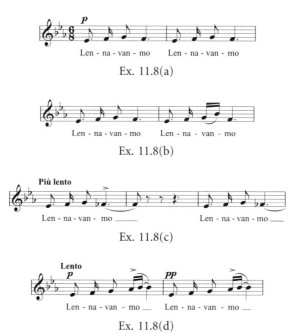

Ex. 11.8(a)

Ex. 11.8(b)

Ex. 11.8(c)

Ex. 11.8(d)

In the final short song, 'At the last', Bax attempts a tour-de-force. Over the *Lento* tread of a funeral march, the words are sung throughout to a monotone B-flat until the very last syllable, when there is a rise of a major 3rd to the dominant, D. It means that, for once, Bax can justifiably give all his attention to the piano, which he does in rich chords and textures; the singer is left with rhythmic declamation – which, one must admit, Bax does not fully exploit. (It is a technical trick which songwriters should allow themselves no more than once in their careers.) Even so, in attempting this *trompe-d'oreille*, he has failed to illuminate an important aspect of Macleod's verse, namely its strong sea-tidal imagery.

A *Celtic Song Cycle* is an uneven work, typical of early Bax in both subject matter and technique. In its emphasis on virtuoso piano writing, far more elaborate and demanding than the norm, it is, one must admit, original. The result is that the piano has a more prominent role in the proceedings than the voice, which goes against the very spirit of the art of solo song. One is inclined to sympathise with Sir Hubert Parry who, on hearing the work, exclaimed, 'Young Bax's stuff sounds like a bevy of little devils' (Bax, 1943: 27).

A curiosity amongst Bax's early songs is 'The flute (Ideala)' (1907, *1923*). The poem by Björnsen was originally set in the Norwegian but later supplied with an excellent English translation by Edmund Gosse – a fine poem in its own right. It describes a boy wandering through a forest who hears a wonderful song and carves himself a flute on which to play it; he falls asleep to the tune, but when he wakes, the music has faded away. Bax makes of the poem an extended, through-set song, almost a little scena, with the flute as an obbligato on the piano forming a natural counterpoint.

An even greater curiosity is *The Bard of the Dimbovitza* (1914, rev. 1946, *1948*), a song-cycle for mezzo-soprano and orchestra. (There is a piano arrangement by the composer, but the orchestral version is the preferred one; we lose the essential Baxian colour otherwise.) The provenance of the text is unusual. According to Bax's title page, the poems were 'collected from the Roumanian Peasantry by Hélène Vacaresco, translated [into English] by Carmen Sylva and Alma Strettell'. 'Carmen Sylva' was the pseudonym of Queen Elizabeth of Romania (1843–1916) and may well have been the author of the 'peasant poems'; Alma Strettell was a noted author whose poetry was set by both Stanford and Somervell. These Romanian peasant verses were published in this country in two volumes in 1892 and 1897 and became extremely popular, satisfying the current vogue interest in folklore and the picturesque, and vying in popularity with Fitzgerald's *Rubáiyát of Omar Khayyám*. Indeed, as indicated earlier, even Hubert Parry drew on the verses for the text of his orchestral scena 'The soldier's tent' (1900) (q.v.). In choosing these texts, Bax could hardly have moved further away, geographically and culturally, from his Celtic preoccupations. But the turn-of-the-century vogue for such exotic subject-matter was attracting many of his songwriting contemporaries, notably Bantock and Amy Woodforde-Finden. Bax captures the Romanian folk origins of the texts in his music, as in the shepherd 'fluier'-player's arabesque figures and the cadential falling 4ths, though in an impressionistic way rather than by conscious imitation. Idiomatically the music is closer to Delius and Warlock than anything; the rich chromatic harmonies that suffuse the work with its sad melancholy look forward to *The Curlew*. In the final 1946 version, the order of the five poems is:

1. 'Gipsy song'
2. 'The well of tears'
3. 'Misconception'
4. 'My girdle I hung on a tree-top tall'
5. 'Spinning song'

(In the original version the order was: 2, 1, 4, 5, 3 – a far less satisfactory arrangement.) The poems give plenty of scope to the song-composer, with their refraining lines and burdens, their bold, direct imagery and language and their use of dialogue-form in the last two songs. The imagery of the spinning-wheel and spindles pervades several of the poems, not just the last one. (Indeed, the first poem could also have been called 'Spinning song'.) Bax takes full advantage of these poetic offerings, as well as underlining the title of the cycle by giving prominence to the harp, with its traditional bardic associations, in his scoring (e.g. the spread chords before the final verse of the first song).

The cycle contains some of Bax's most attractive music: lyrical vocal lines – the main themes of songs 1 and 4 have a directness that one wishes Bax could have always adopted – and a great deal of zest and humour. 'The well of tears' is of interest as an example of the composer's use of self-quotation, for he includes a phrase from his early tone poem *Into the Twilight* (1908) immediately after the words 'The night is coming, let thy spindle be'. Clearly the nocturnal mood of the poem reminded him of his earlier work. 'Misconception' is a tightly structured song. The opening idea – parallel chromatic thirds that expand into parallel triads – suffuses the entire piece, giving it a darkly brooding, *Curlew*-like quality (Ex. 11.9).

Ex. 11.9

Ex. 11.10

In the dialogue-song 'My girdle I hung on a tree-top tall', the plaintive questions of a love-sick youth are mockingly answered by the coquettish girl, progressing from 'capriciously' through 'resentfully' and 'heartlessly' (her mocking laugh carefully notated), to 'loud and unfeeling', the song preceded and closed by a delightful refrain-tune to the title words (Ex. 11.10). It is a tour-de-force of controlled irony.

The final 'Spinning song', setting off with a spinning figure on low flute, is a conversation between a girl and her mother, the girl's enthusiastic questions about her mother's earlier life answered by the mother's banal, listlessly-tolling refrain: 'Thy father cometh home, leave the door open' (Ex. 11.11).

Ex. 11.11

Bax cunningly links the final two songs together, interpreting them as 'Before' and 'After' narratives: the mother and father of song 5 = the girl and boy of song 4. This is underlined by ironical musical cross-links, the passage in song 5 where the (absent) father is mentioned (Ex. 11.11) reflecting the boy's dirge-like chords in song 4 (Ex. 11.12).

Ex. 11.12

Bax considered *The Bard of the Dimbovitza* to be one of his best works. Yet it is little known and seldom performed. A cycle of poems based on late-Victorian translations of Romanian folk-poetry does not seem to have the makings of an attractive song-sequence or the potential for a masterpiece, but with its imaginative word-setting and colourful orchestral accompaniment, it is literally one of the unsung masterpieces of English Romantic song, and certainly Bax's major achievement in the medium. It also reopens the question of the over-elaborate, over-noted accompaniments in his songs for voice and piano. Clearly he was a songwriter who benefited from the full colour palette and resources of the symphony orchestra. In his songs for the monochrome medium of voice and piano, he had to find a *res media*, between his natural impulse for ornamental and textural elaboration, and the practical requirements of the songwriter's art: to balance the piano with the voice and to balance the two with the primary concern of a song, the conveyance of the text. That he realised this himself can be seen in the songs that he was to write immediately after *The Bard of the Dimbovitza*.

Bax's post-war songs show greater simplicity and directness. They include settings of Housman and Hardy as well as some fine settings of Irish poets, notably Campbell, Colum, Stephens and Joyce. Of his three Housman settings, the first two were written in 1918 and published with the 'Sheila MacCarthy' setting, 'Lullaby', in *Three Songs* (1920). In 'Far in a western brookland' the sadness of the young man exiled in London from his native Shropshire is caught in an attractively spacious setting. 'When I was one-and-twenty' is an over-blown setting of what is essentially simple verse. The second stanza has a particularly intricate accompaniment, and the final 'Oh, 'tis true' is far too

Ex. 11.13(a)

Ex. 11.13(b)

fraught. The remaining setting, 'In the morning' (1926, *1926*), taken from Housman's *Last Poems* (1922), is, however, one of his finest songs. It is a good example of Bax's ability to give spaciousness to a relatively short poem; he does not rush the words, but allows the music time to evoke the poignancy of the situation. Housman's poem is set out in two balancing stanzas that echo each other almost exactly with subtle alterations of word and emphasis, all faithfully echoed by Bax in his varied strophic setting. The major-minor mode tension inherent from the very outset is memorably frozen at the singer's final cadence, 'And they looked away', with its A-flat instead of the half-expected A-natural (Ex. 11.13(a) and (b)). It is one of the most memorable of all Housman settings, and it leaves you wishing that Bax had made further explorations into the Shropshire landscape.

The same can be said of the Dorset landscape of Thomas Hardy's poems, though rather strangely his three Hardy settings – 'The market girl' (1922, *1922*), 'Carrey Clavel' (1925, *1926*) and 'On the bridge' (1926, *1926*) – all have an Irish flavour to their music. 'The market girl', with its simple two-verse strophic setting and pentatonic tune, has a Warlockean charm and is far superior to Finzi's later setting. 'Carrey Clavel' is more sophisticated. Carrey's coquettishness is caught in the sad little Irish-jig-of-a-tune, unashamedly in the Dorian mode, which haunts the entire piece. (It makes one wonder whether the lass had Irish rather than Dorset ancestry.) A rich Delian interlude interrupts the jig momentarily in the final verse, leading to one of Bax's most sensuously beautiful passages, as the poet 'sips' a kiss from Carrey (Ex. 11.14) before the jig takes the song to its rousing conclusion.

Ex. 11.14

'On the bridge' can justify its Irishness: two young girls are making eyes at an Irish lancer from the Casterbridge barracks. It is a jaunty narrative song, the piano's ritornello again haunting the entire setting, with an appropriate military touch for the lancer. The vocal line is a continuous patter of semiquavers, perfectly in keeping with Hardy's long, racy stanzas. The whole song has a popular ring to it and deserves to be better known. These three Hardy settings are amongst Bax's most attractive songs: modest in aim, but hitting their target perfectly.

Bax's settings of contemporary Irish poets hold a special place in his output. The first Irish poet that he appears to have set was Moira O'Neill, one of Stanford's main sources of Irish lyrics, in the song 'The grand match' (1903); but the bulk and finest date from the 1920s, notably the two songbooks published in 1922, *Three Irish Songs* and *Five Irish Songs*. In *Five Irish Songs* – all except the third, 'I heard a piper piping', written in February/March 1921 – he sets poems by Padraic Colum (2), Joseph Campbell (2) and J. M. Synge (1). 'The pigeons' (Colum) is almost expressionist in its intensity. Tonal clusters evoke the murmuring coos of the pigeons stirring within their nests at night. The song moves briefly into a rocking lullaby for the poet's final words, 'a childless woman hears', before cadencing back to the cooing accompaniment. 'As I came over the grey, grey hills' (Campbell) is a marching-song with a strong Celtic flavour. The first two stanzas are set to the march-tune, the third to a gentler nocturnal idea before the piano leads us back to a full rendering of the march for the final verse. In 'I heard a piper piping' (also by Campbell) he incorporates the flute referred to in the poem as a basic aural image, just as he had done in his earlier song 'The flute'. Its plaintive pentatonic solo arabesques drift down, like a robin's song out of nowhere, leaving the singer to sing the first two lines of the poem unaccompanied: 'Never have I heard so plaintive a song'. From then on, the two – the piano's piping right-hand and the singer – run in tandem, though completely differentiated, the piper continuing his pentatonic line, the singer in a Dorian modality. At the end the 'flute' concludes on an unresolved dissonance, leaving the singer alone 'to listen to his song'. The second Colum setting of the group, 'Across the door', is one of Bax's finest. In four short pages he manages to create a miniature operatic scene, of a woman enticed from a dance by her lover. The song begins with a fiddler playing a bright Irish reel at the dance. The singer enters halfway through the dance measure, describing the scene and how she is seduced by her lover. This move 'Across the door' is marked after the first verse by a sudden change in the music: a spread chord (A-flat minor over a low pedal G) takes us from the gaiety of the dance-floor to the mystery of the outside world: 'Ah strange were the dim wide meadows' (Ex. 11.15(a)). The strangeness of this outside world is evoked in the change in the music: *Molto Lento*, rich chromatic harmonies and rich textures which reach a pianissimo climax when he kisses her on the mouth, the whole-tone harmonies giving the music a disembodied effect (Ex. 11.15(b)). (Snatched kisses for some reason brought out a strong musical response from Bax: there is a similar moment in 'Carrey Clavell'.) What happens afterwards is left to the piano, which cadences inconclusively on an unresolved 9th. It is an unusual song, which perfectly evokes the strange, dream-like situation.

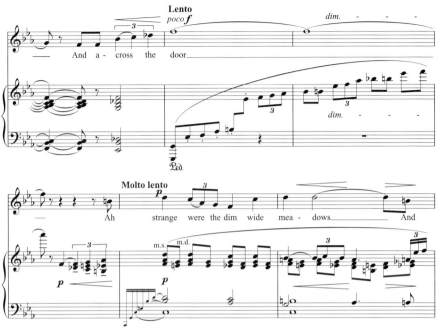

Ex. 11.15(a)

Ex. 11.15(b)

'Beg-Innish' is Bax's only setting of the poetry of J. M. Synge (1871–1909). The poem describes yet another Irish dance scene, here with no amorous interruption. 'Fierce and reckless (To be played throughout with a harsh and crude accentuation)' is Bax's marking, which he underlines with percussive chords and open (fiddle-string) 5ths. And when the poet says 'I'll play you jigs', the composer duly obliges with just that, a skirling 6/8 jig-tune above a duple vamping bass (Ex. 11.16).

Ex. 11.16

The final verse begins at a slower tempo, 'Heavy and Emphatic', ironically underlining the references to 'priest and peeler', before resuming the original fierce and reckless tempo. The song ends with a reeling coda, bringing both it and the songbook to a gloriously upbeat conclusion. Reels, jigs, a March, a Piper, the hint of a Lullaby: they are all here in one of Bax's most varied and satisfying vocal works.

The author of two of the texts in *Five Irish Songs*, Padraic Colum (1881–1972), was a close personal friend of Bax, and the *Three Irish Songs* (1922, *1922*) are all to his poetry: 'Cradle song' – a charming setting of Colum's most famous poem, 'O, men from the fields' – 'Rann of exile' and 'Rann of wandering'. Of the three, 'Rann of exile' is outstanding. Colum's poem (see epigraph) describes in anguished terms the effect of exile, and receives from Bax a forceful, committed interpretation. It begins with a single melismatic line on the piano, marked 'in the manner of a Caoin' (= 'keen' = lament) (Ex. 11.17).

Ex. 11.17

This 'keening' is taken up by the singer in the second verse, as the sorrowing wail 'Ocón', and it is this 'caoin', in a dark, 'chalumeau' pitch, that brings the song to an end. Bax made another setting of Colum, 'Dermott Donn

MacMorna', at the same time as the *Three Irish Songs,* but it was not published until 1994. It is one of his most disturbing songs. Colum's poem describes a woman praying for her lover to rescue her from her loveless marriage. Bax matches this text with a passionate, Dorian-mode vocal line and a piano accompaniment with a low-trilling, menacing pedal-note, which represents the woman's fear of her husband and her despair at her fate. The fateful reiteration of the refrain, 'Dermott Donn MacMorna', as she calls upon her lover, rings like a litany bell throughout the song. The music tells us far more than the poem ever could: we know that she will not escape and that the story will end in tragedy. What a tragedy, then, that this fine song had to wait so long – 72 years after it was written, 41 years after its composer's death – to be published.

James Stephens's mysterious poem, 'Out and away' (1926, *1926*), receives from Bax equally mysterious treatment. It is one of his most experimental songs, closer to the sound world of Holst's Humbert Wolfe settings or the later songs of Frank Bridge. One must disagree with Jacobs (1960: 169) that Bax was 'pursuing harmonic complexity to an extent that seems to smother rather than illuminate the singer's message'. Though harmonically complex, the lucid, 4th-based chords that drift upwards on the piano do not obscure the singer, and Bax supplies a vocal line that is both agreeable to sing and is faithful to the text.

Another unjustly neglected song, neglected this time because of its obscure and (until recently) only publication, is his one and only setting of the poetry of James Joyce, 'Watching the needleboats'. This was Bax's contribution to *The Joyce Book* (1933), whose other contributors included John Ireland, Herbert Howells and E. J. Moeran (q.v.). It is one of the best songs in the anthology and, indeed, one of Bax's finest. Joyce's rather wan, unspecific lyric emanates from the hazier recesses of the Celtic Twilight, but supplies the composer with a neatly varied refrain, 'No more, return no more'/'Return no more return', which Bax matches with equal adroitness. The singer has a wide, arcing melody over a chromatic motive, which droops down over a tonic-anchored piano bass. The final cadence, echoing the vocal line's opening arc, rises to a dissonance (G-sharp minor triad above the A/E pedal drone) before gradually dissolving note by note onto a plain A minor triad: an exquisite cadence that sums up the entire song (Ex. 11.18).

Ex. 11.18

At the beginning of the chapter, mention was made of Arnold's settings of the poetry of his brother Clifford. Though he seems to have made at least seven settings, one is a very early work (1900), one a translation of a poem by Dehmel, two are part of incidental music to Clifford's play, *The Golden Eagle* (both are translations) and two are lost. The remaining song, 'Youth' (1918, *1920*), is a little gem, however. The poem is reminiscent of Robert Wever's famous, often-set lyric, 'In an arbour green', and, indeed, Arnold's setting is similar in mood to E. J. Moeran's version of the lyric, 'In youth is pleasure', written a few years later (1925). A dreamy, lyrical accompaniment sets the mood of the 'blue day of spring' when the lover watches his beloved gathering flowers, and their tender dialogue is captured in the easy-flowing vocal line. The touch of doubt in her reply to his admiring words, 'O Love, my love, /May you remember that/When I am no more beautiful', is caught, characteristically, in the ambiguity between major and minor 3rds, heard first in the vocal line and mulled over and finally resolved in the piano coda (Ex. 11.19). There can be few finer sibling collaborations in the history of song.

Ex. 11.19

In one of his poems, W. B. Yeats wrote:

> The fascination of what's difficult
> Has dried the sap out of my veins, and rent
> Spontaneous joy and natural content
> Out of my heart.
> (*The Green Helmet and Other Poems*, 1910)

As a songwriter, Bax might well have heeded his friend's words. His desire, particularly in his early songs, for complexity, whether in the use of chromaticism or in texture, did not perhaps rend spontaneous joy from his songs, but led to unnecessary overwriting and raised an impregnable fence round them not only for singer and pianist but listener too. Such complexities, as Morley and Campion reminded us 400 years ago, are the domain of instrumental music, not of song, because they can only detract from the primacy of relaying the sense of the words. Fortunately, in his later songs, Bax managed to curb this tendency to prolixity and ornament. At the same time, the merits of his early songs – the spaciousness of his text-setting, his exploration of the poetry of the Celtic Twilight and Irish Nationalist poets, and his advanced harmonic idiom – are maintained, explored and distilled in his later songs, with the result that in works such as 'In the morning', 'Across the door', 'Rann of exile' and 'Watching the needleboats', we have truly modern, 20th-century masterpieces of song.

12

George Butterworth (1885–1916)

> With rue my heart is laden
>   For golden friends I had,
> For many a rose-lipt maiden
>   And many a lightfoot lad.
>
> By brooks too broad for leaping
>   The lightfoot boys are laid;
> The rose-lipt girls are sleeping
>   In fields where roses fade.

A. E. Housman:
'With rue my heart is laden'

Like Henri Duparc, George Butterworth is a songwriter whose reputation rests on a mere handful of songs, but the circumstances of their composing careers were quite different. Duparc's 16 extant songs were written over a period of 16 years, and though he stopped writing music at the age of 36, he lived on for another 50 years. Butterworth's song-career lasted a mere five years; he was, like Denis Browne and Ernest Farrar, a casualty of the First World War, killed at the Battle of the Somme on 5 August 1916 at the age of 31. Excluding the folksong arrangements, there are 18 surviving songs, eleven of which are settings of A. E. Housman, and it is these Housman settings which guarantee his place in the history of English song.

How, it might be asked, can this slender *oeuvre* deserve a separate chapter? Butterworth's achievement, it will be argued, is in quite different ratio to his slender output and his importance as a songwriter lies in the entirely new conception of what English art-song could be. He wanted to shed the claustrophobic clutter of so much late romantic song and replace it with a new directness of expression and simplicity. His was the musical equivalent of Thoreau's great dictum, 'Simplify! Simplify!' and he found his model in folksong, of which he was, with Vaughan Williams and Grainger, one of the pioneer composer-collectors in this country. Here he found lyrical ease and melodic directness as well as the forgotten tonal world of modal music, which would replace what, to him, were the exhausted resources of late 19th-century musical language. By keeping his ear on the melody, he rethought the traditional role of the song accompaniment, with its long keyboard introductions and codas and intricate keyboard figurations. This he replaced with simple, uncluttered accompaniments developed from those he and his mentors, Cecil Sharp and Vaughan Williams had been using in their folksong arrangements. 'To him, as to me, the folksong was not an inhibiting but a liberating influence,' Vaughan Williams wrote (1963: 193). His words could stand as Butterworth's epitaph.

Before he enlisted in the army in 1914, Butterworth destroyed many of his early works. As well as the two Housman song-cycles and the Henley song-cycle, three separate solo songs survived the bonfire: 'I fear thy kisses' (Shelley, 1909, *1919*), 'Requiescat' (Wilde, 1911, *1920*) and 'I will make you brooches' (Stevenson, c.1909/1910, *1920*). Though written at the same time as the Housman songs, they can be seen in retrospect as a final staging-post to them. The Shelley and Wilde settings share many similarities: melancholy sentiments – one a wan little love-song, the other an epitaph for a young girl – which the poets have set out in tiny quatrains and which are expressed in music of great delicacy and economy. 'I fear thy kisses' is dominated by a tiny motive (a descending third followed by a tone) which threads voice and accompaniment together. The tonality is unusual: F minor but cadencing modally onto B-flat. An unexpected excursion in the second verse into E major is neatly explained in the song's coda. In 'Requiescat' he solves the technical problem of Wilde's tiny stanzas by portmanteau-ing stanzas 1 and 2, and 3 and 4 into longer strophes. A characteristic Butterworth idea is heard at the end of the first strophe when the piano picks up the singer's opening line in thirds – a pre-echo of the clarinets in *A Shropshire Lad* Rhapsody (Ex. 12.1).

Ex. 12.1

Already we see the importance of silence, which can so often speak so much louder than sound, in his telling use of rests in the piano part. Both songs show that Butterworth had not completely thrown off traditional 19th-century ideas, the 'mother's milk' attraction of secondary 7ths (Shelley) and sequences (Wilde), but they indicate the way ahead. Though 'I will make you brooches' has 'a rather catchy tune' (Rippin, 1966: 769), it does not (*pace* Copley, 1985: 156) stand comparison with the Vaughan Williams and Warlock settings of the same text. He seems to be in two minds, caught halfway between modality and conventional diatonic harmony. The setting is mainly in a bright Mixolydian modality, which 'retreats' at decisive moments to a normal major tonality, as though he were unsure of the freedom he is allowing himself.

If these three songs were all he wrote, Butterworth would not be remembered even as a parenthesis in English song, for they give only a small hint of what was to come when he found a poet who not only gave him the type of verse to match his musical ideas, but, equally important, a subject-matter which emotionally reflected his own. The 63 poems published by Housman as *A Shropshire Lad* (1896) have produced a response from composers unparalleled in English song. In a brief twenty-year period straddling the First World War, major song-cycles were written by Somervell (1904), Vaughan Williams (1909), Butterworth (1911), Moeran (1920), Ireland (1921) and Gurney (1923 and 1926), as well as scores of fine separate solo songs by songwriters as diverse as Balfour Gardiner, Bax, Orr and Burrows. But many consider that Butterworth, particularly in his first cycle, comes nearest to the heart of Housman than any other composer. Certainly the folk-like simplicity and directness of the verse was matched by the straightforward, folk-like style which Butterworth was developing. (Housman the Cambridge Professor of Latin paradoxically preferred language based on Anglo-Saxon words in his poetry and never used a long, Latinate word where a short Anglo-Saxon one would do.) The language of the old folk ballads which Housman admitted were his models are reflected in Butterworth's modally-inflected songs with their straightforward, unfussy piano accompaniments. Some have accused Butterworth of simple-mindedness rather than simplicity, but there is in his settings a balance between passion and poise, artlessness and artifice. Gerald Finzi, in a nicely chosen analogy, pinpointed the essence of Butterworth's settings when he described them as 'reminiscent of English water colour . . . saying far more in its few strokes than any words could do' (Crees lecture, 1955: 7).

The background to the composition of the two cycles was complex, as Stephen Banfield has shown (1981: 261–7). The songs were written between 1909 and 1911 and Butterworth clearly gave much thought and planning to their composition. In his own copy of *A Shropshire Lad* he listed numerous possible choices of poem, eventually selecting fourteen, which he placed in an order that suggests that he was thinking, like Somervell before him, in terms of one large-scale song-cycle with a narrative outline. By the time he had made his first MS copy (early 1911) he had cut out four of the original poems, but was still intent on a single cycle, beginning with 'O fair to see' and ending with 'Bredon Hill'. In the end he divided the songs into two groups, adding to the second a setting of a poem not on the original list, 'On the idle hill of summer'.

Though Butterworth himself never called *Six Songs from 'A Shropshire Lad'* a song-cycle, it is one to all intents and purposes, in that each song leads naturally to the next through careful juxtaposition of poem and tonality. Individual songs *can* stand independently, but they make a stronger impact when heard in the sequence that Butterworth devised. Songs about the fleetingness of life (1 and 5), the folly of falling in love (2 and 3) and the unimportance of being earnest (4) lead to the final dialogue between the Lad and his dead friend. The sequence is reinforced by a subtle arrangement of tonalities: E major – E minor (Dorian) – F major – G-sharp minor – F-sharp major – C minor (Dorian).

The opening song, 'Loveliest of trees', is the key to the sequence and the key to all of Butterworth's Housman settings in that it forms the basis of his orchestral rhapsody, *A Shropshire Lad* (1912). Motives from this song reappear in later songs; indeed, the opening vocal lines of the first four songs bear a remarkable kinship (Ex. 12.2).

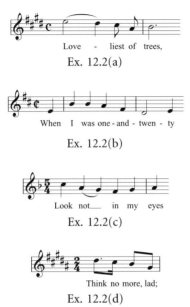

Ex. 12.2(a)

Ex. 12.2(b)

Ex. 12.2(c)

Ex. 12.2(d)

Though the song gives the impression of improvisation, its structure is highly organised and subtle. The three stanzas are set as a bow-shaped ternary form in which the final verse mirrors the first. This mirroring is reflected within the verse itself, where the opening phrase is inverted in the third line of the poem (Ex. 12.3).

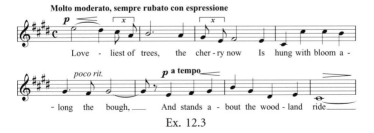

Ex. 12.3

In the third verse these two phrases change places: the second heard first ('And since to look at things in bloom'), the opening phrase last. The clue to this can be found in the text itself: Housman has framed his poem with references to the cherry trees; Butterworth has simply (i.e. artfully) followed Housman's lead. In the second verse Butterworth picks up the 'cuckoo' motive 'x' for both the vocal line and the sparse piano accompaniment. All is low-key – a sensible solution to a tricky stanza, where the Lad's emotions are at a standstill whilst he does some finger counting. (It is as though the cuckoo is calling unheard whilst the Lad is caught up in his mathematical reverie.) Yet despite this careful control of structure, the final result is not of intellectual cleverness but of an almost dreamy extemporisation, and in giving the singer the weight of responsibility, Butterworth makes us concentrate on Housman's words.

'When I was one-and-twenty' finds Butterworth at his most simple and folk-like. Under the song's title he has written 'Tune Traditional', but does not identify it. Nor has anyone so far been able to do so. It is in the Dorian mode and has the A B B A pattern typical of so many English folksongs (e.g. 'The Lincolnshire Poacher'). This corresponds perfectly with Housman's poem. The modal tune, however, is harmonised tonally, predominantly with first inversion chords and with implied 'modulations'. Taking a hint from Housman's own repetition of the poem's final phrase, ''tis true, 'tis true', Butterworth extends the music by a further repetition, intoned *pianissimo* over a bald plagal cadence. In 'Look not in my eyes' he chooses not the expected duple or triple metre, but an irregular 5/4 time signature, which he shifts flexibly between 2 + 3 and 3 + 2. This gives him an 'extra note' to play with, which he uses to give two-note melismas to important words. During the song these two-notes-a-syllable appear at almost every point in the bar, but instead of a metric straitjacket we hear a flexible, flowing line. The vocal line is again modal (here Mixolydian) and, as with the second song, the accompaniment some-times agrees with it, sometimes not. Butterworth again uses *tonal* devices: the 'modulation' to the dominant at the end of the first verse and the song's unexpected final cadence into F major, when the ear has been expecting B-flat major. Butterworth treats the cynical verses of 'Think no more, lad' in appropriate mock-jolly style, but rather naughtily makes a ternary pie out of Housman's two stanzas by repeating the first verse, with slight variations, at the end. There is, for the usually reticent Butterworth, some explicit word-painting at the phrase 'falling sky' (Exs. 12.4(a) and (b)). Of the many fine settings of 'The lads in their hundreds', Butterworth's is to my mind the best. Housman's poem, a spine-chilling foreboding as the Lad sits drinking at Ludlow Fair, uses a dactylic, folk-like metre and monosyllabic language, which is perfectly matched in Butterworth's music. There is no introduction: the voice leads the way from the outset, and the accompaniment is kept to a minimum to allow the vocal line to speak for itself. The piano's predominantly high tessitura

until the final cadence, the lowest note is G-sharp below middle C – imbues the setting with a trance-like aura.

Exs. 12.4(a)

Exs. 12.4(b)

The outstanding song, and the one that best defines Butterworth's attitude to songwriting, is 'Is my team ploughing?', which concludes the set. Butterworth characterises the catechetical dialogue between the dead youth and his living friend in both vocal line and accompaniment:

Q: high tessitura of vocal line, marked *molto moderato, senza rigore; pianissimo;* the piano a legato chain of 7ths chords drifting downwards over the span of an octave, with a conclusion unresolved but pointing towards B-flat major.

A: lower-pitched vocal line: *poco più mosso; forte;* an accompaniment of block triads and purposeful bass, ending conclusively with a plagal cadence in C minor.

These musical cadences effectively mirror the question and answer of the poem by the simplest means. How does Butterworth deal with the poem's 'problem ending' (discussed in the Introduction, p. 5)? Firstly, by making a break between the last two lines, slowing down the tempo and reducing the friend's dynamics to *piano*; next, by cadencing the voice onto the final of the mode (C) instead of G as previously; and finally, by gently slipping from the stark triads of the friend's accompaniment into the chromatic chain of chords associated with the 'dead man' (Ex. 12.5).

Ex. 12.5

The effect of the passage is elusive – it is as if the ghost and the living man, the Lad and his Doppelgänger, are fused into one spirit. The chromatic chords, instead of dropping down the octave as before, come to a halt halfway down the scale, suspended, as it were, in air. A 'cadence' is effected by the deep anchoring note of the piano's lowest C, forming an added 6th chord which is only resolved when the upper notes are removed, leaving the low C 'vibrating in the memory'. But is this the resolution that Housman would have wished? As so often, Butterworth leaves the final interpretation to the singer. That concluding phrase can be (and has been) sung in a variety of ways: with a smile on the lips, or with guilty sadness. Whatever the view, Butterworth has found a satisfying answer to a difficult problem. Of the other composers who have set this poem, only Charles Orr has found such a convincing solution.

The *Six Songs from 'A Shropshire Lad'* has homogeneity and unity: directness of expression, folk-like simplicity of vocal line and a piano accompaniment pared down to the bone. It was something new for its time and highly welcome in English music, after the overwrought complexities of much late romantic music.

But no-one should misinterpret this simplicity; it is art concealing art. Butterworth's second Housman sequence, *Bredon Hill and Other Songs*, lacks this homogeneity. Of the five songs, numbers 2, 3 and 5 share the folk-like character of the first cycle. Indeed, 'With rue my heart is laden', which he quotes at the end of the *A Shropshire Lad* rhapsody, is one of the most hauntingly beautiful of all his songs. The remaining two songs, however, are quite different, being far richer in both harmony and texture, and more complex in tonal organisation. 'Bredon Hill' is one of the weakest of the set. It lacks the intensity of Vaughan Williams's setting, and the continuous shifts of key centre break down the poem's unity. 'On the idle hill of summer', on the other hand, is one of Butterworth's most profound songs, anecdotally assured – the summer haze, the drums, the bugles and the fife are brilliantly evoked and integrated – and harmonically one of his most advanced inventions. In this it looked forward to the Rhapsody but, by the same token, away from the style of its companion songs.

Had he lived, would Butterworth have gone on to set more Housman exploring further the bittersweet musings of the Shropshire Lad, doing for Housman what Finzi was to do for Hardy? Hopefully not: such a monopolistic attitude on the part of a song-composer reveals a lack of breadth and adventure. (The monopoly on Housman was to become the prerogative of C. W. Orr.) Butterworth as a songwriter moved on, slightly unexpectedly to W. E. Henley, a poet of quite different cast to Housman, unfairly remembered today as the author of the jingoistic, ultra-Victorian 'Pro Rege Nostro' ('What have I done for you,/England, my England?'). Henley, though, was a fashioner of extremely effective lyrics, often choosing, as in the 'In Hospital' sequence, a very modern subject-matter handled in a post-Victorian manner. Many of his lyrics, particularly those from his collection *A Book of Verses* (1888), have been set to music by composers including Delius and Quilter.

Butterworth's song-cycle *Love Blows as the Wind Blows* was written in 1911–12 and originally consisted of four songs for baritone and string quartet. In this version it comprised (1) 'In the year that's come and gone', (2) 'Life in her creaking shoes', (3) 'Fill a glass with golden wine' and (4) 'On the way to Kew'. All four lyrics are eminently suitable for musical setting: concise, direct and with plenty of metric and stanza variety, which Butterworth acknowledges and takes full advantage of in his music. In 1914 he rescored the work for small orchestra, omitting the third song and revising the other three. In 1921 the original four-song string quartet version was published in a piano solo reduction, almost certainly provided by Vaughan Williams, and this version makes a very attractive alternative. Unlike the Housman settings, the work is designated as a song-cycle; the four songs are conceived as an entity, each song leading directly on to the next, as the directions *attacca* and *piccola pausa* indicate. The songs do not stand alone: for example, the first song sets out from E-flat major and modulates to D major for its cadence in readiness for the A major tonality of the second. More importantly, the work is bound together by a motto theme, associated with the music for the refrain of the second song, 'Love blows as the wind blows', from which, of course, the work takes its title. This theme is heard, on solo cello, at the very outset of the work before the singer enters, at the climax of the final song, at the crucial words 'And old immortal words/Sang in my breast like birds', and (very subtly) in the short coda to the cycle (Exs. 12.6(a), (b) and (c)).

Ex. 12.6(a)

Ex. 12.6(b)

Ex. 12.6(c)

The style is noticeably more contrapuntal than in the Housman sequences, and not just as the result of the string quartet accompaniment. This can be heard in the first song, where the singer's opening phrase is used in subtle imitation and half-imitation in the accompaniment, giving the setting a 'Finzian' flavour. As in the Housman songs, Butterworth takes his cue from the shapes of the poems for his musical structures. He does this most obviously in the second song's refrain, but most tellingly in the final song, 'On the way to Kew'. Here we have a remarkable matching of words and music. Henley's poem consists of three ten-line stanzas, each with four refraining lines:

1. 'On the way to Kew'
2. 'By the river old and gray'
3. '. . . in the Long Ago'
4. 'Coming up from Richmond'

But except for (4), they are never in the same order. ('Coming up from Richmond' is always the penultimate line.) With minor adjustments, Butterworth sets these lines to the same musical phrases, producing a marvellous kaleidoscopic pattern to the song, which, with the insouciant jauntiness of the musical ideas, admirably captures the 'promenade' that Henley is describing.

Butterworth was killed near Pozières, during the Battle of the Somme, in August 1916. There is something ironic about his death: it is almost as though he were living out the fate of his (and Housman's) Shropshire Lad, with its numerous references to and images of soldiers going into battle. This feeling of irony is nowhere more apparent than in the last two songs of the second Housman sequence. In 'On the idle hill of summer', the poet, half-asleep on a hillside (Bredon again?) describes the distant sounds of marching soldiers. He reflects on the folly of war, but decides nevertheless to join the soldiers himself. In 'With rue my heart is laden' (see epigraph), a sadder, wiser young man reflects on the 'golden friends' whom he will never see again:

> By brooks too broad for leaping
>   The lightfoot boys are laid;
> The rose-lipt girls are sleeping
>   In fields where roses fade.

Butterworth's death robbed us of potentially one of the finest British composers of his generation. His surviving output is small and was written over a period of less than five years, between 1909 and 1914, for in the last two years of his life he had little time or opportunity to write music. The stark simplicity of his songs came as a much-needed breath of fresh air into the stuffy drawing-rooms of English song. His impact on English song was similar to that of Edward Thomas – another First World War casualty – on English poetry: a fresh vision on old, deep-rooted subjects, a new way to express ageless thoughts. His surviving works are 'few, but roses'.

13

Denis Browne (1888–1915)

So did she move; so did she sing,
Like the harmonious spheres that bring
  Unto their rounds their music's aid;
Which she performèd such a way,
As all th'enamour'd world will say:
  'The Graces danc'd, and Apollo play'd.'

Richard Lovelace:
'To Gratiana dancing and singing'.

If George Butterworth's artistic legacy was small, then Denis Browne's was minute. But the handful of songs that he wrote in his brief career is worth all the outpourings of lesser songwriters. For this reason he deserves his own slender chapter amongst the larger chapters devoted to others. Like Butterworth, Browne was a casualty of the First World War. On 28 February 1915 he left England with the Hood Battalion on board the *Grantully Castle*. With him were Rupert Brooke, Arthur Asquith, son of the Prime Minister, and the Australian-born composer and pianist, Frederick Kelly. Brooke died from blood-poisoning on April 23rd and was buried on the island of Skyros; Browne was one of his pall-bearers. Six weeks later, on June 4th, Browne himself was killed at Achi Baba on the Gallipoli peninsula: he was only 26. His premature death, coupled with a busy musical life as pianist, critic and conductor, makes it hardly surprising that his output as a composer was so small: a handful of choral and orchestral pieces, an incomplete ballet, *The Comic Spirit*, and eleven songs. Of these songs, only two, both Tennyson settings, were published during his lifetime, 'Move eastward, happy earth' and 'The snowdrop' (*1909*), written when he was barely 21. Not surprisingly they give no hint of the originality to come. Two Yeats songs, dating from 1909, 'Had I the heavens' embroidered cloths' and 'The fiddler of Dooney', are disappointing, as is 'Parting', to an anonymous translation of a poem by Arno Holz. 'The isle of lost dreams' (1909, *1990*) is more effective and makes an attractive song; its Anglican hymn-like response to William Sharp's Celtic musing is unexpected but is compensated by a memorable vocal line. The finest of these early songs is a setting of Francis Thompson's 'Dream-tryst' (1909, *1990*). It is dated 27 December 1909, two weeks before 'Parting', yet here Browne evokes a quite original sensibility. With its experimental bitonal and quartal harmonies and dream-like oriental atmosphere, it anticipates the mature achievement of 'Arabia' (Ex. 13.1)

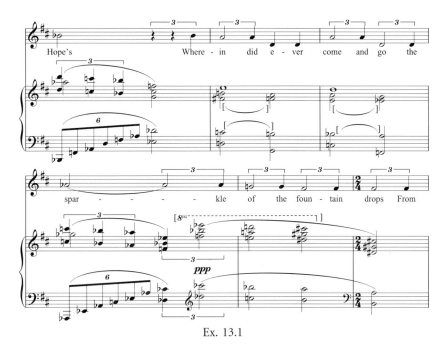

Ex. 13.1

Browne's reputation, however, rests on his last four songs, published after his death. 'Diaphenia' (1912, *1923*) sets a lyric which first appeared in the anthology, *England's Helicon* (1600), over the initials 'H. C.', where it is entitled 'Damelus' Song to his Diaphenia'. 'H. C.', for a long time thought to be Henry Constable, is now considered to be Henry Chettle (c.1560–?1607), a playwright-contemporary of Shakespeare and the author of the satirical pamphlet *Kind Harts Dreame* (?1593). Francis Pilkington set the lyric in his *First Booke of Songs* (1605). Though Browne's setting lacks the profundity of the other three songs, its artless charm conceals real art. Notice, for example, its irregular three-bar phrasing and the way in which the melody and harmonies are wittily subjected to dislocation (bars 16–17/28–9), as though the bass were cheekily deciding to go its own way, then sneaking back for the cadence (Ex. 13.2). The sly humour of its oompah accompaniment and the insouciance of its chromaticism link it, as Banfield points out, as much to the vaudeville as the Lied tradition (1985: 154).

Ex. 13.2

'Epitaph on Salathiel Pavy' (1912, *1927*) was written a month after 'Diaphenia' and Browne had intended that they should be performed in tandem as *Two Elizabethan Songs*. The subject of Ben Jonson's epitaph (from *Epigrams*, 1616) was a famed boy chorister-cum-child actor and member of the Chapel Royal. The contrapuntal textures of the piano accompaniment remind us of the consort accompaniments to Orlando Gibbon's verse anthems, whilst the chromatic bass of the ritornello recalls an even more famous elegy – Dido's Lament, from Purcell's *Dido and Aeneas* (1689). Notice the skilful way in which the two elements of the ritornello – upward moving inverted triads and downward-moving chromatic line – are later inverted (Ex. 13.3 (a) and (b)). The subtle chromatic touches to the modality, linked with the singer's expressive, wide-ranging vocal line, give the song the force of genuine elegy. This blending of classical restraint and modern sensibility, of modality and texture that hark back to Jacobean England with 20th-century harmonies, poignantly links the death of that 'Child of Queen Elizabeth's Chapel' with the present time, pre-echoing what Peter Warlock was to do a decade later (Ex. 13.3(c)).

Ex. 13.3(a)

Ex. 13.3(b)

Ex. 13.3(c)

Browne's setting of Walter de la Mare's 'Arabia' is dated 22 June 1914, six weeks before the outbreak of the First World War, and was first published in the December 1919 number of *The Monthly Chapbook* alongside songs by Browne's contemporaries, Armstrong Gibbs and Clive Carey. Odd as it may seem, it is the earliest-known setting of de la Mare's poetry. It was Browne's last song and also his most 'advanced', remarkably close in spirit to the later music of Debussy, which, of course, he could not have known. Its unusual harmonies of super-imposed, unrelated triads, anticipate techniques which Frank Bridge was to use in his music of the 1920s and 1930s, whilst the non-synchronisation of the final lines anticipates music of an even later date. This experimentation is not used for its own sake, however, but to evoke the strange, dream-like spirit of de la Mare's poem (Ex. 13.4(a)). Formally, the song is extremely subtle, the piano carrying the weight of the structure. The main motive, of unrelated triads, acts as introduction, ritornello and coda to the song. At its first appearance, it cadences onto sonorous G minor triads, from which the first verse is launched, over a simple texture of slowly moving minims (Ex. 13.4(b)). The verse closes with a reprise of the ritornello, which closes this time onto an off-beat dominant pedal-note (D). The second verse, marked *Poco più mosso* and beginning in the tonic major, is poised over this pedal-note, and the off-beat rhythm continues for the first half of the verse. In the second half, the texture changes to widely-spaced, strange-sounding bitonal chords – 'Hear the strange lutes on the green banks/ Ring loud' – which continues to the end of the verse when the ritornello reappears, transformed into flowing arpeggios, as the accompaniment to the final verse. At the final lines of the setting, the synchronisation between voice and piano breaks down, the singer *Tempo perduto* (= desperately), the piano *Molto più lento* (see Ex. 11. 4(a)). The ritornello than reappears in its original form, bringing the song to a close on the sonorous G minor triads. Across this piano 'landscape', the singer has a free, through-composed arioso line, with little repetition of material and in which the declamation of the words is the priority.

Ex. 13.4(a)

Ex. 13.4(b)

The pinnacle of Browne's achievement, however, is his setting of Richard Lovelace's lyric, 'To Gratiana dancing and singing' (1913, *1923*), written in February 1913 for his friend Steuart Wilson. As a basis for the accompaniment he uses an anonymous *Allmayne* from Elizabeth Rogers's Virginal Book (c.1656) which he had come upon during the Milton Tercentenary performance of *Comus* at Cambridge in 1908, in which he (and Rupert Brooke) had taken part (Ex. 13.5(a)).

Ex. 13.5(a)

He dresses the tune up in rich harmonies and textures, with characteristic hand-crossing and, in the second verse, the use of harped 10ths and an 'echo chord'. The whole effect is remarkably reminiscent of the style of Percy Grainger, a composer whom Browne greatly admired (Ex. 13.5(b)). Above this slow, stately dance measure, the singer has a subtle, melodious descant, almost in the style of Welsh penillion (Ex. 13.5(c)). Together, singer and accompanist exquisitely capture the spirit of Lovelace's poem, of the admiring poet watching his beloved across the dance-floor. Browne regularises the pattern of the *Allmayne*, which plays in the background throughout the song, by repeating the first two bars of the second strain and cutting out its repeats, so that both of its strains are of equal length (8 bars = 8 bars). Above this, the six lines of Lovelace's stanza (3 + 3) are counterpointed in a delightfully asymmetrical way. Thus, in verse 1, the first two lines fit the first four bars, whilst the third line, through long melismas on 'Gratiana' and 'steers', manages to fill the next four. The singer does not join the second strain until its second bar and by this and other delays, the fourth line of the verse fills the next four bars, leaving the last two lines to fit the final four bars. The same cross-counterpointing of word-setting and music continues through the two ensuing verses. Combined with the flowing *Allmayne* tempo that Browne stipulates the result is one of spaciousness and grace, completely in keeping with the conception. As with 'Epitaph on Salathiel Pavy', by using 17th-century musical material (a 17th-century poem and a 17th-century allemande) and 20th-century musical techniques, Browne imaginatively creates a link across Time.

Ex. 13.5(b)

Ex. 13.5(c)

Browne's achievement as a songwriter, even compared with Butterworth's, is embryonic, his potential unfulfilled. The final songs stand as separate, isolated pinnacles, each quite distinct in mood, technique and sensibility. They are like four precious gems, a sapphire, a diamond, a ruby and an emerald, which together hardly make up a bracelet, let alone a necklace. The eclecticism of his choice of poets underlines this. We have a lament and a love-song from the Elizabethan age (Jonson and 'H.C.'), a sophisticated Cavalier lyric (Lovelace), two poems by Tennyson, an example each from the Irish and Scottish Celtic Twilights (Yeats and Sharp), an opium-incense reverie by Francis Thompson and a dream-landscape by Walter de la Mare. It is tempting to speculate which direction he might have taken had he lived. Would he have set the poetry of his friend Rupert Brooke? (The nearest they came to collaborating was on board the

Grantully Castle when Brooke drafted a poem for Browne to set on the improbable, but clearly topical, subject of dysentery, with the ironic title, 'The dance'.) Would he, like Ivor Gurney, have found inspiration in Georgian contemporaries such as Edward Thomas or Robert Graves? Or would he have discovered, like Finzi and Ireland, the harder-edged lyrics of Thomas Hardy? Or would he have continued the 'historical' songs of 'Salathiel Pavy' and 'Gratiana' and, like Warlock, explored further the poetry and music of England's first Golden Age of Song? We can only speculate and be glad that we have this precious handful of songs, magical fragments from a never-fulfilled career. There can be few composers whose reputations rest on so slender an output. 'Gratiana', 'Diaphenia', 'Salathiel Pavy' and 'Arabia' deserve to be included in any respectable anthology of English song. Many would claim 'Gratiana' as one of the half-dozen best songs in the English repertoire, and its influence on later English song-composers can never be over-estimated. In these few precious songs, indeed:

The Graces danc'd, and Apollo play'd.

14

Armstrong Gibbs (1889–1960)

Slowly, silently, now the moon
Walks the night in her silver shoon;
This way, and that, she peers, and sees
Silver fruit upon silver trees;
One by one the casements catch
Her beams beneath the silvery thatch;
Couched in his kennel, like a log,
With paws of silver sleeps the dog;
From their shadowy cote the white breasts peep
Of doves in a silver-feathered sleep;
A harvest mouse goes scampering by,
With silver claws and silver eye;
And moveless fish in the water gleam,
By silver reeds in a silver stream.

Walter de la Mare: 'Silver'

Cecil Armstrong Gibbs was a relative latecomer to songwriting. There is an early surviving song, 'Near and far' (poem by 'A. R. Ropes' = Adrian Ross; MS at CUL, Add. MS 6590), dated 'Xmas 1909', and a handful of settings of Shelley, Blake, Stevenson and Sidney in the years preceding World War 1, but it was not until 1917, when he was in his late twenties, that he began writing songs in earnest – significantly, as it turned out, when he discovered the poetry of Walter de la Mare. Over the next 40 years he wrote over 150 solo songs, an enormous output for a composer who composed music for other media, choral, orchestral and chamber, and spent much of his professional life teaching and adjudicating. Like Quilter, Gibbs's best songs were written in the early part of his career, during the period 1917–33. In the songs of his later years, inspiration is intermittent. His was a minor talent; he happily accepted the traditions and restrictions of song composition as he found them and there is no radical attempt to break new ground, as with his close contemporaries Butterworth and Warlock, or even his older contemporaries Vaughan Williams and Ireland. Nor did he possess the instantly recognisable voice of Quilter or Warlock. Yet, at his best, in such songs as 'The witch', 'Hypochondriacus', 'The ballad of Semmerwater', 'By a bierside', 'The fields are full' and the finest of his de la Mare settings, he is outstanding.

He turned to over 50 different poets, but the majority of these were set only once; just three poets are set more than five times: John Irvine (7), Mordaunt

Currie (17) and Walter de la Mare (38). His poets are drawn from all periods, ranging from Tudor Anon. to his younger contemporaries; some, such as Congreve and Landor, are most unexpected, and many are obscure and very minor. Who were Leon Eeman, Margery Agrell, Edith Harrhy and Bernard Martin? But if a text inspired him he was able to turn even the most indifferent poem into a fine song. Above all others, he preferred Walter de la Mare. His tally of 38 settings exceeds any other song-composer and makes the dozen or so set by his nearest rival, Herbert Howells, appear modest. Like Finzi with Hardy and Orr with Housman, Gibbs's songs will always be associated with de la Mare's poetry. But this should not blind us to the merits of his other songs.

If his choice of poet is wide-ranging, his choice of song-text is limited. He rarely tackles the big, time-honoured subjects such as death and unrequited love (Hancock-Child, 1993: 38); rather he favours magic and romance, night, sleep and dreams, silence and shadows. There is a childlike quality in nearly everything he sets – hence his penchant for de la Mare. His treatment of his texts is bold and sensitive, even if, on occasion, one feels he 'acts out his poem's swiftly changing moods too obviously and explicitly', as in 'Titania', for example. As with Quilter, he was the supreme professional. His piano accompaniments are deft and expressive, written by someone who understood the instrument; his vocal lines, though often far from simple, are always eminently singable. He is an expert technician, knowing how to vary word-setting, whilst finding the unexpected but invariably 'right' rhythmic shape for a line. Take, for example, a simple early song such as 'Five eyes', where the opening line etches itself on the mind immediately, or 'Silver', where he avoids the monotony of the repeated eponym by giving it almost every conceivable variety of shape and rhythm.

Gibbs's style represents a typical British compromise between old and new, tradition and change. In harmonic and tonal matters, he adheres to more traditional techniques, though not so conservatively as his contemporary Gurney; one has only to listen to songs as diverse as 'Hypochondriacus', 'The fields are full', 'The witch' and 'Love is a sickness' to realise that they could not have been written by a 19th-century composer. But his adoption of newer techniques is limited. There are constant modal inflections, but of a modest character, usually limited to flattened 7ths and the occasional English cadence, picked up from his acquaintance with Tudor music. This shows especially in pastiche-based songs such as *Two Elizabethan Songs* and 'Amaryllis', which remind us strongly of Warlock, though lacking Warlock's pungency and wit. He displays little interest in folksong; even a folk-like poem such as 'When I was one-and-twenty', where you might expect it, smacks of church modality rather than folksong. He does enrich his basically traditional tonal and harmonic palette with the use of whole-tone scales and harmonies, absorbed from French composers such as Debussy, and augmented triads (see *Songs of the Mad Sea-Captain*) and scales of major thirds (as in 'Dream song' and 'The witch') are familiar hallmarks. Very occasionally he introduces 4th-based harmonies; these appear as early as *Crossings*, in the ritornello to 'Candlestick-maker's song' (itself a key motto from the play's overture).

The characteristic Gibbs song contains Fauré-like side-steps to remote keys which always come safely home again; often whole-tone harmonies are used to effect these unexpected modulations (see 'Lullaby' in *Crossings*). Sometimes one feels that he falls into 'easy' formulae, as, for example, in the many songs that travel down through a cycle of fifths in their penultimate phrases ('The mountain').

His melodies 'lie comfortably on the voice', though are not always simple to pitch. Like those of Delius and Bax, his vocal lines are rarely self-contained, like a folksong, but rely on the context of their accompanying harmonies. His word-setting is, characteristically for his time, basically syllabic, so that the occasional use of melisma comes as a delightful surprise, as in the cadences of 'Beggar's song' and 'In youth is pleasure'. His piano accompaniments, like those of Roger Quilter, are deft, expressive and a delight to play, clearly written by someone who understood the instrument. They are always technically within the range of the good amateur pianist: none of the intimidating virtuosity of Bax or the thick chordings of Warlock. He has a penchant for off-beat pedal-notes (in 'Silver', most famously) and for delicate treble-register sounds (see 'The fields are full' and 'Philomel').

Gibbs's reputation as a songwriter rests on his settings of the poetry of de la Mare, which almost exactly coincided with the period of his finest work, from 'Five eyes' and 'Song of shadows' written in 1917 to the *Five Children's Songs from 'Peacock Pie'* of 1933. Writing in 1956, Gibbs said of de la Mare's poetry that it 'opened magic casements' for him (Gibbs, 1956). He was attracted by the childlike quality of de la Mare's verse and the world of the 'far-away', romance and enchantment that it evokes, and it is significant that the poetry of other writers that he set – Mordaunt Currie's 'The witch' and Bernard Martin's *Songs of the Mad Sea-Captain* – strove to attain that same de la Mare magic. Gibbs's particular genius matched de la Mare perfectly and in his settings he supplied the 'tiny music' that the poet so loved.

The early settings went through various arrangements and regroupings. Some began as partsongs: 'Five eyes' and 'Song of shadows' are still popular as such. 'Nod' (initially turned down by Novello) was the first to be published, in Harold Monro's *The Monthly Chapbook* (December 1919) alongside Denis Browne's 'Arabia'. In the following year Stainer & Bell issued a group of five, and from that point the songs were also taken up by Winthrop Rogers and Curwen. The *Five Songs* (*1920*) were originally envisaged as three separate groupings: 'Love in the almond bough' and 'The mountains' (written in 1918) as *Two Songs*, op. 19, 'The linnet' and 'The stranger' (1919) as *Two Songs*, op. 21; and 'The bells' (1918) as the second of *Two Songs*, op. 14. In the Stainer & Bell publication they appear in the following order, with dedications to Gibbs's early mentors and the poet himself:

1. 'The stranger'   (Adrian C. Boult)
2. 'The linnet'   (Prof. H. P. Allen)
3. 'The mountains'   (Walter de la Mare)
4. 'Love in the almond bough' (Edward J. Dent)
5. 'The bells'   (Dr Ralph Vaughan Williams)

They vary in quality, almost corresponding to their original groupings. 'The mountains', with its characteristic off-beat pedal-note, is the weakest, and 'Love in the almond bough' no more than a nondescript waltz song. 'The linnet', like so many of Gibbs's songs, is inspired by a harmonic idea, here two unrelated chords, B minor and an augmented 6th on A-flat, spread out in an upward arpeggio ending with a linnet-like twitter. 'The stranger', too, takes its character from a harmonic idea, in this case a piquancy of supertonic chord over tonic bass. The outstanding song of the group is 'The bells', a setting of one of de la Mare's most evocative poems. In it the poet gives us an oblique perspective of the countryside as seen from a bell-tower, with its eight ringers, over a field to the ploughman and his team and his children playing nearby. Gibbs sets the narrative as a through-composed song with an unusual shape: starting loud and clamorous it gradually grows calmer and quieter, until it achieves complete stillness in the final bars (Ex. 14.1).

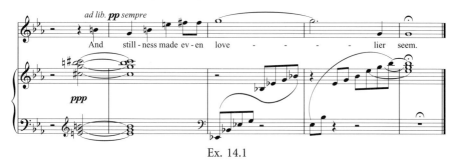

Ex. 14.1

Not unexpectedly, bell-sounds dominate – it would have been perverse had they not. The bell-ring ostinato begins in the middle register and continues through to the final couplets, when it suddenly stops at the words 'Soon night hid horses, children, all,/In sleep deep and ambrosial', only to begin again, higher and more distant, to depict the bells echoing in a dream.

   Three other memorable settings from this time are 'Five eyes' (1917, *1922*), 'Song of shadows' (1917, *1922*) and 'Nod' (1918, *1919/1921*). 'Five eyes' is one of Gibbs's best known songs, deservedly so. With its scampering accompaniment and perky vocal line, it is a perfect match for the five eyes of Hans the miller's cats, 'Jekkel, and Jessup, and one-eyed Jill'. 'Song of shadows' begins unexpectedly, with the piano making an unusual harmonic move, from a rich 'out-of-key' chord on the mediant (9th with flattened 7th) to the dominant, before the E-flat tonic is established. We then seem to be taken into the cosy drawing-room, with piano arpeggios lapping around a rather ordinary tune.

But halfway through the stanza, when 'The old hound whimpers couched in sleep', things change: the arpeggios cease and are replaced by *pianissimo* block triads that sink chromatically down before meeting up again with the lapping arpeggios (Ex. 14.2). The song finds its logical fulfilment at the very end where, in the briefly echoed final words 'Home once more', the unusual flattened chordal sequence from the beginning is reprised and justified.

Ex. 14.2

'Nod' is notable for the control of pace and rhythm of Gibbs's word-setting. Note the skilful way with which he deals with the first stanza, with hardly a repetition of rhythm from bar to bar, and the way in which he manages to slow down the pace of the fifth verse without interrupting the gently-rocking quaver flow of the accompaniment (Exs. 14.3(a) and (b)).

Ex. 14.3(a)

Ex. 14.3(b)

The four songs that comprise *Crossings* (1919, *1921*) are part of the incidental music that Gibbs wrote for de la Mare's fairy play, which was mounted to mark the retirement of the headmaster of The Wick preparatory school, Hove, where Gibbs was teaching at the time. De la Mare's libretto was specially written for the occasion. The production, on 21 June 1919, was a memorable affair, with Gibbs and his wife in the orchestra, E. J. Dent stage-managing and Adrian Boult conducting. As they had to be sung by children, the songs had to be tailored carefully, but despite these technical restrictions, Gibbs produced some of his most inventive songs: direct and simple, tuneful yet haunting. He was aided by de la Mare's words, which are varied in verse shape and full of vivid, dream-like imagery. 'Araby' is one of de la Mare's characteristic dialogue poems, here set out as question and answer between a ship's captain and a sailor. Gibbs neatly characterises the two speakers by setting the sailor's answer a 3rd higher than his master's question, all heard over a rocking barcarolle. In the final verse, when the dialogue ceases, the spirit of exotic adventure dashed by the elements, the music becomes unsettled too, and only reaches haven in the final bars, with the singer's final, downward arpeggio (Ex. 14.4).

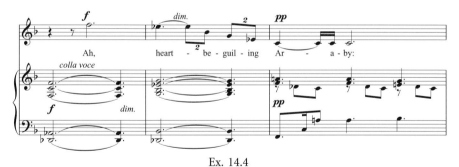

Ex. 14.4

'Ann's cradle song' ('Now silent falls' in *Collected Rhymes and Verses*) is an unusual lullaby, set in common time over a walking bass. De la Mare subtly alters the usual verse-and-refrain pattern by adding an extra stanza to the third verse, which enables Gibbs to expand his music for the final strophe. The music of verse and refrain are strongly differentiated, the C-sharp minor of the verse and the memorable rocking D-flat major refrain linked by pivotal augmented

6th chords (Ex. 14.5). In the extended third verse, the lullaby mood is briefly broken by 'cries in the brake, bells in the sea'.

Ex. 14.5

This Gibbs sets to new melodic material with a simple arpeggiated accompaniment, which reaches a rich chromatic passage (pedal-notes enclosing parallel secondary 7ths) when the landscape fills with leaping foxes and hooting owls. But he draws the threads together when he reaches the pivotal augmented 6th, to take us safely into the final lullaby-refrain. 'Beggar's song' ('Now all the road' in *CVR*) is the nearest Gibbs comes to writing a folksong-inspired tune, complete with a memorable little melisma at the end of the first phrase. But it is more wide-ranging than any folksong, roaming from the initial E tonality through B-flat and C-sharp before returning home. The bustling accompaniment is built on reflecting arpeggios that radiate from either side of the tonic E – a tonic that cannot decide whether to be major (as in the introduction) or minor (as it is when the Beggar sings). 'Candlestick-maker's song' ('The flower' in *CVR*) is sung by the character in the drama who represents 'Dream, Romance, the other World' (Gibbs, quoted in Banfield, 1985: 226). Gibbs sets de la Mare's three five-line stanzas as a ternary song, the music following the Candlestick-maker's story with deceptive ease, as he leads us to his land of enchantment. Many commentators feel that Gibbs never surpassed these songs. *Crossings* stands as a remarkable example of empathy between poet and composer, a true collaboration.

These early de la Mare settings represent Gibbs at his best. A later song which rekindled the magic is 'Dream song' (1932, *1933*). This is yet another incursion into fairyland, full of those potent de la Mare images of dream and sleep. The opening lines of the three stanzas act as a chiming incantation to different kinds of light:

Sunlight, moonlight,
Twilight, starlight . . .

Lantern-light, taper-light,
Torch-light, no-light . . .

Elf-light, bat-light,
Touchwood-light, toad-light . . .

Gibbs colours the tonality of the song with modal inflections, notably the fragment of whole-tone scale at the cadences of verses 1 and 3 (Ex. 14.6).

Ex. 14.6

The gentle walking-crotchet motion of the outer strophes – reminiscent, as is the whole song, of Warlock's early 'Lullaby' – is cleverly differentiated by the scherzando textures of the second verse, which are neatly reprised in the song's coda.

Another fine de la Mare setting, dating from 1924, is 'The galliass'. De la Mare's mysterious poem is set out as an allegorical dialogue between a 'Landsman' and an 'Unknown Stranger'. The former is seeking the Ship (= Galliass) of Sleep, and the word 'Sleep' acts as a refrain to all four verses. Gibbs gives appropriately different musics to the two speakers – static chords and G major tonality for the Landsman, a pulsing pedal-note for the Unknown Stranger, with E-flat minor tonality for verse 1 and E major for verse 2. But symmetrical squareness is skilfully avoided. The piano's opening ritornello – a gently bitonal opening chord (D minor on C minor) resolving onto G major – returns before verse 2, but is subsequently dispensed with. But at the end, after the music is left high and dry in a C-sharp minor tonality, the ritornello returns, to modulate the song, Poulenc-wise 'through a mousehole', to the desired G major cadence (Ex. 14.7). The outstanding de la Mare setting is 'Silver' (1920, *1922*), the poet's famous invocation to moonlight. The four strophes that Gibbs fashions from the poet's rhyming couplets are set in masterly tour-de-force over a tonic pedal E. Tolling off-the-beat like a bell low down on the keyboard, it matches the insistent repetitions of the word 'silver' in the poem.

Ex. 14.7

Above this there is, minim-slow, a two-chord ostinato, a silvery chordal mixture of E minor and C major, rocking to and fro with an added 6th on E minor, so that, despite the insistent presence of the pedal E, there is tonal ambiguity throughout (Ex. 14.8).

Ex. 14.8

Though not technically an 'air over a ground', this is the effect produced. Just before the end, the chords and tolling tonic momentarily disappear – like a moon behind a cloud – so that the image of the harvest mouse 'scampering by,/ With silver claws, and silver eye' can be sung *parlando*: a magical moment in a magical song. The music ends unresolved, with that ambiguous E minor/C major chord settling for eternity over its pedal E. Many other composers have set 'Silver' but, as Stephen Banfield has said, Gibbs's setting comes 'as near as is possible to what one might desire as a "definitive" setting of the text' (1985: 214). It is arguably Gibbs's finest and most characteristic as well as most frequently performed song.

Not all of the de la Mare settings are successful. In 'The mountains' he finds no significant music for de la Mare's mystical evocation of 'the icy hills' with their 'untroubled snows'; all the more sad, in view of the fact that the song is dedicated to de la Mare. 'John Mouldy' (1920, *1922*), written at the same time as 'Silver', fails to capture the macabre nature of the text – it should be a frightening song; it isn't – whilst 'The ship of Rio' (1932, *1933*) verges closer to the childish than the childlike. With its hornpipe-like accompaniment and

'Yo! Ho! my hearties' atmosphere, it looks forward to *Songs of the Mad Sea-Captain* (*1946*) with its predictable shanty-based music. Nevertheless, viewed in total, Gibbs's de la Mare settings represent a considerable achievement.

The only other poet who stimulated Gibbs to song in any comparable way was Mordaunt Currie (1894–1978), a baronet (the fifth of his line) who lived not far from Gibbs, at Bishop Witham in Essex. Currie supplied Gibbs with the texts for 17 songs, culminating in his only song-cycle, *Joan of Arc* (1944, *1947*). For Gibbs to write a song-cycle was an unexpected move; even more unexpected was the subject-matter. One can only think that the date of composition was significant in the choice of such a subject, the life of the Maid of Orléans symbolising patriotism in a time of war. The theme is unusual in English song and was a far leap from Gibbs's usual territory. He treats Currie's heroic texts to appropriately heroic music: five dramatic songs for soprano, set out like a series of operatic *scena*: Vision – Victory – Vanquished. Not surprisingly, the songs are disappointing, the music pompous and overblown. Such matter for songwriting was beyond Gibbs's call of duty. Of all the Currie settings, the best is undoubtedly 'The witch' (*1938*). This gruesome little poem, very much in the de la Mare mould, could well be retitled 'Death and the witch'. It consists of a conversation between the witch, 'Tib', and her two familiars, a cat and a dog. They predict their mistress's demise, but when she questions them, they keep mum. The song's invention springs from the opening piano figuration, which curls chromatically round itself like a cat.

Ex. 14.9(a)

Ex. 14.9(b)

This memorable little idea stops abruptly, uncadenced, when the singer enters, an unexpected move which is repeated at the end of the song, where the music is cut off in mid-flight, as in Holst's 'The floral bandit' (Ex. 14.9(a)). The witch's final agonising outburst is one of the best things in Gibbs (Ex. 14.9(b)). Of the many 'one-off' settings of poets that line Gibbs's career like poetic scalps, those of Edward Shanks, William Watson and Charles Lamb are particularly noteworthy. His setting of Shanks's 'The fields are full' (*1920*), though lacking the intensity of Warlock's 'Late summer', has proved popular with singers. As with Shelley's 'Music, when soft voices die', the problem for the songwriter in this poem is to avoid getting waylaid by the extended simile (stanza 2) at the expense of the central image (stanza 1). Warlock avoids it in his setting; Gurney gets ensnared by it in his; Gibbs teeters on the edge. The change of texture in the second verse momentarily takes attention away from the image of summer fields, but he manages to retrieve the situation as, *come primo*, he returns to the high liquid triads of the opening verse. The setting of Watson's 'The ballad of Semmerwater' (*1930*) shows a rarely encountered aspect of Gibbs's songwriting, the narrative ballad. This is a most effective song, with its sinister tolling of sunken bells and its fine control of changing textures, and Gibbs captures well the onward thrust of the narrative. Hear how he exploits the singer's lowest notes to full effect (Ex. 14.10).

Ex. 14.10

'The tiger-lily', to a poem by Dorothy Pleydell Bouverie (1921, *1924*), is one of Gibbs's most profound songs. In text and mood, the song bears similarities to Warlock's 'The frostbound wood', composed some eight years later. Tonally the music veers between C minor and E major, a conflict apparent from the opening bar and only finally resolved in the unexpected final cadence, where 'the expected resolution is side-stepped and the final chord is desolate and unforgiving' (Hancock-Child, 1993: 63) (Ex. 14.11). The balance between vocal line and piano in this song shows Gibbs at his finest. His two Hardy settings – 'Lyonnesse' (*1921*) and 'The oxen' (1951, *1952*) – are disappointing. 'Lyonnesse', a poem that above all others needs to have magic shining from its eyes, is pedestrian in its solid 3/4 march. Nor does 'The oxen' capture the spirit of Hardy's familiar, oft-set poem; its ending is spoilt by sentimentality. Far more impressive is his setting of the 'Song of the Chief Centurions' from Masefield's play, *Pompey the Great*,

Ex. 14.11

a lyric that has also inspired songs from Gurney and Whittaker. 'By a bierside' ('This is a sacred city', *1924*) is a powerful, succinct setting of this noble elegy, more focussed than Gurney's overlong, diffuse version, more direct and memorable than Whittaker's.

Some of the 'Elizabethan' songs, to poems by Daniel, Wever, Barnfield, Munday and the ubiquitous Anon., have their attraction, but lack the pungency and wit of Warlock's songs in the same vein, with which they inevitably beg comparison. Gibbs slips neatly into his doublet and hose, but he hasn't Warlock's innate understanding and knowledge of his models. The late setting of Munday's 'Lament for Robin Hood' (*1956*) contains some imaginative moments.

But outstanding amongst these 'one-off' songs is 'Hypochondriacus' (*1949*), to an obscure poem by Charles Lamb. Lamb, who is remembered as a poet for one poem, the much-anthologised 'The old familiar faces', has rarely been set to music. 'Hypochondriacus' was published with his play, *John Woodville*, in 1802, where it is described as 'A Conceipt of Diabolical Possession':

> . . . Black thoughts continually
> Crowding my privacy;
> They come unbidden,
> Like foes at a wedding,
> Thrusting their faces
> In better guests' places . . .

It continues with a catalogue of the foul fiends that possess the poet:

> Fierce Anthropophagi,
> Spectra, Diaboli,
> What scared St. Anthony,
> Hobgoblins, Lemures . . .

and concludes with an apostrophe in Latin (slightly incorrect – which only adds to the madness):

> 'Jesu! Maria! liberate nos ab his diris tentationibus Inimici.'

It can be seen why a composer would be attracted to such wild verses, the couplets tumbling over each other in mad confusion. Though Gibbs is not perhaps the first composer you would expect to accept the challenge, he produces a mad song worthy of Purcell. To deal with the racing couplets, he adopts patter-song technique; starting quietly and low down in the singer's register, with clipped cadences to each phrase ending, the music rises gradually to a frenetic climax, at which point, over a dissonant chord, the Latin tag is spat out *senza misura* (Ex. 14.12).

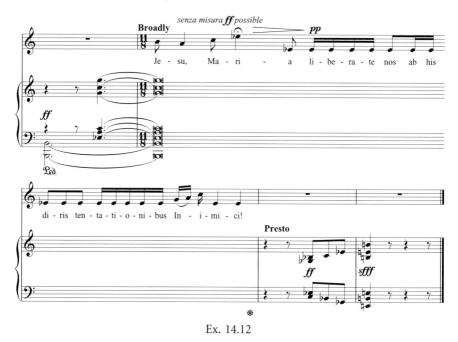

Ex. 14.12

The accompaniment – the composer at his most 'modernly' dissonant – is cued by the opening words ('By myself walking,/To myself talking'), striding along in unrestrained, unvaried beats, with a chromatic bass and full of augmented chords. It is a truly terrifying song, and one of Gibbs's most original. It is sad that he wrote no more in this vein.

Like Roger Quilter, Armstrong Gibbs is a composer of 'light conceits': not 'of lovers' perhaps – he wrote few love-songs and those that he did are two moves from reality, classical myth clothed by 16th-century poets – but of light subject-matter conceived with a grace and lightness of touch. He rarely used song to express deep spiritual concerns; 'high seriousness' was not his forte, as his only song-cycle, *Joan of Arc*, demonstrates. His subject-matter, one he shared with his Georgian poet-contemporaries, was the sensuous pleasures of this world, of the more benign aspects of the English countryside: church bells, the moon, birds, flowers, trees, in which joy for their beauty is tinged with melancholy sadness for their transience. What he evoked best of all, however, was the land of enchantment, the faraway land of dream and romance, which was crystallised in verse for him by his favourite poet, Walter de la Mare. Sometimes this lightness of touch leads to a lightness of another kind. Works such as *Songs of the Mad Sea-Captain* are essentially 'light music', not attempting to do anything more than titillate and amuse. That he could, on occasion, plumb greater depths is demonstrated in songs such as 'Hypochondriacus' and 'By a bierside'. It will have been noted that, with the exception of *Joan of Arc*, he made no attempt to write large-scale solo vocal works. *Crossings* and *Songs of the Mad Sea-Captain* are no more than song-books, collections of single songs under one title with no attempt made to give them more profound structural unity. We have no *Curlew* or *Maud* or *On Wenlock Edge*. The bulk of his output consists of separate solo songs, many of them, as we have seen, one-and-only settings of poets. The exception is his settings of the poetry of de la Mare. Separate or not, these are a major achievement taken together, worthy to rank Gibbs amongst the other leading English songwriters of his time.

15

Ivor Gurney (1890–1937)

Only the wanderer
Knows England's graces,
Or can anew see clear
Familiar faces.

And who loves Joy as he
That dwells in shadows?
Do not forget me quite,
O Severn meadows.

Ivor Gurney:
'Only the wanderer'

You would expect the son of a tailor of Gloucester to be born with a silver thread in his jacket, and Ivor Gurney was blest with the dual talents of poet and composer. Though several composers have been Sunday poets and a few writers Sunday composers, an artist who is accomplished equally at both and recognised as such by his peers is a rare bird indeed. In this country the only person comparable with Gurney is Thomas Campion (1567–1620). Campion was unique amongst composers of lute-song in that he set only his own words; Gurney rarely set his own words and kept his creative activities as poet and composer discrete. He himself felt that his true vocation was music and in his essay 'The Springs of Music', wrote: 'The brighter vision brought music; the fainter verse' (Boden, 1986: 121). In his letters from the front during the First World War, to his Gloucestershire friend and fellow-composer, Herbert Howells, he is stoically cheerful despite the fact that life in the trenches made it virtually impossible for him to write music. He had to be content with second best – his own implication – and write poetry (Thornton, 1991: 191 *passim*). Yet many would argue that, *pace* his own assessment of himself, his poetry is more original than his music. Whereas his music is firmly anchored in the 19th century, his poetry has an unmistakable 20th-century sensibility. His music embodies his ideals and dreams; his poetry shows the man himself, almost nakedly so at times.

Gurney's first songs date from c.1904. The first reference we have to him as a poet is in a letter dated June 1913 to another Gloucester friend, the poet F. W. Harvey, though it is clear from the context that he had been writing poetry for some time (Thornton, 1991: 4–5). By 1913 he was devoting as much time to writing poetry as music. As a poet Gurney was extremely prolific and between 1913 and 1926 wrote nearly 900 poems (possibly more: with so ill-organised a person it is difficult to be precise). During his lifetime, 46 were published in *Severn and Somme* (1917), 58 in *War's Embers* (1919) and a few in various journals and magazines, including *Music and Letters*. He continued to write poetry long after his ability to compose coherent music ceased. As he himself so poignantly wrote:

> Had I a song
> I would sing it here
> Four lined square shaped
> Utterance clear
>
> But since I have none,
> Well, regret in verse
> Before the power's gone
> Might be worse, might be worse.
>
> 'Had I a song'

The *Collected Poems of Ivor Gurney* (1982), edited by P. J. Kavanagh, includes more than 300 poems. The quality of his poetry shows that he was no mere dabbler. There is a clear progression from *Severn and Somme* to the post-war poems, and there can be little doubt that his wartime experiences stretched him and fundamentally affected his poetic technique. His early influences were varied: he read Tennyson, Kipling and Housman, but the strongest influences were the Elizabethan and Jacobean poets and dramatists, particularly Ben Jonson, for whom he retained a lifetime's affection. Later influences were Hopkins (whose poetry he had come upon in Robert Bridges' popular wartime anthology, *The Spirit of Man* (1916)) and Walt Whitman (his friend Marion Scott had sent him a pocket edition of Whitman whilst he was in France). Reading his mature poems, one is struck by their singularity. 'Gnarled', 'knotty' and 'craggy' are epithets that have been used to describe his style. He telescopes ideas – what Hurd calls 'a kind of stutter in the thought process' (1978: 200) – cuts corner in his syntax – something he shares with Hopkins – and is cavalier with punctuation, all idiosyncrasies which can lead to obscurity and ambiguity on an initial reading. Yet he possesses the gifts of the true poet: the ability to write the striking opening line, to find the unexpected but just-right word, to imbue common, everyday objects and experiences with magic. And on a purely technical level, he is a master of his craft; his poetry is full of subtle rhymes and varied stanza-shapes, and he can turn his hand to a sonnet or rondel or narrative ballad with apparent ease. His subject-matter is very individual. The title of his first volume, *Severn and Somme*, sums up his main preoccupations: the contrast between peacetime, boyhood Gloucestershire, and wartime, soldiering in France. When in the trenches the recitation of Gloucestershire place-names was a litany that kept him sane, whilst several of his poems have musical subject-matter; musical imagery abounds, slipping naturally into his way of thinking. Few poets have been so successful at evoking a response to music as in 'The motetts [*sic*] of William Byrd', 'Masterpiece' – a brilliant attempt to describe the act of composition – and 'Hedger', where he somehow manages to entwine his admiration for a hedger at work and for Mozart's A major Piano Concerto:

> To me the A Major Concerto has been dearer
> Than ever before, because I saw one weave
> Wonderful patterns of bright green, never clearer
> Of April; whose hand nothing at all did deceive
> Of laying right
> The stakes of bright
> Green lopped-off spear-shaped, and stuck notched, crooked-up;
> Wonder was quickened at workman's craftsmanship
> But clumsy were the efforts of my stiff body
> To help him in the laying of bramble, ready
> Of mind, but clumsy of muscle in helping; rip
> Of clothes unheeded, torn hands. And his quick moving
> Was never broken by any danger, his loving
> Use of the bill or scythe was most deft, and clear –
> Had my piano-playing or counterpoint
> Been so without fear
> Then indeed fame had been mine of most bright outshining;
> But never have I known singer or piano-player
> So quick and sure in movement as this hedge-layer
> This gap-mender, of quiet courage unhastening.

His achievement as a poet is enormous. Of the poets of the First World War, his star has risen higher than any over the past 20 years. Today he is justly acclaimed, with Owen, Sassoon and Rosenberg, as one of the finest poets of that war. Yet 'he never doubted (or had reason to doubt) that his true vocation was music, or that it was the supreme form of all self-expression' (Hurd, 1978: 199). He himself wrote, 'The chief use of Poetry [seems] to be, to one, perhaps mistaken, musician, to stir his spirit to the height of music, the maker to create' (Boden, 1986: 121).

Of Gurney's songs, over 250 have survived in manuscript. The amazing fact is that the bulk of this enormous song output was written in a period of four years, between 1919, after he left the army, and 1922, before he was admitted to the asylum: and all this despite increasing mental instability and a most erratic lifestyle. The 150 or so songs written or half-written over this period represent an almost Wolfian frenzy of inspiration: a considerable achievement for a man who 'dwelt in shadows'. Including the four major song-cycles (the 'Elizas', *Lights Out* and the two Housman cycles), just under 100 of Gurney's songs have been published. Gurney's creative methods were extremely haphazard and impulsive, and this is reflected in his songs. Many are only half-conceived and others lack final artistic polish, as though he could not be bothered to follow up the fine frenzy of initial inspiration. In order to bring his work into the public domain, an editor is needed and that editor's task is not so much to extract the good from the rubbish – that is easily done – but to decide which of the flawed material is worth keeping. Over the years his various editors – Marion Scott, Gerald Finzi, Howard Ferguson and Michael Hurd – have understandably erred on the generous side (see Hurd, 1998). Even so, one is drawn to the sad conclusion that some of the songs should not have been selected for publication. It does Gurney's reputation no good to have such masterpieces as 'The folly of being comforted' and 'The singer' cheek-by-jowl with half-baked conceptions such as 'Snow' and 'Ploughman singing'. The five volumes published by OUP between 1938 and 1979 could be condensed to three without artistic loss.

Gurney's choice of poet is, not unexpectedly, discriminating and wide-ranging. As well as Anon. and himself, he set to music more than 80 different poets. At a period when the serious English song-composer, following Parry's example, was ransacking the anthologies of Elizabethan and Jacobean verse, it is not surprising that Gurney should choose Shakespeare, Fletcher, Campion, Jonson, Nashe and Raleigh. Similarly, the vogue for Shropshire Lads and Celtic Twilights during the first two decades of the century caught his imagination and sent him to Housman and Yeats. But the majority of poets he sets are his own close contemporaries, many of whom, like him, had served in the war zones of 1914–18: Wilfrid Gibson, Francis Ledwidge, Edward Thomas, Edward Shanks, John Freeman and Robert Graves (aka 'John Doyle' as well as under his own name). These, with Hilaire Belloc, J. C. Squire, John Masefield and Walter de la Mare, formed what has conveniently been described as the Georgian movement. Gurney became, in effect, the unofficial 'Master of the Music' to the movement, and a collection of the poetry he set by these poets would produce a fairly representative anthology of Georgian verse.

Stanford, Gurney's teacher at the RCM, once remarked that Gurney was 'potentially . . . the most gifted man that ever came into my care. But he is the least teachable' (Howells, 1938: 14). But something must have rubbed off from his contact with Stanford, for many of the essential ingredients of Gurney's harmonic style are to be found in a song such as Stanford's 'The fairy lough'. He may well have caught from his teacher a love of Irish pastoral poetry; and there is an Irish turn-of-phrase in some of his melodic lines, not only in an 'Irish' song such as 'Down by the salley gardens' but also de la Mare's 'Bread and cherries'. With Parry, he shares a fine taste in poetry and a meticulous ear in setting English words. Some commentators have stressed the fact that his music is little influenced by the folksong movement, but many of his songs, whether advertently or not, have echoes of folksong in their melodic lines, both in their modality and in their contours, as, for example, 'I will go with my father a-ploughing' and 'Walking song'. Though they may roam into harmonic regions well beyond the orbit of the folksong, one feels that they have taken their initial cue from such material. Considering that he was a close contemporary of Bax, Butterworth, Browne, Bliss and Warlock, Gurney's idiom is extremely conservative, if not old-fashioned. For all the influences mentioned above, Gurney's style, like that of Parry and his teacher Stanford, is rooted in the German classics: Schubert, Schumann and Brahms.

In his thesis, 'The solo vocal music of Ivor Gurney (1890–1937)', C. W. Moore gives an amusing 'statistically based' description of the typical Gurney song – like some composite creature invented by a committee of zoologists (see Banfield, 1985: 182). There are, indeed, certain identifiable fingerprints in his songs, recognisable 'Gurneyisms'. Take, for example, his final cadences, which give us an insight into their composer, like the signature at the end of a letter (Exs. 15.1(a), (b), (c), (d) and (e)).

Ex. 15.1(a)

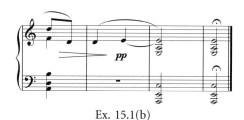

Ex. 15.1(b)

Ex. 15.1(c)

Ex. 15.1(d)

plough-song That bless - es the cleav - ing share.

mf

Ex. 15.1(e)

The tonality of Gurney's music is extremely fluid: the music hovers around rather than settles onto a key. 'Ha'nacker mill' is ostensibly in F major but hovers around G, whilst 'Severn meadows', ostensibly in D major, is pulled towards G major. Many songs avoid any reference to a root-position tonic chord for as long as possible, and several songs, like 'The singer', begin 'out-of-key'. Others are made tonally ambiguous by his penchant for 1st and 2nd inversion chords, notably 'Desire in spring'. In this, his music reminds us of a composer who, though rarely bracketed with Gurney, resembles him in certain temperamental aspects – Elgar. But despite its restless tonality and continual modulation, Gurney's idiom is essentially diatonic; in fact, his melodic train of thought is essentially modal. (There is, for example, not one accidental in 'Carol of the Skiddaw yowes'.) Indeed, he often manages to modulate from tonic to dominant without recourse to accidentals (see bars 9–10 of 'I will go with my father a-ploughing'). A chromatically fraught song like 'Last hours' is most unusual.

Gurney's unstable personality is reflected in his songs. Many are only half-conceived and others lack final artistic polish. Some potentially fine songs are spoilt by technical flaws; beautifully-shaped vocal lines and exquisite word-setting are too often marred by clumsy or plain dull piano accompaniments, unconvincing harmonic movement and (a recurrent fault) unsatisfactory conclusions. (That cadential 'fingerprint' referred to earlier often leaves a feeling of inconclusiveness rather than finality – an inconclusiveness not sought but simply arrived at.) His writing for the piano is often thick, over-noted and over-knotted, and at odds with his vocal lines. Take, for example, 'Most holy night': the vocal line, one of Gurney's most hauntingly simple, is completely ruined by the over-written piano part. (The same flaw can be found in 'The Latmian shepherd'.) Lack of textural variety is another weakness: too often he succumbs to vague arpeggiated figurations which give his accompaniments an aimless, meandering feeling, which neither enhances the vocal line nor helps to underline the meaning of the text. (Listen, for example, to the interlude between verses 2 and 3 of 'Most holy night'.)

His range of song-types is also limited. His attempts to write a swashbuckling ballad in 'Hawk and buckle' lacks both swash and buckle, and he has not the extrovert flair of Stanford or Warlock to write a rousing narrative ballad: 'The

night of Trafalgar' is very small beer. Nor has he the requisite art to bring off
light, humorous songs, as is shown by 'Nine o' the clock' and 'Goodnight to
the meadows'. His attempts to enter the Royalty Ballad market under the
pseudonym 'Michael Flood' failed. For all its individuality, his harmonic
language is extremely conservative, firmly rooted in Brahms and Stanford.
Vaughan Williams and Holst – despite his great admiration for the former –
might never have happened; the new music from the continent certainly
hadn't, for he seems to have been impervious even to Debussy and Ravel, let
alone Schoenberg, Bartók and Stravinsky. And for a specialist songwriter, he
lacks a crucial talent – the ability, when needed, to write a memorable tune.
But, you may ask, what about 'Carol of the Skiddaw yowes' or 'Down by the
salley gardens' or 'Black Stitchel' or 'Sleep'? These are the exceptions, whereas
other song-composers such as Warlock, Quilter and Bridge manage it time
after time.

But in his finest songs – and I would list some 20 which rank amongst the
outstanding achievements in English Romantic Song – he had qualities which
are bequeathed to very few songwriters. Amongst these are his ability to deploy
unusual, often unexpected, but telling modulations in the context of the poem.
Very occasionally these modulations do not work – for example, the linking
passage between verses 1 and 2 of 'Love shakes my soul' – but, as Howells has
said, 'At best it is the rich source of a pervading, wandering beauty in his work'
(1938: 15). Take, for example, the piano's link to the final verse of 'Black
Stitchel' or the musical phrase (so very appropriate) to the words 'silent
changes' in 'Desire in spring' (Ex. 15.2).

Ex. 15.2

Most unusually for a songwriter, Gurney rarely uses word-painting – the eponymous aural references in 'The penny whistle' are exceptional – and the use of such side-stepping modulations to capture the *chiaroscuro* of changing moods may be seen as his equivalent.

There is, too, a delightful waywardness about his music; it rambles like an unkempt English hedgerow. Here is both strength and a weakness. In some instances, it becomes mere haphazard meandering, as in 'Ploughman singing' (his only, but disappointing, setting of John Clare), whilst at its best, in its harmonic unexpectedness and avoidance of the obvious cadence and modulation, it can produce subtle and elusive effects, as in 'I will go with my father a-ploughing' and 'The Lent lily'.

What I personally admire most in his songs is their spaciousness and impeccable sense of timing. So many songwriters, once they embark on a song, seem to have only one concern: to set the words as quickly as possible, as they race to the final cadence in blind panic. More than any other English songwriter, Gurney had the ability to allow his poems to *breathe*. He is not afraid of silence: 'those silences that amount to genius', as Howells perceptibly put it (1938: 15). He breaks up the vocal line between phrases and sentences to allow the music to fill in what he reads as the poet's unsaid, inexpressible thoughts. But then, he was a poet himself. Listen again to 'Orpheus', 'Cathleen ni Houlihan', 'The scribe', 'Spring' and above all his masterpiece, 'The folly of being comforted', to hear what I mean.

'He was a poet himself'. This is the crux of the matter. As a songwriter, Gurney was, as it were, a 'fifth columnist', a double agent, for not only was he the unofficial composer *to* the Georgian movement, but also was himself a distinguished member *of* it. As a practitioner in both art forms, he had an insight into setting words to music possessed by few other composers, and this raises two paradoxes. It has always struck me as odd that someone who was a poet and who so clearly loved the poetry he chose to set to music could be so cavalier and careless in his treatment of texts. It would appear to be the result of his habit of setting poems from memory. Marion Scott has described this:

> When he meant to set a poem, he liked to carry it about with him, either copied into his pocket notebook or else absorbed direct into his memory. When the work of actual setting came along, he depended almost entirely on memory (1938: Preface).

This method would not have mattered if Gurney's memory had been good, but it wasn't, and time and again he misremembered his texts. On one occasion he even misremembered his poet's name: the author of 'Carol of the Skiddaw yowes' is *Edmund* (not Ernest) Casson. Most of these slips of memory are trivial: 'does' for 'dost', 'that' for 'this', 'there' for 'here'; the transposition of words in phrases, as for example 'heart and step' for 'step and heart' in de la Mare's 'An epitaph'. Some are more serious. When he set Yeats's poem 'The folly of being comforted', he left out two crucial lines and it was not until he had completed his initial sketch that he realised his mistake. Fortunately he managed to rectify the situation. He was less fortunate in 'I shall be ever maiden', where he omitted a crucial phrase, 'or hallow'; as it was essential to the poem, his editor had to interpolate a musical phrase to Gurney's original song. Often these misremembrances distort and spoil. In his setting of Masefield's 'On the downs' he not only leaves out two crucial words – he has 'Glitters and hangs' instead of 'Glitters with fire and hangs' – but ruins the rhyming: instead of 'red-eyed kestrels' that *hover*, he has a single kestrel that *hovers* and thus it not only misses its field-mouse as it 'flits like a shadow into *cover*', but also its rhyme. One has to be cautious though; the editors of Gurney's songs in the five-volume OUP edition have carefully inserted the poet's 'correct' words in small type beneath the misremembrances, but on occasion they have been incorrect themselves, for in his setting of Raleigh's 'Even such is time', Masefield's 'By a bierside' and Yeats's 'Cradle song', Gurney has gone to authentic alternative versions for his texts.

The other paradox is that, given his dual gifts as poet and composer, why did he not set to music more of his own poetry? In a letter to Howells (31 July 1917) he writes of the poets he was eager to set 'après la guerre':

What Names! Brooke, Sorley, (I have not read him) Katharine Tynan, Nicholson, Sassoon, Gibson, John Freeman, Laurence Binyon, F. W. Harvey, Masefield, and . . . (but not for me,) Gurney . . .

'But not for me . . .' Clearly Gurney had reservations about attempting to be a Campion. Why this reticence? Was it modesty or something more fundamental – perhaps the realisation that his own poetry was not suitable for musical setting? As has been noted (Introduction, p. 1), though the two arts of poetry and music share certain similarities, notably existence in a time dimension, they differ considerably in other respects. Poetry is an articulate art, working with ideas and everyday images; music is an abstract art, and however strongly it may *suggest* ideas and images, it can never articulate them. In the case of a creator like Gurney skilled in both, it is more than likely that he will use the two arts to complement each other. In doing so, he may emphasise the non-musical side of poetry and (though not, of course, in Gurney's case) the 'abstract' side of music. What, then, is the point of duplication, or of using one art to ape the other? Though the inspiration both for his poetry and his music came from the same source, the kinds of invention differ. Much of his finest, most characteristic poetry is, as we have seen, 'rugged' and 'gnarled', full of syntactical elision, speaking with a wry, questing tone of voice: not features that are particularly conducive to musical setting. And in his later years his poetry grew less, rather than more, lyrical. Gurney himself must have realised this. Of his surviving songs, only 15 are settings of his own poetry, and only one of these, 'Severn meadows', has been thought fit to be published by his editors. (There is perhaps one other which should be published: 'Western sailors', a late song dating from March 1926.) Whether, circumstances permitting, Gurney could have eventually honed his verse in such a way as to 'divert it into lyrical channels' is now a matter of conjecture. It would have required a discipline that Gurney probably didn't possess. We are left with one tiny masterpiece – 'Severn meadows'.

The 'Elizas' and the separate solo songs

The *Five Elizabethan Songs* (1913, *1920*), which Gurney affectionately referred to as 'The Elizas', are his earliest songs of importance. All to familiar lyrics but set with youthful freshness, they remain amongst his finest achievements. From the outset of his career, Gurney demonstrates his great virtues: careful, apposite word-setting and a spaciousness and impeccable sense of timing. The songs were originally conceived with instrumental accompaniment; in a letter to F. W. Harvey early in 1914 he specified: '2 flutes, 2 clarinets, a harp and two bassoons', but he later wrote to Herbert Howells that 'The piano accompaniment is perfectly adequate' (21 June 1916). The instrumental origins of the piano version, however, show through in places. 'Orpheus', using the song lyric attributed to John Fletcher in Shakespeare's *Henry VIII*, is set in varied strophic form. The running accompaniment of semiquavers, with its catchy little syncopations, acts as Orpheus's lute. Notice the neat way he moves from 2/4 to 3/4 for the second half of each strophe, whilst breaking up the running texture for a more declamatory style (Ex. 15.3).

Ex. 15.3

The accompaniment of 'Tears' (= 'Weep you no more, sad fountains', Anon. 16thC) has an Elgarian touch, with gently moving 6ths over a slow-moving bass. 'Under the greenwood tree' finds Gurney in light, popular vein, and the song would not be out of place in an Edward German operetta. He neatly avoids first-beat-of-the-bar emphasis in the accompaniment, leaving the voice to lead.

Some awkward piano writing – as in the interlude between verses and the quick upward runs of thirds doubled in octaves in the second verse – reveals the original instrumental scoring. The throwaway ending is neatly done. 'Sleep' (Fletcher) is justly the most popular song of the set, and perhaps Gurney's best known song. The words are set as a cradle-song over a gently rocking accompaniment. This is a romantic, personal interpretation of the text: indeed, it could well be 'Come Death' rather than 'Come Sleep . . .' that he is invoking. In this it is quite different from Warlock's equally famous setting, which is cool and classically restrained (see Hold, 1980). Notice, for example, the unexpected enharmonic move in the piano coda from D-flat major to a dominant 7th on D natural, before the return to a mellifluous D-flat major cadence chord: a hint that perhaps, after all, joys will have some abiding (Ex. 15.4).

Ex. 15.4

Of all the songs, 'Spring' (Nashe) betrays its origins as a transcription from multi-instrumental accompaniment to piano, as, for example, in the lengthy 'fill-in' character of the interludes between verses and some awkward piano writing (the right hand octaves, bars 63–5), but it is effective nonetheless. It reveals a lively, boisterous, youthful Gurney, something that he was not able to (or didn't wish to) recapture in his later songs. It may be naïve in places – as in the interludes between verses – but what a sweep of conception! – the spaciousness of the word-setting, the breadth of imagination within the narrow limits of this 'light conceit'. One weakness of the set is that all five poems are two stanzas long. This leads inevitably to a uniformity of structure: two verses set in basically strophic manner.

After the 'Elizas', Gurney wisely – courageously – turned his back on the Treasure House of the 16th- and 17th-century English lyric and concentrated instead almost entirely on 20th-century poets and on the Georgians in particular. But one late 'Treasure House' setting that should be noted is the Herrick setting, 'To violets' (1920, *1959*), in which he 'counterpoints' Herrick's short lines with his music: against the grain, but giving a delightful cross-rhythm between the two.

During his composing career, Gurney made 15 settings of the poetry of W. B. Yeats, two of the same poem. Six of these have been published; of the remaining nine, two are early songs, dating from 1909 before he began his studies at the RCM, and two from his asylum years (1925). The published Yeats settings include some of his finest songs. The poetry of W. B. Yeats held a fatal attraction for composers at the beginning of this century, but the fey land of the Celtic Twilight that the poet inhabited in these early poems could prove marshy ground for composers. Gurney, however, was not a person to be lured by fays or will-o'-the-wisps. The best of his Yeats settings go to the heart of the matter and none more so than 'The folly of being comforted' (1917, *1938*), arguably his finest song and one of the supreme masterpieces of English song. That he himself knew that he had written a masterpiece is evident from a letter he wrote to Marion Scott (31 October 1917) from Edinburgh War Hospital, Bangour, where he was recuperating from gassing:

> I have 3 Poems, and O – a new song for mezzo soprano. One of my best, madam; that being a setting of those wistful, magical words of Yeats – 'The Folly of Being Comforted'.
> There is one passage
>> 'O she had not these ways
>> When all the wild summer was in her gaze,'
> which will raise your hair.

He goes on to say that he wrote the song in one sitting after a busy night helping in the hospital wards, only to find that, through tiredness or haste, he had left out two of Yeats's lines:

> 'The fire that burns about her when she stirs
> Burns but more clearly'

'O Blasphemy! My balance upset! . . .' he exclaims. (No mention of Yeats's balance . . .) Fortunately he managed to rectify the situation by a masterly piece of troping. What is especially admirable about the setting is Gurney's dramatic use of rests and the subtle interplay between voice and piano. It is one of Gurney's most closely argued songs, given added strength by its strong contrapuntal drive. The piano's little head motif controls the course of the entire song (Ex. 15.5(a)). It is not until halfway through, at the words 'But, heart, there is no comfort, not a grain', that he gives this motif to the voice; the effect is doubly forceful because it is heard unaccompanied after a lengthy piano interlude. If one were asked to choose one passage from Gurney's output which summed up his special genius, it would be the following (Ex. 15.5(b)). This is the

passage he referred to in his letter to Marion Scott 'which will raise your hair'.
It does just that. And how many songs have such a devastating ending
(Ex. 15.5(c))? The long-held final note, over ruthless reiterations of piano
tonics, will, it seems, never be resolved. It is an extremely difficult passage for
the singer to bring off, particularly at the end of so long and intense a song,
but when it is sung well, it is shattering in its intensity.

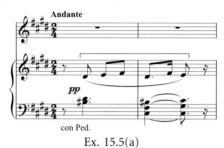

Ex. 15.5(a)

Ex. 15.5(b)

Ex. 15.5(c)

The subject of 'Cathleen ni Houlihan' (1919, *1938*) is the Old Woman who symbolises Ireland in Yeats's eponymous play. (Yeats's title for the poem was 'Red Hanrahan's song about Ireland'.) Like 'The folly . . .' it is another dramatic song, this time set out strophically to match the stanzas of the poem. The vamped accompanimental figure gives it drive and urgency, and it again shows Gurney's fine sense of dramatic timing, in the long pause

Ex. 15.6

(including a whole GP bar) between verses, and the dramatic side-slip down a semitone for the opening of verse 3 (Ex. 15.6). The heart sinks with the sinking tonality!

Quite different in character is 'Down by the salley gardens' (1920, *1938*). Yeats called the poem 'An old song resung', basing it on 'The rambling boys of pleasure'. (Salley gardens means 'willow gardens'.) The song is unusual in his output in that Gurney permits himself a full-blown tune, a folk-like melody of extraordinary beauty that matches the folk-origins of the poem perfectly. The piano underpins the vocal line in an unpretentious but supportive way. Notice the augmentation of the final phrase and the piano's subtle variant of the singer's final phrase as a coda (Ex. 15.7).

Ex. 15.7

'The fiddler of Dooney' (1917, *1959*) had a long gestation. Begun as early as 1917, in March 1918 he was writing to Marion Scott, 'an attempt at the "Fiddler of Dooney" is slowly struggling toward completion'; this, however, was not reached until 1919. (Even so, he must still have been unsatisfied, for in September 1925 he made a second setting of the same poem.) As with 'Down by the salley gardens', he sets the poem to a four-square, catchy tune, here appropriately an Irish folksong of a tune, declaimed above a scampering Irish jig of an accompaniment. But it is only in the first verse that he uses it conventionally, and in the subsequent verses – the five stanzas are strophied A1 B1 C A2 B2 – he characteristically (and delightfully) expands phrases by lengthening notes and adding melismas to reflect the word-setting. Notice the wryly ironic, slightly pompous *largamente* phrase at the words 'To Peter sitting in state' and the extension at 'I read in my book of songs/I got at Sligo fair' – all done without interrupting the ongoing thrust of the jig. It is one of Gurney's few genuinely quick-paced songs.

'Cradle song' (1920, *1959*) is a wistful lullaby, in which the cradle-rocking accompaniment is subtly and sparingly used. It should be noted that Gurney sets an early version of Yeats's poem, so however much one prefers the later words (printed by the editors in small type), the song should be sung to the earlier version.

These five songs represent some of the finest Yeats's settings in the repertoire and together form an effective recital group. The other Yeats's setting, 'The cloths of heaven' (1920, *1979*) is less satisfactory. It shares many similarities with 'Cradle song': a similar melodic line, a similar syncopated rocking accompaniment, a similar mood. Indeed, the two songs were written at the same time and seem almost to be two aspects of the same conception. But the sweet tune of 'The cloths of heaven' is spoilt by a turgid, club-footed accompaniment. It certainly does not compare with the settings of Dunhill and Warlock.

As well as Yeats, Gurney made settings of several other Anglo-Irish poets. 'The County Mayo' (1918, *1921*) sets a poem by the Irish poet Anthony Raftery (1784–1835) in a translation by James Stephens (1882–1950). With its modal melody, running semiquaver accompaniment and tonal shifts in the main verses from E minor to G major, it is in some ways a pre-run for 'I will go with my father a-ploughing' (1921, *1921*) written the same year. This setting of the poem by 'Seomsamh Mac Cathmhaoil' (= Joseph Campbell) is one of his most memorable songs; it *has* to be, else it will fail the words. A farmer's son describes going to the fields with his father, to plough, to sow and to reap, whilst his father sings a song for each seasonal occupation: the plough-song, the seed-song, the scythe-song. Gurney comes up with one of his most attractive melodies, folk-like but infinitely more flexible than a folk-tune, being elusive and wayward in quality, with metric shifts from 2/4 for the verse to 3/4 for the refrain, and continual tonal shifts from E minor to G major. In the third verse there are even more unexpected modulations, from E minor via F major, C minor and A-flat major to G major. The singer cadences in G major only for the piano to re-cadence emphatically in the home key of E minor: unexpected but logical. Yet the song manages to retain its basic joyful, folk-like simplicity for all its sophisticated procedures. The waywardness is reflected in its structure. Though basically a strophic song, its elements rarely coincide. There is little repetition; the accompaniment is always evolving, never exactly the same – compare the introduction (bars 1–4) with the interludes (20–3 and 41–4) (Ex. 15.8(a), (b) and (c)). In places this seems finicky, as in the piano's opening four bars where the same material is given four different treatments, as though Gurney cannot decide on which is the best solution.

Ex. 15.8(a)

Ex. 15.8(b)

Ex. 15.8(c)

Campbell has fashioned for the songwriter a poem perfectly suitable for varied strophic setting, with its 'three-season' triptych, its refraining opening lines, individual details for each season and the varied 'burden'-refrain at the end of each verse. Gurney gives point and character to this final refrain both in the change of metre (2/4 to 3/4) and in the passionate, strong vocal line over strong, solid chords on the piano, to contrast with the rocking figurations and gentler melodic material of the verse.

'Desire in spring' (1918, 1920) was one of the first of Gurney's songs to be published, in Harold Monro's magazine, *The Chapbook*, in December 1920. It is the setting of a poem by Francis Ledwidge (1891–1917) who fought, like Gurney, in the First World War and was killed in action in Flanders; the poem was included in Ledwidge's 1915 publication, *Songs of the Fields*. Out of the gentle Celtic melancholy of the poem Gurney creates a colourful, memorable song. His own preferred title had been 'Twilight song', but his publisher thought otherwise. Gurney was right: 'Desire in spring' gives a quite wrong message. The words are set to a shapely, folk-like melody in the Mixolydian mode, but from the outset the tonality is elusive, resulting from avoidance of tonic root-position chords and a preponderance of 1st and 2nd inversion chords as well as the modal inflection of flattened 7th. The two stanzas are set in varied strophic form and here we have one of the best examples of the way Gurney rethinks his opening strophe in his second strophe, so that vocal line and harmonies can match the new words (Exs. 15.9(a) and (b)). The result is a natural matching of words and music, stanza and strophe.

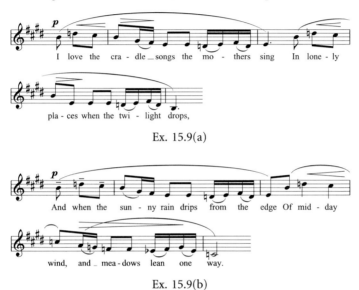

Ex. 15.9(a)

Ex. 15.9(b)

Notice too the subtle way he incorporates a fragment of the opening vocal line in the piano's coda. The song seems to have been a special favourite with Gurney, for phrases echo from it in subsequent songs: 'The singer' (bars 22–4) and 'The boat is chafing' (bars 11–12).

Gurney made a number of settings of de la Mare's poems, of which three have been published. 'The scribe' (1918, *1938*) is the first and most substantial, a song full of variety and imagination. It begins with a rather ordinary, almost improvisatory phrase, but this is deceptive. In his setting Gurney follows the pattern of de la Mare's poem: one short (8-line) stanza followed by a much longer (18-line) stanza – even to the extent of having a complete bar's rest between the two strophes. Following this *Grand Pausa*, a new idea, in triplet rhythm, is set up by the voice and taken up by the piano, battering relentlessly through strange, disconcerting modulations, until that magical moment when, appropriately at the words 'All words forgotten', the accompaniment stops, leaving the singer alone for the final phrase, 'Thou, Lord, and I'. At this point the opening motive – almost forgotten by now – returns to bring the music full-circle: simple and calm after the passionate, complex modulations. The final pages reveal some of Gurney's most original vocal writing: long, down-ward-loping phrases (Ex. 15.10).

Ex. 15.10

Though it shares with 'The scribe' (and 'Severn meadows') the same open-spaced 7th chord at its beginning, 'An epitaph' (1919, *1938*) is of quite different character. The wonderful opening vocal phrase captures the mood of the entire poem (Ex. 15.11(a)). One of the marvels of the song is its pacing.

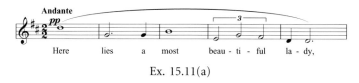

Ex. 15.11(a)

One can only admire the way in which Gurney finds a flexible give-and-take between poem and music, between vocal line and its accompaniment which is so *right*, satisfying sense as well as sound. Note, too, those imaginative and unexpected (not the most obvious) inflections he gives to de la Mare's words, especially '*most* beautiful lady' in bars 12–13 (Ex. 15.11(b)), the way in which he changes mood – not suddenly, but gently, like a cloud temporarily crossing a sunny landscape – and the subtle reprise of the graceful opening melody at the end.

Ex. 15.11(b)

'Bread and cherries' (c.1921, *1938*) is the musical equivalent of an epigram, a difficult sort of song to bring off successfully, for music needs time to establish mood and context. It has a folk-like, slightly Irish aura to it, with a nod perhaps towards 'I will go with my father a-ploughing' at bars 20–21. It is a mere trifle, but neatly, wittily done – note the unexpected cadence into E major instead of G major at the end – and would make an excellent encore piece.

It is not surprising that Hilaire Belloc, in his downs-striding, outdoor mood, should appeal to Gurney. 'West Sussex drinking song' dates from early on (1913, *1921*), and late in his composing career (March 1925) he was working on a setting of 'Tarantella'. But the Belloc settings are disappointing. 'Ha'nacker Mill' (c.1919, *1938*) is totally unconvincing, and cannot compare with Warlock's masterly setting of the same poem. What is more, Gurney commits the unforgivable offence of forgetting the wonderful final line of the first stanza – 'And the sweeps have fallen from Ha'nacker Mill' – replacing it with a repetition of the first line, which sounds awkward and trite. The meandering accompaniment hinders rather than aids the song and what atmosphere is evoked is ruined by a commonplace final cadence into F major. In 'Most holy night' (1920, *1959*), he omits one of Belloc's verses, giving the three remaining verses an A1 A2 B shape. Again, this is not Gurney at his best. There is some unconvincing note-spinning between verses 2 and 3, a heavy-booted accompaniment, and a quirky melisma on the word 'from' (verse 3), as well as quite unacceptable 'misrememberings': 'sweet dreams' instead of 'new dreams' and 'O fold thy wings' instead of 'Fold your great wings'. But the old Gurney magic reappears momentarily at the end, in a long coda culminating in a sensuously beautiful cadence.

The three published Masefield settings are also of mixed quality. 'Captain Stratton's fancy' (1914/1917, *1920*) – a eulogy to rum – is dedicated to Gurney's friend and fellow poet, F. W. Harvey, 'singer of this song in many prison camps'. It is by no means *echt* Gurney: rather, as if he were trying his hand at a popular Royalty Ballad. 'On the downs' (1919, *1959*) is much more typical. Masefield's haunting poem, full of the mystery of time and place, in strong, vivid imagery, is the sort of poem one would expect Gurney to transform into a haunting song. But he fails to do so. The word-setting is awkward and uncharacteristically hurried as he fails to allows phrases and words to breathe. Mention has already been made of a crucial misremembering in this song, where, instead of 'kestrels hover', he has 'kestrel hovers', thus nullifying the rhyme with 'cover' two lines later. He also loses the sense of Masefield's original in the verse:

> Once the tribe did thus on the downs, on these downs burning
> Men in frame
> Crying to the gods of the downs till their brains were turning
> And the gods came.

by breaking the flow of the vocal line between 'frame' and 'Crying'. Why is there such urgency in the setting? It sounds more like a song about going into battle than the mysteries of time. 'By a bierside' (1916, *1979*) is a setting of the words of the Chief Centurions from Masefield's play *Pompey the Great*. It is one of the handful of songs – 'Severn meadows' and 'In Flanders' – written when he was on active service, which would account for the 14 misremembered words (a record, I think, for this man of faulty memory). In a letter to Marion Scott (September 1916) Gurney wrote: 'That setting of Masefield was written in two sittings, almost without effort, and only the first part had been premeditated upon'. Gurney always revered such spontaneity. The accompaniment suggests that he had an orchestral accompaniment in mind rather than a piano, though more than orchestral resources would be needed to make sense of the reiterated passage at bars 35–42. (Indeed, Herbert Howells orchestrated it (and 'In Flanders') for a performance at the RCM on 23 March 1917.) Nonetheless, it is an impressive song in the grand manner. Particularly memorable is the setting of the words 'Death drives the lonely soul to wander under the sky', where the vocal line wanders through an unusual sequence of chords (Ex. 15.12).

Ex. 15.12

The wild, craggy, outdoor imagery of the Northumbrian poet Wilfrid Gibson (1878–1962) was bound to appeal to Gurney and he made several settings, including five amounting almost to a song-book in the 1920s; sadly only one was fit for publication, but that is the masterly 'Black Stitchel' (1920, *1938*) The title of the poem, taken from Gibson's 1918 collection *Whin*, refers to a hill. Each of the four verses takes up a different compass bearing: South – West – North – East.

Ex. 15.13

Gurney effortlessly moves us from the simple pastoral mood of the first two verses, through the 'black wrath' of verse 3, with its dark, restless harmonies, suddenly coming out into the sunlight to rejoin the song's original ritornello for the final verse. The setting of the final lines, 'And I could think no more for pity/ Of man and beast', is one of the most plaintive moments in Gurney (Ex. 15.13). Quite different in mood, but equally fine is 'All night under the moon' (1918, *1938*), one of his most atmospheric songs. Still, hushed, rarely rising above *pianissimo*, it captures the nocturnal mood of Gibson's poem to perfection: long sustained phrases so slow that time and metre are almost obliterated. Note how, in each strophe, Gurney breaks the setting before the refrain with a sudden move from G-sharp minor tonality onto a D major dominant 7th (Ex. 15.14). The song has the same rapt atmosphere as 'Sleep'.

Ex. 15.14

Another close contemporary who inspired Gurney was Edward Shanks (1892–1953), one of the youngest and longest surviving of the Georgians, whose neatly turned lyrics attracted many songwriters, including Gibbs and Warlock as well as Gurney. 'The singer' (1919, *1938*) takes pride of place in the first of the Finzi-Scott-Ferguson volumes published by OUP (1938); appropriately, for it is a song about music. Warlock also set the poem, but his version, fine as it is, pales beside the intensity and imagination of Gurney's setting. The song demonstrates Gurney's ability to create a supple but shapely melodic line out of the ebb and flow of the words (note particularly his setting of the central stanza, and the subtle interplay between voice and accompaniment at the end of the song: see Ex. 15.15(b)). The continuity of the piano accompaniment – a toccata-like figuration, Bach-out-of-Brahms – is here apt, justified by the words. Its little upward-curling arpeggio acts as a motif for the entire song; listen to the way it is picked up in slower notes by the singer in its opening phrase (Ex. 15.15(a)). The singer floats on this continuous cushion of running quavers, until, at the end of the song, Gurney slows the music down by breaking up this continuum, drawing out the length of notes. He hardly needs the '*rit*' in bar 39 to help him (Ex. 15.15(b)).

Ex. 15.15(a)

float-ing bubbles whose col-ours are The col-

oured mel - - o-dies.

Ex. 15.15(b)

The structure of the setting is straightforward (the three stanzas set in ternary form A1 B A2), but the tonality of the song is elusive, caused by a careful avoidance of root-position tonic chords. Shanks's poem 'The fields are full' is a seemingly unambiguous lyric for a songwriter to set, but is in fact deceptive. As Banfield points out (1985: 217), it is not an interplay between observer and observed, but between the observed and its simile: the late summer fields and an old couple. It is, therefore, not a suitable poem for strophic treatment. In his setting (1920, *1928*), Gurney walks into this web and gets himself entangled; taking his eye off the scene, he gets too involved with the old couple, and by doing so almost destroys the serenity that he is trying to evoke. 'The Latmian shepherd' (1920, *1938*) is the setting of 'A song from an unwritten play', which neatly retells the legend of Endymion (the Latmian shepherd) beloved by Selene (the moon) who is thrown by her into perpetual sleep. It is another example of Gurney's 'songs that got away': a delicately attractive vocal line spoilt by thick, over-noted texture and a relentless accompaniment. The effect is claustrophobic, allowing no breathing space.

Gurney made two settings of poems by John Freeman (1880–1929), one of the poets mentioned in his 'litany' of writers to set to music 'après la guerre'. In 'Last hours' (1919, *1938*) the dreariness of a grey winter's day is caught in the thickly muffled accompaniment with its constant hemiola plod in the bass line. There is some felicitous word-setting to underline the dreariness: the way he detaches words from each other (bars 27–8/31–2) and that long, slow descent to the final cadence as the last hours of slow winter 'slowly pass', ending with an uncompromising bare fifth (Ex. 15.16). The song has a slightly menacing atmosphere and, in its rich chromaticism, a hint of Duparc.

Ex. 15.16

The author of 'Carol of the Skiddaw yowes' (1919, *1920*), Edmund Casson, was a Cumbrian author who published several books of poetry between 1905 and 1947. The lyric appears as 'A carol of the Skiddaw shepherds' in his collected *Poems* (1938). It is an attractive carol text, in its local North country analogies reminiscent of the nativity sequence in the medieval Wakefield Mystery Cycle. Gurney's setting is untypical in many respects: in its simplicity, of both vocal line and piano accompaniment, and in the strophic setting of the verses; it is as though he were aiming for a more popular market. (It works most effectively as a carol for unison voices.) The idiom is modal – indeed, a tour-de-force of modality, with not one accidental. Yet Gurney's fingerprints are recognisable throughout, including the 'signature' of the final cadence (see Ex. 15.1(b)).

F. W. Harvey (1888–1957) was Gurney's friend from boyhood: his poet-mentor as Howells was his composer-mentor. Born in Hartpury, he grew up in Minsterworth, fought in the front-line trenches of Flanders and France with the 5th Battalion of the Gloucestershire Regiment and was captured and made a prisoner-of-war in 1916. During the war he published two volumes of poetry, *A Gloucestershire Lad at Home and Abroad* (1916), written in the trenches, and *Gloucestershire Friends and Poems from a German Prison Camp* (1917), and after the war produced several other collections, including *Ducks and other verses* (1919), the title poem of which is his best known. Gurney set several of his poems, and the two published examples were both taken from the 1916 volume. 'Walking song' ('Cranham Woods') (1919, *1928*) is a brief, epigrammatic song, less than a minute in length, with a typical Gurneyan walking accompaniment to match the words. More substantial is his setting of Harvey's epigraph to *A Gloucestershire Lad*, 'In Flanders' (1917, *1959*), in which the poet compares the 'huge imprisoning O' of the Flanders landscape with the hills of his native county. The opening line returns at the end like a refrain, 'I'm homesick for my hills again/My hills again', and this, together with the passionate cry of the exile for home, makes it ideal for musical setting. It was one of the poems that Gurney set whilst on active service in Flanders – his MS indicates that it was composed at 'Crucifix Corner, Thiepval; finished 11 January 1917' – and the poem must have had a particularly significant personal meaning for him. Harvey could almost have written it specifically for Gurney to set and at the time Gurney considered it to be, with 'By a bierside', his finest song. Gurney is always at his best when he has tight control over his material, when he restricts and restrains himself. The tough fibre he could give his songs is evident here. After a brief piano introduction, the singer introduces a strong musical idea (Ex. 15.17)).

Ex. 15.17

This gives impetus to the whole song. Notice the way bars 13–21 are recapped in bars 43–51: in the first passage in E-flat major tonality, in the second starting from the remoteness of B minor and bursting back into E-flat major at the keyword 'homesick'. This is followed by a long coda; the music dying away before the final phrase, 'My hills again', is echoed (the echo-repetition is Harvey's) and the song cadences serenely in E-flat major. For some reason Gurney misreads, or misinterprets, the lines 'Where the land is low/Like a huge imprisoning O'. These refer, of course, to Flanders, not Gloucestershire, and one would have expected them to be set in a harsher manner. But, as Banfield points out (1985: 192), they receive the warmest music in the song; an intelligent singer, however, can rectify this. 'In Flanders' is one of the greatest songs in the English repertoire, overwhelming in its emotional effect. It stands as a poignant celebration of the Gloucestershire Cotswolds by two Gloucester-shire men exiled by war in Flanders.

Finally, in this survey of Gurney's separate solo songs, we turn to Gurney the composer *and* poet. 'Severn meadows' (1917, *1927*), dedicated to Miss Dorothy Dawe, who later became Mrs Dorothy Howells, was completed a couple of months after 'In Flanders': the MS is placed and dated 'Caulincourt, March 1917'; the poem itself (see epigraph) was published simply as 'Song' in *Severn and Somme* (1917). It is the only setting by Gurney of his own poetry that has so far been published. Twenty-six bars long, hardly a minute's worth of music, it is a passionate love-song for his native county. The tonal centre, as is eventually made clear, is D major, but the song opens (like 'An epitaph') with an E-minor 7th chord, and in the second line there is a strong pull towards the subdominant, G major. The accompaniment consists almost entirely of 'floating' 3rds and 6ths, the motion occasionally suspended on strong beats of the bar (15–16), sometimes on mild dissonances (21–2). The two short verses are set strophically, with a neat variation in the second verse, in which the melody is inverted in the third line and mightily augmented in the final line (Exs. 15.18(a) and (b)). The understatement of the setting makes the exile's cry-from-the-heart even more poignant. It ranks as one of the most remarkable poet-composer achievements in English song, a perfect example of the marriage of poetry and music.

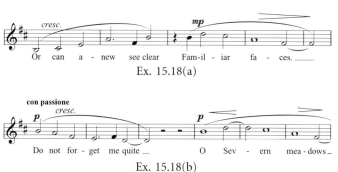

Ex. 15.18(a)

Ex. 15.18(b)

The song-cycles

Gurney made his first Housman settings as early as 1908 – 'On your midnight pallet lying' has recently been published (*Eleven Songs, 1998*) – but it was not until after the war that he embarked on his major Housman works. The two Housman song-cycles, *Ludlow and Teme* (seven songs for tenor) and *The Western Playland* (eight songs for baritone) were published in 1923 and 1926 respectively. Like Vaughan Williams's *On Wenlock Edge*, a work on which they are clearly modelled, both call for an accompaniment of string quartet and piano. As well as familiar poems already set by Somervell, Vaughan Williams and Butterworth, Gurney chooses two poems that songwriters have usually ignored: 'Reveille' and 'Twice a week the winter thorough'. Though both works are called song-cycles, there is no attempt at continuous narrative and no musical cross-references between songs. Whereas the songs in *Ludlow and Teme* all date from 1919, the later publication, *The Western Playland*, contains two songs, 'Loveliest of trees' and 'Is my team ploughing', which Gurney had originally composed in 1908; the rest date from 1919–20. Both Northcote (1966: 105) and Marion Scott (1954: III 856) consider these to be Gurney's finest achievement, but others are less enthusiastic. Banfield (1985: 405) thinks that *The Western Playland* borders on structural and textual incoherence in many places, possibly due to damaging revision during the composer's asylum years, whilst Michael Hurd describes its textures as 'too busy and self-defeating, and the cycle is finished off, disastrously, by a singularly vague instrumental coda' (1978: 209). Its most attractive song is 'Is my team ploughing?', a spacious and airy setting, though with little attempt to differentiate the ghost from his living friend. *Ludlow and Teme* is more effective. If 'Ludlow fair' ('The lads in their hundreds') fails to match the settings by Somervell and Butterworth, or 'On the idle hill of summer' compare with Butterworth's version, the cycle possesses Gurney's greatest qualities as songwriter: lyrical intensity and sensitivity of word-setting, nowhere more apparent than in the final song, 'The Lent lily'.

Ex. 15.19

It is conceived on a big scale, and he allows the light to shine in, as it were, filling in the spaces between the poet's text with musical commentary. Notice, for example, the way in which he isolates the final line of the poem, separated from the previous line by nine bars (Ex. 15.19). It is difficult to explain why, but emotionally this is exactly right.

From early on, Gurney recognised the achievement of Edward Thomas (1878–1917), the quality of whose poetry places him high above the rest of his Georgian contemporaries. He made 19 settings, the earliest, 'Sowing', in the summer of 1918, the last, 'Words' and 'Out in the dark', in 1925 during his asylum years. Nine have been published: three as separate songs and the other six in the song-cycle *Lights Out*. On the face of it, Edward Thomas and Ivor Gurney were an ideal match – in 1990's jargon, a 'dream ticket' – but sadly the songs are variable in quality. 'Cherry trees' (1922, *1952*) is nondescript and shapeless, 'Sowing' (1918, *1925*) suffers from over-complexity of harmonic language, whilst 'Snow' (1921, *1952*), a turgid little song, utterly fails to reflect the child's magical vision of the falling snow. The song-cycle *Lights Out* (1918–25, *1926*) is scored for baritone and piano. Pilkington (1989: 34) says that 'it may well rank as Gurney's finest work', but the mixed quality of its invention precludes this. As with the Housman cycles, it is a song-cycle at its very basic level, with no narrative thread, of course – Thomas's poems are all separate pieces – and no attempt to make musical cross-references. What holds the songs together is the simple fact that they are all by the same poet. 'Scents' opens with an almost identical idea to 'The fields are full', but has a rather tedious, unremitting accompaniment. It ends with an odd little coda – why? (Is it the robin of the poem singing over again 'sad songs of winter mirth'?) 'Will you come?' is a 'light conceit', the sort of song at which Gurney was never very successful; the vocal line is again spoilt by an unrelenting accompaniment. 'The trumpet' was an attempt by Gurney, now an inmate of Dartford Asylum, to supply a rousing conclusion to the cycle. But, sadly, he was by now incapable of composing music coherently, and the song is only half-conceived. 'Bright clouds' is far more effective, its gossamer-like arpeggios – an unusual texture for Gurney – reflecting the falling may-blossom. But by far the best songs are 'The penny whistle' and 'Lights out'. In 'The penny whistle' Thomas describes a family of charcoal-burners camped out in the woods. The little boy is playing a penny whistle, which is hinted at in trills at the beginning of the song and comes into its own in the final verse. Note also the piano's little sequential interlude (bars 37– 41) after the words 'First primroses ask to be seen', and the way the accompaniment's semiquaver momentum is characteristically broken in the final verse. It is a memorable, evocative song. 'Lights out' is one of Thomas's most personal poems and Gurney clearly wanted to make of it an equally memorable song. The reminiscences of his earlier song 'Sleep' are not unexpected, considering the subject-matter of the poem: 'I have come to the borders of sleep/The unfathomable deep/Forest where all must lose/Their way . . .'. Even in his setting of Fletcher's poem, one feels that Gurney is over-reacting to the text; it could be Death he is invoking, rather than Sleep. Here again, the setting is overblown, inflatedly over-romantic compared with the quiet serenity of Edward Thomas's words. But there are some fine moments, including an unexpected cadence chord that leaves the music suspended in the air (Ex. 15.20).

Ex. 15.20

When considering the songs of Ivor Gurney, it is important to remember that they show only one aspect of the man. They are the old-fashioned, dreamy, solemn-sided, romantic, backward-looking Gurney; they lack the humour and originality and 20th-century sensibility of his poetry or the self-revealing, knockabout humour of his letters. In some respects his achievement as a poet is more original than his achievement as a composer. As a songwriter he is restricted in scope, and uneven. Many of his songs are technically flawed and lack polish; in this respect he is the complete opposite of a songwriter such as Roger Quilter. But his virtues place him in a unique position in the Pantheon of English Song. His sense of pace and timing when setting English poetry has never been surpassed. Songs such as 'Sleep', 'Desire in spring', 'In Flanders', 'The folly of being comforted', 'Black Stitchel' and 'I will go with my father a-ploughing' rank amongst the enduring masterpieces of English song.

16

Herbert Howells (1892–1983)

King David lifted his sad eyes
Into the dark-boughed tree –
'Tell me, thou little bird that singest,
Who taught my grief to thee?'
But the bird in no wise heeded;
And the king in the cool of the moon
Hearkened to the nightingale's sorrowfulness,
Till all his own was gone.

Walter de la Mare: 'King David'

Howells's career as a composer was severely affected by the sudden death, from polio in September 1935, of his nine-year-old son, Michael. It was something from which he never recovered, and though he gradually returned to composition, his music was never the same again. The idiom was different: richer, more mystical, his concerns mainly spiritual rather than secular. The *Requiem* and *Hymnus Paradisi* mark the beginning of this new phase, and his familiar anthems and services were all written in the years after 1940.

The effect on his songwriting was profound. Of his 40 or so published songs, the majority were written before 1935. The last song to appear in his lifetime was 'Lost love' (*1934*). For the remaining fifty years of his life he published none, but instead tinkered around with one final, major project, a book of songs to poems by his chosen poet, Walter de la Mare. At his death (1992) more than half of his songs remained in manuscript. His career as a songwriter leaves us with a question mark. Christopher Palmer has said that 'He was quintessentially a *vocal* composer. His music *sings*, is melodic in impulse' (1986: Preface). But unlike his friend, Ivor Gurney, his song output was small and intermittent, giving the impression that he was not fully committed to the craft. Why was this? Palmer suggests that for him English poetry was 'a lifelong recreation . . .I think he may have regarded song-writing as a relaxation, a hobby, something he did for the sheerest love of, and joy in, doing it' (1995: Prefatory note).

He certainly lacked Gurney's appetite for poetry. Gurney, of course, was himself a poet and it would be unrealistic to expect all songwriters to match his literary enthusiasm. Yet for composers to specialise in songwriting, it is almost *sine qua non* that they have a deep love and knowledge of poetry: Parry,

Somervell, Quilter, Warlock and Finzi all demonstrate this. One suspects that Howells did not have this commitment, and his choice of poets for setting suggests that he was not particularly widely read in English poetry. He concentrated his attention on one poet, Walter de la Mare. Except for Wilfrid Gibson and Fiona Macleod (five early settings have recently been published (1999)), the remaining poets are mostly one-off liaisons, with Skelton, Shakespeare, Shelley, Dobson, Newbolt, Stephens and Joyce, as well as some minor, off-the-beaten-track writers like H. Burkitt Parker and W. L. Courtney. For a man who acknowledged throughout his career his indebtedness to his native Gloucestershire, its countryside and history, and which was celebrated by him in so many instrumental works, there are surprisingly no settings of Ivor Gurney and only one of F. W. Harvey.

All this is regrettable, for, potentially, Howells was one of the most talented song-composers of his time. He had a fluent technique, a wide and rich harmonic range, a rhythmic sprightliness and an individual lyrical gift, which mark him out amongst all his British contemporaries. His music inhabits a landscape thoroughly English, but 'off-the-main-tracks', like the goat paths he describes in one of his songs. One has only to listen to 'King David', 'Come sing and dance' or 'The Lady Caroline' to appreciate this. How did he come to create this unique sound world? Some of the influences on the *style Howells* are self-evident. His teacher at the RCM was Stanford. Of all his pupils, Stanford had the highest regard for Howells, calling him his 'son in music' (Palmer, 1978: 12). His setting of Austin Dobson's 'Madrigal' is very much the work of the 'son of Stanford', with its deftly-tripping accompaniment, even down to the 'Irish' outline of the melody. Vaughan Williams, however, was probably the greatest influence on his style. Howells spoke of the revelation of hearing the first performance of the *Tallis Fantasia* at the Gloucester Three Choirs Festival in 1910 and of the *Pastoral Symphony* ten years later. He said that he felt an 'intuitive affinity' with Vaughan Williams (Palmer, 1978: 12), and this can be seen in their joint love of church and folk modes, pentatonic scales and Tudor polyphony. But his indebtedness to Vaughan Williams is qualified by other quite different influences, as diverse as Delius, Ravel and Stravinsky. Howells himself stated that he 'didn't think there's much Delius in my own work' (Palmer, 1978: 16), but others may disagree. If ever there was a composite of Delius and Vaughan Williams, it is Howells. Certain little arabesque figures and rich chromatic harmonies in *In Green Ways* and 'King David' have strong Delian echoes. There is, too, a strong link between Ravel and Howells in their penchant for antique dance forms and dance rhythms and in their love of rich, bittersweet diatonic dissonances. This comes through clearly in songs such as 'The Lady Caroline' and 'The three cherry trees'. (The impressionist romantic sound world of these two songs is close to that of Howell's younger contemporary, Walton, but that is probably because of a common debt to Ravel.) Howells acknowledged the impact of Stravinsky's *Petrushka* on him, and his *Peacock Pie* songs, with their stark textures and reliance on ostinatos, have a very Stravinskian ring to them. So too do the Stravinskian 'wrong-notes' in 'The mugger's song'. But this was a passing phase, and not an area that he was to explore further.

Another important influence, not a composer but a single song, was Denis Browne's 'To Gratiana dancing and singing'. In a BBC conversation with Arthur Bliss in 1977 (quoted in Palmer, 1992: 373), Howells acknowledged the impact that this song had on him. The penillion technique employed by Browne – a self-contained dance over which the singer embroiders a quasi-improvised line – appears in some of Howells's finest songs, notably 'Gavotte' and the minuet and siciliana that respectively underpin 'The Lady Caroline' and 'The three cherry trees'. In his later songs, from 'Come sing and dance' onwards, the richness of *Hymnus Paradisi* is evident, textures in which the imitational impulse is deliberately blurred by 'impressionistic' polyphony. But Howells was nothing if not eclectic in his technique, and his influences are by no means restricted to earlier music. He borrows tonal clusters (probably from Bartók, a composer he admired) and 'bluesy', falsely related 3rds from jazz, which gives such unexpected piquancy to songs like 'Flood' and 'The old soldier'.

There are, throughout his work, fingerprints that are immediately recognisable. Take, for example, those little arabesque figures, sometimes very brief, such as the four semiquavers which crop up throughout 'The goat paths', but often longer, as in the roulades of notes in 'Come sing and dance'. 'Under the greenwood tree' has examples of both (Ex. 16.1).

Ex. 16.1

Then there is the sudden movement from rich harmony to bare octaves, as in 'The old soldier', 'King David' and 'A queer song'; these become very bleak octaves indeed in 'The old stone house'. His writing for his two performers is always generous and inventive. As mentioned earlier, Howells's music is essentially melodic in impulse. Small surprise, then, that his writing for his singers is natural and unforced, yet at the same time bold and imaginative. In his word-setting he is not afraid to use melisma, which gives his vocal lines a rapturous lyricism unusual in English song-composers of his generation. Witness the ecstatic melismatic 'Eias' in 'Come sing and dance' and the words 'sing', winging down from a high A-flat, in 'The Lady Caroline', or those ever-rising sequences in 'Merry Margaret' at the words 'Far, far passing'. His piano accompaniments are not mere harmonic cushions for his singers, but an essential part of the conception. There is a true partnership between these two completely different sound sources; voice and keyboard are thoroughly integrated, not only in obvious imitations and echoes, but also in more subtle ways, as in 'Andy Battle' where the two effortlessly take over from one another (Ex. 16.2).

Ex. 16.2

In any consideration of Howells's songs, his settings of Walter de la Mare call for special attention. (This would be by sheer weight of numbers alone, for they form nearly half his output.) De la Mare was Howells's favourite poet: they knew each other personally and were lifelong friends. In the setting of de la Mare's poetry, only Armstrong Gibbs bears comparison with Howells for the number and quality of settings. In 1919 Howells completed several settings from the poet's 1913 collection, *Peacock Pie*, six of which were published under that title in 1923. He intended to incorporate the remainder, which included 'Andy Battle', 'King David' and 'Poor Jim Jay', into a second set, but this never materialised. 'King David' was published as a separate solo song in 1923. Until 1969 he worked sporadically on further settings, by which time he had decided on a title and which songs to include, but no definitive order or even (for certain songs) a definitive text. Nor did he make any serious attempt to publish them, primarily because, as he told Christopher Palmer, 'King David' had to be part of the collection, and that was already published (Palmer, 1992: 177). *A Garland for de la Mare* had to await publication until 1995, twelve years after the composer's death. It is by no means *Peacock Pie* Set 2 as originally envisaged. The poem-texts come from far wider de la Mare sources, and the musical idioms used are quite different. Whereas the *Peacock Pie* songs are starkly simple and laconic, rooted on ostinato figures, with sparse textures and abrasive harmonic idiom, the songs in *A Garland* are harmonically and texturally rich. What Howells has done in these two songbooks is create two quite different 'portraits' of de la Mare. 'King David', which would have appeared like an alien duckling amongst the original *Peacock Pie* songs, fits perfectly happily in the second collection.

What drew Howells to de la Mare? There are strong similarities between the two artists. Both inhabited in their minds a mysterious world of shadows and night and dreams; both were concerned with craftsmanship, to encapsulate with deliberate, exquisite 'tiny perfection', a music almost aiming for silence:

> Tiny, clear, discrete:
> The listener within deems solely his,
> A music so remote and sweet
> It all but lovely as silence is.
>   De la Mare: 'Clavichord'

Peacock Pie (1919, *1923*) is a remarkably original set of songs for an English composer to have written in 1919. Its songs are far closer in sensibility to those that Stravinsky was writing at the time – e.g. the *Souvenirs* of 1913 – than to the English tradition of Ireland, Quilter and Gurney. In their abrasive harmonies and reliance on ostinato, one feels that the young Howells was being deliberately experimental. The songs are clearly intended for children to listen to rather than perform and in this they are comparable with Warlock's *Candlelight* rather than Britten's *Friday Afternoons*, to Schumann's *Kinderszenen* rather than *Album des Jugends*. At the same time there is no question of condescension: the young listeners are not being written down to, patted on the head. Some of the songs are disquieting, as indeed are de la Mare's verses. The textures are sparse, often no more than two-part writing for the piano and in places just a single line. 'Tired Tim', 'Alas, alack!', 'The dunce' and 'Miss T' are the most radical. Howells's imaginatively penned tempo directions tell us much about the interpretations: 'Languid' for 'Tired Tim', 'Deliberate and unyielding' for 'The dunce', 'Precise, and rather quick' for 'Miss T'. 'Mrs MacQueen' (of the Lollie-Shop), with its pentatonic tune, is the most conventional of the set. Howells cunningly develops the tune, unwinding it, like a ball of wool, in longer and longer strands over subsequent verses. 'Full moon' is a gentle nocturne, Holstian in flavour: over a limpid, arching ostinato of bare 5ths in 5/4 metre over a static bass, a sustained, lyrical vocal line floats and swims, as Dick watches the moon. 'The dunce' is an odd little song, though perfectly in keeping with the poet's portrait of a juvenile paranoiac. Its textures are Stravinskian, its tonality deliberately bitonal (Howells has given a single flat for the vocal line, nothing for the piano). The piano's two-stranded texture picks up the aural imagery from the poem: a ticking clock in the heavy, angular 'atonal' basso ostinato, and in the right hand the 'dunce, dunce, dunce' reiterations of the thrush and the bluebottle buzzing in his head – an appropriately gangling, clumping accompaniment for this dunderhead (Ex. 16.3).

Why does that thrush   call, 'Dunce, dunce, dunce!'?

Ex. 16.3

Equally Stravinskian is the final song, 'Miss T', whose lean texture could come straight out of *Les Cinq Doigts*. Single strands on the piano, using pentatonic ostinatos pivoting round middle C, are picked up and elaborated by the singer: nothing could be more fitting for this person, who is what she eats. The song (and the sequence) ends on an unresolved dissonance (Ex. 16.4).

Ex. 16.4

'Alas, alack!', the lament of a fish sizzling in a frying-pan, has a pent-up vehemence, characterised by sustained notes sounding through staccatissimo chords. The listlessness of 'Tired Tim' in the opening song is neatly summed up: weary chromatic chords frame the simplest ostinato of all – ladders of notes (C minor in origin), two octaves apart, onto which the weary words are pinned. These songs are not the Howells that we have since come to know. They are by way of an experiment in 'minimalism' and ostinato, a cul-de-sac that he needed to explore but from which he immediately retreated. But there is a stark simplicity about them which, for all their harmonic richness and textural detail, the later de la Mare settings miss.

Even in its published form (1995), *A Garland for de la Mare* still gives the impression of 'work in progress'. Apart from minor textual queries, two of the songs, 'A queer song' and 'Andy Battle', have substantial alternatives in different MS copies, whilst 'Before dawn' exists in two quite distinct versions. Though Howells took the majority of poems from *Peacock Pie*, he also resorted to other de la Mare publications: 'The Lady Caroline' comes from *Songs of Childhood*, 'Before dawn' from *The Veil*, and 'The three cherry trees' from *The Listeners*. In accordance with Howells's wishes, 'King David' is also included. Most of the other songs date from 1968–73. The final published tally, counting the two versions of 'Before dawn', is thirteen: a baker's dozen which would have appealed to de la Mare. All are imbued with the mature

Howells style, the *angst*-suffused, bittersweet world of *Hymnus Paradisi*. The
textures are elaborate and intricate, the pace leisurely, almost timeless. The
songs vary from brief lyrics ('Some one') to lengthy narratives ('A queer
story'). The best rank amongst Howells's finest songs.

The technique of placing a poem within the context of a self-contained musical
form, such as a dance or a march, has a hallowed ancestry: Schumann's 'Das ist ein
Flöten und Geigen' from *Dichterliebe*, Fauré's 'Clair de lune'; in English song,
Somervell's 'Come into the garden, Maud' (*Maud*) and 'The street sounds to the
soldiers' tread' (*A Shropshire Lad*), and, of course, Denis Browne's 'To Gratiana
dancing and singing'. Browne's song, as we have seen, had a strong impact on
Howells, and in 'The Lady Caroline' he uses a similar technique for a similar
situation, though not perhaps for such strongly justifiable reasons: the lady in
question is not dancing, but binding up her hair, Belinda-like, in front of her
looking-glass. The only music alluded to is that of the Christmas Waits, but
Howells chooses to ignore their rustic carol and graces the occasion with a richly
ornamented minuet. (However, at the words, 'I heard the Waits their sweet song
sing', he cannot resist unrolling an ecstatic vocal line.) The poem's three verses are
through-set, the only reprise coming halfway through the final verse. He leaves the
minuet to form the structure of the song, with clear-cut cadences to each of the
verses, thus freeing the vocal line. It is an exquisitely subtle song (Ex. 16.5).

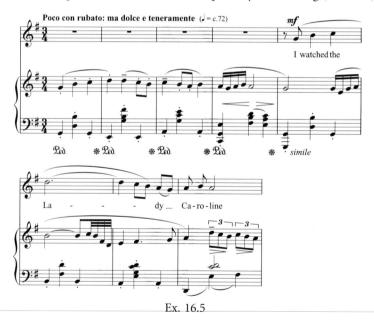

Ex. 16.5

He uses the same technique in 'The three cherry trees', here replacing the
minuet for an intricately detailed siciliana. The gently-swaying, dream-like tread
of the dance captures to perfection the 'Ghost of a beautiful lady/Who walks in
the garden all shady'; indeed, another ghost, that of Ravel, hovers amongst the

bittersweet harmonies. One is also reminded how closely the sound-world of those two inveterate English Romantics, Howells and Walton, came in their later music: there is the same impressionistic haze and glitter in the highly ornamental writing, with its tone-clusters and ambiguous note relationships. If this song is less successful than 'The Lady Caroline', it is because the ideas are too elaborate and diffusely focussed, and because the dance takes too great a precedence over the singer.

Quite different in character is 'The old soldier', though again a self-contained accompaniment lurks in the background, here, appropriately, a march to match the old soldier described. Typically for Howells, it is a seamless song, defying the strophic treatment suggested by the parallel stanzas of the poem; even the 'Fol rol dol' refrain is given varied treatment at each recurrence. It shows the composer in his neatest scherzo vein, an aerated texture – Howells always knew when to leave notes out – with elastic rhythms and voice and piano neatly entwining (Ex. 16.6). But for all the 'Fol rol dol' and bluster, his harmonic idiom remains intact; indeed, one almost senses a reminiscence of *Hymnus Paradisi* in the final page.

Ex. 16.6

Two other songs deserve special comment. 'The song of the secret' opens in the key of A-flat major with beautiful sonorous chords to the question, 'Where is beauty?', only to be destroyed utterly by the answering, 'Gone, gone' on an A-sharp set over a bleak B minor triad (Ex. 16.7). This answer is echoed later on in the words, 'Gone/Is beauty from me': over rich, blue-note-impregnated harmonies which tug at the heart, the word 'beauty' is caught up in a long melisma, as though the composer were loth to let it go.

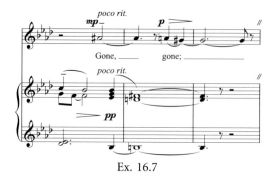

Ex. 16.7

The song ends, 'Secret as a dream', on an unresolved chord, which tries vainly to reach G-sharp minor as it fades away. 'The old house' – a metaphor for Death: 'a very, very old house I know' – has inspired one of Howells's most poignant songs. The piano's mellifluous 3rds set up the 'extremely tranquil'atmosphere that Howells asks for. But these 3rds have a tonal ambiguity at odds with this tranquillity: all is not as it seems, for this is a house, into which people go but never return. The only point of beauty and light in the gloom is the Evening Star, which inspires the composer to some of his most sensuously beautiful music, in which he makes an old textural cliché – rich arpeggios rising from deep bass notes to a sustained, high melodic line – sound new and fresh (Ex. 16.8).

Ex. 16.8

Of the remaining songs, 'Andy Battle' and 'A queer song' are both narratives: 'Andy Battle' is a sea story, with brisk shanty-ish setting of the first three verses describing Andy's colourful adventures, followed by a slow, enigmatic final verse for his 'sorrowful end'; whilst 'A queer song' is a long, rambling narrative (114, albeit short, lines) of three jolly farmers who 'bet a pound/Each dance the other would/Off the ground', resulting in a watery end for the winner. In its spare textures and jig-like tread, it is very close in character to the scherzo movements in *Howells' Clavichord* (1961). 'Some one', a setting of one of de la Mare's most famous lyrics, 'Some one came knocking/At my wee, small door', is an example of Howells's ability to capture in 'faint music' the 'tiny' world so beloved by the poet; he does this through a hesitant vocal line, a deliberately sketchy piano accompaniment and mysterious pauses and silences. The ending is particularly effective, the voice fading to nothing against the final piano chord (Ex. 16.9).

Ex. 16.9

But for all the fine qualities of these later songs, the sensitivity of word-setting and rich, allusive accompaniments, the gem of the collection is 'King David', the song written fifty years earlier, though in retrospect the very work which heralded his later style. If one were forced to choose just one song by Howells, it would probably be this. It is the definitive version of the de la Mare poem; of it Howells himself said, 'I'm prouder to have written 'King David' than almost anything else of mine', adding, 'de la Mare once said he didn't want anyone else to set it' (Palmer, 1978:16). The subject-matter of the poem is perennial: Art or Nature, here represented by the relative power of the King's harpists or of the Nightingale to assuage the human spirit. It is a profound subject and one that Howells treats in an appropriately profound manner. This can be seen in his handling of the tonalities. Ostensibly the song is in E-flat minor – which is what the vocal line implies – but the piano's chordal accompaniment continually pulls the music towards the subdominant (A-flat minor). These rich chords (9ths on A-flat minor) over a brief but pregnant rhythmic pattern, act as a ritornello throughout the song: act, as it were, as the 'tuning-up' chord for the hundred harps that the sorrowful King calls for to ease his melancholy. But they are powerless to charm, and in the silence that ensues, the King rises; the A-flat left hanging in the air turns, through the simple magic of enharmonic change, into a G-sharp, and thus the ritornello returns in the key of E major, this time with the Nightingale singing above (Ex. 16.10).

Ex. 16.10

The device is a simple one that has been used many times, but Howells imbues it with a new magic which still affects us today, over 70 years after the song was written. The song is a masterpiece of pacing and organisation, itself the perfect artefact to vie with King David's Nightingale. But for all its rich sensuous harmonic language, it is the pregnant use of silence that one remembers after the song has finished.

Howells's only other surviving song sequence is *In Green Ways*, op. 43. This has a complicated history. It began as *Five Songs*, with the opus number 16, in 1915/16, scored for voice, flute and clarinet, string quartet and string orchestra, and consisted of settings of poems by Goethe and Theodor Storm (both in Howells's own translations), Skelton and Shakespeare, ending with a triolet by H. Burkitt Parker. In this version it was performed at a concert at the RCM in February 1916. No MS of this prototype survives. In 1928 the composer revised it, substituting a setting of James Stephens's 'The goat paths' for the Storm song and adding a new final verse for the Burkitt Parker triolet to words by his friend and RCM colleague, Claude Aveling, and scoring it for an orchestra of woodwind, timps and percussion, harp, piano and strings. In this new version it was performed at the 1928 Three Choirs Festival at Gloucester by the dedicatee, Joan Elwes. Later that year, OUP published a voice and piano score, in which form it is best known today. The final sequence of songs is:

1. Under the greenwood tree (Shakespeare)
2. The goat paths (Stephens)
3. Merry Margaret (Skelton)
4. Wanderer's night song (Goethe)
5. On the merry first of May (Parker and Aveling)

The title *In Green Ways* is borrowed from Stephens's volume of poems, which contains 'The goat paths'. Though not specified as a cycle by Howells – he calls it simply 'five songs for high voice' – the careful grouping of the songs and the very title indicate that he thought of them as a songbook if not a cycle. Palmer writes that 'memories of the [original] instrumental textures – if we have any – are banished permanently within a few bars of the first songs' (1992: Introduction). With this one must disagree: the orchestral nature of the original shows through in several places in what are, for Howells, unidiomatic piano textures, as, for example, in the final cadence of 'Merry Margaret', the widely-spread textures of 'Wanderer's night song' and the awkward piano-writing of 'Under the greenwood tree'. The songs are mixed in quality, moving from the sublime ('The goat paths') to the slightly ridiculous ('On the merry first of May'). The Shakespeare setting has an unexpected Arabian sound to it, as though Hassan were inviting us to rest under a tree on the road to Samarkand, rather than Jaques in the Forest of Arden. 'Merry Margaret' is a graceful, if somewhat skittish portrait of a young lady, encapsulated in the delicious final melisma on 'Gentle as a falcon' (Ex. 16.11).

Ex. 16.11

'Wanderer's night song', though capturing the dark profundity of Goethe's verse – Howells's tempo marking is 'Slow: with great quietude' – suffers from an opaqueness of texture and, as already mentioned, an orchestrally conceived idiom. 'On the merry first of May' is unique in Howells's output: the setting of two triolets by two different poets each using the same opening refrain-line. Palmer calls the poems 'saucy parody' but surely this is the real thing! Howells had little chance with such nondescript, featureless verse.

The outstanding song is, in fact, the new one that Howells wrote for the songbook's 1928 relaunch. 'The goat paths' is a big song both in conception and length, with the composer using a colourful palette of ideas. Stephens's poem is a summer idyll, describing a herd of goats following their crooked paths through the hillside furze and heather; the poet then imagines what he would do if he were as free as they, dreaming until he found:

> Something
> I can never find;
> Something
> Lying
> On the ground
> In the bottom
> Of my mind.

The poem is laid out in 'clipped, close-cropped lines', to borrow Banfield's neat phrase (1985: 218), with frequent use of assonance and word-repetition. The haze of the summer day is captured in the mesmeric way in which refraining lines chime throughout the poem:

> 'Of a quiet Sunniness'
> 'To the sunny Quietude'
> 'In a sunny Solitude'

as though everything was dazed and dazzled by the noon-day heat. All this gives the poem a fast-moving quality in keeping with its 'capricious' subject-matter. In fact, the composer portrays this as 'the summer leisure of high noon' (Palmer, 1992: 406), a conception quite different from the poet's, as Howells discovered when he heard Stephens recite the poem: 'He made of it something unbelievably like a dynamo, utterly unlike the leisurely pastoral idyll I'd conceived it as' (Palmer, 1978: 16).

Though the word-setting is always his paramount consideration, Howells plans the song almost as an instrumental movement. The analysis of the musical form that follows shows the subtlety of his scheme. It is set out in five large paragraphs, which correspond with the sections of the poem. The piano's introduction presents a striking musical phrase: an upward 7th arcing back down a major triad and treated imitatively (Ex. 16.12(a)). At first the singer ignores this, entering with a sustained line based on a subtle modal scale (E F A B C-sharp D-sharp) (Ex. 16.12(b)). The section cadences (fig. 3) on a plain G major chord, from which, unexpectedly, the singer re-enters in C-sharp tonality and to which the accompaniment immediately adjusts. At fig. 4, the opening instrumental ritornello figure returns on the piano and the music again cadences in G major. The next paragraph of verse, beginning 'If you approach/They run away!', starts as unaccompanied recitative and, indeed, there is minimal accompaniment until fig. 6. The recitative, however, is not as 'free' as all that, for at the words 'To crouch again, /Where nothing stirs', Howells reintroduces the singer's opening phrase. The last two sections of the poem are more personal, the poet-observing becoming the poet-musing: 'Were I but/As free/As they', and Howells deftly marks this crucial transition in musical terms. Commencing from the E on which the singer has cadenced, the piano plays its original ritornello. Now, at last, the singer picks up the figure, developing and decorating it in an imaginative variety of ways (Ex. 16.12(c)). The section cadences into quiet A major tonality (fig. 9). A short interlude takes us to a richly-added dominant chord on E for the short final section, 'In that airy/Quietness/I would dream', in which there are final echoes of the ritornello and an instrumental cadence onto a single, mid-register E. Over this the singer then declaims the final lines of the poem (those quoted on p. 00), but with the very last phrase, 'In the bottom/Of my mind', heard unaccompanied (Ex. 16.12(d)). It is a remarkable song, equally effective in its piano as its orchestral version, one of Howells's finest achievements and (literally) one of the unsung masterpieces of 20th-century English song.

Ex. 16.12(a)

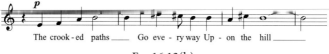

Ex. 16.12(b)

Ex. 16.12(c)

Ex. 16.12(d)

Sadly Howells never completed his planned six-song-cycle to poems by the Northumbrian-born poet Wilfrid Gibson, which he had intended to name after the poet's 1916 collection, *Whin* (= gorse, or furze). Only two – 'Old skinflint' and 'The mugger's song' – were published; of the remaining four, 'Blaweary' has been recorded (Chandos CD, 1994 CHAN 9185/6), 'Pity me' and 'Stow-on-the-Wold' were never completed, and 'Fallowfield Fell' is 'missing'. 'Old skinflint' and 'The mugger's song' are country portraits and show an earthy and rumbustious side to Howells's personality – much to be welcomed for, as Paul Spicer has remarked, Howells was not particularly good at being light-hearted (1998: 166). 'The mugger's song' (1919, *1924*) is a humorous depiction of an itinerant countryman ('mugger' = a hawker of earthenware). The piano has a suitably lurching D major tune with a gipsy-like triplet twiddle, played out roughly over a Stravinskian 'wrong-note' bass. Above this the singer is given an appropriately folksy melody (Ex. 16.13).

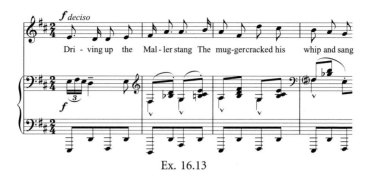

Ex. 16.13

There is some neat word-painting at the reference to his rival, 'A sweep whose legs are odd and even'. The song makes a good pairing with another Gibson setting, 'Girl's song' from three years earlier. 'Blaweary' (1921) – a poem which Gurney also set – is a magical little lullaby, which opens with a simple pentatonic line to accompany another folk-inspired melody and ends with the voice left on its own.

Many other single solo songs deserve mention. One of the most popular of all Howells's songs – justly so – is 'Come sing and dance' (1927, *1927*). It is the setting of an anonymous carol text consisting of three seven-line stanzas, only two lines of which have changing texts, the rest being refraining lines. Howells takes advantage of this to concentrate on the music and makes of it an ecstatic

Ex. 16.14

dance-song, in the tradition of 'This is my dancing day', with a swinging, almost insolent dance movement. The music is 'cross-gartered' throughout, ostensibly in 3/4 time but with 2/4 rhythmic patterns counterpointing across it to set up continuous hemiola tension. Its joyful vocal line soars like a bird (Ex. 16.14). It is rich in harmony and hidden detail, and in this respect looks forward not so much to the later songs as to the wonderful anthems and church services that Howells was to compose in the 1940s. 'A madrigal' (1916, *1919*), to a poem by Austin Dobson, has a deft, tripping accompaniment with a catchy little cadence and a vocal line full of duplet melismas (Ex. 16.15).

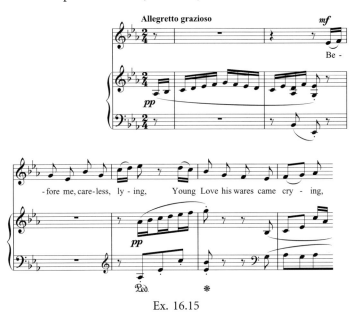

Ex. 16.15

There is a slightly Irish air to it, reminding us that Howells was a 'son of Stanford' if ever there was. 'Gavotte' (1919, *1927*), to the poem by Sir Henry Newbolt, is an early essay in the penillion manner that he was to explore more subtly in 'The Lady Caroline'. He catches well the frills and trills of the allusions in Newbolt's 'Old French' poem; not unexpectedly and more than in any other of his songs, it shows overt indebtedness to Ravel. Quite different is his setting of Clifford Bax's 'Lost love' (*1934*). The entire song is based on a simple pentatonic melodic line, either used as a single unison line or doubled in octaves; only occasionally does he resort to harmony, and then in the form of drones or simple ostinatos. This gives the song a strongly oriental feeling – not surprising as Bax's poem comes from his *Twenty Chinese Poems*, but unexpected in the context of Howells's output. His single setting of Blake's poetry, 'The little boy lost' (first published in *Music and Letters* in 1920) is another unusual song. There is to begin with hardly any music, just a murmuring two-chord ostinato that fades away to almost nothing. Above this, Blake's sad little verses are set in broken phrases that add to the desolation. Only towards the end, at three key phrases, is the placid E-minor-Aeolian modality broken: a B-flat on 'The mire was *deep*', a G-sharp on 'And the child did *weep*', and an F-natural on 'the vapour *flew*'. It is a disconcerting but effective song, and one wishes that the composer had explored Blake further. 'Goddess of night' (1921, *1921*) is his only setting of the poetry of his friend and fellow Gloucestershire-man, F. W. Harvey. The song is based on two ambiguous key centres: A-flat major, which opens the song, contradicting E major, which is the song's basic tonality. The singer picks up the one note in common (A-flat/G-sharp) on the opening word, 'Calm', and cadences on the same note, on the word 'eyes'; this A-flat/G-sharp gives rise to the Lydian curve of the vocal line (Ex. 16.16).

Ex. 16.16

Ex. 16.17

The two chords/key centres rock gently together in this exquisite little nocturne, the slow, calm 3/4 tread continually pushed out of kilter by inserted 2/4 bars. 'Flood' (1931, *1933*) was Howells's contribution to *The Joyce Book*. It is one of his most chromatically adventurous songs, each of the four vocal phrases set to a different mode: a whole-tone mode, the tone-semitone (Messiaen's 2nd) mode, a pentatonic mode, and back again to a whole-tone mode. This bewildering diversity is held together by watery arpeggios full of cross-rhythms, which rise to a fine climax at 'Love's full flood,/Lambent and vast and ruthless'. Like 'Come sing and dance', it looks forward to the mystical, ecstatic style of Howells's later works (Ex. 16.17).

Howells's songs range widely in subject-matter, from the sorrowful ('King David') to the ecstatic ('Come sing and dance'), from still nocturne ('Goddess of night') to rumbustious rustic portrait ('The mugger's song'), from delicate, old-world courtesies ('The Lady Caroline') to earthy rough humour ('The old soldier'). In common with many other English songwriters, he was particularly good at writing lullabies. They date from as early as 'An old man's lullaby' ('Golden slumbers') of 1917, through 'O my deir hert' (1922, *1923*, the song he dedicated to his infant daughter, Ursula) and 'Blaweary'; the lullaby mode even rocks its way sadly through the song 'The little boy lost'. In his contribution to a symposium of essays on Ivor Gurney, Howells commented on Gurney's use of silence in his songs: 'those silences that amount to genius' (1938: 13). He too possessed this genius. He knew exactly how to use the pause and the moment of 'no-music': take those pregnant silences between verses in 'Lost love', 'The little boy lost', 'The girl's song', 'King David' and 'The goat paths'. Closely allied to this is the way he so often leaves his singer alone at the end of a song, as in 'Blaweary', 'Some one' and, again, 'The goat paths'. There is no better way to give primacy to the singer, and, in consequence, primacy to the poet's text. Howells was potentially one of the finest English songwriters of the 20th century; he had all the technical skills and an immaculate instinct for suitable texts. It is a matter of great regret that he did not devote more of his talents and compositional time to songwriting.

17

C. W. Orr (1893–1976)

In valleys green and still
  Where lovers wander maying
They hear from over hill
  A music playing.

Behind the drum and fife,
  Past hawthornwood and hollow,
Through earth and out of life
  The soldiers follow.

The soldier's is the trade:
  In any wind or weather
He steals the heart of maid
  And man together.

The lover and his lass
  Beneath the hawthorn lying
Have heard the soldiers pass,
  And both are sighing.

And down the distance they
  With dying note and swelling
Walk the resounding way
  To the still dwelling.

A. E. Housman: 'In valleys green and still'

Charles Orr's song output – 35 songs in 82 years – is a meagre harvest for a man who regarded himself as a specialist song-composer. Ill-health; painstakingly slow craftsmanship; a reliance on inspiration coming to him, rather than he seeking it out; disillusionment with his musical career and lack of recognition: all these factors can help explain this low tally. Butterworth and Browne, because of their tragically short careers, wrote even less, yet their achievement is considerably more. In the end, one feels that Orr lacked a vital spark of imagination. And yet there is a quality to his songs, recognised early on by Delius and Warlock, which demands our serious critical attention.

Orr had a lifelong passion for German lieder: 'No English songs have ever given me the thrill that German lieder have done', he once said (Wilson: 17). His early love of Schubert, Schumann and Brahms was augmented and displaced when he discovered the music of Hugo Wolf. Wolf became Orr's songwriting mentor; indeed, Orr himself became an authority on the composer and made English translations of his song-texts. He admired Wolf not only for his discriminating choice of text and immaculate word-setting, but also for the unity of his conception of vocal-line and accompaniment, in which the two elements are intertwined and interdependent – equal partners as in an instrumental duo sonata. The other major influence on his style was Frederick Delius, whom he met in 1915. As with Delius, the harmonic element in Orr's music takes precedence over everything else, flowering in continuous chromaticism from fundamentally diatonic roots; thus he strove to capture every nuance of the text, every shade of meaning, in chromatic chiaroscuro. In other respects, particularly as far as the techniques of songwriting are concerned, Orr's debt to Delius is far less. Certainly he would have learned little from studying Delius's piano accompaniments: here Wolf was his main teacher. A third, lesser though still important, influence was Peter Warlock, whom he met through Delius. Warlock, a year younger than Orr, was highly impressed by Orr's early songs and persuaded Chesters to publish them. The two composers showed their mutual admiration by dedicating songs to each other: Orr with 'The carpenter's son' (1922), Warlock in the following year with 'Consider'. 'Consider' stands out in Warlock's *oeuvre* for its untypically 'pianistic', one might even say 'Orr-like', accompaniment; it is close to the sort of figurative textures that Orr was using in his first published song, 'Plucking the rushes'. 'The carpenter's son' again is atypical of its composer: large-scale and far more dramatic and aggressive than his later Housman setting, though certainly not Warlockean. Orr and Warlock were in fact following quite individual paths towards their songwriting ideals. With Warlock, it was the example of the Elizabethan lutenist-songwriters, Dowland, Campion and Daniel, who opened his ears to future development. With Orr, it was Wolf – a composer for whom Warlock showed little interest – who showed the path ahead. There are occasions, however, when the two composers do come within touching distance and nowhere more so than in Orr's 'Tryste Noel', a song which could be mistaken for Warlock. In its siciliana-based rhythms and richly chromatic chording and modal-diatonic framework, it reminds us of such carol-songs as 'Balulalow', 'The first mercy', 'Chanson du jour de Noël' and 'Bethlehem Down'. Warlock, for his part, is closest to Orr in his most Delius-influenced phase: *Saudades* and 'The sick heart'. But whereas Warlock moved on, Orr continued throughout his career to explore this particular, rather circumscribed ground.

Orr's main shortcoming as a song-composer is this restricted vision, which is apparent in his limited choice of text and in the setting of those texts. Of his 35 songs, 24 are settings of one poet, A. E. Housman; the first, ''Tis time, I think', dates from 1921, the last, 'In valleys green and still', from 1952. Orr possibly set more Housman than any other major songwriter: indeed, the poet became almost an obsession with him. His remaining eleven solo songs show a wide, if curious choice of English poetry: translations from the Chinese by Arthur Waley (1889–1966) and from the Latin by Helen Waddell (1889–1965) – two of the favourite text-sources for 20th-century British composers – and settings of poems by George Digby (1612–77), Patrick Hannay (? d. 1629), Thomas Hood, Dante Gabriel Rossetti, Robert Bridges, Louise Imogen Guiney and James Joyce. The techniques he uses in his songwriting hardly evolve at all – place 'Plucking rushes' and 'When the lad for longing sighs' side by side with 'The time of roses' and 'In valleys green and still': could you tell that thirty years separate them? What has been said in the early songs is being repeated (albeit with grace and refinement) in the later ones. This would not matter if Orr had a strong individual musical personality, but he lacks an instantly recognisable tone-of-voice.

Yet, there are hallmarks to be found on deeper acquaintance, of a subtle, unostentatious kind. First and foremost is the way vocal line and accompaniment are integrated; singer and pianist, are equal partners with equally important musical material. Neither dominates the other, and without one, the other does not make sense. The timing of the poem-setting and the word-setting are immaculate; here Orr has few peers. His vocal writing can sometimes (as with Bax) be awkward, especially in the use of angular intervals, for he is clearly much more at home in the piano-writing. His piano parts are idiomatically conceived, highly demanding, as both Walter Legge and Eugene Goossens remarked (Foreman, 1987: 171 and 182); yet for all their difficulty, they fit the hands like a glove. (He had a penchant for crossing the hands, l.h. over r.h., and intertwining the fingers, which can be seen in his first published song, 'Plucking the rushes'.) At their best these piano accompaniments are an essential commentary on the poem being set, underpinning the vocal line and supplying commentary on the texts when the voice is silent. Occasionally they can be fussy, harmonies and modulations subjected to unnecessarily finicky alteration. Warlock was quick to spot these weaknesses. In a letter to Orr (June 1922), written after receiving copies of his early Housman settings, Warlock wrote:

> . . . there are small details I find disquieting – little angularities in the melodic line of the accompaniment and an occasional feeling that the chord changes when it needn't, which – with the continual 7ths and 9ths, to 11ths and 13ths by addition of a note rather low down, makes the harmony, for my ear, rather cloying (Wilson: 31).

Other critics have made similar comments. Northcote refers to 'Orr's nervous chromatic harmony' (1937: 359), Banfield to 'discursive chromatics or rambling modulations' (1985: 303).

To illustrate the 'hallmarks' discussed above, I have chosen 'The Isle of Portland'. The title of the poem (no. LIX from *A Shropshire Lad*) refers to the island off Weymouth in Dorset, where convicted criminals were sentenced to hard labour. Here, we may read, in Housman's elusive narrative, that one of the Lad's companions has been sent to work at 'the felon-quarried stone' – possibly the Ned of the previous poem (no. LVIII, 'When I came last to Ludlow'). Orr sets the three quatrains in varied strophic form; the tempo marking is *Lento, sostenuto* and the metre Orr's favourite 3/4, across which is laid an uneasy barcarolle-like rhythm (Ex. 17.1(a)). This rhythmic pattern, clearly depicting the smooth 'star-filled seas' described in the first verse, can be heard, often subtly suggested but always there, in every bar of the song until the final cadence, where the metre is augmented into 12/8 (= 4/4). Though sweetly harmonised, this rhythmic ostinato acts as a disturbing undertow to the setting and its ebb and flow unifies the ebb and flow of other elements in the song.

Ex. 17.1(a)

Though basically strophic, the vocal line is reprised from verse to verse in an extremely flexible manner (Ex. 17.1(b)). What holds these three statements together is an underlying harmonic progression, itself undergoing continuous modification, but recognisable enough to make its point.

Ex. 17.1(b)(i)

Ex. 17.1(b)(ii)

Ex. 17.1(b)(iii)

Typical of Orr is the swift movement from the song's home key of E-flat major (already modally modified with a D-flat) to a dominant 7th on D major (the enharmonic pun of D-flat/C-sharp acting as crucial common ground), all accomplished before the first line of the poem is sung. The music remains here in D major until halfway through the final line of the stanza, when it returns, via E major, to its E-flat major base to cadence. Again an enharmonic pun of D-sharp/E-flat and G-sharp/A-flat ensures the modulation's effectiveness. Orr also avoids symmetrical regularity in the piano interludes between verses: that between verses 1 and 2 is less than two bars long; between verses 2 and 3 there is an extended interlude of four bars, which summarises the tonal polarity between the flat (E-flat) and sharp (here E major) (Ex. 17.1(c)). In the four-bar piano coda, the 12/8 not only establishes once and finally the E-flat major tonality, but also brings the rhythmic ostinato serenely to a halt.

Ex. 17.1(c)

These technical procedures are used solely to underline what the poem is saying. Thus the dramatic interlude between verses 2 and 3 is placed there because it comes immediately after the poet has made his first personal statement, which links him with the Portland prisoner:

> Far from his folk a dead lad lies
>   That once was friends with me.

Note how he re-emphasises this personal connection by opening the third verse with exactly the same notes that ended verse 2 (Ex. 17.1(d))

Ex. 17.1(d)

and how, by the time we reach the words of the final verse, the obsessive rhythmic ostinato has taken on the function of a lullaby as well as the gentle movement of the sea:

> Lie you easy, dream you light,
>   And sleep you fast for aye;

The song displays many other hallmarks of Orr's style: the use of fermatas to mark the ends of strophes and even phrases (see bars 18 and 38); the subtle rhythmic caste of the vocal line, with its avoidance of strong, first-beat stresses (see the opening of the 2nd strophe); a predilection for low cadence notes (final cadence); a chromatic vocal line which often gives rise to slightly angular intervals (e.g. bars 47–50); the repetition, brief but tasteful, of the final lines of text (something he does in several of his songs); the rich harmonic palette – the 7ths, 9ths, 11ths and 13ths that Warlock refers to (there are particularly rich dissonances in bars 36–7 and 51–2, and there is hardly a simple triad in the entire piece. The song even begins with a dominant 7th and the final E-flat chord is coloured with an added 6th!). But most of all, it is the writing for the piano that is so characteristic: elegant, sonorous, beautifully conceived for the instrument, yet working in partnership with, never against the voice. See how, for example, the piano aids and underpins the voice at the enharmonic modulation in bars 13 and 14 (Ex. 17.1(d)). Lyrical, compact, completely in tune with the text, and, in spite of the subtleties of technique, simple, direct and unpretentious, this is Orr at his best.

As has already been noted, Orr's 24 Housman settings account for nearly three-quarters of his song output. In this specialisation he would appear to have been inspired by Ernest Newman's exhortation to English songwriters, to do 'for Mr Housman what Wolf did for Mörike, for Goethe, for Eichendorff' (1918: 393) and he himself stated that his fervent wish was to leave behind 'only one setting of which Wolf would not be ashamed' (Northcote, 1937: 355). He was understandably upset when the BBC ignored his settings in a series of programmes devoted to Housman songs (Banfield, 1985: 301). Clearly Orr's reputation as a songwriter stands or falls by these songs, just as no consideration of Housman settings can be made without reference to Orr. Critics have been divided. Some, including Eric Sams and Christopher Palmer, claim that no songwriter has served Housman better. Others are less convinced. Arthur Jacobs tartly commented that Orr had 'set Housman almost exclusively, and less memorably than some other composers' (1960: 172). Jacobs's comment is provocative and perhaps unjust. But, after repeated experience of these songs, one is nonetheless left questioning whether Orr *was* the man whom Newman had in mind for the task. Edmund Rubbra put his finger on the matter when he wrote: 'I cannot help feeling that this composer's natural idiom, compounded as it is of caressing Delius-like harmonies, is not a suitable vehicle for the starkly direct statements of the chosen poems' (1941: 297).

A further problem about the Housman canon is that Orr set the poems piecemeal – possibly because of his slow style of working and his determination not to set a poem unless he was fully inspired. So we do not have a comprehensive 'Housman Songbook', like Wolf's Goethe, Mörike or Eichendorff songbooks, let alone a song-cycle. The *Cycle of Songs from 'A Shropshire Lad'* (*1934*) is not a song-cycle in the accepted sense, but a songbook of just seven songs; the other settings are in even smaller groupings: *Two Songs from 'A Shropshire Lad'* (1923), *Three Songs from 'A Shropshire Lad'* (1940) and *Five Songs from 'A Shropshire Lad'* (*1959*); the rest are separate songs. However fine the individual songs, they cannot compare with the major achievements of Somervell, Vaughan Williams and Ireland in their song-cycles. The songs vary in quality, too. The earliest, *Two Songs from 'A Shropshire Lad'* (*1923*), are not very promising; ''Tis time I think' (1921) suffers from a dense harmonic style and words which are not so much set as pegged onto a siciliana rhythm, and 'Loveliest of trees' again is marred by a clotted harmonic accompaniment. It is saved from oblivion by the setting of the word 'bloom' in verses 1 and 3, an unexpected harmonic plunge from the home key of F minor to an added 6th on A-flat major (Ex. 17.2). Some of the songs fail to reach the heart of the poem.

Ex. 17.2

The darkly ironic 'Hughley steeple' is treated like a simple folksong; its mood is light and breezy with no attempt to interpret the darkness of Housman's text. Similarly, 'The lads in their hundreds' (1936, *1937*) is a rather jolly setting of a not particularly jolly poem, redeemed, it must be said, by the splendid treatment of the final line. (It was evidently Orr's own favourite amongst his Housman songs.) Other settings lack striking ideas: the textures of such songs as 'On your midnight pallet lying' and 'Into my heart an air that kills' are too abstract, lacking what Edmund Blunden referred to as 'particularity'. It is as though Orr had decided to eschew the use of word-painting or any recourse to aural imagery. Why? Housman's poetry is essentially defined and required a similar response from the composer. It is when Orr gives clear-cut definition to his songs, through the use of aural imagery and word-painting, that he best succeeds, as in 'Is my team ploughing?', 'Along the field', 'The isle of Portland' and especially 'The carpenter's son' (1922, *1923*). This is one of his earliest Housman settings and one of the most striking. It is an unusual poem to set to music, and according to Gooch and Thatcher (1976), Orr is the only composer who has so far attempted it. The poem has strong biblical undertones: the life of a Shropshire boy is paralleled with that of Christ, told in the first person, which makes it all the more harrowing:

> 'Here hang I, and right and left
> Two poor fellows hang for theft:
> All's the same the luck we prove,
> Though the midmost hangs for love.'

Orr underpins the song with a march-like accompaniment, in which an insistent rhythmic motto is heard over ambiguous harmonies. This is not just a pegboard for the words, as the siciliana rhythm was in ''Tis time, I think', but acts as an ever-present backcloth to the tragic story (Ex. 17.3(a)).

Ex. 17.3(a)

Ex. 17.3(b)

The seven stanzas are given different tonal centres, each pivoting over a pair of chords, until the song eventually returns full circle back to its D major/B-flat opening. This leads into an almost hysterical coda, which ends with dissonant, hammered chords (Ex. 17.3(b)). Orr uses simple but telling imitation – note how the piano's 'motto' echoes the singer's opening words – and the word-setting is particularly dramatic and searing at the climaxes to the refraining words, 'Live, lads, and I will die' which end both the first and final stanzas (Ex. 17.3(c)).

Ex. 17.3(c)

Orr dedicated the song to Warlock who thought it 'magnificent', and this masterly, haunting song is well worthy of its dedicatee. For the normally unassertive Orr, it is a strikingly forceful song – something that, sadly, he never sought to emulate again.

Of the five Housman songs written and published between 1924 and 1927 and later brought together as *Five Songs from 'A Shropshire Lad'* (1959), two are particularly fine. 'With rue my heart is laden' has been praised by both Northcote (1937: 356) and Warlock (Wilson, 1989: 34): Warlock described it as 'one of the loveliest songs any English composer has written.' The poem is set to a gentle, limpid *Andante*, the vocal line subtly counterpointing the 3/4 metre. The two short quatrains are through-set, the final lines echoing the opening. The effect of this reprise is emphasised by the relatively long piano interlude between the two halves of the second strophe. 'Is my team ploughing?' is one of Orr's finest achievements. Of the many settings of this problematic poem, Orr's interpretation reaches the heart of Housman's intentions best of all, avoiding on the one hand the hysteria of Vaughan Williams and on the other the elegiac melancholy of Butterworth. He treats the poem with an almost casual innocence, though the gentle tension of the singer's 6/8 against the piano's 2/4 reproduces the unease behind the dialogue. There are several subtle details to note: the strange little 'knocking' figure which marks each question and answer and which develops into an ironic, mocking question-mark by the end of the song (Ex. 17.4); the way in which Orr reverses the tessitura of question and answer in the final verse; and the way in which the final unresolved dominant 7th echoes the unresolved statement of the poem. No other setting succeeds so well in capturing the irony of that final stanza.

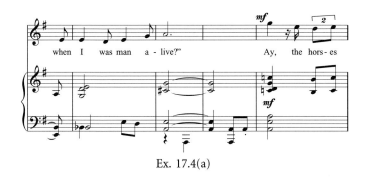

Ex. 17.4(a)

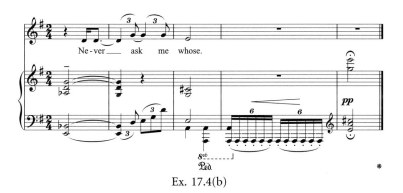

Ex. 17.4(b)

Another fine song from the period, not incorporated in the 1959 re-publication, is 'When I was one-and-twenty' (1924, *1925*). Though set strophically, Orr manages to contrast the 'experience' of verse 2 with the 'innocence' of verse 1 by alteration of vocal line, the slowing down of tempo and the prolongation of notes and of text. The vocal line soars up from its folk-modal roots, ranging far wider than any folksong, and shows how Orr could give rhythmic variety to the simple metres of the poem without destroying its folk-like character.

The seven songs that make up the *Cycle of Songs from 'A Shropshire Lad'* (*1934*) vary in quality. Northcote (1937: 358) and Palmer (1973: 691) praise 'When I watch the living meet', a song over which the shadow of Hugo Wolf certainly hovers, but its contorted, almost tortured chromatic vocal line leads in places to some uncomfortable vocal writing. 'Hughley steeple' is another Housman poem that has rarely been set to music. Its theme, contrasting those friends of the Shropshire Lad buried to the south of the steeple (who died from 'natural causes') with those buried to the north (i.e. suicides) is perhaps too gruesome for most tastes. Orr's setting has many attractive features. He sets the words simply, as though it were a folksong, the voice leading straight in (with no piano prelude) and each verse ending with a *caesura*. But Orr makes no attempt to interpret the darkness of the text. With its lilting 6/8 metre and *Poco Animato* direction, it is too bright and breezy: the setting is almost cynical. There is even more folksong in 'Farewell to barn and stack and tree' (another poem featuring violent death) which, with its pentatonic melody and 'Scotch snaps', has a slightly Celtic aura. No surprise, then, that Arnold Bax should have praised this song and earned the dedication. But what is the reason for the Celtic idiom? With its reference to the 'Severn shore' it is essentially an 'English' poem: as little Celtic as the Hardy poems that Bax himself set. One feels that, untypically, Orr is adapting words to a pre-conceived tune rather than finding a melody to match the words. It is, nevertheless, an attractive song. The four verses of 'Oh fair enough are sky and plain' are set to alternating musical material (A B A B). In the second strophe, Orr repeats the final line, which he extends to two repeats in the final strophe – musically effective and poetically justified, as the words 'And wishes he were I' fade away like an echo. The song is an example of Orr's ability to write a delicate, pianistically effective accompaniment that moulds and enhances the singer's line as well as reflecting the watery reflections of the poem. The outstanding song of the set, however, is the first, 'Along the field', in which Orr brilliantly captures the 'sad condition of humanity' of Housman's poem. A 'waldenweben' accompanimental figure ripples its way in the r.h., like a hidden underground stream, over a rising arpeggiated counter-tune with a subtle 'cuckoo' refrain in the l.h. (Ex. 17.5). Above this is a shapely vocal line, with perfectly placed climaxes, encompassing the long stanzas with fluent ease. It is a song at the heart of the English Romantic Song tradition, with its unconscious echoes of and homages to Delius and Gurney.

Ex. 17.5

The *Three Songs from 'A Shropshire Lad'* (*1940*), dedicated to Gerald Moore, are disappointing. 'Into my heart an air that kills' (dating from 1932) shows Orr at his least effective: over-fussy harmonies (the opening fidgets through six key centres in eight bars) and, more seriously, a failure to capture the deep melancholy of the text. The setting is too dream-like, lacking definition. 'Westward on the high-hilled plains' is a stronger song, the four verses set A B C A. But why the *caesura* at the end of the second lines of verses 1 and 4? They make no poetical point, but merely halt the flow of the music. 'Oh see how thick the goldcup flowers', with the courting words of the lovelorn youth put down by the maid's curt, sceptical replies, is one of the few songs in Orr's output that dances along. But the modulations (from E major to E-flat major and back again) are unconvincing, and the introduction of new material in the third verse is out of place: it sounds as if we are embarking on an entirely new song.

Two remaining Housman settings deserve attention. 'Soldier from the wars returning' is taken from *Last Poems* (1922) and therefore outside the main *Shropshire Lad* canon, but it stands almost symbolically as the song at the heart of all his Housman settings, with its symbols of Soldiers, War and Death. Clearly the poem moved Orr strongly, as its dedication (Lieutenants R. L. and L. C. (Coldstream Guards) 1917) and epigraph ('These in the glorious morning of their days/ For England's sake lost all but England's praise') indicate. In essence it is an elegiac hymn, simple in texture to allow the words to sing through, and erupting suddenly into highly charged dramatic textures in the third verse. But the *nobilmente* ending is perhaps too easily achieved. That same preoccupation with soldiers and war is at the heart of Orr's final Housman setting, 'In valleys green and still' (1952, *1954*). Housman's poem is artfully ambiguous: the sound of drum and fife attract two lovers, and a soldier steals the hearts of both lover and his lass, for different (or is it the same?) reasons. The five verses are set in an effective ternary pattern, A1 B1 C A2 B2. A subtle touch is the way he inverts the opening phrases of A and B on their reprise. The chromatically inflected vocal line, over a rich, dense harmonic background, is, as always, extremely sensitive to word-rhythms and inflections. It is the ending of the song that stays in the mind: the bugle-calls, of mildly bitonal augmented 5ths contradicting the E-flat tonality, echoing into the distance. These augmented 5ths have been pre-echoed earlier in the song, at the words 'hollow' and 'swelling', so that we are aurally and emotionally prepared for them. The song is a fitting conclusion to Orr's Housman settings (Ex. 17.6). Despite Orr's lifelong preoccupation with the poetry of Housman and his averred opinion that his Housman songs were his finest achievement, others may judge his best songs to be those outside the Housman canon. In fact, his two earliest publications, to poems by Arthur Waley and Dante Gabriel Rossetti, are good examples. 'Plucking the rushes' (1921, *1922*) comes from Waley's *170 Chinese Poems* (1918), one of the most influential works of its kind. With their emphasis on the concrete and the particular, unrhymed lines and flexible metres and rhythms, these poems were perfect in every way for musical setting, as is proved by the number of songwriters who have chosen them, including Gibbs, Rawsthorne, Britten and Oldham.

Ex. 17.6

In this 4th-century poem, the poet describes a boy and girl gathering rushes for thatching. The Chinese location is characterised with tact and subtlety – parallel 5ths that dominate the piano's arpeggiated textures and the pentatonic shapes of the vocal line – all within a richly chromatic 20th-century idiom. 'Silent noon' is even more impressive, not only for its intrinsic quality but because it inevitably places itself for comparison with Vaughan Williams's classic setting. Structurally and in mood, Orr's song shows many similarities, but whether this is through deliberate modelling or subconscious echo is difficult to tell. Both composers adopt the same ternary pattern to the sonnet shape – A1: 'Your hands lie open . . .'; B: 'All round our nest . . .'; A2: 'Oh! clasp we to our hearts' – but Orr's is the more subtle. The still serene atmosphere of the summer noon is captured in what was to become the composer's favourite triple-time pulse. Unlike Vaughan Williams, he bravely moves straight into his setting without a preliminary prelude to establish the mood, but recompenses this with a long, serene coda. With its rich, summery harmonies the song catches the idyllic scene to perfection and is a worthy alternative to the Vaughan Williams version.

'Tryste Noel' (1927, *1930*) is a setting of mock-medieval verses by the American-born poet, editor and Catholic apologist, Louise Imogen Guiney (1861–1920). With its use of siciliana rhythms, 1st inversion chords floating over sustained pedal-notes and false relations, this is Orr modelling himself on Warlock; it could well have been subtitled 'P. W. in homage' (Ex. 17.7).

Ex. 17.7

A comparison, however, with such Warlock songs as 'Balulalow' and 'Chanson du jour de Noël' reminds us how superbly conceived and crafted are Warlock's treatments of 'old verse'. Perhaps the Wardour-street pastiche of Guiney's poem lends itself to a slightly contrived medieval air, as opposed to Warlock's use of genuine medieval texts and his firsthand knowledge of the idiom. Yet Orr's song is nonetheless memorable, and far more effective than the stodgy, rhythmically static setting of 'The Earl of Bristol's farewell' (1927, *1930*) and 'Whenas I wake' (1928, *1930*), where he has chosen genuine 17th-century verses.

Orr was one of the 'baker's dozen' chosen by Herbert Hughes to contribute settings of Joyce's *Pomes Penyeach*, published in 1933 as *The Joyce Book*. 'Bahnhofstrasse' (1931) is a tour-de-force, one of his finest songs and certainly one of the most memorable contributions to that mixed-quality collection. The poem is about old age, symbolised by the poet's reference to his failing eyesight. (Bahnhofstrasse = Station Street in Zurich, where Joyce first experienced an attack of glaucoma.) Orr sets the short lyric with a folk-like simplicity that conceals complex undertones. Here for once he gives concrete definition to his song: an inverted tonic pedal-note (G) chimes obsessively against the singer's pentatonic melodic line, underlining 'the passing of time and age with which the poem is concerned' (Banfield, 1985: 304) (Ex. 17.8). If one were forced to choose just one Orr song for a Desert Island, this would have to be a contender. 'Bahnhofstrasse' was subsequently published as the first of *Four Songs for High Voice* (*1959*). The other three are late songs: 'Requiem' (1957), to a late medieval lyric in Helen Waddell's translation, 'The time of roses' (1955), by Thomas Hood, and 'Since thou, O fondest and truest' (1959) by Robert Bridges, all poems which have been memorably set by other songwriters.

Ex. 17.8

The Hood poem (dating from 1827) was originally entitled 'Ballad', and Orr seems intent on writing one. Its fussy harmonic changes are unconvincing. The Bridges setting, the last he completed, is full of bombast and finicky, over-refined word-setting: a disappointing conclusion to a songwriting career. 'Requiem' is more direct and thereby more effective, though the restlessly twitchy harmonic changes seem at odds with the serene mood of this sad elegy. Far more appealing is his setting of the same poet's 'Hymn before sleep' (1953, 1954).

As so often, Peter Warlock went to the heart of the matter when, in a letter acknowledging the safe arrival of Orr's earliest Housman settings (quoted on page 316), he voiced disquiet at angularities in the melodic line of the accompaniment, meretricious harmonic changes and cloying harmony. The angularities Warlock criticises apply to the vocal lines as well as to the accompaniment, and, with the cloying harmony, derive from the same source: Orr's over-reliance on harmonic resources in his songs at the expense of other parameters. It was a fault that Warlock recognised in his own early songs and mitigated through his study of Jacobean lute-song. Orr, however, never found a way out; his basic technique hardly altered throughout his career. Another weakness in Orr's songs is a lack of defining 'particularity', symbolised by his eschewing of word-painting or any other aural means to match the visual imagery of the poetry he sets. In this he is at odds with his favourite poet, Housman, whose poetry is full of strong topographical associations and concrete images. There is nothing wrong with abstraction in songwriting and certainly nothing to praise in the song-composer who dots every 'i' and crosses every 't' of a poem, but, as composers as dissimilar as Parry, Ireland, Warlock and Britten have demonstrated, such aural analogy works wonders in the setting of English poetry. When Orr does match the visual aspects of the poem in his music, as in 'Along the field', with its 'rustle of spring' and cuckoo calls, or 'The carpenter's son', with its dead march, or 'Oh fair enough are sky and plain', with its watery, toccata-like accompaniment, his songs immediately come to life. At their weakest, Orr's songs are 'worthy' – conscientious but lacking an essential vital spark. In his finest songs, however, his qualities are self-evident: wide and colourful harmonic resources which give his best songs 'that subtle and never-cloying elegiac sweetness' that Palmer speaks of (1974: Prefatory note); melodic subtlety coupled with sureness of text-setting, which make his songs so 'poet friendly' and so enjoyable to sing; and finely-wrought, idiosyncratic piano-writing that makes his accompaniments a pleasure to play.

18

Peter Warlock (1894–1930)

At 'The Fox Inn'
The tattered ears,
The fox's grin
Mock the dead years.

High on the wall
Above the cask
Laughs at you all
The fox's mask . . .

Bruce Blunt: 'The Fox'

Few 20th-century musicians led a life more carefully calculated to become a legend than 'Peter Warlock'. He was born Philip Heseltine at the Savoy Hotel in 1894; he died 'Peter Warlock' by gas poisoning in December 1930. In those 36 years he accomplished more than most of us manage in three-score-and-ten. He was scholar, editor, music critic, biographer, anthologist and concert-promoter. He was the writer of brilliant limericks and clerihews and had a fine line in barbed invective. The riotous bohemian existence that he led in London and Eynsford in the years immediately after World War One have been captured for posterity in at least four famous works of fiction – notably D. H. Lawrence's *Women in Love* where he appears as the obnoxious Halliday – as well as flashing like a comet through many autobiographies of the period. In addition to all this, he happened to be one of the finest songwriters that this country has ever produced. Roy Campbell, in his beautiful memorial poem ('Dedication of a Tree: To "Peter Warlock"', *Mithraic Emblems*, 1936), aptly likened him to a cicada:

Who in one hour, resounding, clear, and strong,
    A century of ant-hood far out-glows,
And burns more sunlight in a single song
    Than they can store against the winter snows.

Such a life inevitably gives birth to myths and legends, and few English composers have been demonised by myth as much as he has. One of these – a hare set running by Cecil Gray in his pioneering study of the composer (1934) – is that the so-called 'Heseltine' songs are superior to the 'Warlock' ones: that Heseltine *Dolens* is better than Warlock *Boisterens*. Arnold Whittall has suggested that 'Despair, as in *The Curlew*, lay behind Warlock's best music'

(1966: 123). Many years earlier, Gerald Cockshott had convincingly refuted this idea. 'There has', he wrote:

> been an . . . unfortunate tendency . . . to take it for granted that the personal, 'Heseltine' songs are of necessity superior to the rest. 'What a pity he wrote only one 'Frostbound wood' and all those songs about beer', is the implication. In England we still tend to rate the personal lament above the generalized utterance, partly because we feel that a work of art cannot be in the highest class unless its *subject-matter* is desperately serious . . . and partly, no doubt, because in the former meretriciousness is less easy to detect. An emotion is of no particular significance unless it is one that is generally experienced; and to explore the unusual circumstances or the extraordinary situation is a symptom of decadence (1940: 256).

He goes on to suggest that:

> while 'The fox' and 'The frostbound wood' remain two of the finest songs that have ever been written, there is, I feel, something rather unhealthy about the crying curlews and full hearts of Yeats and Nichols . . . In contrast, fresh air blows through the 'Warlock' ballads (1940: 257).

As with all great songwriters, Warlock's talent was not restricted to one species of song. He wrote good songs in every vein that he chose to essay, and it would be impossible to prove that the 'Heseltine' were superior, technically or otherwise, to the 'Warlock'. As this chapter will show, Warlock's finest songs span his entire career and cover a variety of poets and moods.

It would be of no service to Warlock to lay extravagant claims for him as a composer. He seems to have deliberately set himself a modest target, and his range of song-forms is a limited one. With the exception of *The Curlew*, whose four songs must be regarded as a single, extended composition, all are separate solo songs. The song-sets, such as *Lillygay, Candlelight,* and shorter groups like the *Peterisms* and the *Three Belloc Songs*, do not claim to be song-cycles. Even in his separate solo songs, Warlock has limited his choice of texts to simple lyric poetry. There is no dramatic 'Erlkönig' in his output and, with the exception of 'Away to twiver', 'Yarmouth fair' and *Lillygay*, there are no narrative songs.

He also limits himself in his choice of poet and poetic subject-matter. Of his mature output of just over 100 songs for solo voice and piano, less than 20 are to texts by 20th-century poets. There are over 40 anonymous poems from the 15th to 17th centuries, seven by Shakespeare, and 26 by other 16th- and early 17th-century poets. Hardly surprisingly, there are none at all to poems from the late 17th or the 18th centuries. From the 19th century there are two by Stevenson, one by Clare, one by Moore, one translation by William Cory and a Blake epigram. That is to say that over 80 per cent of his songs are to texts written before he was born. The 20th-century poets can all be described as 'Georgian' and minor Georgian at that, and include Bruce Blunt (5), Hilaire Belloc (4), Robert Nichols (2) and Edward Shanks (2). Just as interesting are the poets from the 20th century whom he does *not* choose. There is no Housman – surprisingly in some ways, considering Warlock's *penchant* for the melancholy – and, significantly, no Hardy, de la Mare or Kipling: all lyric poets working contemporarily with him and whose poetry has appealed to other songwriters. It is also interesting to note that the Yeats poems selected for *The Curlew* date from the poet's early period, the latest, 'The withering of the boughs', from the 1904 collection, *In the Seven Woods*. It cannot be claimed that Warlock was out of touch with the literature of his day. His circle of friends and acquaintances included, at one time or another, writers such as D. H. Lawrence and Aldous Huxley (both of whom caricatured him in novels), and he professed great admiration for the work of James Joyce. It would appear that, in Warlock's case, the avoidance of 20th-century poetry was not so much through lack of appreciation as through a natural inclination towards the literature of the Elizabethan and Jacobean periods, of and for which he had particular knowledge and affection. With Warlock we have a genuinely 20th-century phenomenon: the composer-scholar; the musician who not only composes music himself but also studies and edits music of a previous period; a composer, moreover, who may well have been inspired to compose his own settings of earlier lyrics through his acquaintance with the original settings. His choice of Shakespeare and other Elizabethan poets seems, in part, to have been an attempt to reinterpret the lyrics for the circumstances of his own day and age. Indeed, they *do* possess, amongst other things, 'the atmosphere and charm of the period', as one publisher's publicity blurb states (1967: Preface). This is inevitable – Warlock the scholar peeping over the shoulder of Warlock the composer – but it is incidental. Songs such as 'Mockery' and 'Away to twiver' are completely 20th-century and characteristically Warlockean in sensibility.

The main musical influences on Warlock the songwriter were Delius, Quilter, van Dieren and 17th-century English lute-song. He had first encountered Delius's music in 1920 when at Eton and had been overwhelmed by the experience. He met the composer during the latter's visit to London in the following year and the two began a correspondence. The older man became almost a father figure to the young Philip, who in return did much to promote Delius's music in England, including writing the first full-length study of the composer (1923). Though his youthful enthusiasm later abated somewhat, Delius remained an important figure in his life, and it was Warlock who, with Beecham, organised the great Delius Festival of 1929. His earliest attempts at songwriting, however, were indebted not to Delius but to the songs of Roger Quilter, whom, again, he met whilst at Eton. By October 1913 he was extravagantly acclaiming Quilter's virtues: 'His setting of Shakespeare's "O mistress mine" is the most exquisite and entirely lovely lyric I know . . . one feels absolute perfection in its three brief pages' (Smith, 1994: 29). His enthusiasm for Quilter, especially the early songs, remained throughout his life, and years later he acknowledged his debt by sending him a copy of 'Late summer' inscribed, 'To Roger Quilter without whose genial influence there would have been no songs by Peter Warlock'. He met the Dutch-born composer, Bernard van Dieren, in 1916 and was immediately drawn to the music of this original, if somewhat over-refined composer, with its highly chromatic and contrapuntally-complex idiom. The shadow of van Dieren is most noticeable in the songs of Warlock's early maturity, *Saudades* (1916–17) and *The Curlew* (1915–22), though later works, such as 'Sorrow's lullaby' and 'And wilt thou leave me thus?', show trace influences. Van Dieren replaced Delius as Warlock's 'father-confessor', and Warlock's involvement in promoting the Dutchman's music became almost obsessional.

But by far the most important and beneficial influence on his songwriting was Elizabethan and Jacobean music, with which he first became acquainted in 1915 and which he began to transcribe and edit in earnest in the early 1920s. From the English lutenist songwriters, Warlock learned a great deal. It was not limited to what might be termed 'archaisms', such as a fondness for melodic sequences, the use of the 'Elizabethan cadence', or modally-inflected melodies. Far more importantly he learned to free his music from the tyranny of the bar-line and to inject new life into what was basically a diatonic idiom, both factors which contributed to the rhythmic vigour and sprightliness which was to characterise his mature songs, even including those in doleful mood. The first fruits of this crucial discovery came with the songs that he sent under the pseudonym 'Peter Warlock' to the publisher Winthrop Rogers in 1918; these were published in the autumn of 1919 and included 'As ever I saw' and 'The bayly berith the bell away'.

But such very English influences are by no means the whole story. Warlock's tastes were wide and certainly not insular, and in many of his songs one can detect the impact of contemporary European composers: the colourful dissonances of Bartók and of Schoenberg (particularly in the 'atonal' interlude of *The Curlew*); even Stravinsky, a composer whom he professed to dislike, seems to lurk behind the drunken smith in 'Away to twiver'. All these diverse influences, strange bedfellows but typical of the wide-ranging eclecticism of the man, make up what we recognise as the songwriter Peter Warlock.

Though he never committed himself to words on the subject of his own songs, Warlock's comments on the songs of other composers and on songwriting in general, in his prefaces and articles, give us an insight into his own attitudes. Amongst the 'Aphorisms' that he contributed to *The New Age* (1917: 46) are the following:

> If words are set to music, the music must be as independent an entity as the poem.
> The poem must be recreated rather than interpreted.
> To underline a poem word by word is the work of a misguided schoolmaster.

In a later article in *The Sackbut* (1921: 421), he wrote:

> One should never lose sight of the fact that song is *in essence* unaccompanied tune.

His own practice bears this out. His vocal lines hold the song's quintessence and are usually a satisfactory entity in themselves. This is nowhere more evident than in 'Sleep' (1922, *1924*), which starts from, and cadences onto the tonic and needs no accompaniment to make tonal sense. He is concerned in his word-setting with the interpretation of the general emotion of the poem rather than a particular succession of images within it. For this reason, specific word-painting is seldom found. He rarely indulges in melisma, except for the 'tripping duplets' which he effects in a song such as 'The lover's maze'. In fact Warlock is surprisingly conformist to the Cranmerian doctrine of 'one syllable, one note'.

Despite the diversity of influence on his music, there are certain hallmarks that characterise the Warlock song. Some of these have already been suggested; here are others. One notable melodic feature is the stepwise progression of thirds – the 'steps up' and the 'steps down'. 'Piggesnie' provides the most striking examples of the 'steps up', 'Mr Belloc's fancy' of the 'steps down', whilst 'Maltworms' combines the two (Exs. 18.1(a), (b) and (c)). But the motive is also to be found in 'My own country' and developed with more sophistication in 'Mockery' and 'The fox' (see Ex. 18.31(b)).

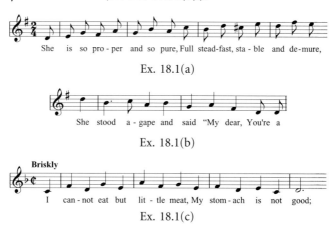

Ex. 18.1(a)

Ex. 18.1(b)

Ex. 18.1(c)

Another melodic feature is the way in which some of his melodies hover around one note or a handful of notes, in the style of an intonation. In 'The night' the vocal line of the first verse does not move from the insistent E-tonic until the leap to the octave E on the very last syllable. With constant moving of chords around this pedal, it has the feeling of hushed incantation (Ex. 18.2). An extension of this intonation, from one note to two notes, can be heard in 'There was an old man' (*Candlelight*) and the device is taken a step further in 'The frostbound wood', where Warlock limits himself throughout the song to only four pitches (see Ex. 18.29). Such use of pedal-notes and ostinatos, though striking, is unusual in a composer whose vocal writing is usually extremely wide-ranging and varied. His melodic lines are frequently modally based, but with an ambiguity to the modality. Songs with vocal lines as modally 'pure' as 'Sleep' and 'Chanson du jour de Noël' are uncommon. Chromatic alterations are usually made to the basic modes, particularly to the 3rd, 6th and 7th degrees, so that melodies hover between major and minor, Mixolydian and Ionian; see 'O my kitten'/'As ever I saw' (7th degrees), 'Balulalow'/'Ha'nacker mill' (6th degrees) and 'The first mercy' (3rd degree). One striking feature of his accompaniments is Warlock's fondness for chains of parallel 6ths or 10ths, usually associated with a bass pedal-note. 'As ever I saw' and 'Balulalow' are classic examples, but it is also heard in the sad, rocking accompaniment of 'Sleep' and as one of the key motives in *The Curlew* song-cycle (see Exs. 18.9(b) and 10(a)).

Ex. 18.2

Warlock's cadences are one of his most characteristic hallmarks. Like so many early 20th-century composers, he strove, almost 'officiously', to avoid the conventional V-I cadence, that feature of European tonal music which was used like a rubber-stamp to conclude pieces of music from the mid 17th century to the late 19th century. His endeavours to avoid it show considerable imagination:

(a) avoidance of the dominant chord, modulating instead to a remote tonality, as in 'Sleep' and 'Cradle song' – a move usually followed by an unadulterated tonic triad (Ex. 18.3(a));
(b) avoidance of a simple final chord, as in 'And wilt thou leave me thus?' (Ex. 18.3(b));
(c) avoidance of a full close altogether, ending on an indefinite chord, as in 'The frostbound wood' and 'Along the stream' (Ex. 18.3(c)).

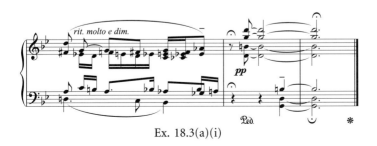

Ex. 18.3(a)(i)

Ex. 18.3(a)(ii)

Ex. 18.3(b)

Her face was love-ly and care-la-den Un-der a white hood. ___

Ex. 18.3(c)(i)

whis-per-ing   Fare - well!

ritenuto al fine   *pochiss.*

Ex. 18.3(c)(ii)

If he does use a conventional full close, he may disguise the dominant chord with chromatic added notes (as in 'Rest, sweet nymphs'), Bartókian crushed chords (of which there are several examples, as in 'Tommy Tucker', 'There was an old woman' and 'Jillian of Berry') or an adaptation of a modal 'English 7th' cadence ('Sweet content' and 'As ever I saw'). Occasionally he reverses the procedure: after a chromatically rich passage he ends with a simple V-I – almost a 'cock-a-snook', 'I told you so'. 'Sweet-and-twenty' and 'Whenas the rye' are examples of this (Ex. 18.3(d)). These cadences show Warlock in a nutshell: they are utterly characteristic of the man. Another important fingerprint is his use of quartal harmonies, noticeable as early as *Saudades*. Whether he learnt this from contemporary European composers or from lute tuning, is difficult to decide: probably a mixture of both, though it would have been impressed on him through his studies of 17th-century lute-song.

Ex. 18.3(d)(i)

Ex. 18.3(d)(ii)

I have left full discussion of Warlock's piano accompaniments until last in order to view them as a whole and, at the same time, to answer the criticisms that are often directed against them. Gerald Cockshott has said: 'If Warlock is kind to the singer, he is often exactly the reverse to the pianist' (1940: 257). There is no disputing the fact that some of his accompaniments are overwritten. Fewer notes would achieve the same effect *and*, importantly, would still sound authentically Warlock. This he himself proved in his two versions of 'Mr Belloc's fancy' (1921 and 1930). The final version shows how he could prune out unnecessary difficulties yet retain the essential character of the music. I am sure that over-elaborate piano-writing is a factor that dissuades recitalists from performing certain of his songs more frequently. 'Rutterkin', one of his most original songs, is virtually precluded from performance by the demands of its piano accompaniment, and how often have we heard performances of 'Captain Stratton's fancy' where notes have been left out in order to maintain the song at its correct pace?

Another criticism that has been levelled against his piano parts is that they are unidiomatic. Warlock's most characteristic writing for the instrument is, as his early *Folksong Preludes* show, linear in conception. Though harmonically rich, it is contrapuntally directed, with the individual strands carefully maintained.

This explains why he chose on occasion to make string quartet versions of songs (e.g. 'Sleep' and 'Balulalow'). In an early song such as 'The bayly berith the bell away', the piano as an instrument is rarely exploited in its own right and often sounds – as the composer intended – like a keyboard transcription of a lute accompaniment. The consequent return of emphasis to the singer and the words is, of course, one of Warlock's most important contributions to the art of songwriting in the 20th century. Even in his later songs, where he achieves a more positive and idiomatic piano accompaniment and a closer integration of vocal and accompanimental elements, the voice is always given precedence. But these factors do not mean that his piano-writing is ineffective or 'unpianistic'. One must beware of preconceptions as to what constitutes a 'pianistic' style. It was this conventional conception that marred a large number of English songs written at this period: arpeggiated accompaniments, meretricious flurries of notes, all covering up poverty of invention. On the few occasions when Warlock does use this kind of piano-writing – for instance, 'Consider' (1923) and 'The contented lover' (1928) – the result sounds uncharacteristic. On the other hand, the difficulties that the accompanist must meet in songs such as 'Mockery' and 'Sigh no more, ladies' are entirely 'pianistic'.

In the following survey of Warlock's songs, I have chosen for discussion those that I consider particularly outstanding in an outstanding *oeuvre*. In doing so, I have endeavoured to choose a group which covers his entire mature songwriting career and is representative of a variety of poet, subject-matter and mood.

Early songs, to 1920

Warlock began writing songs soon after leaving Eton. Some of these early works have been published (*Eight Songs*, 1972) and subsequently included in the Collected Edition of his songs (Vol. 1, 1982). Though they show a considerably sophisticated harmonic vocabulary, very much influenced by his mentors of the time, Delius and Quilter, they are hardly more than juvenilia. The vocal lines are often uningratiating and the piano accompaniments ponderous, as this passage from 'A lake and a fairy boat' (1911, *1972*) shows (Ex. 18.4). (It should be noted that the tempo marking is 'Fast: very soft and light'.) Over-noted piano-writing was something that he had to work against throughout his career. The most fruitful outcome of his contact with Bernard van Dieren was that it released Warlock's music from its cramping reliance on harmony. He learned to conceive his musical lines contrapuntally, while retaining his rich harmonic palette. This process can be observed in the song collection *Saudades* (1916–17, *1923*), completed during his stay in Ireland (1917–18). Warlock appended a footnote to the first song, quoting from an essay by L. Cranmer-Byng: '. . . that haunting sense of sadness and regret for days gone by which the Portuguese call *Saudades* – a word which has no equivalent in the English language'; 'nostalgia' is probably the nearest we shall get.

Ex. 18.4

This mood permeates all three songs: 'Along the stream', a setting of a poem by Li-Po translated by Cranmer-Byng, 'Take, O take those lips away', the first of two settings of Shakespeare's lyric that Warlock was to make, and 'Heracleitus', William Cory's famous translation of the lyric by Callimachus. The Shakespeare setting is the most conventional, having both key signature (here the four flats = a Dorian-mode B-flat minor) and time signature (3/4); vocal lines keep metrically to the 3/4 and the tonality, despite chromatic blurring, to the Dorian-mode, whilst the piano has a harmonically conceived texture, with use of broken arpeggios and pulsing chords. The other two songs, however, show the influence of van Dieren: no key signatures, no bar-lines, a highly chromatic idiom verging in places on the atonal, and contrapuntally motivated textures. This is particularly noticeable in 'Along the stream' which is dedicated to van Dieren. But, at a stroke, Warlock out-masters his mentor. The song is held together by a motto theme, heard at the outset in the piano and recurring throughout in both voice and accompaniment ('x'), and a motto chord, of the secondary 7th ('y') (Ex. 18.5, (a), (b) and (c)). These combine at the crucial phrase, 'Where no birds wake' and at the song's short postlude, where the chord 'y' acts as an unresolved question mark (see Ex. 18.3(c)). It is at once one of Warlock's most highly organised and most 'atonal' songs. The motto chord 'y' reappears four times at crucial moments in the final song, 'Heracleitus' with which it shares the same gloomy mood, thus lending musical unity to the group.

Ex. 18.5(a)

Ex. 18.5(b)

Ex. 18.5(c)

Quite different in mood, but foreshadowing the Warlock of later songs, is the setting of Blake's epigram 'I asked a thief to steal me a peach', a piece of *joie-de-vivre* penned on the final day of the year 1917 (*1972*). The epigram is one of the most difficult poetic forms to capture in music: its brevity, which is its *raison d'être*, leaves little time to establish a mood or create a satisfactory form. Here Warlock carries out the process brilliantly, with wit and perfect timing. His music (as do Blake's words) says in refined musical terms what Warlock declared in one of his more salacious limericks:

> I once knew a girl from Bermuda
> Who thought she was shrewd – I was shrewder . . .

The other songs from Warlock's 'Irish' year, those published in 1919 by Winthrop Rogers, are the first to show the influence of his study of Elizabethan and Jacobean music; all use texts from the 15th and 16th centuries. They established Warlock as an individual, original voice in English song. 'As ever I saw' (1918, *1919*), the first of three settings he made of this poem, has proved to be one of his most popular songs. It owes its individuality to an ambiguity of mode (major/minor/Mixolydian) which permeates both vocal line and accompaniment. He sets the first three verses strophically; then, in verse 4, introduces a new tune. Or is it? If your ears are capable of listening backwards, you will realise that it is an exact palindrome of the original tune (Exs. 18.6(a) and (b)). (He does a similar thing, though less convincingly, in 'Love for love' (1919, *1920*) where verses 3 and 4 are cancrizan mirrors of verses 1 and 2. Though the palindrome works, the tune is rather ordinary.)

Ex. 18.6(a)

Ex. 18.6(b)

'The bayly berith the bell away' (1918, *1919*) is a setting of a late 15th-century text, whose enigmatic meaning has bemused and baffled many commentators (see Cox and Bishop, 1994: 166–170 and 171–4). Warlock himself, in a letter to the singer Jane Vowles (28 November 1928) says: 'For me the charm of the fragment lies precisely in the fact that it *means* nothing, but suggests the loveliest images with a verbal music that foreshadows the procedure of the French *Symbolistes* of the nineteenth century ... "The Bayly" should be sung meaninglessly, as a child (but not as a grown-up!) sings a nursery rhyme.' Perhaps so, but though I think we can turn a deaf ear and blind eye to what the bayly, the bell and the lily and the rose are, I think we can take it that the poem is *about* a young girl on her wedding morning, and that is the heart of the matter. In its text and the atmosphere that Warlock conjures up, it bears many similarities to the *Corpus Christi* carol, which he set for soloist and orchestra in 1919. In both, he manages to reconcile a feeling for the 'period' of the text with an imaginative 'contemporary' interpretation. Usually 'period flavour' can be taken to be synonymous with pastiche, but in this setting Warlock avoids such glibness. In these early songs Warlock shows most clearly his indebtedness to the lutenist songwriters. The vocal line is given prominence over the accompaniment, which functions almost solely as a harmonic and rhythmic underpin to the voice. Rarely is the piano exploited in its own right, and it contributes a minimum of interludes and the briefest of codas. The whole texture of the accompaniment is reminiscent of the Jacobean lute ayre, as though it were an elaborate keyboard transcription of a lute part (Ex. 18.7(a)).

Ex. 18.7(a)

The vocal line is narrow in range but makes telling use of the singer's lower notes, particularly in the refrains of verses 1 and 2. Often it is embedded in the middle of a contrapuntal texture, which gives the song an introspective quality, as though the singer were singing to herself. The outward simplicity of the song is, however, deceptive. The regularity of the metre – in all three verses a constant 3/8 barring is maintained, with no use of cross-rhythm – is balanced by a *rubato* use of the tempo and by asymmetrical phrasing of the vocal line. In the first verse, for instance, the first phrase is six bars long, the second, four bars and the third, nine bars. Though clearly based on an E-flat tonality, the music hovers continually between E-flat major, E-flat minor, C minor and C major. This ambiguity of mode pervades the whole piece, culminating in the third verse where the conflicting tonalities are combined linearly (Ex. 18.7(b)).

Ex. 18.7(b)

Here the piano begins in C minor, whilst the voice maintains its original E-flat vocal line. The modulation at bars 39–41 is unusual and the effect surprising but totally in keeping with the text. It is as though the music, with the words, were moving out of the window and briefly into the sunlight. Though Warlock's use of 'period' flavour as part of his compositional technique is evident in this song, the total effect is completely original, not only in such obvious fingerprints of parallel 3rds and 6ths in the inner parts of the texture, but in the delicacy of the mood that he evokes. The final impression is difficult to define: it conveys gentle unease, wavering between sadness and joy, and, in doing so, manages to embody the mystery of the poem.

Other outstanding songs of this period (1918–19) include 'My gostly fader', 'Lullaby' and 'Balulalow'. 'My gostly fader' (1918, *1919*) is a setting of an early 15th-century rondel attributed to Charles d'Orléans. Warlock's song acknowledges the rondel shape and captures the confessional character of the poem in a hymn-like simplicity and a plainchant-imbued vocal line. It makes an excellent companion piece to 'The bayly'. 'Lullaby' (1918, *1919*) is one of two settings of poems by Dekker, both with 'Golden Slumbers' imagery, and the first in a line of fine cradle-songs. He manages to create an entirely convincing duple-time alternative to the traditional triple-time song. Again, there is a mixture of the old and new: a diatonic melody veers modally from minor to major to Dorian; an accompaniment full of subtle chromaticism hints at a consort of viols, particularly in the long, graceful postlude (Ex. 18.8).

Ex. 18.8

'Balulalow' (1919, *1923*), too, is a lullaby, here a sacred cradle-carol, setting a text by Luther translated into Anglo-Scots by the brothers Wedderburn (1567). Except for the final chord, the accompaniment is steadfastly anchored throughout to a tonic pedal. The effect of this final chordal change, to an exotic chord on the subdominant suggesting perfect and plagal cadences at the same time, comes as a magical shock. With its chromatic inflection to a basically modal melody and its use of tonic pedal above which sweet, sonorously spaced tonic triads wander, it is one of Warlock's most characteristic songs.

The 'Welsh' period, 1921–4

Warlock spent the years 1921–4 mainly at his mother's home at Cefn Bryntalch in Montgomeryshire. It was one of his most productive and fruitful periods, during which he wrote over 40 songs and completed *The Curlew* song-cycle.

The Curlew as it appears in its final, published, four-song version (*1924*) had a long gestation. Warlock is known to have set at least eight of Yeats's poems; the first songs, written in the winter of 1915, included 'He reproves the curlew', and this reappeared with four other songs, 'The lover mourns for the loss of love', 'The cloths of heaven', 'Wine comes in at the mouth' and 'He hears the cry of the sedge', in the first performance of the first version of the song-cycle in October 1920. When Philip Wilson performed the second, definitive version in November 1922, 'The cloths of heaven' and 'Wine comes in at the mouth' had been withdrawn and replaced by a new song, 'The withering of the boughs'. All the poems come from Yeats's early collection *The wind among the reeds* (1899), with the exception of 'The withering of the boughs', which is from *In the Seven Woods* (1904). They show Yeats at his most self-pitying, his Celtic Twilight robes at their most damp and wan. The theme of *The Curlew* is ageless: a poet remembers his lost love as he wanders through a bleak, desolate landscape of moorland, marsh and lake. Throughout Yeats's poems the same images recur: curlew – sedge – peewits – the wind; reinforced by the same strongly emotive words: 'weeping' – 'crying' – 'despair' – 'pale' – 'dim' – 'withered' – 'desolate'. The accompanying sextet of instruments – flute, cor anglais and string quartet – sets *The Curlew* apart from Warlock's other songs. He himself said that the work 'should not be regarded as a set of songs but rather as a piece of chamber-music in one continuous movement' (see Tomlinson, 1973: 2) and he referred to it as 'a kind of symphonic poem' (Smith, 1994: 205). Considerable scope is given to the instrumental episodes; indeed, the prelude and interludes are as important to the overall effect as the settings of the poems. The string quartet bears the main burden of accompanying the voice, whilst the two woodwind instruments play their most prominent role in the prelude and interludes.

The cycle's structure is subtle and superficially free, but it is held together by motives which recur in various guises throughout the work. The most important of these are:

(a) the opening bars (cor anglais) which transform into the first bars of the vocal part (letter E) (Ex. 18.9(a));
(b) the passage consisting of a theme in parallel 10ths moving over a sustained pedal, which first appears at A (Ex. 18.9(b)). Copley calls this the 'gloom' motive (1979: 174) and Banfield the 'wind' motive (1985: 266). It is, of course, one of Warlock's most characteristic ideas, which recurs in many of his mature songs.

In addition there are two other motives which suggest calls of birds mentioned by Yeats in his poems:

(c) the curlew, depicted by a rising 7th (violin I, 3 bars before A) (Ex. 18.9(c));
(d) the peewit, characterised by repeated notes followed by falling intervals (flute, bars 3 and 4 of B)(Ex. 18.9(d)).

Minor 3rds (and minor triads) haunt the entire work – they are particularly noticeable in the Interlude between the second and third songs – and give rise to many of the motives as well as the unusual chords and scales used in the piece. An important technical feature is Warlock's consistent use of a mode built up of alternating tones and semitones (= Messiaen's '2nd Mode of Limited Transposition'), a mode 'obsessed' by the minor 3rd and, by extension, the diminished 5th and diminished 7th. The melancholy character of the mode pervades the entire work (it can be heard in its simplest, scalic form on violin II, 7 bars after Y). Two forms of the mode can be heard in the final, sung lines of the third song, before the closing *sprechstimme* (Ex. 18.9(e)). Another, closely related mode, that of alternating minor 3rds and semitones, is also prominently used (see flute, 6 bars before M; see also at S and Z+11)(Ex. 18. 9(f)). The rhythmic language is elusive and sophisticated, far closer to *Saudades* than the neat 'diatonic' rhythms of Warlock's shorter, extrovert songs of the period. (For a fuller discussion of the technical background to *The Curlew*, see Banfield, 1985: 263–8, and Collins, 1996: 22 *et seq.*)

Ex. 18.9(a)(i)

Ex. 18.9(a)(ii)

Ex. 18.9(b)

Ex. 18.9(c)

Ex. 18.9(d)

Ex. 18.9(e)(i)

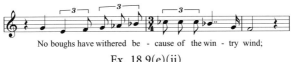

No boughs have withered be - cause of the win - try wind;

Ex. 18.9(e)(ii)

Ex. 18.9(f)

Although conceived as one continuous movement, the work falls naturally into eight smaller sections:

1. Beginning to E. Instrumental prelude, conjuring up the mood of desolation and the haunting sense of regret that permeates the whole work.
2. E–H. Setting of the first poem, 'He reproves the curlew'.
3. H–J. Interlude, in which we hear echoes of ideas from the prelude, the 'peewit' and 'gloom' motives, ending with two mysterious chords on the upper strings in harmonics.
4. J–K. Setting of the second poem, 'The lover mourns for the loss of love': 12 bars long accompanied by muted strings in sad, plodding chords.
5. K–N. Interlude, characterised by the use of minor 3rds, marked *quasi recitativo*, in which the string quartet acts as accompaniment to solo woodwind phrases. The return of the 'floating 10ths' of the 'gloom' motive heralds the return of the singer.
6. N–X. Setting of the third and longest poem, 'The withering of the boughs'. In each of the three long verses, a phrase from the poem is characterised musically:
   vs. 1 the peewit and curlew
   vs. 2 the witches's ride
   vs. 3 the 'sleepy country'
   The final verse acts as a brief respite from 'the encircling gloom', but the cor anglais soon disturbs the serenity with its recall of the opening theme (a) (4 bars before W).
7. X–Z+14. This Interlude is one of the most extraordinary passages that Warlock ever wrote. It is technically very advanced for a British work of its time: a chordal build-up of intervals of the 4th; almost atonal; extremely contrapuntal in places; a kaleidoscope of ideas and textures within a few bars. Taken out of context it could be by Schoenberg or one of his more advanced pupils. Yet Warlock's use of the work's basic motives (notably the 'peewit' and its associated falling minor thirds) ensures that it fits into the overall picture. After this interlude, the cor anglais is heard no more: 'exorcised', as it were.
8. Z+15–end. The setting of the short final poem, 'He hears the cry of the sedge'. The voice sings unaccompanied until the last few bars, when the lower strings enter to provide the final cadence.

The Curlew is a bitter, broody bird, not a work to be listened to too often, but one to be saved for special moments. Except for that 'solitary ray of sunshine' in the third song, it is filled with dark despair. Yet this singleness of purpose and of mood is its great virtue. *The Curlew* is one of the finest of English song-cycles: most other British song-cycles appear frivolous by comparison.

Warlock too considered *The Curlew*, with the *Corpus Christi* carol, to be his finest achievement (Lambert, 1938: 12); he certainly never wrote another solo vocal work as sustained and on so large a scale. Nevertheless, the songbooks and separate solo songs of the 1920s represent a substantial if quite different achievement. If just one song had to be chosen, the one by which the general public best knows Warlock, it would have to be 'Sleep' (1922, *1924*). (It is significant that OUP placed 'Sleep' as the very first song in its [*First*] *Book of Songs* published immediately after the composer's death.) Warlock's setting inevitably invokes comparison with Ivor Gurney's, written ten years earlier. Both are considered to be amongst their composer's best, yet they are quite different in character. Gurney's is a 'romantic' interpretation: a passionate *cri de coeur*, as though he were making an analogy between 'Sleep' and 'Death'. His opening line could well have been 'Come away, Death' rather than 'Come, Sleep'. Warlock's is a 'classical' interpretation: calm, still and contemplative, reflected in the classical balance of melo-poetic phrases, such as the way in which the framing outer lines act as inverse reflections of each other, and in the long, sustained *legato* of the vocal line. The influence of Jacobean music is nowhere more noticeable than here. It could be the transcription of a Jacobean consort-song. The vocal line, though *prima inter pares*, is one strand in a homogenous contrapuntal texture. At the same time, it is self-sufficient and, if sung unaccompanied, would still make its point. It is a perfect example of the composer's dictum that 'Song is in essence un-accompanied tune' (Ex. 18.10(a)). Note how, like a folksong, it begins and ends on its tonic note. The function of the accompaniment is to point up and emphasise what the voice is doing, as in the way it underlines the phrase 'but a sliding' (Ex. 18.10(b)).

Nothing could be further from the calm, intricately introverted setting of 'Sleep' than the boisterous, extrovert setting of 'Mr Belloc's fancy' (1921, *1922/ 1930*). This is the first of a series of Warlock songs extolling the virtues of alcoholic drinks, the others being 'Captain Stratton's fancy' (1921, *1922*), 'Good ale' (1922, *1922*), 'The toper's song' (1924, *1926*), 'Peter Warlock's fancy' (1924, *1925*) and 'Maltworms' (written in collaboration with E. J. Moeran: 1926, *1926*). They are the finest of their kind and together make up a unique *Toper's Song-Book*. Indeed, 'Mr Belloc's fancy' (Beer) was intended to be paired with 'Captain Stratton's fancy' (Rum) as *Two True Toper's Tunes to Troll with Trulls and Trollops in a Tavern*, though they never appeared in print as such. Though 'Captain Stratton's fancy' (setting Masefield's invocation to the 'tipple' and 'Heart's delight' of the old, bold mate of Henry Morgan) has always been the most popular with singers, the others are equally effective, and from a musical point of view 'Mr Belloc's fancy' is the finer song. J. C. Squire's poem burlesques Hilaire Belloc's love

Ex. 18.10(a)

Ex. 18.10(b)

of beer and of Sussex (and, *en route*, his anti-semitic views). Warlock's setting has great swing and panache, and makes an excellent curtain raiser. The final refrain, where 'Belloc' gets fuddled between Roman Catholic texts and his earlier nonsense words, is wittily painted in pious chromaticisms (Ex. 18.11).

During his 'Welsh' period Warlock wrote three song collections: the two sets of *Peterisms* (1922–3, 1923/1924), *Lillygay* (1922, 1923) and *Candlelight* (1923, 1924). The *Peterisms* are settings of 16th- and early 17th-century lyrics, some of which he had already used – Peele's 'Chopcherry' (= 'Whenas the rye') – or was to set again later – Wever's 'Lusty Juventus' (= 'In an arbour green'). Some of the songs are marred by over-demanding accompaniments, 'Rutterkin' and 'Lusty Juventus' in particular, and require wrists of steel combined with delicate fingers to bring them off. The pick of the group are 'A sad song' and 'Rutterkin'. 'A sad song' sets Aspatia's Song ('Lay a garland on my hearse') from Beaumont and Fletcher's *The Maid's Tragedy*.

Ex. 18.11

Ex. 18.12

Warlock captures the Ophelia-like sadness of the text with seemingly artless simplicity over a gently rocking 6/8 dance measure; the broken phrases of the final line are particularly moving (Ex. 18.12). 'Rutterkin' sets an anonymous early 16th century poem (possibly by Skelton, possibly by Cornish) describing a ragged, drunken Dutchman 'come into our Town'. Warlock treats it with verve and spirit, the rhythmic thrust partly achieved by irregular metres (7/8 with occasional 5/8, 3/8, 3/4, 4/8 and 5/4 thrown in). This, with its drones, contrapuntal textures, quartal harmonies and highly percussive chords, remind us of Warlock's admiration for the music of Bartók. It is one of the composer's most brash, 'modern'-sounding songs, well worth the effort despite the challenges of its tough accompaniment.

The five *Lillygay* songs again show little sympathy for the pianist, though the vocal writing is much more considerate; the songs make an ideal group for a soprano. Warlock found the poems in an anthology of the same name edited by Victor Neuberg. Though ostensibly 'anonymous' poems, Neuburg was, in fact, the author of the text of the final song 'Rantum tantum', and may well have been responsible for the others. Warlock treats them in appropriate folk style, with modally caste melodic lines (including a 'Scotch snap' for the Old Scots poem, 'Johnnie wi' the tye'). The songs are set strophically, the voice retaining the original melody virtually unaltered, whilst the piano accompaniment varies considerably from verse to verse. This is especially noticeable in the two longest poems, 'The distracted maid' and 'Burd Ellen and young Tamlane'. The former is particularly impressive, the accompaniment evolving naturally to fit the ongoing narrative. Warlock shows considerable invention in his piano textures. The ending of the song, when the maid realises that her dreams are in vain and the piano breaks off its hitherto continuum of notes, is very moving (Ex. 18.13(a)). If 'Burd Ellen and young Tamlane' is less successful, it is because Warlock's tune for the brief stanzas is less striking. The piano accompaniment, however, in following the grim tale of the forsaken mother, embarks on an extraordinary harmonic odyssey: it begins suspiciously subdued, over a drone, and gradually undergoes some strange bitonal contortions worthy of Prokofiev or Stravinsky at their most radical (Ex. 18.13(b)).

Ex. 18.13(a)

Ex. 18.13(b)

The 'cycle of nursery jingles', *Candlelight*, is one of Warlock's most delightful works. Setting traditional nursery rhymes to new music was by no means a novelty, but few previous – or later – attempts have produced music of such imagination and invention. Most of the songs are only a page long – the whole cycle of twelve is over in less than six minutes – and they show Warlock to be the master of the epigram. Nor does he have to curb his natural style. What could be simpler or more Warlockean than the opening song, 'How many miles to Babylon?', short enough to quote in full (Ex. 18.14)? Here we have *multum in parva*: Warlock-in-a-nutshell: a miniature masterpiece.

Ex. 18.14

Several separate solo songs from this fecund period deserve attention. 'Late summer' (1919, *1922*) is a setting of Edward Shanks's song lyric 'The fields are full', a song of 'high summer' in both the countryside and human life. Both

Gurney and Gibbs set it (q.v.), but neither achieved the rich serenity of
Warlock's song. In its richly-sweet chromatic harmonies, it harks back to his
earlier Delius-influenced songs – a 'late summer' homage to his first master –
yet it has a compactness and feeling for the solo voice that Delius never achieved
in his mature songs. (Notice how the vocal line and the pianist's countermelody
run hand in hand, as if reflecting the two lovers 'who in youth/With love were
filled'.) Moreover, Warlock manages to encapsulate the meaning of Shanks's
deceptively simple lyric and, unlike Gurney, avoids confusion of image with
imagery. The relatively long coda gives musical unity to the piece, by reprising
not only the piano's opening bars but the singer's too (Exs. 18.15(a) and (b)).

Ex. 18.15(a)

Ex. 18.15(b)

'Rest, sweet nymphs' (1922, *1924*), an anonymous text set by Francis Pilkington
in his *First Booke of Songs or Ayres* (1605), is another of Warlock's inimitable
cradle-songs with the sweetest of sequences for its lullaby refrain. He seems to
have recalled his rejected Yeats setting, 'The everlasting voices', and reuses the
opening descent of parallel 2nd-inversion chords to memorable effect. In 'Hey,
troly loly lo' (1922, *1922*) he again sets an anonymous 16th-century lyric, this

time a pastoral dialogue between a lecherous gentleman and a coy milkmaid.
The repartee – he keen and amorous, she shyly reticent, alternately concerned
with milking her cow and with fear that her mother will see them – is brilliantly
caught in Warlock's witty setting, with upward roulades of arpeggios at every
cadence and a lumbering rustic bass at the maid's coquettish refrains (Ex. 18.16).

Ex. 18.16

No-one but Warlock could make such a silk purse out of such doggerel. Other
fine songs of the period include 'Piggesnie' (1922, *1922*), a 'light conceit'
perennially popular with singers, whose melody epitomises the composer's
trade-mark of 'steps up', 'Milkmaids' (1923, *1924*), whose insouciant, ambling
melody could so easily be a genuine folk-tune, and 'Little trotty wagtail' (1922,
1923), his only setting of John Clare, and the best of the many settings of this
popular poem. (Though published as a unison song, it is equally effective as a
solo song.)

The 'Eynsford' period, 1925–8

In June 1924, Warlock returned to London and in the following year moved to
the Kent village of Eynsford, where he stayed until 1928. Here he completed his
masterly monograph, *The English Ayre*, and wrote *Capriol Suite* as well as some
of his finest songs, including the *Three Belloc Songs* and his mature Shakespeare
settings. Though the Belloc songs were intended as a set, for some reason they
were published separately. (Even in OUP's *A Second Book of Songs* (1967) they

are scattered.) Warlock chose three contrasting poems, which together make a varied recital group. 'Ha'nacker mill' is a moving, time-haunted elegy to a place that has irretrievably changed and to inhabitants who have long departed: 'Sally is gone that was so kindly . . . Ha'nacker's down and England's done'. Warlock conjures up the atmosphere with a downward sequence of widely spaced, unrelated minor triads, later chromatically altered with added 6ths (Ex. 18.17(a)).

Ex. 18.17(a)

The three verses are set strophically but with subtle asymmetries to both vocal line and accompaniment. Notice, for example, how the phrase used as a brief interlude between verses 1 and 2 (straight out of *The Curlew*) becomes the accompaniment for the third line of verse 3, whilst the introductory chords to verse 1 become the accompaniment of verse 2 (Exs. 18.17(b) and (c)). 'The night' has the rapt simplicity of a prayer, pivoting on the tonic note E (see Ex. 18.2).

Ex. 18.17(b)

Ex. 18.17(c)

Again, the relationship between voice and accompaniment is subtle and varied. The singer intones this single E for the whole of the first verse, only rising up an octave on the final syllable of 'repose', whilst around this intonation the piano plays a series of chords, mirroring outwards from the tonic E and cadencing into the subdominant. In the second verse, the singer takes up the piano's melodic line, the music again cadencing in the subdominant. In verse 3 this idea is expanded, the music this time cadencing in the tonic major. In the final verse, the singer has the same melody as in verse 2, this time underpinned with a rich, strummed chordal accompaniment with a tonic pedal below and dominant above; the music cadences as in the opening verses on to the subdominant, which the piano, somewhat grudgingly, converts to E (bare 4ths, B and E). As Ivor Gurney had expressed his *Heimweh* for his native Gloucestershire in 'Severn meadows', so Belloc expresses his homesickness for the trees and downland of his adopted Sussex in 'My own country'. Warlock gives the poem a syllabic setting, regular quavers for almost every syllable, but avoids monotony by occasional changes of metre from the basic 4/8, to 2/8 and 3/8. This gives the song a dream-like serenity, similar to that achieved by Quilter in his song 'Dream valley'. But there is no dreaminess about the word-setting: Warlock follows every important emotional move in the poem. For example, after an excursion into A major at the words 'And some stand few', the music magically returns to the home key of F major at 'All the woods are new' (Ex. 18.17(d)). Note, too, the slowing down of pace and disintegration of texture in the final lines (Ex. 18.17(e)).

Ex. 18.17(d)

Ex. 18.17(e)

Ex. 18.17(f)

Warlock makes no attempt to unify the three songs into a cycle, though, subconsciously perhaps, he has linked the first and last through their introductory preludes, each of which descends twice through a sequence, first plain, then coloured (Ex. 18.17(f); cf. Ex. 18.17(a)).

In March 1924, whilst still living in Wales, Warlock made a setting of Shakespeare's 'O mistress mine' – the lyric set by Quilter in his first set of Shakespeare songs, op. 6, for which Warlock had expressed such admiration. Until then he had set only one Shakespeare lyric, 'Take, O take those lips away', though that on two occasions, as the second song of *Saudades* (1917) and as a separate song in 1918. 'Sweet-and-twenty', however, was to release any inhibitions that he might have had about tackling Shakespeare, whose lyrics had been set so often that comparisons would inevitably be made with his own. Over the next four years he made four further settings; with 'Sweet-and-twenty', these are amongst the finest 20th-century interpretations of the Bard. Even so, he differentiated his own settings from others by giving his songs 'hand-crafted' titles, taken from key phrases in the poems, so that 'When daisies pied' becomes 'Mockery', 'It was a lover and his lass' becomes 'Pretty ringtime', 'When daffodils begin to peer' 'The sweet o' the year', and 'O mistress mine' emerges as 'Sweet-and-twenty'. 'Sweet-and-twenty' (1924, *1924*) is one of the most beautiful love-songs in the repertoire, catching the poignancy of youthful love better than any other setting. Though never over-emphasised, every inflection of the text is caught within a memorable melodic line. Notice the ease with which he uses cross-rhythms, making a hemiola of two 3/8 bars into one 3/4 (Ex. 18.18). There are no unnecessary notes in the setting: a brief introduction, interlude and coda, with the simplest, almost throwaway V-I cadence.

Ex. 18.18

'Pretty ringtime' (1925, *1926*) is probably the most popular of these Shakespeare settings. One of the problems facing the songwriter setting this familiar text is the preponderance of refraining lines: of the eight lines of each stanza, only two are 'verse', the rest 'refrain'. Warlock solves this by giving maximum variety and character to the three main refrains ('With a hey and a ho . . .'/'In the spring time . . .'/'When birds do sing . . .') so that they can be repeated happily without causing aural tedium. In 'Sigh no more, ladies' (1927, *1928*), he creates one of his most sardonic songs. The irony and unease is underlined by the continuous juxtaposition of 6/8 and 5/8 metres. Notice the caustic bitonal treatment of the words 'your sounds of woe', which are 'converted' into smooth, parallel-6th chords (6/4s in verse 1, 6/3s in verse 2) of the 'hey nonnies' (Ex. 18.19). Again he sets the stanzas strophically but with subtle alterations: observe, for example, the way he uses the piano's introductory bars to underlay the opening of verse 2, neatly catching up with the original texture at line 3. The final 'pattered' 'hey nonnies' are a superb piece of invention.

Ex. 18.19

'Mockery' is a setting of Ver's song, 'When daisies pied', from *Love's Labour's Lost*. Warlock's title is significant: here, as if to redress the bowdlerised, 'pretty' version by Arne, he goes out of his way to emphasise the cuckoldry behind the words, with cuckooing 3rds and a sly allusion to Mendelssohn's 'Wedding March' (see Ex. 18.20(c)). The two stanzas are set strophically, without alterations to either vocal or piano parts. This is itself unusual for Warlock, who normally prefers a much-varied strophe, but the variety and subtlety of the melodic, harmonic and rhythmic devices are ample justification for his decision. The song is one of the composer's most mercurial and, harmonically, one of his most adventurous. Of pastiche there is no hint, though his debt to the lutenist composers is evident in the delightful cross-rhythms of the refrain. The piano's introduction, with its rapid descending chain of 3rds, gives the listener no chance to anticipate the key of the song (Ex. 18.20(a)). This sequence of notes is no mere *trompe-d'oreille*, for the entire song owes its construction to these 'cuckooing' 3rds. The words of the verse are set to a jogtrot accompaniment, which cunningly supports the vocal line and clarifies its implied harmonies, to present a picture of the 'bustle of spring'. The refrain, however, though maintaining the basic quaver pulse, breaks down the duple metre into smaller units by means of cross-rhythm, as can be seen in the vocal line (Ex. 18.20(b)). The song uses bitonality to add spice to the words and some of the resulting chords are extremely complex and dissonant, as in the converging 7ths and augmented 5ths at the words 'Mocks married men' (Ex. 18.20(c)). Notice, too, the pianist's coda. After a repeat of the downward flight of 3rds, Warlock compresses them into chords, ending with a final cock-a-snook G (tonic) in the bass (Ex. 18.20(d)). The score is marked 'Fast and in strict time: *sempre staccatissimo e senza Ped*', and though this makes the song difficult to perform, the challenge is well worth the effort.

Ex. 18.20(a)

Cuck - oo,   cuck - oo!   O word of fear, Un - pleas - ing to a mar - ried ear!

Ex. 18.20(b)

Mocks mar - ried men, for thus sings he,

Ex. 18.20(c)

Ex. 18.20(d)

After the wit and originality of 'Sigh no more, ladies' and 'Mockery', his final Shakespeare setting, 'The sweet o' the year' is disappointingly tame and conventional. It relies too much on the technique of earlier songs, new then but growing tired here. He does at least realise that Autolycus's 'aunts' are not quite of the family sort, providing cuckooing 3rds to prove it (Ex. 18.21).

Ex. 18.21

Warlock intended Autolycus's song to be part of the collection *Seven Songs of Summer* which he wrote in 1928, but which eventually appeared (*1929*) as separate songs under the imprint of two different publishers. All seven are settings of 16th- and 17th-century verse, ranging from Marlowe and Shakespeare to Wever, Mabbe and the ubiquitous 'Anon.' They do not compare in quality with his earlier settings of similar verse: they are lighter, less demanding, more popular in appeal. Indeed, one suspects that they were written as potboilers to pay for the rent and beer.

Ex. 18.22

'Youth', his third and most memorable setting of Robert Wever's poem, 'In an arbour green', has a catchy tune and accompaniment which would not be out of place in an English Edwardian musical comedy (Ex. 18.22). 'The contented lover' (James Mabbe's translation of a poem by Fernando de Rojas) is, like the earlier song 'Consider', uncharacteristic both in method and subject-matter. It sounds like the work of another composer. Its companion, 'The droll lover' (Anon. 17th century), is, on the other hand, pure Warlock, full of dancing cross-rhythms, false relations and tangy bitonal harmonies. 'Elore lo' (another 17th-century Anon. text) is the gem of the collection. Here Warlock ingeniously sets the text in even quavers to a 6/8–3/4 vocal line, with continual cross-rhythm against the basic metre and the accompaniment. He borrows Hamlet's advice as a footnote: 'To be sung "trippingly upon the tongue"' (Ex. 18.23).

Ex. 18.23

Higher in quality of invention are the four separate songs to Tudor verse from the same period: 'Away to twiver', 'The lover's maze', 'Cradle song' and 'And wilt thou leave me thus?', songs which alone would justify Warlock's status as one of the finest songwriters of the 20th century. He found the text of 'Away to twiver' in the anonymous 16th-century play, *The Famous History of Friar Bacon*, where it is sung by Friar Bacon's manservant, Miles, to the tune of 'I have been a fiddler'. This saucy description of 'the morrow after the wedding day' is little more than doggerel. Warlock, however, transforms it into something much greater, and the song is one of his most original achievements. It indicates a line of development that he was not, unfortunately, to explore further: the narrative ballad. For each verse the singer has the same basic melodic line, which is varied rhythmically but only to match the new text. In contrast, the piano acts as a continually changing backcloth to the wedding proceedings, beginning as a bagpipe drone (note the augmentation when the voice enters (Ex. 18.24(a)) and later incorporating an imaginative series of cameos: a 'consort of fiddle-de-dees' (a passage which could come straight out of *Capriol Suite* (Ex. 18.24(b)), 'the drunken smith' lurching chromatically from chord to chord (Ex. 18.24(c)) and, finally, the 'simpering women' who could 'eat no more', where the E-Dorian mode of the voice is given bimodal accompaniment in C-sharp (Ex. 18.24(d)).

Ex. 18.24(a)

Ex. 18.24(b)

Ex. 18.24(c)

Ex. 18.24(d)

The technique adopted is very much in the tradition of early English variations, one that Warlock had already used successfully in 'The distracted maid', where a basic theme (here the vocal line) remains constant whilst 'every possible device of harmonic decoration is expended on it' (Gray, 1934: 246). It is a procedure that Delius had used in a number of works, notably *Brigg Fair*, and one that Warlock would also have come across in his study of Elizabethan music. But, in spite of the great variety of texture and harmonic device within a comparatively short span, the song remains a satisfactory and unified experience. (Performers and scholars have always had a problem with the song's refrain 'Away to Twiver, away, away!' What does 'Twiver' mean? Is it a verb (the infinitive of a verb – alas! not in OED – which describes part of the bridal nuptials)? – or a place-name (perhaps an imaginary town in, say, Essex)? – or is it just nonsense? In all the original published versions, Twiver is given a capital letter, but in those days many nouns were capitalised.

In 'The lover's maze' (1927, *1928*) Warlock sets a poem attributed to Thomas Campion, which he had discovered in *Giles Earle, His Booke* (1615) and later edited. It has much in common with 'Sigh no more, ladies' and 'Mockery', written at the same time. Here Warlock makes one of his most successful 'across Time' forays. On one level he is paying homage to Campion, in the song's basic modality, its clear-cut cadencing, false-relations and cross-rhythms, and in its vocal line full of tripping two-notes-to-a-syllable (cf. Campion's 'Fain would I wed'); but on another level, in its frenetic imitation, intricate canonic comments on the vocal line and acerbic, bitonal harmony, it is indisputably 20th century. One of the many felicitous touches is the way in which he adapts his music to the new texts in his strophic setting: compare the lady's coquettish replies in verse 2 with the poet's growing despondency in verse 3 (Exs. 18.25(a) and (b)). Some might feel that the setting is merely ingenious and clever, but it is entirely appropriate to the burden of the text: 'For love is like an endless maze,/More hard to get out than to enter'. It is – dare one say it? – an amazing song.

Ex. 18.25(a)

Ex. 18.25(b)

'Cradle song' (1927, *1928*) is a setting of John Phillip's lullaby lyric from *The Comedy of Patient and Meek Grissill* (c.1566) – Britten, too, was to set it as the finale of *A Charm of Lullabies* (1947) – and it has much in common with Warlock's earlier lullabies, 'Balulalow' and 'Sleep'. Here both the verses, with their internal refrain, and the burden-refrain give scope for an extended song. Amongst the song's subtleties is the manner in which the preludial rocking figure, which acts as a ritornello between both verses and burden-refrain, is varied (Exs. 18.26(a) and (b)), and the rich chordal cadence chords before the burdens of verses 2 and 3.

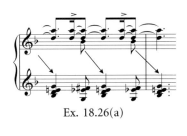

Ex. 18.26(a)

Ex. 18.26(b)

Notice, too, how Warlock 'justifies' these at the end of the song when, as in 'Sleep', he places a strange, 'out-of-key' chord before cadencing onto the final, consoling tonic chord (see Ex. 18.3(a)(ii)).

No song of Warlock's shows better how he could capture both the natural inflection of words and create a shaped musical line than 'And wilt thou leave me thus?' (1928, *1929*). Here he manages to fuse the freedom of recitative with the formality of aria (Ex. 18.27(a)). The song begins, unusually for Warlock, with a fragment of imitation on the piano (Ex. 18.27(b)). This memorable idea, whose questioning line is the perfect counterpart to the opening words, acts as the basic material for the entire song, both in voice and accompaniment.

And wilt thou leave me thus? Say nay, say nay, for shame! To save thee from the blame Of all my grief and grame. And wilt thou leave me thus? Say nay, say nay!

Ex. 18.27(a)

Ex. 18.27(b)

In the latter it appears not only in the interludes between verses but also during the song itself: in transposed form (bar 3, etc.), in mirror form (bar 10) and in mirrored augmentation (bars 19–21) (see Ex. 18.27(c)). The four verses are arranged in ternary shape (A A1 B A2). In the third verse the voice, after opening with the piano with an inversion of the main motive, goes its separate way, flowering lyrically at the words 'given thee my heart', which the accompaniment underlines with characteristic floating 10ths (Ex. 18.27(c)). The final verse is an elaborate variation of the first.

And wilt thou leave me thus, That hath given thee my heart Nev-er for to de-

Ex. 18.27(c)

At the end the main motive reappears, after an unexpected side-step, in the remote key of A major, reflecting the lover's final, passionate attempt to attract his love's attention. On the printed page the song, with its continuous metre changes, looks complicated, but Warlock instructs the singer to sing the words 'flowingly, in strict accordance with the punctuation of the poem and without regard for bar-line accents'. In this way he captures the breathless intimacy of the lover's exhortations, from the questioning of the opening line to the protestation of the refrain. Where dissonance and chromatic harmonies appear (e.g. in bars 6–7: 'of all my grief and grame', and bars 29–30: 'Alas thy cruelty'), they are used to underline the sense of the words. There is no better example of Warlock's ability to come to terms with a poem from an earlier period and yet avoid the pitfalls of archaism and pastiche. Music and poetry here make a perfectly 'harmonious meeting': the resulting song sounds inevitable.

The last songs, 1928–30

Warlock left Eynsford in the autumn of 1928 and, after a brief return to Wales, settled again in London. His output of songs in the last two years of his life was small. This was due to several factors. Much of 1929 was taken up with the organisation of the large-scale Delius Festival, which entailed a visit to Delius in France, writing the prospectus (May) and two articles for *Radio Times* (October) as well as various programme notes and music copying jobs for the six concerts. Moreover, the market for songs was not as healthy as it had been five years earlier, and this coincided with a fallow period in his own creativity. The only new solo songs that he wrote in his last two years were 'The frostbound wood', 'After two years' and 'The fox'.

From 'After two years', a delicate love poem by his contemporary, Richard Aldington (1892–1962), Warlock creates one of his most subtly profound love-songs (1930, *1931*). The three verses are through-composed, the music held together by a siciliana-like ritornello consisting of a characteristic falling figure (Ex. 18.28(a)). Contrapuntal textures mix with sophisticated modern harmonies, the 'early music' element by now completely absorbed (Ex. 18.28(b)). The author of the words of both 'The frostbound wood' and 'The fox' was Warlock's journalist friend, Bruce Blunt (1899–1957), who had already supplied him with texts for three other songs: 'The first mercy', 'The cricketers of Hambledon' and 'Bethlehem Down'. Though Blunt was by no means a poet of genius – after Warlock's death he wrote very little poetry, an exception being 'The long barrow', a poignant elegy for his dead friend – a creative spark seems to have been ignited between him and Warlock, and their collaboration produced a handful of varied songs: three carols, an elegy and a drinking-song.

Ex. 18.28(a)

It is God's will That I shall
love her still As he loves Ma - ry. And

Ex. 18.28(b)

'The cricketers of Hambledon' (1928, *1929*) is a *pièce d'occasion par excellence*, written to celebrate a famous cricket match between J. C. Squire's 'The Invalids' and J. C. Whalley-Tooker's 'Hampshire Eskimos' at Broadhalfpenny Down, Hambledon, on New Year's Day 1929. (The Invalids won by 89 runs to 78.) The song is, appropriately, a beery toast to the founding fathers of modern cricket, the villagers of Hambledon, and was originally performed with brass band accompaniment. The piano version retains the broad brush-strokes of the original, an extrovert piece much in the style of the earlier drinking-songs, with a rousing unison chorus. Though it can be effective in the right setting, it remains a period piece, albeit it a very engaging one. One can understand, however, why *Curlew*-loving Warlockeans such as Cecil Gray deplored it.

The three carol-songs are a quite different matter. 'The first mercy' (1927, *1927*), the first of the collaborations, tells the Christmas story as seen through the eyes of animals at the stable in Bethlehem: not the ox and ass – 'ye know of them' – but lesser beasts: swallow, moth and mouse. The lullaby character of the song links it with 'Balulalow' and 'Cradle song', both of which are echoed in the music. What distinguishes it is the way in which Warlock gives variety to Blunt's five verses by setting them to alternating strophes, each beginning with the same opening phrase. The childlike simplicity, particularly in the final verse, makes this one of the most moving of all Warlock's carols.

The only solo song written in 1929 was 'The frostbound wood' (1929, *1929/ 1930*), originally published in *Radio Times* on December 20th of that year. In his last songs, Warlock seems to be aiming for greater simplicity and economy, both in vocal line and accompaniment. The singer has only four different pitches – D E G A – which are pre-echoed in the piano's opening bar (Ex. 18.29).

Ex. 18.29

Only at the very end of the song does he allow the singer to rise to the upper octave E (cf. 'The night', Ex. 18.2). The musical interest, therefore, relies on the rhythmic setting of the words. The piano part underpins the rhythms of the voice and emphasises certain key words and phrases, such as the final 'lovely and care-laden'. The setting has the austerity and remoteness of an antique chant, a perfect match for the 'frosty' sentiments of the poem.

'Bethlehem Down' (1930, *1931*) began life as a 4-part carol and was published as such in the *Daily Telegraph* on 24 December 1927. Three years later Warlock made a solo version, dated 1 December 1930 – less than three weeks before he died. In his poem, Blunt once again takes an oblique look at the traditional carol text. The young Mary's thoughts on the birth of her son ('Myrrh for its sweetness, and gold for a crown') are contrasted with the future reality ('Myrrh for embalming, and wood for a crown'). The melody is one of Warlock's most hauntingly memorable; the keyboard accompaniment one of his most fussy and intricate (Ex. 18.30). I say 'keyboard', for though ostensibly for either organ or piano, it fits neither particularly well. The original simple homophonic choral version is the most effective, but it is worth the trouble to disentangle the accompaniment of the solo version if only for the beautiful vocal line.

Ex. 18.30

And so to Warlock's last and, in the view of many, finest song, 'The fox' (1930, *1931*). Though Blunt's poem (see epigraph) has charm and atmosphere, it does not in itself possess the 'depth' of meaning or allusion subsequently given it by Warlock. It has, however, some great virtues: the imagery is clear, direct, precise – in primary colours, as it were – and the words are short and uncomplicated; it

hints at deeper things and Warlock responded to that hint. The six short stanzas
fall into three sections, which the composer himself follows in the music:

1. stanzas 1 and 2: a description of the stuffed fox at the inn;
2. stanzas 3, 4 and 5: evoking the atmosphere of haunting and foreboding;
3. stanza 6: a final, personal comment by the poet.

The first two stanzas run into each other without a break, as do stanzas 3, 4 and
5, and the three main divisions are punctuated by short piano interludes. These
three strophes are handled in a deceptively straightforward manner. The piano
has two motives: a ghostly 'call' ('x') answered by two chords descending
chromatically ('y') (Ex. 18.31(a)). During the verses the piano remains
discretely in the background – a series of remotely connected chords based
on the minor triad – with the minimum of rhythmic, contrapuntal or colour
interest, its function simply to underpin the vocal line.

Ex. 18.31(a)

Gerald Cockshott has said that 'The fox', with its companion song 'The
frostbound wood', breaks new ground for Warlock and represents 'a definite
psychological advance on his earlier conceptions' (1940: 258, fn 33). Both songs
are of a deeper, more serious nature, and this is reflected in a more sophisticated
technique. 'The frostbound wood' is almost Stravinskian in its delimited melodic
material, its vocal line restricted to four notes throughout. The vocal line of 'The
fox' is more wide-ranging, yet it is one of the most tightly-organised that Warlock
ever wrote (Ex. 18.31(b).

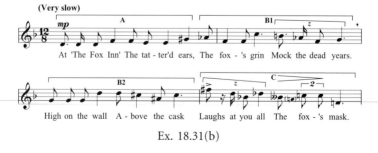

Ex. 18.31(b)

It will be seen that he has expanded his use of modality from the earlier songs to
encompass almost every semitone. Out of the 20 different pitches of the first

strophe (see above), 11 semitones are used. One of the least important notes is the dominant (A), yet the music remains clear in its tonality and is punctuated by strong cadences. It will also be noted that the vocal line is extremely symmetrical in shape, consisting of an arc of four component phrases (A-B1-B2-C). The two opening phrases consist of ever-widening intervals (minor 3rd, major 3rd, perfect 5th) – an extension of the recurrent Warlockean fingerprint of the 'steps up' – answered by a motive of three falling notes ('z'). The second part of the phrase is then repeated, transposed up a tone, and itself answered by a final phrase (C) which contains the previous motives in compressed form: the falling notes ('z') followed by an inversion of the 'steps up'. The vocal line of the second and longest strophe is almost entirely concerned with the development of phrases A and B, and in particular with the intervals of the minor and major 3rd. These ideas gradually coalesce at the words 'Beneath this roof/His eyes mistrust', when the opening phrases are repeated, transposed up a tritone, to reach a climax at the words 'The crumbled hoof,/The hounds of dust' (Ex. 18.31(c)).

Ex. 18.31(c)

The final stanza is a direct recapitulation of the opening phrases of the first strophe. In no previous song had Warlock fused spontaneous reaction to text with such a tightly unified vocal line. It was rare for him to use technical procedures in a deliberate manner in order to create formal unity – the use of palindrome in 'As ever I saw' and the canonic writing of 'The lover's maze' are exceptional. Here, the thematic unity that he imposes helps to contain the extreme freedom of tonality and pitch.

It cannot be stressed too firmly that the presence of such technical details in no way guarantees the success of the music. Only too often, the more one can 'see' in a work – the more complex the inner machinery appears to the eye – the less there is to 'hear' in the end. But in 'The fox', as in all great songs, the elements of structure, word-setting and atmosphere – the whole fabric of the song – are inextricably interwoven. Somehow we feel the 'The fox' could not be other than what it is: in the terms that Warlock has chosen, there seems to be no alternative to his conception. Some things defy analysis: for example, the opening 'call' on the piano (see Ex. 18.31(a)). I purposely avoid labelling it a '*horn*-call', even though this is obviously one of its functions; for it can also be regarded as the 'laugh' of the fox and as the 'call' that 'you will not call'. Such tiny details take on a wealth of allusion by the end of the song. 'The fox' is not only Warlock's finest achievement; it is also one of the supreme masterpieces of English song.

No extravagant claims need be made for the songs of Peter Warlock: indeed, I am sure that he would have been amused at the very idea. He imposed a limit on what he was prepared to do, yet within that limit he achieved a quality and perfection that few song-composers can equal. At times one regrets that he did not explore larger musical forms – his only true song-cycle, *The Curlew*, is a clear indication that he could weld songs into a larger format if he wished – or that he did not explore further the possibilities of the narrative song, of which 'The distracted maid' and 'Away to twiver' are such fine examples. His later songs, 'The fox' and 'The frostbound wood', mark a new tautness and muscularity in his song structures. If 'The fox' is any indication of what he was capable of doing later, then English song did indeed suffer irretrievable loss on that December morning in 1930. Yet Warlock, like his French counterpart, Duparc, and his fellow-countryman, Thomas Campion, will hold a special place in the history of music for the very fact that, within his self-imposed limits, he produced a body of songs that is as perfect as we mortals can expect: love-songs, lullabies, drinking-songs, elegies, songs of contentment and songs of regret. Constant Lambert was not exaggerating when he said that 'this achievement entitles him to be classed with Dowland, Schubert, Mussorgsky and Debussy as one of the greatest song writers that music has known' (1938: 13).

19

E. J. Moeran (1894–1950)

I will go out and meet the evening hours
And greet them one by one as friend greets friend,
Where many a tall poplar summit towers
On summit, shrines of quietness that send
Their silence through the blue air like a wreath
Of sacrificial flame unwavering
In the deep evening stillness, when no breath
Sets the faint tendrils floating on light wing
Over the long dim fields mist-islanded.
I will go out and meet them one by one,
And learn the things old times have left unsaid,
And read the secrets of an age long gone,
And out of twilight and the darkening plain
Build up all that old quiet world again.

Seumas O'Sullivan: 'Evening'

The First World War affected E. J. Moeran's career radically. When hostilities began, he was 19 and a student at the Royal College of Music. He immediately enlisted as a motorcycle despatch-rider in the Norfolk Regiment and was later commissioned. In May 1917 he was severely wounded by shrapnel at Bullecourt, which rendered him unfit for further active service and permanently affected his health. By the time he resumed his musical studies in 1920, he was in his late twenties.

His first songs, *Four Songs from 'A Shropshire Lad'*, were written in 1916; one of them, 'When I came last to Ludlow', was to be his first publication. His mature songs date from 1920, and between then and his death he wrote 52, setting over twenty different poets, from Robert Wever to James Joyce. Many of these poets were set only once and included such a poetic rarity as Dorothy L. Sayers ('The bean flower', 1923, *1924*). The poets set most frequently were A. E. Housman (11), James Joyce (10), Seumas O'Sullivan (7) and Shakespeare (6). It is interesting to note that until 1924, all the poets chosen were contemporary. In that year he met Peter Warlock and between 1925 and 1928 the two men shared a house at Eynsford in Kent; from then on Moeran began to turn to 16th-century poems, many already set by Warlock himself: 'In youth is pleasure' (Warlock: 1922/1923/1928 – Moeran: 1925); 'Lay a garland' (1922–1933); 'It was a lover and his lass' (1925–1934); 'When daisies pied' (1927–1940); 'When daffodils begin to peer' (1928–1930); and 'The passionate shepherd' (1928–1934). This points us to an important facet of Moeran's musical personality: its chameleonic nature. Unlike Quilter, Gurney or Ireland, whose characteristic plumage is recognisable even in their earliest songs, Moeran seemed to need the example of others to spur him on. His influences are extremely eclectic and (one might think) mutually exclusive: Stanford (his pre-war teacher), John Ireland (his post-war teacher), Vaughan Williams, Delius, Warlock – and folksong. In the case of Ireland and Warlock, the models had too individual an idiom to be imitated and had an unhelpful effect on his progress as a composer. (A strong influence on Moeran's instrumental music – Sibelius – is not detectable in his songs.) Traces of Stanford are slender (that of a strong teacher personality on a receptive young pupil) but can be detected even in a late work such as the O'Sullivan song-cycle; perhaps not surprising, considering the Irish provenance of the texts. John Ireland's shadow is most noticeable in the works written before 1924, particularly the first song of *Ludlow Town*, but also re-emerges in some later songs. Moeran followed the example of Vaughan Williams by incorporating folk-idioms into his concert music, and the bi-modality of a seminal work such as the Pastoral Symphony made a particularly strong impression on him, as it did on his contemporary, Herbert Howells. The influence of Delius and Warlock is recognisable from the mid-1920s, at its strongest between 1924 and 1930. Like so many English composers of his generation, Moeran was captivated by the sensuous chromatic harmonies of Delius; two of the most direct examples in his songs are 'In youth is pleasure' and 'When daisies pied'. But Moeran more often received his Delius through the prism of Warlock. He adopted many of Warlock's already-established musical procedures: a penchant for siciliana rhythms ('Strings in the earth and air'/'Where the bee sucks'), richly-spiced chromatic chords and such highly-familiar Warlockean hallmarks as floating, parallel 10ths between inner parts ('Now, O now, in this brown land'/'The dustman') and 'weeping 9ths' (the first and last songs of *Seven Poems by James Joyce*). A song such as 'The lover and his lass' could easily be mistaken for Warlock, so flattering is it in its homage. But it was an overwhelming, stultifying influence, a ghost that, after Warlock's death, had to be exorcised. Far more beneficial was the influence of his folksong activity, both as a collector and arranger. In particular, his *Six Folksongs from Norfolk* (*1923*) were to have a positive effect on his own original solo vocal music. Indeed, that superb setting of 'The shooting of his dear' was to cast a long-lasting spell, not only on his later songs but on his *Symphony in G minor* (1937). From 1930 onwards came the influence of another Ireland – the Emerald Isle. Moeran was himself half-Irish and in later life Ireland became virtually his adopted home. He collected folksongs – seven of which he arranged for voice and piano as *Songs from County Kerry* – and, like Stanford and Bax earlier, the shapes and special quality of Irish folk-melodies affected much of his music, particularly in the 1930s and 1940s. The weight of so many diverse influences might be though too over-whelming for a composer to forge an individual style, but in his finest songs Moeran emerges as a distinctive songwriter with a recognisable voice of his own.

As we have already seen, A. E. Housman's slim volume of poems, *A Shropshire Lad* (1896), held a strong fascination for a whole generation of English songwriters. Moeran was no exception and set eleven of the poems in all. The four early settings of 1916 have been published as an appendix to the Centenary Edition of his Collected Songs, Volume 3 (*1994*). They are juvenilia, and though the second song, 'When I came last to Ludlow', appeared (in MS facsimile) in the Autumn 1919 number of *Arts and Letters*, Moeran never saw fit to republish it or to publish the other three during his lifetime. Indeed, his dissatisfaction with the set can be gauged by the fact that, nine years later, he rewrote the fourth song, 'Far in a western brookland'; (1925, *1926*), modifying the vocal line and completely recasting the piano part, turning an elaborate, fussy texture into one of almost Butterworthian simplicity (Exs. 19.1(a) and (b)).

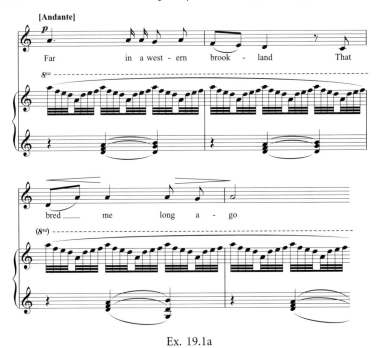

Ex. 19.1a

Ex. 19.1(b)

The four songs that comprise *Ludlow Town* (1920, *1924*) were written during his period of study with John Ireland, who himself was embarking on his own Housman song-cycle, *The Land of Lost Content*. Moeran's settings owe a strong debt to his teacher's songwriting techniques, particularly in the keyboard writing. Though the songs show an intensity of response to the texts and a variety of textures, they lack the memorability of the settings of Vaughan Williams, Butterworth or Ireland himself. There is no attempt to unify the poems into a true song-cycle, either by thematic cross-reference, or by tonal connections between the songs (D major – C minor – E-flat major – A major), though the contrasting tempi (alternating slow and fast) ensure variety. 'When smoke stood up from Ludlow' is a wan interpretation, the vocal line too dourly folk-modal for the text in question. Nor does he capture the poem's shape: the Lad's crucial change of mood after aiming a missile at the singing blackbird in the fourth verse needs to be more positively marked, as in Orr's setting. (Moeran obviously sensed the significance of this, for his original title for the song was 'The blackbird'.) 'Farewell to barn and stack and tree' opens with an unusual chordal progression, which returns in epitomised form in the piano coda. Here one can detect the presence of Vaughan Williams. But the music is too disjointed to be effective, the flow broken by continual stops and starts. The last two songs adopt abstract musical devices, in the form of a march and a jig. 'Say, lad, have you things to do?' is set to a march-like tread; its steady crotchet dominates the song, its basic 4/4 metric pattern varied by 3/4, 5/4 and 3/2 bars, and above this the singer declaims a fidgety vocal line. The effect is fussy, whilst the sudden move back to the tonic E-flat, after the singer has made a perfectly satisfactory cadence into C minor, is disconcerting and unnecessary. The final song, 'The lads in their hundreds', is the most memorable. It is a patter-song placed above a clumping Irish jig, entirely appropriate in mood if not geography for the country-fair scene described. The vocal line – which almost begs for an Irish brogue – is set to a lilting Mixolydian mode on A (the two sharps in the key signature carefully acknowledge this). Sadly, however, Moeran allows the dancing to go on too long, and thus misses the pathos of the poem. The dance does slow down to effect a melancholy cadence, but by then it is too late. Butterworth, in his setting, managed to suggest both the fun of the fair and the melancholy.

Moeran's three remaining Housman settings were written between 1925 and 1934. ''Tis time, I think, by Wenlock Town' (1925, *1926*) is basically a waltz-song with a simple diatonic melody, whose F major tonality veers continually towards D minor. The three verses are set in ternary form. As with 'Say, lad, have you things to do?', the ending is unsatisfactory. The words have a melancholy drift, the Shropshire Lad in exile nostalgically remembering spring-time in his native county:

> Spring will not wait the loiterer's time
>   Who keeps so long away.

Moeran, however, interprets this with an added 6th in F minor which simply sentimentalises the situation. 'Loveliest of trees' (1931, *1932*) has a more chromatic accompaniment and a far more wide-ranging vocal line. Again, the three short verses are set in a ternary pattern. One of Moeran's most distinctive fingerprints – openly-spread 9th chords over a minor triad, yearning downwards in resolution – appears in the second verse (Ex. 19.2(a)) and at the end of the final verse the piano suddenly and memorably blossoms out at the poet's description of 'the cherry hung with snow' (Ex. 19. 2(b)).

Ex. 19.2(a)

Ex. 19.2(b)

'Oh fair enough are sky and plain' has a complex history, going through three different versions in three years. (All can be found in *Collected Solo Songs*, vol. 3.) The first dates from 1931 and was subsequently published in 1957. For some reason Moeran was dissatisfied with it and between 1931 and 1934 made two further versions in which he made superficial alterations to both vocal line (which became more folkily ornamented) and the harmonies of the accompaniment (which became more chromatically tinged). But the alterations in the second and third versions are mere tinkering – the first works perfectly well. Moeran's first version has a crystalline simplicity worthy of Butterworth. Gone are the opaque textures of *Ludlow Town*. It is the best of all his Housman songs, simple but not simplistic, with effective use of bi-modality (Ex. 19.3), and sounds like Moeran and no-one else. Equally importantly, it perfectly encapsulates Housman's text.

Ex. 19.3

Whether inspired or not by Warlock's example, from the mid-1920s Moeran made several settings of 16th- and 17th-century poets, including Robert Wever, Thomas Dekker, Thomas Campion, John Fletcher and William Browne, as well as Shakespeare. Certainly he seems to be modelling himself on Warlock in some of these settings, adopting his costume but not wearing it convincingly. This applies particularly to the *Four English Lyrics* (1933–4, *1934*), which lack Warlock's superior melodic invention, often covering up indifferent vocal lines with exotic or off-beat harmonies, as in 'Willow song' and 'Cherry ripe'. 'The constant lover', whilst a pleasantly tripping love-song, is far too close to Warlock for comfort. More effective is 'Troll the bowl' (Dekker: 1925, *1925*), a drinking-song written for John Goss. It is a strange and original addition to the toping repertoire, starting out in emphatic B minor, but changing for its eponymous refrain to B major where it remains for the rest of the song. Despite Warlock's virtual monopoly of the genre, it is quite unlike Warlock's own examples. The *Four English Lyrics* show also the influence of his own infinitely more memorable choral settings of 16th-century lyrics, *Songs of Springtime* (1929, *1933*), which include two Shakespeare poems, 'Under the greenwood tree' and 'Sigh no more, ladies'. The year after these were published he made a two-part setting of 'It was a lover and his lass' which he reworked as a solo song in 1940, adding three more Shakespeare poems to form *Four Shakespeare Songs* (*1940*). This is one of his most effective works, full of variety and showing his individual style in all its facets. 'The lover and his lass' is perhaps his most thoroughgoing homage to Warlock, with its 'lute-string' 4th-chords and its variation on the 'steps-up' formula in the piano ritornello (Ex. 19.4).

Ex. 19.4

The model, however, is not so much Warlock's own version of the same lyric, 'Pretty ringtime', but 'Piggesnie' (see Ex. 18.1(a)). It is, nevertheless, a fine song: bright, rhythmically alive and economical, and deservedly one of the composer's most popular. 'Where the bee sucks' is more individual, set to a gently flowing siciliana rhythm with its associated minor-triad 9th, an idea which features prominently in the James Joyce songs. The final burden, 'Merrily, merrily shall I live now', contains tiny problems: the downward interval D-flat – F on 'merrily' (bar 17) is difficult to achieve (and, if achieved, to make sense of) against the prevailing chords – most singers opt for an F-sharp; and the accentuation of the phrase 'shall I live now' is strange and unconvincing. However, these are minor quibbles, and the song has an appealing atmosphere, quite unlike other settings of this lyric. The cuckoo song of Ver and the owl song of Hiems from *Love's Labour's Lost* make a neatly contrasting diptych. In 'When daisies pied', Moeran returns stylistically to the Ireland influence of his early songs and piano pieces. A rich, arpeggiated accompaniment, reminiscent of *On a May morning* (1921), is used to float the shapely vocal line of the verses. The refrain is particularly imaginative: at the reference to the cuckoo, the music suddenly darkens and fragments, whilst at the phrase 'O word of fear' the harmonies turn sour, before finding their equilibrium again for the second verse (Ex. 19.5). 'When icicles hang by the wall' is one of the few Shakespeare lyrics that Warlock didn't get around to setting, so there should be no need for comparison were it not for the fact that another Warlock song, 'Mockery' (= his setting of 'When daisies pied') lurks amongst Moeran's refrain chords (Ex. 19.6). With its realistic owl-calls and vividly pointed details, it makes a spirited finale to the group.

Ex. 19.5

Ex. 19.6

Moeran, as we have seen, was on somewhat dangerous ground when setting
16th-century poets: invidious comparisons with Warlock are almost inevitable.
There is, however, one poem, Robert Wever's 'In an arbour green', where

Moeran 'beareth the prize'. Warlock set this poem three times – 'In an arbour green' (1922), 'Lusty Juventus' (1923) and 'Youth' (1928) – but Moeran's one setting, 'In youth is pleasure' (1925, *1925*) is arguably superior to all three. It is also the first of the composer's songs to show his own individual voice. The musical interpretation at a first hearing might seem to be at odds with the text. Here is no bright, bustling youthfulness; instead a voluptuous hedonism tinged with bittersweet melancholy, as the youth daydreams in his green arbour. We are in the sensuous realms of *L'Après-midi d'un faune*. Moeran effects this through the drowsy lulling of the pedal-note in the introduction and interludes, and the improvisatory character of the accompaniment, with its arabesque-like arpeggios and sensuous chromatic harmonies, whose tonal ambiguities continue to the final cadence (Ex. 19.7). For all its apparent calm, it is a disturbing song, which echoes long afterwards in the memory.

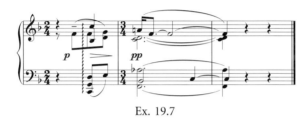

Ex. 19.7

Moeran's choice of song-text, as has already been mentioned, was entirely from contemporary poets in the early part of his career. In addition to Housman, he set Masefield ('Twilight', 1920, *1936*), Bridges ('Spring goeth all in white', 1920, *1924*, and 'When June is come', 1923, *1924*) and Yeats ('A dream of death', 1925, *1925*). None of these is of special interest. Two poetic contemporaries, however, inspired Moeran to some of his finest songs: James Joyce (1882–1941) and Seumas O'Sullivan (1879–1958). In these poets Moeran found material which suited his genius. Despite both being Irish-born, their poetry is quite different in character. Whereas O'Sullivan's texts are Irish in subject-matter, language and imagery, there is not a trace of nationalism in Joyce's poetry, unless, cynically, you count the imagery of falling rain that continually drips through the poetry.

Moeran's ten songs constitute one of the finest bodies of Joyce settings in the repertoire, and some consider the *Seven Poems by James Joyce* (1929, *1930*) to be his crowning achievement (Northcote, 1966: 108). The texts are taken from the poet's early volume of poetry, *Chamber Music* (1907), which consists of thirty short poems which Joyce modelled on Elizabethan song-lyrics but, one suspects, with half an ear to the contemporary neo-medieval verse experiments of Dobson, Lang, Swinburne and Henley. Joyce, himself a capable trained singer, knew exactly what was needed in words-for-music, and the poems are full of references to music, musical instruments and natural sounds (the wind, falling rain, the sea). As with all song-lyrics, they sound better than they appear on the printed page. His compatriot, W. B. Yeats, published a volume of poetry towards the end of his life entitled, *Words for Music, Perhaps*; there is no 'Perhaps' for Joyce. *Chamber music* is not a haphazard collection of verse – the Great Shaper would not have been content with that – but a sequence of love-poems, autobiographically based on his own love for his future wife, Nora Barnacle, with an 'artified' ending tacked on. As with Tennyson's *Maud* and Housman's *A Shropshire Lad*, the sequence is too long for one song-cycle, and most composers have been content to set individual poems or smaller groupings, as did Moeran and Eugene Goossens. It is interesting to compare and contrast the poems that Moeran set with those chosen by Goossens for his song-cycle, *Chamber Music*, written in the same year. (Numbers in brackets refer to Joyce's original numbering in his 1907 publication. Moeran's own song titles are given in brackets after Joyce's original):

MOERAN	GOOSSENS
1. (1) Strings in the earth and air (Dm)	1. (33) Now, O now, [in this brown land]
2. (8) Who goes amid the green wood? (E Mixolydian) ('The merry greenwood')	2. (28) Gentle lady, do not sing sad songs
3. (10) Bright cap and streamers (AM) ('Bright cap')	3. (29) Dear heart, why will you use me so?
4. (16) O cool is the valley now (FM) ('The pleasant valley')	4. (16) O cool is the valley now
5. (31) O, it was out by Donnycarney (FM) ('Donnycarney')	5. (35) All day I hear the noise of waters
6. (32) Rain has fallen [all day] (E Dorian)	6. (36) I hear an army
7. (33) Now, O now, in this brown land (→Dm)	

There are just two settings in common: 'O cool is the valley now' and 'Now, O now, in this brown land'. Whereas Goossens re-orders the sequence, Moeran keeps to Joyce's published order, and so preserves, in miniature, the essential (albeit minimal) narrative of the original, as it follows the 'excitement of young love to the nostalgic retrospect after love has ended' (Banfield, 1985: 271). He matches and contrasts this in his chosen sequence: a slow, lilting opening song, through two sprightly optimistic songs, followed by two more gently paced songs, and ending with two slow, melancholy songs. As will be seen from the basic tonalities given beside the songs listed above (necessarily imprecise due to the modal inflections), they are well contrasted tonally, making a 'cyclic' return to the initial D minor tonality at the end. There are also subtler cross-references, notably the recurrence of the minor-triad 9th chords of the opening song in the final two songs. Except for the final song, all are extremely brief, bagatelle-like in size.

Music permeates the opening poem, 'Strings in the earth and air':

> There's music along the river . . .
> All softly playing,
>   With head to music bent,
> And fingers straying
>   Upon an instrument.

Moeran encapsulates it in a 'sad siciliana', with major 9ths drooping over a minor triad, resolving onto a major 6/4 chord (Ex. 19.8).

Ex. 19.8

This melancholy dance measure clouds the entire cycle, despite the rays of optimism in some of the earlier songs. Moeran gives his setting plenty of air, and the dance measure acts, save for one small break (bars 24–5), as a continuous backdrop throughout, tying up the song with a neat reworking of the opening ritornello. 'The merry greenwood' and 'Bright cap' are quick, scherzo songs in contrasting metres, a brightness in the encircling gloom. 'The merry greenwood' is set to a duple metre and Mixolydian E, with pentuplet arabesques, a characteristic feature of Moeran's piano-writing, buoying up the mood. Over this the singer has a trimly enclosed tune based on the 'steps-up' formula. The four verses are set strophically, with an adroit variation in the third verse which cadences onto the dominant rather than the previous tonics. The elf-like individual described in 'Bright cap' dances to a 3/8 metre in A major, again with Mixolydian (G-natural) inflections. Again, there is a well-sculpted, folk-inspired vocal line, with effective use made of duplet melismas on the semiquavers. The two stanzas, set strophically, are over and done with in less than a minute. In 'The pleasant valley' the ghost of John Ireland looms and glooms. The opening, with its irregular 5/8 metre and sombre chromatic-modal chords, could have come from the slow movement of one of Ireland's instrumental works. It is another extremely brief song; the eight-line poem is through-set and Moeran ignores Joyce's refraining of the opening lines at the end of the poem. Equally brief is 'Donnycarney', a poem very similar in shape, mood and subject-matter to Yeats's 'Down by the salley gardens'. Like Yeats's famous poem, Joyce's could well have been modelled on an Irish folk-original:

> O, it was out by Donnycarney
>   When the bat flew from tree to tree
> My love and I did walk together
>   And sweet were the words she said to me.
>
> Along with us the summer wind
>   Went murmuring – O happily! –
> But softer than the breath of summer
>   Was the kiss she gave to me.

Indeed, Moeran takes up the cue, and the song opens with a melody that is, perhaps, the most Irish inspired of all the songs (Ex. 19.9). Gloom and mist from the Land of the Curlew, however, darken the second verse: this is odd, for the

O,— it was out   by Don-ny - car - ney When the bat   flew from tree to   tree

Ex. 19.9

mood of the text is light and happy. (Perhaps Moeran wanted to suggest
something that had personal significance?) The drooping 9ths of the siciliana
return for the penultimate song, 'Rain has fallen', but this time in duple metre,
its obsessive melancholy entirely in keeping with the rain-soaked text of the
poem. The two short stanzas are through-set, though Moeran marks the end of
each verse with a rich, bitonal cadence chord (Exs. 19.10(a) and (b)).

me - mor - ies. ___   Stay- ing a lit - tle by   the way Of

Ex. 19.10(a)

Ex. 19.10(b)

The final song, 'Now, O now, in this brown land', is by far the most substantial.
With its autumnal imagery and references to the 'sweet music' of the first song, it
forms an appropriate and impressive conclusion to the cycle. The siciliana rhythm
returns, this time not lilting but in slow, sustained chords. For the singer, the three
verses are set to a varied strophic melody that undergoes subtle inflections as it
follows the nuances of the text; the accompaniment, however, varies its texture for
each verse. At the end of the siciliana-based first verse, the music cadences into A,
and the note A continues as a pedal for the whole of the second verse (bars 15–31).
The autumnal image of the 'Rogue in red and yellow dress . . . knocking at the tree'
and the whistling wind are depicted in the falling chromatics of the vocal line and
Curlew-esque parallel 10ths in the accompaniment. Then, at the end of the verse,
the gloom is shattered by an unexpected arpeggiated A major chord and a new,
richly textured accompaniment, until the singer's penultimate line. The music
then breaks off, and when it resumes it has rediscovered not only the siciliana
rhythm but also its appoggiatura 9ths, and these accompany the setting of the final

line of the cycle, 'The year, the year is gathering'. It is to this sad little motive, with a delicate ornament added, that the music comes to a close, inconclusively, though appropriately, on a D minor 9th chord (Ex. 19.11(a)). This is one of Moeran's most sensitive songs, in which he shows how well he could mould his music to the requirements of his text. Note, for instance, how he alters the inflections of his vocal line during the three verses (Exs. 19.11(b), (c) and (d)).

Ex. 19.11(a)

Ex. 19.11(b)

Ex. 19.11(c)

Ex. 19.11(d)

Seven Poems by James Joyce is a work that occupies a significant place in Moeran's vocal output, a work that, Janus-like, looks forwards and backwards, as it refers back to earlier songs and is itself to be quoted in later songs (cf. 'Now,

O now, in this brown land' with 'Loveliest of trees' written two years later).
There is no doubt that Warlock's *The Curlew* hovers like a ghost in many places.
Indeed, *Seven Songs* could be regarded as Moeran's *Curlew*, but the fact that the
comparison can justifiably be made indicates the quality of the music.

In the same year that he wrote the *Seven Poems*, Moeran made a setting of
another Joyce poem, 'Rosefrail' (1929, *1931*), taken not from *Chamber Music*
but from the recently published *Pomes Penyeach* (1927). (Joyce's own title for
the poem was 'A flower given to my daughter'.) Moeran opens the song with the
ornamented 'x' from the coda of 'Now, O now, in this brown land' (see
Ex. 19.11(a)), as though he were taking up from where he had broken off.
'Rosefrail' is, in fact, another siciliana-based song, as slight and as frail as the
child it depicts. It was to be the first of three settings of poems from *Pomes
Penyeach*. The second, 'Tilly', was in fact commissioned by Herbert Hughes for

Ex. 19.12(a)

Ex. 19.12(b)

The Joyce Book (1933). (The French composer, Albert Roussel, made the 'official' setting of 'A flower given to my daughter'.) The title 'Tilly' refers not to the boy who urges the cattle along the cold red road in the poem, but to the thirteenth ('milkman's extra') poem of the collection, which had originally retailed at a shilling (= 12 old pence). In the Dublin of Joyce's childhood, when the milkman left milk at the door in a jug, he added a bit extra, called a 'tilly'. It is the extra *and* earliest-written (1904) poem of the collection, and was originally called 'Rumi-nants' – a typically Joycean double-edged title, referring as it does to the cattle being driven home and the poet's reflection about his family after the death of his mother. Here, appropriately, Moeran's idiom is more advanced than in *Seven Poems*, and is, indeed, the most sophisticated of all his Joyce settings. The writing for both singer and piano is spacious, and he is generous in his ideas, with each of the three verses given a completely different accompaniment. The song opens with a chain of minor triads (1st inversions in close position) which continue, sphinx-like, for the first five long bars of this *Lento*-paced setting. Above this, the singer's line consists of pentatonic fragments, homed around A minor, C minor, E major and D major. These two ideas drift around each other, sometimes coinciding, more often not (Ex. 19.12(a)). At the phrase 'a cold red road', this accompaniment breaks off and verse 2 begins accompanied by pentatonic arpeggios and a more familiar Moeran idea of rich chromatic chords in parallel motion (Ex. 19.12(b)). There is yet another texture for the third verse: richly spread root triads, spiced with added notes, which reach a sharply dissonant bitonal chord (C-flat major over C minor) for 'I bleed by the bleak stream' (Ex. 19.12(c)). In the coda of the song, he at last begins to reprise some of the earlier ideas, finally cadencing on a bleak, third-less D: clearly the 'key' of the song, though it had not been heard until the end of the first verse.

Ex. 19.12(c)

If 'Tilly' is a fine song, 'Rahoon' (1946, *1947*) is a great song: Moeran's masterpiece and one of the finest of all Joyce settings. The poem – poet's original title was 'She weeps over Rahoon' – refers in its imagery back to poem 32 of *Chamber Music*, 'Rain has fallen all the day', which Moeran had, of course, set in *Seven Poems*. Here, however, the musical ideas are much stronger and more memorable. The piano opens with a sequence of bittersweet chords, minor triads with a major 7th, with appoggiaturas 'resolving' in the inner parts, though not necessarily onto concords. Above this the r.h. has a fixed ostinato figure, which drips down through the texture like the falling rain of the poem (Ex. 19.13(a)). The appoggiatura motive, 'x', is then developed in more familiar Moeran textures, rich chords and arpeggiated figures (Ex. 19.13(b)). The singer's extremely chromatic vocal line ranges across the poem in a free, flexible arioso span, with no attempt at direct reprise. It is left to the accompanist to mark out the formal progress of the music, which it does by recapping (i) the 'falling rain' idea ('w') at the end of verse 2 and (ii) the chordal idea during verse 3. At the words 'the black mould/And muttering rain', the chordal idea, 'x', becomes involved in a rhythmic ostinato, which gradually unwinds itself to reach some sort of cadence in the final *una corda* bitonal chord (Ex. 19.13(c)). This chord underlines, if it does not satisfy, a C minor tonality, but the intense chromaticism of the music renders the song virtually atonal in places. 'Rahoon' was written for and dedicated to Kathleen Ferrier, who gave the first performance in a BBC broadcast in 1947; it was to be Moeran's final song. It shares its brooding intensity with the Cello Sonata written in the same year, and in its dark-hued pessimism is Moeran's equivalent of Warlock's 'The fox'. For once the comparison does Moeran no shame: it possesses all of the composer's virtues as a songwriter – flexible rhythms, sophisticated harmonies, memorable ideas, assured writing for both voice and piano.

Ex. 19.13(a)

Ex. 19.13(b)

Ex. 19.13(c)

Six Poems by Seumas O'Sullivan (1944, *1946*) is Moeran's major solo vocal work and arguably his finest. Seumas O'Sullivan – the pen name of the poet and editor, James Starkey (1879–1958) – was a friend of the composer, and his poetry, with its strong Irish accent, straightforward language and vivid imagery, attracted several leading songwriters. His most popular poem, 'The piper' ('A

piper in the streets today') has been set by Peter Crossley-Holland, Michael
Head, Ivor Gurney, Norman Peterkin and Vaughan Williams. Moeran himself
made seven settings of O'Sullivan's poetry, the first of which, 'Invitation in
autumn' (1943, *1946*), was published separately. He also sketched an eighth
song, 'If there be any gods', originally intended for the song-cycle but not
completed. (The pencil MS of the first page is reproduced in Self, 1986: 172.)
For the cycle Moeran chose poems with a range of subject-matter – landscape
descriptions, portraits of country people, poems about children – all imbued
with an autumnal quality. It is very much the subject-matter that Stanford had
found in the poetry of Moira O'Neill and Winifred Letts. Indeed, 'The poplars'
and 'The dustman' are strongly reminiscent of Stanford's Irish songs. In keeping
with the poetry, Moeran's music shows a strong influence of Irish folk-music in
both melody and accompaniment, skilfully intermixed with more sophisticated,
chromatic elements. Despite passing reminiscences of John Ireland ('A cottager'), Warlock ('Lullaby') and Stanford, such echoes are faint, and in these
songs Moeran has forged a far more personal style than in the earlier Joyce cycle.
They show a wide range of melodic, harmonic and textural ideas and an
imaginative handling of song-forms. If the Joyce songs are restricted in textures
and word-setting, the O'Sullivan settings are spacious and clear-cut. There is no
attempt to unify the cycle tonally (the basic key centres are: A-flat major – A
major – D-flat major – A-flat minor – G minor – B minor) or by thematic cross-
reference, but the final song draws together motives from earlier in the work.
The opening song, 'Evening', shows how Moeran can skilfully intermingle
pentatonic and chromatic material, linking them together through a common
(here arpeggiated) accompaniment.

Ex. 19.14

In O'Sullivan's sonnet (see epigraph), the evening mood is pinpointed by the image of poplar trees, 'shrines of quietness that send/Their silence through the blue air'. In the second song, 'The poplars', the grey poplars become the subject and, indeed, narrators of the poem. Moeran contrasts the poet's musings (outer strophes) and the poplars talking (central strophes) by a contrast of pace, texture and tonality. The Irish character of the song is established in the piano's opening bar, and subsequently endorsed in the vocal line (Ex. 19.14). 'A cottager' is a description of an old Irish peasant and his cottage, each verse ending with the refrain-line, 'Yet who has count of the years between', which Moeran matches in his music. The melodic line has a strong Irish flavour – some would say that another Ireland, John, is lurking there too: the tune closely resembles that of 'The holy boy' – and the accompaniment evokes Irish bagpipe music (Ex. 19.15). 'The dustman', subtitled 'Child's fancy', is a delightful, Stevenson-esque poem, written from a child's-eye perspective. The music, too, is suitably childlike in its ideas, reflecting every change of mood and image:

(a) a 3/4 piano introduction sets the night scene ('everyone asleep/It must be very late'), a little Irish pipe tune in A-flat minor in canon, which the singer takes up and adapts;
(b) a soft tread 'down the darkened stairs' in 4/4;
(c) a more animated, jokey idea, back in triple time (*con spirito*) in D minor for the dustman, with a jig-like fragment leading to
(d) a sombre E-flat minor ('the lights are dim,') at which the *Curlew*-like gloom motive appears before the music
(e) trips away on the opening pipe fragment to its final cadence.

Ex. 19.15

After these lighter interludes, 'Lullaby' returns us abruptly to a sombre, reflective mood. O'Sullivan's fine poem uses clear, evocative imagery: 'Husheen the herons are crying/Away in the rain and the sleet'. Moeran's setting is a typically distraught 20th-century lullaby, with metric tension between voice (12/8) and accompaniment (4/4) and tonal tension in the underlying harmonies (the G minor tonic is continually pulled by its F-sharp 7th downwards to F-sharp minor tonality) (Ex. 19.16).

Ex. 19.16

Again, there are swift changes of idea, following the progress of the poem, yet Moeran manages to keep the song unified. Particularly fine are the soaring vocal line at the words 'the wild wings that wrestle', the deft move back to D-flat major for the final verse and the bitonal roulade of notes at 'the winds ever blowing'.

The final song, 'The herdsman', expresses the melancholy thoughts of the poet as he watches a herdsman driving his flock at twilight. (Moeran seems to have had a special affection for the herdsman figure: in 'Tilly', a boy is herding cattle – here a man is herding sheep.) The poem consists of two short quatrains, but Moeran builds it into a large-scale, arch-shaped song. It opens with a characteristic harmonic idea, a minor triad with a major 7th, here ornamented with the arabesque from 'The cottager'. The sad mood is underlined by a sequence of strange bitonal chords (Ex. 19.17(a)). Against this the singer intones an F-sharp, which acts as an inner pedal-note for the first six lines of the setting: even when the singer does move briefly away from it, he is drawn back immediately, as though by a magnet (Ex. 19.17(b)). The mood created could not be more fatalistic or dour. But then, halfway through the final verse, there is a wonderful transformation. At the words 'O happy meadows and trees', there is a sudden blaze of light: the piano breaks from B minor into bright E-flat major in a roulade of arpeggios, whilst the singer, freed at last from the pedal F-sharp, ranges wide and free (Ex. 19.17(c)). It is similar in effect to the move into E major at the words 'O past! O happy life!' in Delius's *Sea Drift* – and like that, just as short-lived. As quickly as it came, the music subsides, first onto the sequence of bitonal chords, to accompany the final line 'The twilight and all its flocks will pass you by', and finally onto the B minor-7th chord and its accompanying arabesques, which slowly resolve into a cadence on an added 6th, thus completing the arch-shape. It is one of Moeran's most memorable songs and a haunting conclusion to a fine song-cycle.

Ex. 19.17(a)

Ex. 19.17(b)

Ex. 19.17(c)

In a letter to his future wife, Peers Coetmore, in December 1943, Moeran wrote, 'I think I am better at songs than at anything else, i.e. some of my songs are my very best work.' Moeran was a composer with a magpie mind; he does not, like a squirrel, bury his influences out of sight, but happily displays them for all to see. Just as one cannot listen to the G minor Symphony without being reminded of the impact on him of Vaughan Williams and Sibelius, so in his songs the influences of his mentors, John Ireland, Delius and Peter Warlock, shine through in harmonic style, choice of text and songwriting techniques. But in his finest songs, there is a special element which sets them apart from other English songwriters of the period; the Joyce and O'Sullivan settings alone earn him an important niche in the history of 20th-century English song.

20

Gerald Finzi (1901–56)

I who am dead a thousand years,
And wrote this sweet archaic song,
Send you my words for messengers
The way I shall not pass along . . .

O friend unseen, unborn, unknown,
Student of our sweet English tongue,
Read out my words at night, alone:
I was a poet, I was young.

Since I can never see your face,
And never shake you by the hand,
I send my soul through time and space
To greet you. You will understand.

James Elroy Flecker:
'To a poet a thousand years hence'

If asked to introduce Finzi's songs to someone who had never heard them before, what are the characteristics that you would identify? His music is unashamedly in an English tradition; contemporary continental models are almost entirely absent and one cannot detect Wagner, Strauss or Debussy influences as one can in the music of Elgar, Delius, Bridge or Bax. Though his attitude to word-setting can be (and has been) compared to that of Hugo Wolf, there is no evidence that he was familiar with Wolf's songs. Any discernible cross-channel influences, such as J. S. Bach, are diffused, as it were, through an English prism. Furthermore, the ideas of any cross-ocean influences are slightly absurd; he bypassed them all: Jazz and Gershwin might never have happened. Finzi's models were almost entirely English, and of a fairly circumscribed kind. His early love was for the music of Vaughan Williams, Holst, Butterworth and Gurney, but perhaps his greatest debt was to Hubert Parry. Parry's Arnoldian 'High Seriousness' towards song-composition, with its emphasis on the importance of detailed attention to choice of poetry and meticulous scansion and word-setting, was the model for Finzi's own songs. Parry also bequeathed not only a contrapuntally based diatonic idiom but also that 'nobilmente' strain which so often occurs in Finzi's music.

For composers of Finzi's generation, Vaughan Williams was an impossible influence to avoid. The impact on Finzi of hearing *On Wenlock Edge* at the 1919

Glastonbury Festival was equivalent to the impact of the Tallis Fantasia on Howells and Gurney at the Gloucester Three Choirs Festival nine years earlier. It is, therefore, surprising how little Finzi makes use of folksong and folk modes. The traditional major and minor modes, with occasional chromatic inflections, are his stock in trade. When he goes into 'folk mode', as in 'The sigh' or 'Ditty', it is, as Banfield has observed, 'that sort of folksong that is closest to the homeliness of the hymn tune' – the sort of 'folk-tune' that Vaughan Williams invented in 'Linden lea' (1985: 281). But his use of modal inflection, when he does use it, can be unexpectedly telling, as at the end of 'Summer schemes' (Ex. 20.1).

Ex. 20.1

Hymn tunes are far more discernible an influence, particularly as perorations to songs – see the conclusions to his Milton sonnet, 'How soon hath Time', and 'To a poet' – and noticeable from his earliest works, such as *By Footpath and Stile*. Finzi's agnostic devotion to the music of the Anglican Church is summed up in his setting of Hardy's 'So I have fared', where the psalm-inspired text is matched by the composer's mock Anglican chant (see Ex. 20.4).

Closely linked with this is his use of chorale-prelude textures, something which he would have learned from J. S. Bach: a singing, ornamented 'chorale' melody in the pianist's r.h. and a walking bass in the l.h., over which the singer 'floats' a quasi-improvised arioso line. The final song of *Dies Natalis* and the 'Aria' from *Farewell to Arms* are two of the most obvious examples. However, Bach's contrapuntal way of thinking influenced Finzi beyond such overt examples, and the basic element of chorale-prelude technique – an elaborate upper-part (= vocal line) over walking bass with contrapuntal inner-parts – is to be found in a large number of his songs.

Finzi was introduced to the songs of Ivor Gurney by his teacher, Edward Bairstow, and the song 'Sleep' was a key influence on his songwriting career. From the mid-1920s, together with Marion Scott and Howard Ferguson, he began a lifelong crusade to bring public attention to Gurney's music by assembling and editing the chaotic manuscripts for publication. As far as his own songs are concerned, this devotion to the cause of Ivor Gurney must have taught him something, but what he learned is difficult to pinpoint. Both composers approached song-composition in a spacious, unhurried manner, attempting to reach the unspoken words between the poet's lines. They allow the piano to comment between vocal phrases and, in doing so, allow genuine interplay between singer and accompanist. Compare, for example, Gurney's setting of 'The folly of being comforted' with Finzi's setting of 'Proud songsters'. Both poems are quite short; the composers, however, have explored every facet and allusion in the poem to produce substantial songs.

Howard Ferguson has said that 'English poetry was probably [Finzi's] deepest interest' (1957: 131). Finzi's love of songwriting sprang from his love of poetry. For a composer he was unusually widely read; his personal library, now permanently housed in the Finzi Room at the University of Reading, consists of over 4,000 volumes, the majority of them editions of English poets. As with every song-composer, his choice of poets for setting to music inevitably reflects his own philosophy of life. Like Vaughan Williams, he could be described as an agnostic with Christian leanings. Thomas Hardy's fatalistic agnosticism attracted him enormously, but he was also aware of 'intimations of immortality' and the 'Lost Edens of Childhood'. It was the expression of these ideas that drew him to the poetry of Thomas Traherne. Though one immediately thinks of these two poets when considering Finzi's vocal music, he found texts in a wide variety of poets – many of them expected, well-known names, such as Milton, Bridges, Blunden and de la Mare, some, like Knevet, obscure, others, like George Barker, unexpected.

Finzi was an extremely slow, meticulous worker. Howard Ferguson has observed that 'Writing was never a fluent business for him, and even the most spontaneous sounding song might have involved endless sketches with possibly a break of years between its opening and closing verses' (1968: sleeve-note). This would have been impossible with composers such as Stravinsky or Britten, whose styles evolved radically over the years. But Finzi, like Ravel and Rawsthorne, was one of those whose musical sound world is recognisable from an early stage. It *is* possible to tell an early Finzi song from a later one (the early ones are harmonically simpler, the accompanimental textures smoother), but early and late can stand side by side without any noticeable jarring – witness, for example, the posthumous collection *Oh fair to see* (1966). The Shanks setting, 'As I lay in the early sun' was written as early as 1921; on the other hand, the Robert Bridges setting, 'Since we loved', was the last song he completed, dated 'August 28 1956'. Thirty-five years separate them: the time hardly shows.

Certain fingerprints recur time and again in Finzi's songs. The expressiveness of his vocal lines is usually achieved by contour rather than chromaticism, in a mixture of conjunct movement and large expressive leaps. A characteristic shape is one that haunts the cycle *Earth and Air and Rain* and which finds its ultimate expression in 'To Lizbie Browne' (see Ex. 20.2(c)). This shape occurs frequently throughout his songs, as, for example at the end of 'To a poet a thousand years hence', to the words 'you will understand' (see Ex. 20.14). It is interesting to note that, quite unlike his contemporaries Tippett and Britten, Finzi rarely uses melisma. The long roulade of notes on the word 'weep' at the end of 'Come away, death' is unusual and has a deliberately 'antique' air about it. But in the main, Finzi assiduously abides by Cranmer's dictum, 'for every syllable a note'.

The piano accompaniment plays a crucial role in a Finzi song. His piano-writing, though lacking the ease or panache of Bax, Bridge or Quilter – he often appears to be thinking in terms of string quartet rather than piano, in the way he follows through his contrapuntal lines – plays an important part in underlining key emotional words and phrases of the text. Particularly recognisable is his use of a minor 9th discord between the upper-part and bass – see 'The clock of the years' (bars 28 and 34), 'In a churchyard' (bar 11), 'O mistress mine' (bar 56), etc. Another characteristic is the way in which the piano echoes the vocal phrases; most songwriters use this device, but few as consistently as Finzi. A song such as 'To Lizbie Browne' is full of such echoes, to the extent that the echoing becomes one of the song's main unifying devices.

But it is Finzi's genius for word-setting which most claims our admiration. Even at the most basic level of scansion, Finzi can instruct us. The genius lies in his subtle handling of rhythm: the imaginative way in which he translates verbal rhythm into musical rhythm. This can be observed from a glance at the score of any song, which will reveal his enormously wide range of note duration. His bass lines may be stiffly static, but his vocal lines are full of variety; rarely does he reproduce the same rhythm from one bar to the next. This rhythmic flexibility – some might say finickiness – enables him to set words with great delicacy, lending his songs the quality of intimate conversation. One has only to follow the poet's original text when listening to a Finzi setting to appreciate this. Such rightness and beauty of scansion is a joy in itself and, in one respect, achieves the melo-poetic ideal. No wonder he has been called the 'poet's composer'.

Finzi had strong views on the prickly problem of words-for-music. In a letter to Ferguson (December 1936), he wrote:

> I do hate the bilge & bunkum about composers trying to 'add' to a poem: that a fine poem is complete in itself, & to set it is only to gild the lily, & so on . . . the first and last thing is that a composer is (presumably) moved by a poem & wishes to identify himself with it & share it.

Despite their different attitudes to songwriting in so many other respects, Finzi and Britten were in agreement here: both felt that, however 'complete' in itself and however great as a work of literature, no poem was outside the song-composer's range of choice if he felt he could identify with and respond musically to it. Thus Britten set T. S. Eliot's *The Journey of the Magi* and a passage from Wordsworth's *The Prelude*, as well as several lyrically intractable poems by W. H. Auden. Finzi was not frightened to tackle sonnets by Milton, Wordsworth's *Ode on the Intimation of Immortality* and poems by Thomas Hardy (e.g. 'Channel firing' and 'The clock of the years') which would seem to defy musical access.

His song-forms range from simple strophic and ternary patterns to complex, through-composed structures. Strophic settings are uncommon, reserved for songs of a deliberately ditty-like nature, such as 'Rollicum-rorum', 'Budmouth dears' or 'Come away, death'. Ternary shapes appear in many songs: 'It was a lover and his lass' and 'Who is Silvia?', from *Let us Garlands Bring*, and 'Wonder', from *Dies Natalis*. He also uses other strophically based designs; for example, the five stanzas of 'For life I had never cared greatly' are deployed in an ABABC pattern. Like Quilter, he treats most short, two-stanza poems, such as 'It never looks like summer' and 'Waiting both', in binary fashion: a single musical paragraph with a caesura in the middle. On the other hand, some of the longer songs, such as 'Ode on the rejection of St Cecilia', are through-composed without any hint of strophic repetition. 'The clock of the years' and 'Channel firing' are in effect miniature dramatic cantatas – operas, almost.

Finzi's great strength as a song-composer is his love and care for the words of the poets he sets. He weighs each phrase, understands each nuance: an attribute in any songwriter, though one that cannot be taken for granted. But can such care for 'just note and accent' in itself be of interest to the listener? May it not be compared to the art of the Elizabethan madrigalist: more rewarding to perform than to listen to? It seems to be just one stage – admittedly an important first stage – in writing a song. A song is not simply written to make clear the syntax and the meaning, but to get beneath the meaning to what the poet has hinted at, but left unsaid, between the lines. This is something that Finzi does not always manage to achieve.

Despite his many virtues as a songwriter, Finzi as a composer has fundamental weaknesses which mar his songs. Some of these relate to specifically songwriting techniques, but many are of a wider compositional nature. Many of his songs lack strong, memorable musical ideas, particularly in their melodies. One does not ask for a catchy musical comedy tune in an art-song; but, as songwriters as diverse as Quilter, Ireland, Denis Browne, Warlock and Britten show, it is perfectly possible to encompass a text with a memorable tune without loss of fidelity. Finzi, one feels, cannot, or will not. His songs are dictated by the *sense* and not necessarily the *shape* of his texts. Faithfulness to a poet's intentions goes beyond 'just note and accent' to the shape of the poem; Finzi is often so concerned with the individual trees that he forgets his wood. Furthermore, his harmonic palette is limited and his sense of tonality weak and circumscribed – once in a key, he stays there and is reluctant to modulate. Such restrictions, if self-imposed, are self-defeating. There are, indeed, examples of effective, dramatic changes of key in his songs (e.g. 'To a poet'), but often his modulations sound awkward and unconvincing. One has only to make comparisons with Howells or Bridge or Ireland in this respect to appreciate how restricted Finzi's harmonic resources are. But perhaps his greatest weakness is his dull sense of rhythm, which lacks the vitality of Vaughan Williams or Warlock or Britten. Admittedly he can divide a crotchet as well as any composer, but rhythm as a fundamental building block in his music is absent. Too often his songs amble blandly along without any inner compunction; when he does make structural use of rhythmic ideas, as in 'Channel firing', with its 'motto' rhythm acting as a ritornello, the music is transformed. Finally, he employs a limited range of accompanimental textures compared with, say, Britten or Warlock. Was it because his mode-of-thought is essentially contrapuntal that Finzi lacked such defining colour and variety? The same basic textures recur throughout his songs. Foremost amongst these is the walking bass line, marching in even, stepwise crotchets – a solecism that he may have picked up from Holst. The tramp, tramp of such basses are fine for songs like 'Budmouth dears' or 'When I set out for Lyonnesse', but become an annoying cliché elsewhere. Four-part contrapuntal textures – the 'SATB sound' so beloved by those English composers conceived in the organ loft – haunt almost every song, whatever the subject-matter, whether relevant or not. On occasions, when he does adopt dance-based textures, they are of a fairly restricted range. Like so many of his British contemporaries, he is fond of siciliana and sarabande – see 'The phantom' and 'Fear no more the heat of the sun'. Less welcome is that bane of English songwriting, the throbbing rhythmic figure: ♪ ♩ ♪ which is too frequently resorted to as a means of reviving flagging interest, or to stimulate excitement artificially, as in the second verse of 'The phantom'. The constant undercurrent of this rhythmic cliché in 'It was a lover and his lass' eventually renders the song extremely tedious. But perhaps Finzi's greatest shortcoming, both as composer and man, is his overbearing solemnity and lack of humour; this is evident from a reading of his life and philosophy as well as his music. We are not lamenting the fact that he was not a 'fun' composer, able to write for the Hoffnung Festivals, but a sense of humour often brings with it a critical awareness, an ability to regard things from oblique angles and to prick the bubbles of pomposity and pretension. It would have been a great asset to Finzi.

I write at length about these matters because Finzi has so often been held up as 'one of the great figures in contemporary English song' (Northcote, 1966: 111). Despite the critical, acclaim bestowed on him by Banfield, Northcote and Howes and the sincere enthusiasm which he inspires in his followers, I find a large number of his songs unmemorable, lacking in dynamism, zest and energy. Nevertheless, amongst his 80 or so published songs there are many fine ones, and it is on these that I shall concentrate in the following pages.

Settings of Thomas Hardy

The poetry of Thomas Hardy preoccupied Finzi's creative imagination throughout his life. Except for the setting of Robert Graves's ballad, 'The cupboard' (1922, *1923*), Finzi's first published work was the Hardy song-cycle *By Footpath and Stile*, op. 2 (1921–2, *1925*), for baritone and string quartet; one of his last completed compositions was 'I said to love', dated 12th July 1956, only two months before his death. In the 35 years between, he completed over 40 settings of Hardy, as well as leaving at least 25 songs in fragmentary form. This devotion to one poet is matched only by that of Charles Orr to A. E. Housman, and Gibbs and Howells to de la Mare. Whatever the quality of Finzi's Hardy settings, they must form the focus of any study of his song output. During his lifetime he published, in addition to *By Footpath and Stile*, three sequences of Hardy settings, each of ten songs: *A Young Man's Exhortation* (1926–9, *1933*) for tenor and piano, and *Earth and Air and Rain* (1928–32, *1936*) and *Before and After Summer* (1932–49, *1949*) for baritone and piano. He had intended to publish at least two more, though neither was completed at his death. Those songs in finished state were published posthumously in two sets, one for tenor, *Till Earth Outwears* (*1958*: seven songs) and one for baritone, *I Said to Love* (*1958*: six songs). In addition there is a further Hardy setting, 'I say "I'll seek her"', in *Oh Fair to See*, a collection of songs for high voice and piano to poems by various writers (*1956*). Although Finzi published his first settings of Hardy in 1925, three years before the poet's death, the two men never met. The Hardy-Finzi canon stands as a ghostly collaboration between poet and composer; at the same time it is a major collaboration, a coming-together of like minds and philosophies.

It has been estimated that, of the 900 or so poems that Hardy wrote, one in eight has musical associations. Hardy's musical tastes were simple: the folk-ballads, reels and jigs of country fairs, the polkas and waltzes of dance-hall and esplanade, favourite piano-duets and parlour-songs, and above all the sturdy old psalm tunes played by musicians of the 'Mellstock Choir'. But, as we have seen, to be inspired by music does not necessarily indicate an ability to write words for musical setting. Few poets wrote more extensively about music than Robert Browning, yet his attempts at writing song-lyrics were, in the main, unsuccessful (see pp. 93–4). Hardy, on the other hand, was a master of the craft, as is proven by the number of composers that he has attracted over the past 100 years. Gooch and Thatcher (1976) list some 300 songs and choral-settings of his poetry by more than 100 different composers; and many more have been added since their catalogue was published. This is a remarkable tally, for in some respects Hardy presents the composer with problems. For one thing, his dour philosophy, a mixture of stoicism and fatalism, is not a sentiment universally held, least of all amongst songwriters. (It is significant that the most frequently set poem is one of his least characteristic: 'Weathers') Another problem lies in his use of language: his poetry is craggy and rugged, deliberately sprinkled with antique phrases, Dorset dialect-words and Anglo-Saxonisms. In most cases these are surface problems, which the composer can easily overcome: the aptness of his poetry for musical treatment far outweighs the difficulties. Few major poets have had such a natural talent for the lyric-writer's art. Many of his poems he conceived with half-an-ear to musical setting – in some cases he even went so far as to specify the *mode* that the composer should adopt – and many of his poems, like those of Burns and Clare, were written to existing folk-melodies.

As has been observed, two features that a song-composer takes into consideration when choosing a lyric poem are line-length and stanza-shape. Short, four-line stanzas, believed by some to be the ideal vehicle for the song-lyric, are the last thing he requires: their very squareness restricts. Hardy appreciated this, and in his poetry invented an amazing diversity of stanza-shapes, varying short lines with long, adopting irregular rhyming patterns and making original use of refrains. Take, for example, the following opening stanzas from regularly stanza-ed poems:

1. When friendly summer calls again,
        Calls again
    Her little fifers to these hills,
    We'll go – we two – to that arched fane
    Of leafage where they prime their bills
    Before they start to flood the plain
    With quavers, minims, shakes and trills.
        'We'll go,' I said; but who shall say
        What may not chance before that day!
            'Summer schemes'

2. When I set out for Lyonnesse,
        A hundred miles away,
        The rime was on the spray,
    And starlight lit my lonesomeness
    When I set out for Lyonnesse
        A hundred miles away.
            'When I set out for Lyonnesse'

3. Simple was I and was young;
        Kept no gallant tryst, I;
    Even from good words held my tongue,
        Quoniam Tu fecisti!
            'So I have fared'

4. When Lawyers strive to heal a breach,
    And Parsons practice what they preach;
    Then Boney he'll come pouncing down,
    And march his men on London town!
        Rollicum-rorum, tol-lol-lorum,
        Rollicum-rorum, tol-lol-lay!
            'Rollicum-rorum'

5. Dear Lizbie Browne,
    Where are you now?
    In sun, in rain? –
    Or is your brow
    Past joy, past pain,
    Dear Lizbie Browne?
            'To Lizbie Browne'

6. The thrushes sing as the sun is going,
    And finches whistle in ones and pairs,
    And as it gets dark loud nightingales
        In bushes
    Pipe, as they can when April wears,
        As if all Time were theirs.
            'Proud songsters'

Though only the opening stanza is given of these six poems, the stanzas that follow have the same pattern of line-length, rhyme and refrain. Hardy, of course, did not choose these stanzas arbitrarily, but to fit the mood and subject-matter of the poem in question. But what a cornucopia they present to the song-composer! It is small wonder that Finzi included all six in his sequence *Earth and Air and Rain*.

Hardy realised, however, that poems using parallel stanzas were by no means the only song-shapes to offer; by their very nature they suggest (though by no means guarantee) a strophic setting to the composer, and in several lyrics he experimented with irregular stanza-patterns, as in 'Shortening days at the homestead':

> The first fire since the summer is lit, and is smoking into the room:
>   The sun-rays thread it through, like woof-lines in a loom.
>   Sparrows spurt from the hedge, whom misgivings appal
> That winter did not leave last year for ever, after all.
>   Like shock-headed urchins, spiny-haired,
>   Stand pollard willows, their twigs just bared.
>
>   Who is this coming with pondering pace,
>   Black and ruddy, with white embossed,
>   His eyes being black, and ruddy his face
>   And the marge of his hair like morning frost?
>   It's the cider-maker,
>   And appletree-shaker,
>   And behind him on wheels, in readiness,
>   His mill, and tubs, and vat, and press.

This suggests a two-part conception for the two stanzas, with their quite different character, shapes, line-lengths and rhyming schemes, and the poem duly receives this from Finzi in his setting in *A Young Man's Exhortation*.

On the other hand, Hardy's verse presents two problems to the aspiring composer – they might be termed 'anti-lyrical factors'. Though Hardy uses formal stanza-patterns, he sometimes does so in order to *destroy* their inherent symmetry, by counterpointing his thoughts through the stanza, so that his sentences come to a rest within a line or flow on from one line to another or, in some cases, from stanza to stanza. This technique is found in 'The phantom' and 'Channel firing', both set by Finzi. In each, Finzi, with his extremely flexible word-setting, follows Hardy's train of thought without difficulty, and creates complex, through-composed song structures which the stanza patterns could never have suggested. The second problem is one of aesthetics rather than verse technique. Like so many 20th-century poets, Hardy's train of thought is often ambiguous, ironic or plain riddling, and he frequently relates a poem from more than one viewpoint or obliquely, at one person removed. This is very effective when read off the page or aloud, but to the composer it can present almost insuperable (insurmountable?) difficulties. Take, for example, 'The self-unseeing', discussed in the Introduction (pp. 5–6). This is a poem that has an inner complexity which music cannot hope to unravel. Finzi, in his setting in

Before and After Summer merely skates across its surface. You need time to stop and think in order to appreciate its full meaning. But the ongoing process of a song does not allow this luxury: the bird has already flown.

It can never be said of Finzi that he shirked his task in his choice of Hardy's lyrics. Most composers have confined themselves to the more pliant lyrics and ballads, such as 'Weathers', 'Her song', 'The market-girl' or 'The oxen'. Finzi tackled some of these, but in addition chose 'tremendous and unlikely poems' (Ferguson, 1968), such as 'Channel firing' and 'He abjures love' (both in *Before and After Summer*), 'At a lunar eclipse' (*Till Earth Outwears*) and 'The clock of the years' (*Earth and Air and Rain*), all poems which, to most composers, would appear to be impossible to set. At the same time, he was able to give new insight into poems that have always attracted composers: 'When I set out for Lyonnesse' and 'Rollicum-rorum'. In his three main songbooks, and particularly in *Earth and Air and Rain*, he effectively balances 'big' poems with lighter lyrics in a satisfying way.

I have deliberately avoided using the word 'song-cycle' when referring to these works, for, with the exception of *By Footpath and Stile*, these Hardy sequences are not song-cycles in the accepted sense. Though assembled with great care, there is no story line and no overall structural device, such as recurrent motives or motto themes, or musical cross-references; variety is more important than unity. Indeed, on the contents page of *A Young Man's Exhortation*, Finzi notes: 'Although designed as a cycle the two parts or any of the numbers can be sung separately'. They are, in effect, songbooks, and can be seen as one ongoing project; as soon as he had netted enough songs, he published them in three batches of ten, in 1933, 1936 and 1949.

On the other hand, *By Footpath and Stile* is a song-cycle, in which the final song, 'Exeunt omnes', draws the work together by references to previous songs. But it is a rather nondescript work. Like Butterworth's *Love blows as the wind blows*, it is scored for baritone voice with string quartet accompaniment, but lacks the incisive characterisation that Butterworth achieves. Harmonically it is wan and unadventurous, lacking any strong characterisation. The setting of the long 'graveyard' ballad, 'Voices from things growing in a churchyard' (the biggest song of the set) is strangely naïve for the usually sophisticated Finzi. The format is a series of disconnected strophes; the tree- and shrub-metamorphosed inhabitants of the churchyard lack any dramatic delineation, whilst the refrain, 'All night eerily', which should strike terror into the listener, is blandly unfrightening. And why does Eve Greensleeves share the same music as Fanny Hurd? There is no dramatic or poetic reason for this; it is a purely abstract musical device. *By Footpath and Stile* is an early work, written when the composer was in his early 20s. It was published in 1925, but Finzi was dissatisfied with it and withdrew it from Curwen's catalogue in 1934, having the stock and plates destroyed. Though he intended revising it, he had, by the time of his death, reworked only two of the six songs. It seems a pity, therefore, that it has been re-issued against the composer's instructions: it is juvenilia and can add nothing to the canon of mature Hardy settings.

Of the three mature sets that the composer published in his lifetime, the first, *A Young Man's Exhortation,* is structurally nearest to a true song-cycle. It falls into two parts, each headed with motto phrases from Psalm 89, the first – 'Mane floreat, et transeat' – consisting of songs showing various moods of youth and love, the second – 'Vespere decidat, induret, et arescat' – more philosophically retrospect, under the shadow of age. The songs range from the hymn-like 'Ditty' and ditty-like 'The sigh' to the graveyard setting of 'Transformations' (a shortened re-run of 'Voices of things growing in a churchyard'), through the rollicum-rorum of 'Budmouth dears' to the bleak, Holstian vision of 'The comet at Yell'ham'. In the latter, Finzi experiments with a texture without bar-lines – as he does in 'At a lunar eclipse' (*Till Earth Outwears*) which dates from the same time; stalking bass crotchets evoke a timelessness, remoteness and sense of distance. The naiveties that marred *By Footpath and Stile* can still be detected in 'Former beauties', where Hardy's words, 'Do they remember those gay times we trod', evoke too obviously a jig-like response. The most effective songs are 'Budmouth dears' and 'Shortening days'. 'Budmouth dears' is an uncharacteristically, but welcome, exhilarating song, each verse crowned with a high A for the tenor, and a tonality that veers cunningly between A major and its relative minor. In 'Shortening days' Finzi effectively accommodates Hardy's two irregular stanzas in his music, the first in a bar-less *senza misura* (cf. 'The comet at Yell'ham'), to capture the onset of autumn, and the second with a jogtrot bass to describe the coming of the cider-maker.

Earth and Air and Rain is the finest of his Hardy sequences. It is at once the most varied, unified and emotionally satisfying, and shows Finzi's imagination at its sustained best. The songs were written over a period of four years (1928–32) and the sequence published in 1936. The title is taken from the final line of the final song, and, after the variety of mood and experience that have been explored, the moment when we at last hear those key words is spine-tingling. The songs have been carefully ordered – starting and ending with references to singing birds – and the sequence centres around the key of D: six songs are in D (major or minor); the rest in keys closely related to D, with the exception of 'To Lizbie Browne' which stands conspicuously – and haughtily – apart in E-flat major. The penultimate song, 'In a churchyard', begins in D minor but ends in B minor in readiness for the final 'Proud songsters'. There are thematic resemblances between some of the songs that give the cycle added unification. The opening phrase of the first song, 'Summer schemes', is echoed (same pitch, same key) by the second phrase of 'Rollicum-rorum', and both find an echo in the refrain of 'Lizbie Browne': in addition, the middle section of the keystone song, 'The phantom', is echoed in the piano ritornello of the final song (Exs. 20.2(a), (b), (c), (d) and (e)).

Ex. 20.2(a)

When Law-yers strive to heal a breach, And Par-sons prac-tise   what they preach;

Ex. 20.2(b)

A tempo

Dear Liz-bie   Browne,

Ex. 20.2(c)

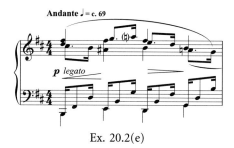

♩ = ♩. **Ma un poco meno mosso** ♩ = 76

mp   *legato*

Ex. 20.2(d)

Andante ♩ = c. 69

p legato

Ex. 20.2(e)

Though the individual songs can be performed separately – 'Rollicum-rorum' was, in fact, published separately – they make their greatest impact in the context of the sequence. Indeed, though Finzi did not call this a 'song-cycle' it is one to all intents and purposes.

'Summer schemes' is deservedly one of Finzi's most popular songs with singers. He sets Hardy's two six-line stanzas in varied strophic form, slowing down the singer's *allegro* momentum at the refrain to match the ironic questioning of Hardy's text, but varying the music of that refrain the second time round. 'When I set out for Lyonnesse' is the first of the two 'popular' songs in the set. Finzi treats the three stanzas as a quiet, mysterious march, over which the singer descants an arioso line. The central verse has an Elgarian ring to it – in atmosphere, it is akin to the 2nd *Pomp and Circumstance March* in A minor. It will be noted that when the singer-poet returns in verse 3 from the fabled land of Lyonnesse, he does so initially not in the key in which he set out (E minor) but in a bright E-flat major, for he has 'magic in his eyes'. 'Waiting both' is one of those spare-textured songs that recur throughout Finzi's output, a texture usually associated with poetry concerned with remote worlds: night skies and stars, as here, indeed. Significantly, the descending phrases of overlapping arpeggios which permeate the song appear in 'To a poet' at the words, 'I send my soul through time and space' (Ex. 20.3(a) and (b)).

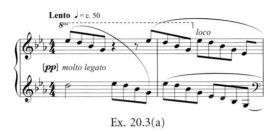

Ex. 20.3(a)

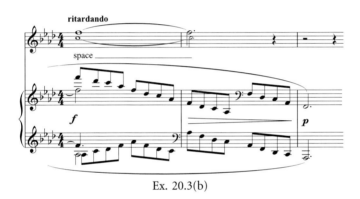

Ex. 20.3(b)

'The phantom' is a brave – perhaps 'fool-Hardy' – poem to set to music. But Finzi skilfully manages to illustrate in vivid musical terms the drama of the 'care-worn' man who sees a vision of a 'ghost-girl-rider', 'a phantom of his own figuring'. In the normally diatonic context of Finzi's idiom, the sliding chromatic harmonies at the words 'And though, toil-tried,/He withers daily' are unexpected and for that reason very striking. However, one cannot help feeling that compared, for example, with Wolf's 'Der Feuerreiter', Finzi's phantom horse-rider seems insipid, lacking horror or fearsomeness. 'So I have fared' – Hardy's own title is 'After reading Psalms XXXIX, XL, etc.' – is one of the composer's finest inventions. Hardy has constructed for this sad little life-story a macaronic text, ending each short stanza with a wryly ironic quotation from the Latin version of the Psalms. Finzi adds the following note to his setting: 'This recitative should be sung with the flexibility and freedom of ordinary speech, and the crotchet should approximate to the reciting tone of Anglican chant'. Anglican chant is the clue to the song, and poem and setting match each other perfectly (Ex. 20.4).

Ex. 20.4

'Rollicum-rorum' is the lyric that Hardy included in chapter 5 of the narrative of his novel *The Trumpet-Major* (1880), set during the Napoleonic Wars:

> Sergeant Stanner . . . who was recruiting at Budmouth, began a satirical song:–
>   'When lawyers strive to heal a breach . . .'

The singing sergeant sang thirteen verses, but fortunately for Finzi – and the rest of us – Hardy printed only four of them: it would otherwise have been a very long song. The setting shows that Finzi, when minded to, could write a genuinely popular ballad, a full-blooded song-with-chorus in the great English tradition running from medieval drinking-songs through 18th-century patriotic sea-songs to the sociable songs of Stanford and Warlock. Characteristic subtleties give it its individuality: the extra beats inserted to break the regular flow; the piano interludes, never the same, which keep the ear guessing. Rather perversely, Finzi himself considered this and 'To Lizbie Browne' 'the two worst songs in the set' (Banfield, 1997: 208). That exquisite love-lyric, 'Lizbie Browne', with its chiming refrains framing each stanza, is on the surface a poem that seems to call out for musical setting. But closer reading will reveal the very refrain to be a problem, for it is repeated *eighteen* times. How does the song-composer counter the monotony which this inevitably presents? Finzi, I think, just manages to avoid it, by skilful rhythmic and melodic variation and in the way he allows the opening refrain-line to run on to the next line, thus breaking the caging symmetry. The winsome, flirtatious nature of Hardy's poem is perfectly encapsulated in the final, questioning piano phrase, 'left in the air' (Ex. 20.5).

Ex. 20.5

Hardy prefaces 'The clock of the years' with words from the *Book of Job*: 'A spirit passed before my face; the hair of my flesh stood up.' In this fantasy poem, the spirit can make time go backwards, but only at his own whim. So the poet's beloved is brought back from the dead, then taken back to her youth and childhood and babyhood until she is 'nought at all':

> And it was as if
> She had never been.

Finzi creates from this disturbing fable a short dramatic cantata in several sections, some of a recitative-like character, others more arioso, framed by a dramatic rush-up-the-scale on the piano. Finzi's genius in handling what for most composers would be an intractable poem is in evidence throughout the song: notice, for example, the masterly way in which he moves from duple to triple metre at the words, 'He shook his head:/No stop was there', and the way he deliberately builds pauses and silences into his texture. 'In a churchyard' is yet another of Hardy's graveyard fantasies, commenting on the lot of those 'whom kindly earth/Secludes from view'. Here it is the church's old yew tree that speaks the first four verses, whilst the poet adds a short final comment in the last. Finzi makes this quite clear in his setting, by a change of texture (lapping arpeggios) and tonality (D major) for the final verse. The song has an unsettled feeling, not inherent in the poem, brought about by its restless tonality: within five short verses the tonal centre travels through D minor, B minor, B-flat minor, D-flat major, D major and back to B minor. Finzi's interpretation of the fourth verse calls for comment. When the dead pray 'That no God trumpet us to rise/We truly hope', the piano underlines the passage with a blazing D-flat major fanfare. This is what might be termed 'phantom word-painting', describing as it does something that does not happen. (It has a perfectly good lineage, including John Dowland's song, 'Sorrow, stay', where there are a series of falling/rising phrases at the words, 'Down and arise . . . I never shall'.) 'Proud songsters' (subtitled 'Thrushes, Finches and Nightingales') was one of the last poems that Hardy wrote – it was first published in *The Daily Telegraph* in April 1928, three months after the poet's death – and one of the poems set by Britten in *Winter Words*. The song is a fine example of the spaciousness of Finzi's songwriting, the two brief stanzas built up into a large-scale song. The setting falls into two distinct parts. The first stanza is framed by a long piano ritornello characterised by the rhythm: ♩ ♩ ; the second stanza is in Finzi's *nobilmente* vein, tenderly elegiac, and the song ends with a brief, heart-rending reference to the music of the opening ritornello. Britten's setting of the poem lasts less than a minute; Finzi's nearly three-and-a-half minutes. Britten's is joyful; Finzi's elegiac. Both are perfectly valid settings of Hardy's text, yet one is left marvelling how the same poem can elicit such completely different responses. Some may feel that Finzi's song is over-extended, but as Banfield has pointed out (1985: 291), it has to bear the weight of the emotions of all the previous songs. [For a fuller comparison of the two settings, see Introduction, pp. 15–16.]

Compared with *Earth and Air and Rain*, *Before and After Summer* lacks variety. The theme of the sequence is summed up in the title, taken from the second song, but the concern is more with *after*-summer than *before*; there is certainly little summer in between. Indeed, *The Curtain Falls* might have been a more appropriate title, and two of the poems pick up this image:

> And night-time calls,
> And the curtain falls
>   'The too short time' ['The best she could']

> But after love what comes?
> A scene that lours,
> A few sad hours,
> And then, the curtain.
>   'He abjures love'

Many of the songs share this dour, fatalistic philosophy, whilst the rest are imbued with a sad melancholy. There are no outgoing, optimistic songs, such as 'When I set out for Lyonnesse' or 'Rollicum-rorum'; the nearest we come to light relief is in 'Epeisodia' which, with its cod pastoral dance (in the outer 'country' verses) and march (in the central 'town' verse), is a little too naïve and facile. 'Amabel', which refrains the girl-in-question's name, is a sequel to 'To Lizbie Browne', but neither poem nor setting are of comparable quality. One questions Finzi's judgement in the choice of some of the poems. 'The self-unseeing' has already been discussed in this context, though one must admit that there is a neat irony in the way it has been positioned next to 'Overlooking the river' in the sequence: in the first poem the poet regrets that he was 'looking away', in the second he wishes that he *had* been looking away. 'He abjures love' is one of Hardy's most revealing poems, a philosophical statement couched in lyrical language, but not the sort of lyricism apt for musical setting. The language is too dense to lend itself easily to singing. What can music do to the complexities of such a poem? It can be no more than meretricious ornament. On the other hand, the big central song, 'Channel firing', appears at first glance a strange choice for song treatment – it describes the effects of gunnery practice at sea on the coffined inhabitants of a churchyard – but does contain in its bleak images a lyrical core which Finzi has skilfully revealed. The 'gun-firing' motive heard in the opening bars acts as a ritornello to draw all the pieces of the jigsaw together (Ex. 20.6). The result if one of his most original songs, at once frightening and, in its black humour, wryly amusing.

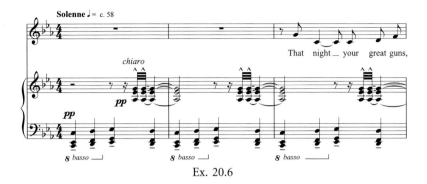

Ex. 20.6

A Young Man's Exhortation, Earth and Air and Rain and *Before and After Summer* have a unity to them. The two Hardy collections gathered together posthumously, *Till Earth Outwears* (*1958*), for tenor and piano, and *I Said to Love* (*1958*), for baritone and piano, have no such accord. The songs in *Till Earth Outwears* span a period of nearly 30 years, the earliest, 'The market-girl', written in 1927 and the latest, 'It never looks like summer', in 1956. Two of the songs are outstanding. 'At a lunar eclipse' is a sequel to 'The comet at Yell'ham'. Unusual for Hardy, the poem is in sonnet-form, and with no stanzas to guide (or restrict) him, Finzi sets it as a through-composed song. The piano has an enigmatic fugally-motivated processional idea, without bar-lines or time signature – something that would have delighted Holst, whose Hardy-inspired tone poem, *Egdon Heath*, had been written two years earlier (Ex. 20.7).

Ex. 20.7

Over this march-like tread the singer declaims the poem, sometimes picking up the fugue subject, at other times, particularly in the final lines, rising to eloquent declamation, a modern version of the Purcellian air-over-a-ground. Of quite different character, but even more successful, is 'In years defaced', one of Hardy's most poignant love-poems (his own title was 'A spot'), from which the sequence takes its title. The song is a good example of Finzi's skill at unifying a through-composed song. The mysterious, somewhat nondescript prelude is the key to the setting (Ex. 20.8(a)).

Ex. 20.8(a)

The motive 'x' is immediately picked up and expanded by the singer; between verses 1 and 3 it is developed as a piano interlude; then, at the words 'O not again/Till Earth outwears', it effects the climax of the song, and by doing so 'explains' the mysterious opening bars. This climax, with its leaning appoggiaturas and a vocal line soaring unexpectedly to a high A on the word 'Earth', is one of the most sublime moments in Finzi's music – a literal 'raising of the voice', as welcome as it is rare (Ex. 20.8(b)).

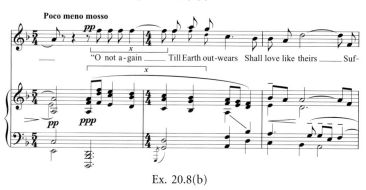

Ex. 20.8(b)

The songs in the baritone set, *I Said to Love,* again differ widely in date, from 'Two lips' (1928) to 'At middle-field gate in February', 'In five-score summers' and the title song, all of which were written in Finzi's last, productive year. In style they range from the folk-like simplicity of 'Two lips' and 'For life I had never cared greatly' to the drama and sophistication of the title song. The three songs written in 1956 call for comment for different reasons. In the case of 'In five-score summers' it is the choice of text. Hardy writing in 1867 is looking forward to life a century later – indeed, his own title for the poem is '1967' – in his most cynical, worm-haunted mode:

> . . . I would only ask thereof
> That thy worm should be my worm, Love!

It is not one of Hardy's best poems, nor is it suitable as a song-lyric. Finzi's setting is nondescript save for the opening vocal line, which is almost Lisztian in its creeping chromaticism. Perhaps it is a satirical response to Hardy's satirical jabs at the novelties of the new century (Ex. 20.9)?

Ex. 20.9

More effective is 'At middle-field gate in February'. Here Finzi captures Hardy's wet, muddy landscape with perfect matching music. The vocal line, centred round a small gamut of notes, drifts up and down over a 'Saturn'-like pendulum swing of chords (Ex. 20.10).

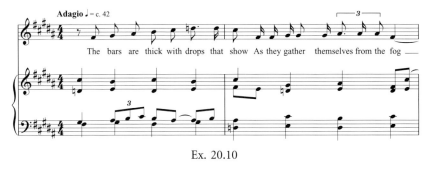

Ex. 20.10

Even the raise of pitch up a tone for the second verse fails to alleviate the dreariness of the scene. As its title suggests, 'I said to love' is a one-way conversation between the poet and Love: perhaps 'harangue' might be a better word. The poet sees Love as ageing like himself and Mankind: no longer 'the Boy, the Bright, the One/Who spread a heaven beneath the Sun', but a being with 'features pitiless,/And iron daggers of distress'. He orders Love to depart, even though it will mean 'Mankind shall cease'. Finzi's song is dated '12 July 1956', which makes it his final Hardy setting, and with hindsight it can be seen to epitomise the entire canon, showing Finzi's songwriting gifts at their best. Music fits the words like a glove: the refrain-lines which, subtly altered, frame each of the four stanzas, receive similar subtle alteration in the music. Beginning with bare 'anonymous' octaves, the piano accompaniment shadows and enlightens every nuance of Hardy's text without obtruding. Then comes a surprise. After the peremptory order, 'Depart then, Love!' at the beginning of the final verse, the piano goes berserk, breaking out into a bravura, double-octave cadenza, *deliberato, pesante*. The effect is unexpected and baffling. But what it does is to focus attention on the searing words of the final stanza: 'Man's race shall perish, threatenest thou,/Without thy kindling coupling-vow?' The element of surprise is not often found in Finzi: it is always welcome.

Finzi's Hardy settings are one of the major contributions to the English Romantic Song repertoire. They were, as we have seen, a coming-together, if not an actual collaboration, of like minds and philosophies. Yet there is something in Finzi's settings of Hardy which leaves the listener unsatisfied. For although Finzi mirrors Hardy's metric patterns and melodic structures so impeccably, he often fails to reach the inner heart of the poems. Finzi's musical idiom is extremely narrow and restricted; Hardy's resources on the other hand are enormously wide-ranging. Finzi smoothes out the ruggedness of Hardy's poetry: he irons out the irony, captures the melancholy but not always the bitterness. There is a marshmallow centre to Finzi's music that does not match Hardy's bleak, granite-like vision. Instead of a bare moorland landscape we have a cosy countryside of hills and dales. Finzi's music emasculates Hardy's verse, drawing all his harsh but colourful moods into a monochrome uniformity. One cannot help comparing Finzi's monochromatic settings with the colourful vitality of Britten's *Winter Words*. In the end, it comes down to this incontrovertible fact: Hardy was a greater poet than Finzi was a composer. It needs a songwriter of the calibre of Britten to do his poetry full justice. Sadly Britten's *Winter Words* was his only excursion into Hardy's poetry. The definitive song-settings of Hardy are still to come.

Settings of poets other than Hardy

Though the Hardy songs form the bulk of Finzi's song-output, he was by no means a one-poet-composer. Indeed, he is probably best known to the general public for his Shakespeare cycle, *Let Us Garlands Bring*, and treasured most for his Traherne sequence, *Dies Natalis*. In many ways the writings of Thomas Traherne (1637–74) match Finzi's musical gifts better than Hardy. If Hardy's vision is a bleak one, of regret for wrong paths taken in youth, the disillusion of old age, and a stoical cynicism about the ways of the world, Traherne's is an ecstatic vision, of the Lost Eden of Childhood and Infancy, one that, despite regrets, can sustain and cheer him through adult life. It is a vision he shared with many other English writers, such as Wordsworth and Clare, but few of these writers achieve the rapture that Traherne manages to bring to his poetry and prose. *Dies Natalis* ('The Birth-Day') sets three of Traherne's poems and an extract from his prose work, *Centuries of Meditation*, all looking back to what Banfield calls 'a personally epiphanic past' (1985: 394). The nearest equivalent that we have in English song to *Dies Natalis* is Tippett's *Boyhood's End* (1943), the setting of a prose passage from W. H. Hudson's autobiography, *Far Away and Long Ago*. But whereas Hudson's words are firmly rooted in the there-and-then of his boyhood on the Argentinean pampas, Traherne's writings are an autobiography of his spiritual life.

Ex. 20.11

Like so many of Finzi's works, *Dies Natalis* (*1939*) had a prolonged gestation. Two of the songs, 'Rhapsody' and 'The salutation', and the instrumental 'Intrada' were composed by 1926; 'The rapture', the central song of the sequence, in 1939. The work is scored for high voice and string orchestra, a choice of accompaniment well suited to Finzi's contrapuntal way of thought. The ternary-form 'Intrada' is based on the musical material of the ensuing song – it was almost certainly written *after* that song, though Banfield (1997: 250–1) thinks otherwise – and leads neatly and naturally into the 'Rhapsody'. Finzi subtitles this 'Recitativo stromentato' (= instrumental recitative). Indeed, he subtitles all of the movements, as though he saw the cycle in formal, almost abstract terms. Though setting prose rather than poetry, Finzi is completely at ease, and the song is one of the finest examples of his gift for fusing vocal line and the inflections of speech. I can think of few examples in the English song repertoire where prose is set with such assurance. Particularly admirable is his treatment of the many polysyllabic words in the text, reminding us that Finzi's great gift as a song-composer was his ability to encompass the natural speech-rhythms of the English language. The setting of the paragraph beginning 'The corn was orient and immortal wheat' is one of the most sublime in English song (Ex. 20.11); anyone who fails to be moved by the disarming simplicity of the coda to this song is beyond all hope. 'The rapture' which follows is one of the composer's most outgoing and joyful songs. It is subtitled 'Danza', and dance it does, with ecstatic trills and bouncing bass to capture the rapturous apostrophes of the poem. It is cast in ritornello form, the music rising to a climax at the words 'O how Divine/Am I!' The effect is made even more telling by the quasi recitative that follows with the final words 'Who mine/Did make the same!/ What hand divine!' 'Wonder', by contrast, is a gentle, contrapuntally-worked song, scored for muted strings with, in the second verse, a solo violin sailing 'The skies in their Magnificence'. Its ternary form is punctuated by exquisitely beautiful cadences into D major. The subtitle, 'Arioso', and the cadences of this G minor-rooted song onto its dominant, suggest a direct link to the 'Aria' that follows. In this setting of the poem 'The salutation', Finzi uses a technique modelled on the Bachian chorale-prelude: a singing 'Air on the G string' over a steady crotchet bass, above which the singer declaims the poem in flowing musical prose, the two elements neatly counterpointing each other up to the final, inevitable cadence. The resulting sound, with its sighing sequential 7ths and *nobilmente* atmosphere, is as close to Parry or Elgar as Bach. In *Dies Natalis* Finzi displays the finest qualities of his craft: a choice of poetry ideally suited to his music, and a balance between musical and poetical demands. It was the work that established his reputation after its initial wartime performances, and is arguably his finest achievement in the field of solo song; many would say it is his masterpiece.

The use of a diptych format in the final two songs links *Dies Natalis* with *Farewell to Arms*, for tenor and small orchestra, which is laid out as a Baroque-style Recitative and Aria. The choice of poems is both unusual and ingenious, for the first, 'The helmet now an hive for bees becomes' by Ralph Knevet (1600–71) is an extended meditation on the second stanza of George Peele's famous lyric, 'His golden locks Time hath to silver turned'. Together they form a commentary on each other, celebrating the end of war and the anticipation of a peaceful future. The idea of a diptych, however, must have been an after-thought. We know that Finzi set Peele's poem in 1926; Knevet's poem only became known to him through Norman Ault's *A Treasury of Unfamiliar Lyrics*, published in 1938: his setting dates from c.1944. In its final form the two songs are linked together: the F-sharp minor of the recitative-like 'Introduction' cadencing in E major in readiness for the A major tonality of the 'Aria'. By working backwards, he makes use of motives from the ritornello of the Aria to furnish accompanimental material for the Introduction, something he had already done with the 'Intrada' and 'Rhapsody' in *Dies Natalis*. Use of a musical 'head-piece', like the beehives/helmets in the poem, binds the two together, and this connection is made even more explicit in the bars before fig. 2. As in the final song of *Dies Natalis*, the Aria uses chorale prelude technique, though it is perhaps a more overt pastiche of Bach than 'The salutation'. This diptych is one of Finzi's most attractive and satisfying works, and unjustly neglected.

Also dating from the late 1920s is *Two Sonnets of John Milton* (1928, *1936*) for high voice and small orchestra, which he dedicated to fellow-composer Edmund Rubbra. Unlike *Farewell to Arms*, these settings – of 'When I consider' and 'How soon hath Time?' – are not united as a diptych, though both poems are linked by the themes of mortality, the loss of youth and the oncoming of physical disability. In their relentless contrapuntal textures, meandering crotchet tread and rather restricted harmonic language, in conjunction with a lack of musical contrast and an overall lugubrious solemn-seriousness, they show the less attractive side of Finzi's art.

Let Us Garlands Bring (*1942*) was begun in 1929 ('Fear no more the heat of the sun') but not completed until 1942 when it was offered as a gift to Vaughan Williams on his 70th birthday. There are two performing versions, one with piano, the other with string orchestra, both with baritone soloist. Though the piano version is the one most often heard, the string version is more effective in places. It is the most popular of all Finzi's vocal works, undemanding to listen to, traditional in conception, with catchy tunes and simple song-forms. Like Quilter's Shakespeare sets, it is a songbook rather than a cycle, the five settings (of song-lyrics from four different plays) arranged to give maximum contrast

Ex. 20.12

and variety. With the Shakespeare settings of Quilter and Warlock, they represent the finest early 20th-century interpretations of Shakespeare's song-lyrics. The 'sad-cypress', 'yew-stuck' imagery of 'Come away, come away, death' is captured in a solemn tread of chords with sharp semitonal dissonances at the key words. The vocal line, characterised by a ♩ ♪ ♩ ♩ rhythm, follows a distinctive Finzi contour, of a musical phrase rising by step followed by a leap. Unusual, however, is the long melisma on the final phrase, 'Weep there', which is almost indulgently histrionic for so normally understated a composer as Finzi (Ex. 20.12). 'Who is Silvia?' – Thurio's song from Act IV of *The Two Gentlemen of Verona* – has been set, some would say, once and for all by Schubert, but Finzi justifies his reinterpretation. The lady-in-question is serenaded in a lilting dance-song, full of Scotch-snap rhythms and with unexpected extensions to the metre at the verse cadences. Its three stanzas are fashioned into a ternary-form song. The famous Dirge from Act IV of *Cymbeline*, 'Fear no more the heat of the sun', is the keystone of the group. He treats the poem as a stately sarabande, which gives the setting a powerful ritualistic quality, like a Dance of Death. This is certainly a song that gains from the rich, sustained textures of the string orchestra; the unvaried rhythms can give the piano version a monotonous plod. 'O mistress mine' (like 'Come away, come away, death', one of Feste's songs from *Twelfth Night*) is one of the finest settings of this often-set lyric. Finzi creates a rustic serenade: over a strummed-*pizzicato* accompaniment, two fiddlers play a perky two-part counterpoint, against which the singer has a slowly moving *legato* line running like a chorale melody (Ex. 20.13).

Ex. 20.13

The onward flow of each verse is halted at the epigrammatic concluding lines that are consequently given prominence:

> Every wise man's son doth know . . .
> Youth's a stuff will not endure.

Despite the completely different nature of the poems, there is a strong resemblance between this rustic love-song and the ecstatic 'infant joy' of 'The rapture' in *Dies Natalis*. 'It was a lover and his lass', the lyric sung to Touchstone by two pages in Act V of *As You Like It*, is another frequently-set lyric. It is the least original song in the sequence – the syncopated rhythmic formula in the piano is too much of a cliché to bear the repetition that Finzi requires of it – but it is eminently singable, and popular with singers. Like Quilter in his earlier setting, Finzi creates a ternary structure from the four stanzas, with new music and a gentler pace for the penultimate verse.

The two posthumously published song collections, *To a Poet* (1965) for baritone and piano, and *Oh Fair to See* (1966) for tenor and piano, are both mixed anthologies, mostly of 20th-century poets, including Flecker, de la Mare, Blunden, Bridges and George Barker. The settings span a period of more than thirty years. The title song of the first collection is a setting of James Elroy Flecker's poem, 'To a poet a thousand years hence' (see epigraph), one of the most haunting of the many Time-haunted poems in English literature, linking as it does Time Present (the poet now writing), Time Past (old Maeonides, i.e. Homer, writing three thousand years ago) and Time Future (the unborn poet who will be writing a thousand years hence). It is also an affirmation of the importance, the 'survival value', of great works of art, whether poetry, music or sculpture. Those words meant a great deal to Finzi. In June 1951, after he had learned that he was suffering from an incurable illness with possibly only another ten years to live, he wrote:

> I like to think that in each generation may be found a few responsive minds, and for them I should still like my work to be available. To shake hands with a good friend over the centuries is a pleasant thing, and the affection which an individual may retain after his departure is perhaps the only thing which guarantees an ultimate life to his work.

It is one of Finzi's biggest songs, four-and-a-half minutes long, and almost a mini-cantata in scale. The piano prelude opens with a fanfare-like idea, like horns and trumpets echoing from a remote past. Each of the six stanzas is set to different music, ranging from recitative-like drama ('How shall we conquer?') to hymn-like simplicity ('O friend unseen, unborn, unknown'), the final verse coming full-circle to the horn-calls of the opening (Ex. 20.14).

Ex. 20.14

Equally large-scale, if not so satisfactory, is the setting of George Barker's 'Ode on the rejection of St. Cecilia' of 1948, a complementary commentary on the full-scale choral-orchestral ode *For St. Cecilia* to Blunden's text that the composer had composed in the previous year. The rather brutal, negative sentiments of the poem – suggesting that silence is preferable to music in an age like ours – are not quite in tune with Finzi's philosophy, but he gives the work as brutal a modernism as he is able within his politely refined style. He sets the poem as a long arioso, the musical equivalent of prose, in contrast to the neat formality of his normal songs, and we hear an eclectic, fragmentary mix of fanfare, funeral march and chorale elements. In its choice of 'big' subject-matter and its histrionic, almost snorting posturings, it reminds us of the philosophical songs of Parry, such as 'When the sun's great orb' and 'Whence?'. *Oh Fair to See* contains, in addition to two settings of poems by Edmund Blunden, a setting of Ivor Gurney's 'Only the wanderer'. Bearing in mind the 'definitiveness' of Gurney's own version of this poem, 'Severn meadows', it seems a strange choice; but Finzi's song dates from 1925, before he was aware of the Gurney setting, which was not published until 1928. The outstanding song of the collection is 'Harvest', written in 1956. In the poem, Blunden sees harvest as a metaphor for his own life: a creative harvest that has not come to its hoped-for fruition. Perhaps Finzi also saw the poem as a reflected metaphor; if so, prophetically, for within a few months of writing it he was dead.

As a songwriter Finzi presents a dilemma to the listener and critic. His musical style is ultra-conservative; his harmonic and textural resources are limited, and at his worse he displays a genius for unmemorability. But his positive attributes more than counter these shortcomings. Of all English songwriters, Ivor Gurney not excepted, he is the 'poet's composer'. If Hugo Wolf had, indeed, set up a *Poetic Supremacy Act* in 1888 with his Goethe settings (Northcote, 1966: 15), then it would have been Finzi who carried his English banner. His care, consideration and almost aristocratic sensitivity towards his texts, not only in interpreting them faithfully but in setting them in music which follows 'just note and accent', is unsurpassed in English song. It is a delight in itself to follow the poet's text whilst listening to a Finzi song, in order to admire the way he magically transforms the contours and rhythms of the poetry into the contours and rhythms of music. Nor was he afraid to set poetry that others might consider too 'perfect' and 'complete' for musical setting – 'self-sufficient' as Larkin's egg. He would set the finest poetry on the understanding that he was moved by it and could find the music within himself to transform it into song. One of his greatest achievements is *Dies Natalis*. Few English composers have been able to evoke the feeling of rapture in their songs as Finzi in this work. Perhaps Michael Tippett is his nearest rival. But whereas Tippett, at the point of ecstasy, has to go beyond words into vocalisation, Finzi manages to achieve the sensation with and through words (Ex. 20.15). In a letter to his fellow-composer, William Busch (8th October 1938), Finzi wrote: 'I shd really feel suicidal if I didn't know that a song outlasts a dynasty'. If any song will outlast a dynasty, then surely it is this one.

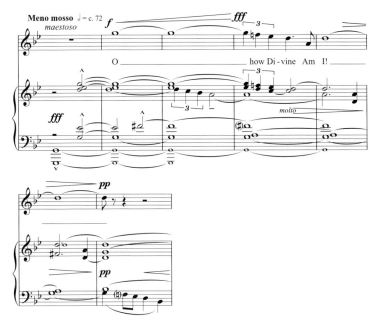

Ex. 20.15

Appendix 1
Chronological Check-list of English Song-Composers, Parry to Finzi

Hubert **PARRY**	(1848–1918)	Norman O'NEILL	(1875–1934)
Frances ALLITSEN	(1848–1912)	Cyril ROOTHAM	(1875–1938)
Arthur Goring THOMAS	(1850–1892)	Martin SHAW	(1875–1958)
Frederick CORDER	(1852–1932)	Donald TOVEY	(1875–1940)
Frederick COWEN	(1852–1935)	William HURLSTONE	(1876–1906)
Charles Villiers **STANFORD**	(1852–1924)	Teresa del RIEGO	(1876–1968)
Maude Valérie WHITE	(1855–1937)	W. G. WHITTAKER	(1876–1944)
Edward **ELGAR**	(1857–1934)	Thomas DUNHILL	(1877–1946)
Marjorie KENNEDY-FRASER	(1857–1930)	H. Balfour GARDINER	(1877–1950)
Robert BRYAN	(1858–1920)	Graham PEEL	(1877–1937)
Ethel SMYTH	(1858–1944)	Roger **QUILTER**	(1877–1953)
Amy WOODFORDE-FINDEN	(1860–1919)	Rutland BOUGHTON	(1878–1960)
Frederick **DELIUS**	(1862–1934)	Joseph HOLBROOKE	(1878–1958)
Edward GERMAN	(1862–1936)	Wilfrid SANDERSON	(1878–1935)
Liza LEHMANN	(1862–1918)	Frank **BRIDGE**	(1879–1941)
Arthur **SOMERVELL**	(1863–1937)	Hamilton HARTY	(1879–1941)
Herbert BREWER	(1865–1928)	John **IRELAND**	(1879–1962)
William Edmonstoune DUNCAN		Harold SAMUEL	(1879–1937)
	(1866–1920)	Cyril SCOTT	(1879–1970)
Charles WOOD	(1866–1926)	Bryceson TREHARNE	(1879–1948)
Herbert BEDFORD	(1867–1945)	John FOULDS	(1880–1939)
Granville BANTOCK	(1868–1946)	Francis George SCOTT	(1880–1958)
Hamish MacCUNN	(1868–1916)	Frederick KELLY	(1881–1916)
H. Walford DAVIES	(1869–1941)	Percy GRAINGER	(1882–1961)
J. Michael DIACK	(1869–1946)	Herbert HUGHES	(1882–1937)
Ernest WALKER	(1870–1949)	Easthope MARTIN	(1882–1925)
Frederick KEEL	(1871–1954)	Haydn WOOD	(1882–1959)
H. Lane WILSON	(1871–1915)	Arnold **BAX**	(1883–1953)
Frederic AUSTIN	(1872–1952)	Gerald (Lord) BERNERS	(1883–1950)
Ralph **VAUGHAN WILLIAMS**	(1872–1958)	Clive CAREY	(1883–1968)
Richard WALTHEW	(1872–1951)	York BOWEN	(1884–1961)
Landon RONALD	(1873–1938)	Christabel MARILLIER	(1883–1976)
Edward BAIRSTOW	(1874–1946)	Felix WHITE	(1884–1945)
Fritz HART	(1874–1949)	George **BUTTERWORTH**	(1885–1916)
Gustav **HOLST**	(1874–1934)	Benjamin DALE	(1885–1943)
Hugh S. ROBERTON	(1874–1952)	Ernest FARRAR	(1885–1918)
H. Waldo WARNER	(1874–1945)	Julius HARRISON	(1885–1963)
Samuel COLERIDGE-TAYLOR	(1875–1912)	Montague PHILLIPS	(1885–1969)

Rebecca CLARKE	(1886–1979)	Greville COOKE	(1894–1989)
Eric COATES	(1886–1957)	E. J. **MOERAN**	(1894–1950)
Norman PETERKIN	(1886–1982)	Peter **WARLOCK**	(1894–1930)
Bernard van DIEREN	(1886–1936)	Gordon JACOB	(1895–1984)
Maurice BESLY	(1888–1945)	Michael MULLINAR	(1895–1973)
W. Denis **BROWNE**	(1888–1915)	Maurice JACOBSON	(1896–1976)
Cecil COLES	(1888–1918)	W. S. Gwynn WILLIAMS	(1896–1978)
C. Armstrong **GIBBS**	(1889–1960)	Harry GILL	(1897–1987)
Ivor **GURNEY**	(1890–1937)	William BAINES	(1899–1922)
Arthur BLISS	(1891–1975)	Hubert FOSS	(1899–1953)
Benjamin BURROWS	(1891–1966)	Patrick HADLEY	(1899–1973)
Malcolm DAVIDSON	(1891–1947)	Mark RAPHAEL	(1899–1988)
Morfydd OWEN	(1891–1918)	Alan BUSH	(1900–1995)
Herbert **HOWELLS**	(1892–1983)	Michael HEAD	(1900–1976)
Reginald REDMAN	(1892–1972)	Maurice JOHNSTON	(1900–1976)
Alec ROWLEY	(1892–1958)	Eric THIMAN	(1900–1975)
D. M. STEWART	(1892–1975)	David WYNNE	(1900–1983)
Arthur BENJAMIN	(1893–1960)	William BUSCH	(1901–1945)
Eugene GOOSSENS	(1893–1962)	Victor HELY-HUTCHINSON	(1901–1947)
Ivor NOVELLO	(1893–1951)	Edmund RUBBRA	(1901–1986)
C. W. **ORR**	(1893–1976)	Gerald **FINZI**	(1901–1956)

Appendix 2
Principal Music Publishers

Many of the original publishers have been taken over by other firms. The present catalogue holders are listed below:

Ashdown = Music Sales Ltd
Ascherberg, Hopwood and Crew = International Music Publications Ltd
Augener = Stainer & Bell Ltd/Roberton Publications
Boosey = Boosey & Hawkes Music Publishers Ltd
Chappell = International Music Publications Ltd
Chester = Music Sales Ltd
Curwen = Music Sales Ltd/William Elkin Music Services
Elkin = Music Sales Ltd
Enoch = Roberton Publications/William Elkin Music Services
Galliard = Stainer & Bell Ltd
Hawkes = Boosey & Hawkes Music Publishers Ltd
Lengnick = Complete Music Ltd
Murdoch, Murdoch & Co. = International Music Publications Ltd
Novello = Music Sales Ltd
Keith Prowse = EMI Music Publishing Ltd
Winthrop Rogers = Boosey & Hawkes Music Publishing Ltd
Thames Publishing = William Elkin Music Services
Tischer & Jagenberg = Oxford University Press Music Department
Weinberger = William Elkin Music Services
Joseph Williams = Stainer & Bell Ltd

Abbreviations used: B&H = Boosey & Hawkes; OUP = Oxford University Press; S&B = Stainer & Bell.

For fuller details of currently available publications, see Michael Pilkington, *English Solo Song: Guides to the Repertoire* (1989–97) and *English Solo Song: a Guide [to] Songs Currently Available* (1997).

PARRY   Augener; Novello.
 Musica Britannica XLIX, S&B, 1982, contains a comprehensive selection of Parry's songs. Other collections: *Seven Songs*, S&B, 1979; *Twenty English Lyrics* (2 vols.), Thames, 1998.
STANFORD   Augener; Boosey; Chappell; Cramer; Enoch; Novello; S&B.
 Musica Britannica LII, S&B, 1986, contains a comprehensive selection of Stanford's songs. Other collections include: *Six Songs*, S&B, 1979.

ELGAR   Ascherberg, Hopwood & Crew; Boosey; Novello.
   Collections: *Sea-Pictures*, Boosey, 1899; *The Elgar Song Album*, Novello, 1984; *Thirteen Songs* (2 vols.), Thames, 1987.

DELIUS   Augener; OUP; Winthrop Rogers; Tischer & Jagenberg.
   Collections: *Twenty-two Songs* (*Complete Works*, vol. 18a), S&B, 1987; *Sixteen Songs* (*Complete Works*, vol. 18b), B&H, 1987; *Nineteen Songs* (*Complete Works*, vol. 19), OUP, 1987; *Song Album*, B&H, 1968; *Ten Songs*, S&B, 1973.

SOMERVELL   Boosey; Thames.
Collections: *Maud*, Boosey, 1898; *Love in Springtime*, Boosey, 1901; *A Shropshire Lad*, Boosey, 1904.

VAUGHAN WILLIAMS   Ashdown; Boosey; Curwen; OUP; Prowse; S&B.
   Collections: *Song Album* (2 vols.), B&H, 1985, 1990; *Collected Songs* (3 vols.), OUP, 1993.

HOLST   Ashdown; Augener; Bosworth; Chester; S&B.
   Collections: *Twelve Humbert Wolfe Songs*, Galliard, 1969; *Rig Veda*, Opus 24, Chester, 1920.

QUILTER   Ascherberg, Hopwood & Crew; B&H; Chappell; Curwen; Elkin; Forsyth; Winthrop Rogers.
   Collections: *Three Shakespeare Songs*, Op 6, B&H, 1905; *To Julia*, Op 8, B&H, 1906; *Seven Elizabethan Lyrics*, Op 12, B&H, 1908; *Five Shakespeare Songs*, Op 23, B&H, 1921; *Twelve Songs*, Thames, 1996.

BRIDGE   Chappell; Winthrop Rogers.
   Collections: *Four Songs*, Galliard, 1974; *[22] Songs*, B&H, 1980; *Five Early Songs*, Thames, 1981; *Three Songs* (for medium voice, viola and piano), Thames, 1982; *Six Songs*, Thames, 1989.

IRELAND   Augener; Braydeston Press; Chester; Cramer; OUP; Schott; Winthrop Rogers.
   Collections: *Eleven Songs*, Galliard, 1970; *The Land of Lost Content and other songs*, Galliard, 1976; *Complete Works for Voice and Piano* (5 vols.), S&B, 1981.

BAX   Chappell; Chester; Murdoch.
   Collections: *Album of Seven Songs*, Chester, 1919; *Five Irish Songs*, Chappell, 1922; *Six Songs*, Thames, 1994; *Twelve Songs*, Thames, 1994.

BUTTERWORTH   Augener; S&B.
   Collections: *Eleven Songs from 'A Shropshire Lad'*, Galliard, 1974; *Love Blows as the Wind Blows*, Thames, 1982.

BROWNE   OUP; Winthrop Rogers; Thames.
   Collections: *Six Songs*, Thames, 1989

GIBBS   B&H; Chappell; Curwen; Elkin; Enoch; OUP; Winthrop Rogers.
   Collections: *Ten Songs*, Thames, 1989.

GURNEY   OUP; Winthrop Rogers; Thames.
   Collections: *Five Elizabethan Songs*, B&H, 1920; *Ludlow & Teme*, S&B, 1923/1982; *The Western Playland*, S&B, 1926/1982; *Five Volumes of Songs*, OUP, 1938–79; *20 Favourite Songs*, OUP, 1996; *Eleven Songs*, Thames, 1998; *Seven Sappho Songs*, Thames, 2000.

HOWELLS   B&H; Music Sales Ltd; OUP; S&B; Thames.
   Collections: *[9] Songs*, B&H, 1986; *In Green Ways*, Thames, 1992; *A Garland for Walter de la Mare*, Thames, 1996; *Five Songs* (9 poems by Fiona Macleod), Thames, 1999.

ORR   Augener; Chester; OUP; Roberton; S&B.
  Collections: *Five Songs from 'A Shropshire Lad'*, OUP, 1959; *Two Seventeenth Century Poems*, Augener, 1930/Roberton, 1974.
WARLOCK   Augener; Chester; Curwen; Elkin; Enoch; OUP; Paterson; Winthrop Rogers; S&B; Thames.
  Collections: *Lillygay*, Chester, 1923; *The Curlew*, S&B, 1924; *Candlelight*, Augener, 1924; *A [First] Book of Songs*, OUP, 1931; *A Second Book of Songs*, OUP, 1967; *Song Album*, B&H, 1967; *Thirteen Songs*, Galliard, 1970; *Eight Songs*, Thames, 1972; *Collected Solo Songs* (8 vols.), Thames 1982–93; *Songs with String Quartet* (*Collected Solo Songs*, vol. 9), Thames, 1997.
MOERAN   Augener; B&H; Chester; Curwen; Novello; OUP; S&B; Joseph Williams.
  Collections: *12 Songs*, Thames, 1988; Collected *Solo Songs* (4 vols.), Thames, 1994–8.
FINZI   OUP; B&H.
  Collections: *A Young Man's Exhortation*, OUP (B&H), 1933; *Earth and Air and Rain*, B&H, 1936; *Let us Garlands Bring*, B&H, 1942; *Before and After Summer*, B&H, 1949; *I Said To Love*, B&H, 1958; *Till Earth Outwears*, B&H, 1958; *To a Poet*, B&H, 1965; *O Fair To See*, B&H, 1966.

Glossary

I have avoided musicological jargon wherever possible, but certain technical terms are inevitable. Most of these are self-explanatory, but, to avoid confusion, here are a few that might be unfamiliar or misinterpreted:

AIR-ON/OVER-A-GROUND   a song constructed over a GROUND BASS.

ALTERNATING STROPHES   a song in which STANZAS are set to alternate STROPHES (A B A B) (e.g. Butterworth's 'Is my team ploughing?').

BINARY SONG   a song consisting of two sections, usually the setting of two stanzas, the first usually ending with a cadence *away* from the tonic (e.g. Quilter's 'Brown is my love', Delius's 'To daffodils', Ireland's 'Epilogue' (*The Land of Lost Content*).

BURDEN   separate, repeated chorus after a VERSE.

CANTATA   the SOLO CANTATA is an extended vocal work, often in a continuous movement divided into several distinct sections. Rare in English Romantic Song, but see Parry's *The Soldier's Tent*.

DA CAPO ARIA   a song in which the opening section (words and music) is repeated after a contrasting central section, creating a ternary-shaped song. Usually referring to songs from the Baroque period but perpetuated in English Romantic Song in e.g. Quilter's 'Cherry ripe' and Bridge's 'When you are old'.

END-STOPPING   the opposite of the following:

ENJAMBEMENT   in poetry, continuation of a sentence beyond the end of a line, couplet or stanza.

GROUND BASS   English term for BASSO OSTINATO.

LYRIC   a short poem specifically intended for musical setting.

MELISMA   a group of notes sung to a single syllable.

MOTIVE   a basic musical idea: a rhythm or melodic figure or, quite often, both.

PENILLION   'canu penillion', a traditional Welsh singing technique, in which the harpist plays a traditional air whilst the singer extemporises a descant against it. Used here to describe songs in which the accompaniment has self-contained music (march, dance, etc.) whilst the singer has a freely-improvised arioso above (e.g. Somervell's

	'The street sounds to the soldiers' tread', Browne's 'To Gratiana dancing and singing'.
OSTINATO	a persistently repeated musical figure or rhythm. BASSO OSTINATO: a bass with this characteristic.
RECITATIVE AND ARIA	a 'double-barrelled' form. RECITATIVE is declamatory (often dramatic or narrative), the ARIA lyrical (contemplative) (e.g. Finzi's *Farewell to Arms*).
REFRAIN	repetition of line(s) within a VERSE, usually, but not always, at the end.
RHYME	identity of sound (assonance) between words at end of poetic line.
RITORNELLO	(It.: 'little return'). An instrumental passage recurring between the verses of a song.
RONDO	a song in which the original strophe alternates with contrasting strophes (e.g. A B A C A) (e.g. Purcell's 'I attempt from love's sickness to fly'). Not a form commonly found in English Romantic Song.
SCENA	extended vocal work, usually of a dramatic kind (e.g. Parry's *The Soldier's Tent*).
SONG-CYCLE	a group of songs (usually more than three) intended by the composer to be sung in a set order, linked either by poet (Quilter's *To Julia*), mood (Warlock's *The Curlew*), theme (Elgar's *Sea Pictures*) or narrative (Somervell's *Maud*).
STANZA	a poetic/verse unit: refers to the *poem*.
STROPHE	a musical unit: the setting (usually) of a STANZA.
STROPHIC SONG	one in which each STANZA is set to the same music. If the music is *identical*, then we refer to it as REPEATED (or SIMPLE) STROPHIC; if varied, as VARIED STROPHIC (e.g. Quilter's 'To daisies', Warlock's 'Pretty ringtime').
TERNARY SONG	song in three musical sections, ABA, where a contrasting central section is followed by a repeat (varied or simple) of original STROPHE (e.g. Quilter's 'How should I your true love know?', Butterworth's 'Loveliest of trees', Parry's 'Good night'). See also DA CAPO ARIA.
THROUGH-SET/ THROUGH-COMPOSED SONG	Ger. 'durchcomponiert': a song without strophic repetition (e.g. Finzi's 'Shortening days at the homestead').
VERSE	the poetic/musical unit: refers to the *song*.

Sources of Copyright Musical Examples

Every effort has been made to contact copyright holders, and the author and publishers are grateful to the following for permission to reproduce copyright material.

Introduction

Example 1   Benjamin Britten, 'The kind ghosts', from *Nocturne*,
               © 1958 Boosey & Hawkes Ltd.
Example 2(a)   Roger Quilter, 'It was a lover and his lass', from *Five Shake-speare Songs*.
               © 1921 Boosey & Co Ltd.
Example 2(c)   Gerald Finzi, 'It was lover', from *Let Us Garlands Bring*
               © 1942 Boosey & Co Ltd.
Reproduced by permission of Boosey & Hawkes Music Publishers Ltd.

Chapter 2

Example 17   Charles Villiers Stanford, 'The aquiline snub', from *Nonsense Rhymes*.
               © Stainer & Bell Ltd. Extract reproduced by permission

Chapter 3

Examples 1, 4–7 Edward Elgar, *Sea Pictures*, Opus 37.
               © 1899 Boosey & Co Ltd.
Example 2   Edward Elgar, 'Speak, music'
               © 1901 Boosey & Co.
Reproduced by permission of Boosey & Hawkes Music Publishers Ltd.

Example 3   Edward Elgar, 'Twilight', from *Song Cycle*, Opus 59.
               © Novello & Co Ltd. Reproduced by permission of Music Sales Ltd.

Chapter 4

Examples 1–7   Frederick Delius, 'Twilight fancies', 'To daffodils', *Cynara*, 'I-Brasil', 'O so white, so soft, O so sweet', *A Late Lark*.
© Oxford University Press. Extracts reproduced by permission

Chapter 5

Example 1   Arthur Somervell, 'Maria at the window'.
© Thames Publishing. Reproduced by permission of William Elkin Music Services

Example 2   Arthur Somervell, 'Into my heart an air that kills', from *A Shropshire Lad*.
© 1904 Boosey & Co. Ltd.

Examples 3–5   Arthur Somervell, *A Broken Arc*.
© 1923 Boosey & Co. Ltd.

Example 6   Arthur Somervell, *Love in Springtime*
© 1901 Boosey & Co. Ltd.

Reproduced by permission of Boosey & Hawkes Music Publishers Ltd

Example 7   Arthur Somervell, 'Shepherd's cradle song'
© Edwin Ashdown. Reproduced by permission of Music Sales Ltd.

Chapter 6

Examples 1, 12, 13 and 14(b) Vaughan Williams 'How can the tree but wither', 'The water mill', *Along the Field* and *Four Last Songs*
© Oxford University Press. Extracts reproduced by permission.

Examples 2–5   Vaughan Williams, *The House of Life*
© Edwin Ashdown. Reproduced by permission of Music Sales Ltd.

Examples 6–8   Vaughan Williams, *Songs of Travel*
© 1905 Boosey & Co Ltd. Reproduced by permission of Boosey & Hawkes Music Publishers Ltd.

Examples 9–10   Vaughan Williams, *On Wenlock Edge*
© 1911 by Ralph Vaughan Williams, revised edition © 1946 by Boosey & Co. Ltd. Reproduced by Boosey & Hawkes Music Publishers Ltd.

Example 11   Vaughan Williams, *Five Mystical Songs*
© Stainer & Bell Ltd. Extract reproduced by permission.

Chapter 7

Examples 1–3   Gustav Holst, *Hymns from the Rig Veda*, Opus 24.
Examples 4–6   Gustav Holst, *Four Songs for Voice & Violin*, Opus 35.
          © Chester Music Ltd. Reproduced by permission of Music Sales Ltd.
Examples 7–9   Gustav Holst, *Twelve Humbert Wolfe Songs*, Opus 48.
          © Stainer & Bell Ltd. Extracts reproduced by permission.

Chapter 8

Example 1   Roger Quilter, 'June'.
    © 1905 Boosey & Co. Ltd.
Example 2   Roger Quilter, 'Come away, death', from *Three Shakespeare Songs*
    © 1905 Boosey & Co. Ltd.
Examples 3, 15–17 Roger Quilter, 'The faithless shepherdess', 'By a fountainside' and 'Fair house of joy', from *Seven Elizabethan Lyrics*
    © Boosey & Co. Ltd.
Examples 5(a), 25 Roger Quilter, 'Why so pale and wan?' and ''The jealous lover', from *Five Jacobean Lyrics*.
    © 1926 Boosey & Co. Ltd
Examples 5(b), 26 'Who is Silvia?' and 'How should I your true love know?', from *Four Shakespeare Songs*.
    © 1933 Boosey & Co. Ltd.
Examples 9–11 Roger Quilter, 'Come away, death', and 'Blow, blow thou winter wind', from *Three Shakespeare Songs*.
    © 1905 Boosey & Co. Ltd.
Examples 13–14 Roger Quilter, 'The night piece' and 'Julia's hair', from *To Julia*.
    © 1906 Boosey & Co. Ltd.
Example 18   Roger Quilter, 'Autumn evening'
    © 1910 Boosey & Co. Ltd.
Examples 20–22 Roger Quilter, 'It was a lover and his lass' and 'Fear no more the heat o' the sun' from *Five Shakespeare Songs*.
    © 1921 Boosey & Co. Ltd.
Example 24   Roger Quilter, 'Arab love song'
    © 1927 Winthrop Rogers Ltd.
Example 27   Roger Quilter, 'I arise from dreams of thee'
    © 1931 Boosey & Co. Ltd.
Reproduced by permission of Boosey & Hawkes Music Publishers Ltd.
Example 4(a)   Frederick Delius, 'Love's philosophy'.
    © Oxford University Press. Extract reproduced by permission.

Example 8 Roger Quilter, 'Moonlight', from *Four Songs of the Sea*, Opus 1
© Forsyth Brothers Ltd. Reproduced by permission of the publishers.

Example 23 Roger Quilter, 'Go, lovely rose'
© 1923 Chappell Music Ltd. Reproduced by permission of International Music Publications Ltd.

Example 28 'Music and moonlight'
© Curwen & Sons. Reproduced by permission of Music Sales Ltd.

Chapter 9

Examples 1, 2, 4, 5, 7–9 Frank Bridge, 'Go not, happy day', 'Come to me in my dreams', 'Strew no more red roses', 'Love went a-riding', 'When you are old and gray', 'What shall I your true love tell' and ''Tis but a week'.
© Winthrop Rogers Ltd.
Reproduced by permission of Boosey & Hawkes Music Publishers Ltd.

Example 3 Frank Bridge, 'Far, far from each other'.
© Thames Publishing. Reproduced by permission of William Elkin Music Services.

Examples 10–13 Frank Bridge, *Three Tagore Songs* and 'Journey's end'
© Stainer & Bell Ltd. Reproduced by permission.

Chapter 10

Examples 1(a)(b)(c)(e), 4, 5, 16, 17 John Ireland, *The Land of Lost Content*, 'My true love hath my heart', 'Sea fever', 'Hope the hornblower' and 'Love and friendship'
© Stainer & Bell Ltd. Reproduced by permission.

Examples 1(d)(f), 6 John Ireland, 'Penumbra' 'Youth's spring tribute' and 'Spleen', from *Marigold*.
© 1916 Winthrop Rogers Ltd. Reproduced by permission of Boosey & Hawkes Music Publishers Ltd.

Examples 2–3 John Ireland, *Songs of a Wayfarer*
© 1912 Boosey & Co. Ltd. Reproduced by Boosey & Hawkes Music Publishers Ltd.

Examples 7 8 John Ireland, *Earth's Call* and 'The sacred flame'
© 1918 Winthrop Rogers Ltd. Reproduced by Boosey & Hawkes Music Publishers Ltd.

Examples 10–11, 14–15, 20 John Ireland, *We'll to the Woods No More, Five Poems by Thomas Hardy* and 'Tutto e sciolto'
© Oxford University Press. Extracts reproduced by permission.

Examples 12–13 John Ireland, 'Summer schemes' and 'Her song'
     © Cramer Music Ltd. Extracts reproduced by permission.
Examples 18–19 John Ireland, *Songs Sacred and Profane*.
     © Schott & Co. Ltd. Extracts reproduced by permission.

Chapter 11

Examples 1–3, 5–8 Arnold Bax, 'The white peace, 'Magnificat', 'The enchanted
     fiddle' and *A Celtic Song Cycle*.
     © Chester Music Ltd. Reproduced by permission of Music
     Sales Ltd.
Example 4   Arnold Bax, 'A lullaby'
     © Thames Publishing. Reproduced permission of Music Sales
     Ltd.
Examples 9–12 Arnold Bax, *The Bard of the Dimbovitza*
     © 1947 Murdoch, Murdoch & Co. Reproduced by permission
     of International Music Publications Ltd
Example 13   Arnold Bax, 'In the morning'.
     © 1926 Chappell Music Ltd. Reproduced by permission of
     International Music Publications Ltd.
Example 14   Arnold Bax, 'Carry Clavell'
     © 1926 Murdoch, Murdoch & Co. Reproduced by permission
     of International Music Publications Ltd.
Examples 15–17 'Across the door', 'Beg innish' and 'Rann of exile'.
     © 1927 Murdoch, Murdoch & Co. Reproduced by permission
     of International Music Publications Ltd.
Example 18   Arnold Bax, 'Watching the needleboats'
     © Oxford University Press. Extracts reproduced by permission.
Example 19   Arnold Bax, 'Youth'.
     © 1920 Murdoch, Murdoch & Co. Reproduced by permission
     of International Music Publications Ltd.

Chapter 13

Example 1   Denis Browne, 'Dream-tryst'.
     © Thames Publishing. Reproduced by permission of William
     Elkin Music Services.

Chapter 14

Example 1   Armstrong Gibbs, 'The stranger'.
     © Stainer & Bell Ltd. Reproduced by kind permission of E
     Ann Rust.

Example 2   Armstrong Gibbs, 'Song of shadows'.
                   © 1922 Winthrop Rogers Ltd.
Example 3   Armstrong Gibbs, 'Nod'.
                   © 1921 Winthrop Rogers Ltd.
Example 6   Armstrong Gibbs, 'Dream song'
                   © Winthrop Rogers Ltd.
Examples 8–9   Armstrong Gibbs, 'Silver' and 'The witch'
                   © Winthrop Rogers Ltd.
Reproduced by permission of Boosey & Hawkes Music Publishers Ltd.

Examples 4–5   Armstrong Gibbs, 'Araby' and 'Ann's cradle song', *Crossings*
                   © Curwen & Sons. Reproduced by permission of Music Sales
                   Ltd.
Examples 7, 10–11 Armstrong Gibbs, 'The galliass', 'The ballad of Semmer-
                   water' and 'The tiger-lily'.
                   © Curwen & Sons. Reproduced by permission of Music Sales
                   Ltd.
Example 12   Armstrong Gibbs, 'Hypochondriacus'
                   © Thames Publishing. Reproduced by permission of William
                   Elkin Music Services.

Chapter 15

Examples 2 & 9 Ivor Gurney, 'Desire in spring'.
                   © Oxford University Press. Extracts reproduced by permission.
Examples 3 & 4 Ivor Gurney, 'Orpheus' and 'Sleep'
                   © 1912 Winthrop Rogers Ltd.
Example 8   Ivor Gurney, 'I will go with my father a-ploughing'
                   © Winthrop Rogers Ltd.
Reproduced by permission of Boosey & Hawkes Music Publishers Ltd.

Examples 5–7, 10–18 Ivor Gurney, 'The folly of being comforted', 'Cathleen ni
                   Houlihan', 'Down by the salley gardens', 'The scribe', 'An
                   epitaph', 'By a bierside', 'Black Stitchel', 'All under the moon',
                   'The singer', 'Last hours', 'In Flanders' and
                   'Severn meadows'.
                   © Oxford University Press. Extracts reproduced by permission.
Examples 19 & 20 Ivor Gurney, 'The lent lily' and 'Lights out'.
                   © Stainer & Bell Ltd.

Chapter 16

Examples 1, 11, 12, 14 & 17 Herbert Howells, 'Under the greenwood tree', 'Merry
                   Margaret', 'The goat paths', 'Come sing and dance' and 'Flood'.
                   © Oxford University Press. Extracts reproduced by permission.

Examples 2, 5–9 Herbert Howells, *A Garland for de la Mare*.
© Thames Publishing. Reproduced by permission of William Elkin Music Services.

Examples 3 & 4 Herbert Howells, *Peacock Pie*.
© Chester Music Ltd. Extracts reproduced by permission of Roberton Publications

Examples 10, 13, 15 & 16 Herbert Howells, 'King David, 'The mugger's song', 'A madrigal' and 'Goddess of night'.
© Winthrop Rogers Ltd. Reproduced by permission of Boosey & Hawkes Music Publishers Ltd.

Chapter 17

Examples 1–3 & 5 C. W. Orr, 'The Isle of Portland', 'Loveliest of trees, the cherry', 'The carpenter's son' and 'Along the field'.
© Chester Music Ltd. Extracts reproduced by permission of Music Sales Ltd.

Examples 4 & 8 C. W. Orr, 'Is my team ploughing' and 'Bahnhoftstrasse'.
© Oxford University Press. Extracts reproduced by permission.

Examples 6 & 7 C. W. Orr, 'In valleys green and still' and 'Tryst noel'.
© Roberton Publications. Extracts reproduced by permission.

Chapter 18

Example 4   Peter Warlock, 'A lake and a fairy boat'.
© Thames Publishing. Reproduced by permission of William Elkin Music Services.

Chapter 19

Example 1   E. J. Moeran, 'Far in a western brookland'
© Thames Publishing. Reproduced by permission of William Elkin Music Services.

Example 2   E. J. Moeran, 'Loveliest of trees, the cherry'
© Curwen & Sons. Extracts reproduced by permission of Music Sales Ltd.

Examples 3, 14–17 E. J. Moeran, 'O fair enough are sky and plain' and *Six Poems by Seumas O'Sullivan*.
© Joseph Williams. Reproduced by permission of Stainer & Bell Ltd.

Examples 4–6   E. J. Moeran, 'The lover and his lass', 'When daisies pied' and 'When icicles hang by the wall'.
© Novello & Co. Ltd. Extracts reproduced by permission of Music Sales Ltd.

Examples 7–13 E. J. Moeran, 'In youth is pleasure', *Seven Poems of James Joyce*, 'Tilly' and 'Rahoon'.
© Oxford University Press. Extracts reproduced by permission.

Chapter 20

Example 1–5 Gerald Finzi, *Earth and Air and Rain*.
© 1936 Boosey & Co. Ltd.
Example 6 Gerald Finzi, 'Channel firing', from *Before and After Summer*.
© 1949 Boosey & Co. Ltd.
Examples 7 & 8 Gerald Finzi, 'At a lunar eclipse' and 'In years defaced', from *Till Earth Outwears*.
© 1958 Boosey & Co. Ltd.
Examples 9 & 10 Gerald Finzi, 'In five-score-summers' and 'At middle-field gate in February', from *I Said To Love*.
© 1958 Boosey & Co. Ltd.
Examples 11 & 15 Gerald Finzi, 'Rhapsody' and 'The rapture', from *Dies Natalis*.
© Carl Fischer Inc.
Examples 12 & 13 Gerald Finzi, *Let Us Garlands Bring*.
© 1942 Boosey & Co. Ltd.
Example 14 Gerald Finzi, 'To a poet a thousand years hence', from *To a Poet*
© 1965 Boosey & Co. Ltd.
Extracts reproduced by permission of Boosey & Hawkes Music Publishers Ltd.

Bibliography

Anon., 'Preface', in *Warlock Songs* (London, 1967)

Auden, W. H., 'Introduction: The poems', in *An Elizabethan Song Book* (London, 1957): vii–xiii

Avison, C., *An Essay on Musical Expression* (London, 1752)

Banfield, S., '"A Shropshire Lad" in the making: a note on the composition of George Butterworth's songs', *Music* Review XLII (1981): 261–7

——, 'Bax as a song composer', *Musical Times* CXXIV (1983): 666–9

——, *Sensibility and English Song* (London, 1985)

——(ed.), *The Blackwell History of Music in Britain: VI. The Twentieth Century* (London, 1995)

——, *Gerald Finzi: An English Composer* (London, 1997)

Barlow, M., *Whom the God Love: The Life and Music of George Butterworth* (London, 1997)

Bax, A., *Farewell, My Youth* (London, 1943)

Beechey, G., 'Walter de la Mare: settings of his poetry, a centenary note', *Musical Times* CXIV (1973): 371–3

Bennett, R., 'Song-writers of the day: II. Roger Quilter', *Music Teacher* V (1926): 409–11

Bernac, P., *Francis Poulenc: The Man and His Songs*, trans. Winifred Radford (London, 1977)

Bishop, J., 'Introduction', in *Frank Bridge Songs* (London, 1979)

Blom, E. (ed.), *Grove's Dictionary of Music and Musicians*, 5th edn, 10 vols. (London, 1954)

Boden, A. (ed.), *Stars in a Dark Night: The Letters of Ivor Gurney to the Chapman Family* (Gloucester, 1986)

Boughton, R., 'Modern British song writers: III. Stanford', *Music Student* V–VI (1913): 65–6

Britten, B., 'Introduction', in E. Crozier (ed.), *Peter Grimes*, Sadlers Wells Opera Books No. 3 (London, 1945): 7–8

Brook, D., *Composers' Gallery* (London, 1946)

Bush, G., 'Introduction', in *Hubert Parry: Seven Songs* (London, 1979) (= 1979a)

——, 'Introduction', in *Charles Stanford: Six Songs* (London, 1979) (= 1979b)

——, 'Foreword', in *John Ireland: the Complete Works for Voice and Piano* (London, 1981)

——, 'Introduction', in *Hubert Parry: Songs*, Musica Britannica XLIX (London, 1982)

——, 'Introduction', in *Charles Villiers Stanford: Songs*, Musica Britannica LII (London, 1985)

——, 'Songs', in Temperley, 1988: 266–87

Campion, T., 'Address to the Reader', in *A Booke of Ayres* (1601)

——, 'Address to the Reader', in *Two Bookes of Ayres* (c.1613)

Carder, R., 'Long shadows fall: a study of Ivor Gurney's songs to his own poems', *British Music Society Journal* 15 (1993): 34–70

Cline, E., 'The composer's use of words: the language and music of Gerald Finzi', *British Music Society Journal* 14 (1992): 8–24

Clinton-Baddeley, V. C., *Words for Music* (Cambridge, 1941)

Cockshott, G., 'Some notes on the songs of Peter Warlock', *Music and Letters* XXI (1940): 246–58

Colles, H. C., *Voice and Verse* (London, 1928)

—— 'Parry as song-writer', *Essays and Lectures* (London, 1945): 55–75

Collett, B., 'Introduction', in *Thirteen Songs* (London, 1987)

Collins, B., *Peter Warlock, The Composer* (Aldershot, 1996)

Copley, I. A., 'An English songwriter: C. W. Orr', *Composer* no. 29 (1968): 12–14

——, *The Music of Peter Warlock: A Critical Survey* (London, 1979)

——, *George Butterworth: A Centennial Tribute* (London, 1985)

Cox, D. and J. Bishop (ed.), *Peter Warlock, A Centenary Celebration* (London, 1994)

Crossley-Holland, P., 'John Ireland', in Blom, 1954, IV: 533–44

Cumberland, G., *Written in Friendship* (London, 1923)

Day, J., *Vaughan Williams* (London, 1961)

Dent, E. J., 'On the composition of English songs', *Music and Letters* VI (1925): 224–35

Dibble, J., *C. Hubert H. Parry: His Life and Times* (London, 1992)

Dickinson, A. E. F., *Holst's Music: A Guide* (London, 1995)

Dryden, J., 'Preface', in *King Arthur* (London, 1691), quoted in Hold, 1994: 315

East, L., 'Roger Quilter (1877–1953)', *Music and Musicians* XXVI no. 3 (1977): 28–30

Elwes, W. and R., *Gervase Elwes: The Story of His Life* (London, 1935)

Evans, E., 'English song and "On Wenlock Edge"', *Musical Times* LIX (1918): 247–9

Fenby, E., *Delius As I Knew Him* (London, 1936)

Ferguson, H., 'Gerald Finzi (1901–1956)', *Music and Letters* XXXVIII (1957): 130–5

——, sleeve-notes to *Hardy Settings of Gerald Finzi*, SRCS 38 and SRCS 51 (Lyrita Records 1968 and 1971)

Ferguson, H. and Hurd, M., *Letters of Gerald Finzi and Howard Ferguson* (Woodbridge, 2001)

Finzi, G., 'The composer's use of words', *Crees Lectures* (RCM, London, 1955, typescript)

Foreman, L. (ed.), *Dermot O'Byrne: Selected Poems of Arnold Bax* (London, 1979)

Foreman, L., *Bax: A Composer and His Times* (London, 1983)

——, *From Parry to Britten: British Music in Letters 1900–1945* (London, 1987)

——, booklet notes to *Bax: 21 Songs* CCD 1046 (Continuum Records, 1992)

Fuller-Maitland, J. A., *The Music of Parry and Stanford* (London, 1934)

Gershwin, I., *Lyrics on Several Occasions* (London, 1977)

Gibbs, C. A., 'Setting de la Mare to music', *Journal of the National Book League* no. 301 (1956): 80–1

Goddard, S., 'The art of Roger Quilter', *The Chesterian* VI (1925): 213–17

Gooch, B. S. and D. Thatcher, *Musical Settings of Late Victorian and Modern British Literature: A Catalogue* (New York and London, 1976)

——, *Musical Settings of Early and Mid-Victorian Literature: A Catalogue* (New York and London, 1979)

——, *Musical Settings of British Romantic Literature: A Catalogue*, 2 vols. (New York and London, 1982)

Graves, C. L., *Hubert Parry: His Life and Works*, 2 vols. (London, 1926)

Gray, C., *Peter Warlock: A Memoir of Philip Heseltine* (London, 1934)

Greene, H. P., *Interpretation in Song* (London, 1912)

—— *Charles Villiers Stanford* (London, 1935)

Hadow, W. H., *Collected Essays* (London, 1928)

Hancock-Child, R., *A Ballad-Maker: The Life and Songs of C. Armstrong Gibbs* (London, 1993) (= 1993a)

——, booklet notes to *Cecil Armstrong Gibbs Songs* 8.223458 (Marco Polo, 1993) (= 1993b)

Hassall, C., 'Music and English poetry', in Arthur Jacobs (ed.), *Music Lover's Anthology* (London, 1948): 151–68

Heseltine, P., 'Predicaments concerning music', in *The New Age* (10 May 1917): 46, reprinted in Smith, 1998: 125–7

——, 'Contingencies: The test of a tune', *The Sackbut* (March 1921): 421

——, *Frederick Delius* (London, 1923)

Hold, T., 'Peter Warlock: the art of the song-writer', *Music Review* XXXVI (1975): 284–99. Reprinted in D. Cox and J. Bishop, *Peter Warlock, A Centenary Celebration* (London, 1994): 87–106

——, *The Walled-In Garden: A Study of the Songs of Roger Quilter* (Rickmansworth, 1978, 2/1996)

——, 'Two aspects of "Sleep": a study in English song-writing', *Music Review* XLI (1980): 26–35

——, '"Words for Music": an old problem revisited', *Music Review* XLVII (1986/7): 283–96

——, 'Introduction' and 'Editorial Notes', in *Six Songs by W. Denis Browne* (London, 1990)

——, 'Words and Music: an anthology of quotations', *Music Review* LV (1994): 311–22

——, '"Flowers to fair": A Shropshire Lad's legacy of song', in A. W. Holden and J. R. Birch (ed.), *A. E. Housman: A Reassessment* (Basingstoke, 2000): 106–33

Holland, A. K., *The Songs of Delius* (London, 1951)

Holst, I., *Gustav Holst* (London, 1938)

——, *The Music of Gustav Holst* (London, 1951)

——, *A Thematic Catalogue of Gustav Holst's Music* (London, 1974)

Howells, H., 'Ivor Gurney: the musician', *Music and Letters* XIX (1938): 13–17

Howes, F., *The English Musical Renaissance* (London, 1966)

Humphreys, G., sleeve-note to *John Carol Case Farewell Recital: Maud*, SHE 527 (Pavilion Records, 1976)

Hutchings, A., 'The Heseltine-Warlock Nonsense', *The Listener* 70 (1963): 34

Hurd, M., *The Ordeal of Ivor Gurney* (Oxford, 1978)

——, 'Gurney's unpublishable (?) songs', *The Ivor Gurney Society Journal* 4 (1998): 7–18

Jacobs, A., 'The British Isles', in D. Stevens (ed.), *A History of Song* (London, 1960): 124–80

Kavanagh, P. J. (ed.), *Collected Poems of Ivor Gurney* (Oxford, 1982)

Kennedy, M., *The Music of Ralph Vaughan Williams* (London, 1964, 2/1980)

——, 'Introduction' and 'Notes' to *Vaughan Williams: Choral Music*, SLS 5082 (Decca, 1977)

Lambert, C., *Music Ho!: A Study of Music in Decline* (London, 1934)

——, 'Master of English song', *Radio Times* LIX (1 July 1938): 12–13

Larkin, P., review, in *Times Literary Supplement*, 27 February 1981

Lawrence, D. H., 'Pornography and obscenity' (1929), in '*A Propos Lady Chatterley's Lover*' *and Other Essays* (Harmondsworth, 1961): 60–84

Leach, G., *British Composer Profiles: A Biographical Dictionary and Chronology of Past British Composers, 1800–1989* (Gerrards Cross, 1989)

Lewis, C. Day (ed.), *A Book of English Lyrics* (London, 1961)

Longmire, J., *John Ireland: Portrait of a Friend* (London, 1969)

——, 'Preface and notes', in *'The Land of Lost Content' and Other Songs by John Ireland* (London, 1976): ii–v

Mann, W., sleeve-note to *John Ireland Songs – Volume One*, SRCS 65 (Lyrita Records, 1975)

Mellers, W., *Studies in Contemporary Music* (London, 1947)

Moore, G., *Singer and Accompanist: The Performance of 50 Songs* (London, 1953)

Moore, J. N., 'Introduction', in *An Elgar Song Album* (London, 1984) (= 1984a)

——, *Edward Elgar: A Creative Life* (London, 1984) (= 1984b)

Morley, T., *A Plaine and Easie Introduction to Practicalle Musicke* (London, 1597)

Newman, E., 'Concerning "A Shropshire Lad" and other matters', *Musical Times* LIX (1918): 393–8

——, 'Mr Housman and the composers', *Sunday Times* (29 October 1922): 7

Northcote, S., 'The songs of C. W. Orr', *Music and Letters* XVIII (1937): 355–9

——, *Byrd to Britten: A Survey of English Song* (London, 1966)

Ottaway, H., 'Ralph Vaughan Williams', in Sadie, 1980 XIX: 569–80

Palmer, C., 'C. W. Orr: an 80th birthday tribute', *Musical Times* CXIV (1973): 690–2

——, 'Prefatory note', in *C. W. Orr: 'The Earl of Bristol's Farewell'* (Wendover, R/1974)

——, *Herbert Howells: A Study* (Borough Green, 1978)

——, 'C. W. Orr', in Sadie, 1980, XIII: 872

——, 'Preface', in *Herbert Howells: A Centenary Celebration* (London, 1986): 3

—— (ed.), *Herbert Howells: A Centenary Celebration* (London, 1992)

——, booklet notes to *Howells: Complete Songs for Voice and Piano* CHAN 9185/6 (Chandos Records, 1994)

——, 'Prefatory note', in *Herbert Howells: A Garland for de la Mare* (London, 1995)

Parrott, H. I., 'Warlock and the fourth', *Music Review* XXVII (1966): 130–2

Parry, C. H. H., 'The present condition of English song-writing', in *The Century Guild Hobby Horse*, no. 10 (April 1888): 69–70

Pattison, B., *Music and Poetry of the English Renaissance* (London, 1948, 2/1970)

Payne, A., with J. Bishop and L. Foreman, *The Music of Frank Bridge* (London, 1976)

Pears, P., sleeve-note to *Twentieth Century English Songs* ZRG 5418 (Argo Records, 1964)

Pilkington, M., *English Solo Song: Guides to the Repertoire*

——, 2. *Gurney, Ireland, Quilter and Warlock* (London, 1989)

——, 3. *Delius, Bridge and Somervell* (London, 1993)

——, 5. *Parry and Stanford* (London, 1997)

——, *English Solo Song: a Guide for Singers, Teachers, Librarians and the Music Trade of Songs Currently Available* (London, 1997)

Pirie, P. J., 'Introduction', in *Four Songs by Frank Bridge* (London, 1974) (= 1974a)

——, 'Introduction', in *George Butterworth: Eleven Songs from 'A Shropshire Lad'* (London, 1974) (= 1974b)

Poulenc, F., *Diary of My Songs (Journal de mes Mélodies)*, trans. by Winifred Radford (London, 1988)

Pound, E., 'On Music', in *The New Age*, 8 February 1912: 343–4, quoted in M. Schafer 1978: 31

Quilter, R., in P. Warlock, ed. H. Foss, *Frederick Delius* (London, 2/1952): 155–6

Raphael, M., 'Roger Quilter, 1877–1953: the man and his songs', *Tempo* XXX (1953–4): 20–1

Rawlins, J., 'Charles Wilfred Orr (1893–1976)', *Composer* no. 74 (1981): 23–8

Richards, F., *The Music of John Ireland* (London, 2000)

Richards, G., *Housman, 1897–1936* (London, 1941)

Rippin, J., 'George Butterworth 1885–1916', in *Musical Times* CVII (1966): 680/82, 769–71

Robertson, A., sleeve-note to *George Butterworth: Settings of Poems from A. E. Housman's 'A Shropshire Lad'* DLP 1117 (HMV, 1956)

Rubbra, E., review of C. W. Orr's *Three Songs from 'A Shropshire Lad'*, *Music and Letters* XXII (1941): 297

Sadie, S. (ed.), *The New Grove's Dictionary of Music and Musicians*, 20 vols. (New York, 1980 and London, 1981)

Schafer, R. M., *British Composers in Interview* (London, 1963)

—— (ed.), *Ezra Pound and Music* (London, 1978)

Scholes, P., *The Oxford Companion to Music*, 9th edn (London, 1955)

Scott, M. M., 'Preface', in *Ivor Gurney: A First Volume of Ten Songs* (London, 1938)

——, 'Postscript', in *Ivor Gurney: A Third Volume of Ten Songs* (London, 1952)

——, 'Ivor Gurney', in Blom, 1954, III: 855–6

Searle, M. V., *John Ireland: The Man and His Music* (Tunbridge Wells, 1979)

Self, G., *The Music of E. J. Moeran* (London, 1986)

Shenton, K., 'Sir Arthur Somervell', in *British Music Society Journal* 9 (1987): 45–54

Short, M., *Gustav Holst: The Man and His Music* (Oxford, 1990)

Smith, B., *Peter Warlock: The Life of Philip Heseltine* (Oxford, 1994)

——, *The Occasional Writings of Philip Heseltine (Peter Warlock), vol. 3. Musical Criticism (2)* (London, 1998)

Spicer, P., *Herbert Howells* (Bridgend, 1998)

Stanford, C. V., *Interludes, Records and Reflections* (London, 1922)

Talbot, J., 'Introduction', in *E. J. Moeran: Collected Solo Songs* (London, 1994)

Temperley, N. (ed.), *The Blackwell History of Music in Britain: V. The Romantic Age: 1800–1914* (London, 1988)

Thornton, R. K. R. (ed.), *Ivor Gurney: Collected Letters* (Ashington and Manchester, 1991)

Threlfall, R., 'Preface', in *Delius Complete Works*, vol. 16 (London, 1990)

Tippett, M., 'Conclusion', in D. Stevens (ed.), *A History of Song* (London, 1960): 461–6

Todd, P., 'Introduction', in *Twelve Songs [of] E. J. Moeran* (London, n.d. [? 1988])

Tomlinson, F., 'Prefatory note', in *Peter Warlock: The Curlew* (London, 1973): 2–3

——, *A Peter Warlock Handbook: I* (London, 1974)

——, *A Peter Warlock Handbook: II* (Rickmansworth, 1977)

——, *Warlock and Blunt* (London, 1981)

Vaughan Williams, R., *National Music and Other Essays* (London, 1963)

Whittall, A., 'The isolationists', *Music Review* (1966): 122–9

Wilson, J., *C. W. Orr: The Unknown Song-Composer* (London, 1989)

Woodward, D. (ed.), *Essex Composers* (Chelmsford, 1985)

Yeats, W. B., 'A note on the setting of these poems to music', in *Later Poems* (London, 1922)

Young, P. M., *A History of British Music* (London, 1967)

Index

(Figures in *italics* refer to musical examples)